Decolonizing Colonial Development Models in Africa

Decolonizing Colonial Development Models in Africa

A New Postcolonial Critique

Edited by
Fidelis Allen and Luke Amadi

LEXINGTON BOOKS
Lanham • Boulder • New York • London

Published by Lexington Books
An imprint of The Rowman & Littlefield Publishing Group, Inc.
4501 Forbes Boulevard, Suite 200, Lanham, Maryland 20706
www.rowman.com

86-90 Paul Street, London EC2A 4NE, United Kingdom

Copyright © 2022 by The Rowman & Littlefield Publishing Group, Inc.

All rights reserved. No part of this book may be reproduced in any form or by any electronic or mechanical means, including information storage and retrieval systems, without written permission from the publisher, except by a reviewer who may quote passages in a review.

British Library Cataloguing in Publication Information Available

Library of Congress Cataloging-in-Publication Data

Names: Allen, Fidelis, editor. | Amadi, Luke, 1978- editor.
Title: Decolonizing colonial development models in Africa : a new postcolonial critique / edited by Fidelis Allen and Luke Amadi.
Description: Lanham : Lexington Books, 2021. | Includes bibliographical references and index.
Identifiers: LCCN 2021043285 (print) | LCCN 2021043286 (ebook) | ISBN 9781666901245 (cloth) | ISBN 9781666901269 (paperback) | ISBN 9781666901252 (epub)
Subjects: LCSH: Decolonization—Africa. | Economic development—Africa. | Postcolonialism—Africa.
Classification: LCC DT30.5 .D425 2021 (print) | LCC DT30.5 (ebook) | DDC 325.3096—dc23
LC record available at https://lccn.loc.gov/2021043285
LC ebook record available at https://lccn.loc.gov/2021043286

Contents

Introduction vii
Fidelis Allen and Luke Amadi

1 Development Paradigms and the Framing of Postcolonial
  Identity: Urbanization, Waterfront Development, and the
  Eko o ni baje Ethos/Slogan in Lagos 1
  Adebisi Alade

2 Nationalism in Postcolonial Studies: A Case for Hybridity 23
  Nick T. C. Lu

3 Maintaining Law and Order or Maintaining Conditions
  Ideal for the Exploitation of Africa? A Counter-Colonial
  Critique of Colonial Development Assumptions 43
  Biko Agozino

4 Postcolonial Development and Nailiyat Dance of Algeria:
  An Unorthodox Approach 65
  Fouad Mami

5 Colonialism and the Destruction of Indigenous Knowledge
  Systems: Daring to Push the Epistemological Frontiers
  for African Re-development Paradigms 91
  Nathan Moyo and Jairos Gonye

6 Deconstructing Colonial Development Models: Rethinking
  Africa's Moral Economy and Social Entrepreneurship for
  Sustainable Rural Development in Postcolonial Africa 113
  Mike O. Odey

7   Decolonization and Deconstruction of Colonial Development in Postcolonial Africa: Alternative Development Initiatives and the Contentions   139
    Victor I. Ogharanduku

8   Challenging the "Colonial Development Model": The Quest for an Indigenous African Model in Ngugi wa Thiong'o's *Petals of Blood*   159
    Solomon Awuzie

9   Nationalism and the Decolonization of the Ideology of Development in Africa   173
    Matthew D. Ogali

10 Women, Resistance Movements, and Colonialism in Africa: Evidence from Egypt, Kenya, and Nigeria   193
    Moses J. Yakubu and James Olusegun Adeyeri

11 African Migrations to Europe: A Historical Appraisal of Transcultural Exchanges and Decolonization in the Age of Globalization   215
    John Ebute Agaba and Emmanuel S. Okla

12 Beyond Colonial Development Model and the Quest for Alternatives in Africa   235
    Olayinka Akanle and Chukwuka Blessing Chidiogo

13 Colonialism and Misconception of Development in Benin Province: The Case of the Oil Palm Industry   253
    Fred Ekpe Ayokhai

14 Decolonizing State Fragility and Forced Migration in Postcolonial Nigeria   269
    Olanrewaju Faith Osasumwen

Author Index   291

Subject Index   297

About the Contributors   305

Introduction
Fidelis Allen and Luke Amadi

Development failure and crisis in postcolonial Africa underline the logic of decolonization of colonial development models. Yet, the concept of *decolonizing colonial development models* remains one of the least studied or interrogated in the study of contemporary postcolonial Africa. None of what could be seen as major works on the subject, particularly in the post–Cold War era, seem to have considered the concept important enough to be a tool for analysis. The significance of this concept stems from the insights it offers in understanding the nature and trends of what can easily be seen as a new postcolonial critique, which is the mandate of this book.

The new postcolonial critique repudiates colonial exploitation, social injustice, and inequity in postcolonial societies. It propagates decolonization. What is decolonization? While there is a lack of consensus among scholars on the meaning of the term "decolonization," in the context of this volume, it refers to counter-intuition against all forms of colonialism. Decolonization, as Agozino (2019:19) argued, is "always a struggle between the colonizers and the colonized by all means necessary . . . sometimes open and sometimes hidden, sometimes violent and sometimes peaceful but always convulsive." Such struggles are aimed at liberation, of indigenous societies from the shackles of colonial exploitation and bondage.

In development contexts, decolonization entails confrontation of Eurocentric/Western-centric methodologies, epistemologies, and, in particular, the historicity and practice of development in postcolonial societies for indigenous alternatives. Decolonization is both a practice and ideology to radically dismantle colonialism and its legacies and free the indigenous people from servitude and underdevelopment. Decolonization entails radical value re-orientation for equity, fairness, and social justice against colonialism.

Decolonization is a crucial element of an inclusive and sustainable development process.

By taking a critical approach, drawing on strands of postcolonial, postmodern, post-developmental, and post-structural theories, the book aims to make a new contribution by identifying the traces and effects of racism, exploitation, imperialism, and injustice among the postcolonial societies, particularly in Africa, and proffer possible ways of redressing them. Thus, at a time of increasing development crises, a postcolonial critique can create an understanding of the historical antecedents of underdevelopment and ways to deal it. Specifically, handling problems such as capitalist exploitation, poverty, and inequality across Africa requires deeper reflections on many issues including extensive postcolonial critique.

The book, in many interesting ways, brings into focus varied levels of analysis of the deconstruction of colonial development models in Africa. Inevitably, the volume will neither provide fully comprehensive coverage of all issues in postcolonial studies nor an entire set of themes on postcolonial studies. What is, however, certain is that the book provides sufficient depth of inquiry in approaching contemporary concerns raised in postcolonial studies. Distinctively, our position is that we can deepen the understanding of the key issues in postcolonial studies and deconstruction of colonial development model for Afrocentric alternatives in particular, through a balanced discourse on some of the debates and issues in the discipline. Furthermore, it provides a new line of inquiry.

The book has fourteen chapters; the first six chapters in the first segment explore the broad conceptual issues around myths and misconceptions of the colonial development model, which have had and continued to have a major impact on development scholarship and the need for alternative models. We begin with a chapter that explores development paradigms and framing of postcolonial identity. This is intended to guide both students and new entrants in understanding the notion of postcolonial urbanization in what the recent literature sees as "urban renewal." The case of *Eko o ni baje* (May Lagos (*Eko*) Be Indestructible) mantra is discussed in postcolonial contexts to confront the issues of modernization, urbanization, local identity distortion, and displacement of the urban poor that inhabit the water front settlements.

Thereafter, chapter 2 elucidates the relevance of nationalism, making a case for hybridity in postcolonial studies, to interrogate the political status quo. The chapter, in particular, argues that hybridity should not be seen exclusively as a postmodern condition but as coextensive with nationalism in modernity. It then suggests the need for constructing a robust counterculture within the debate.

Chapter 3 re-engages with the debate on postcolonial exploitation of Africa by exploring the dynamics of postcolonial "law and order" to substantiate whether such policies are aimed at "maintaining law and order" or "conditions ideal for exploitation and expropriation" of the surpluses produced by African labor for the benefit of Europe, as Rodney argued. The author showed that such an argument remains a relevant theoretical framework for the analysis of the politics of "law and order" and the advancement of decolonization in Africa. Further, the chapter argues that decolonization of Africa is imperative for sustainable development and self-reliance.

Chapter 4 combines a set of approaches that defines a perceptible way of critiquing the colonial development model with regard to the colonial marginalization of Algerian indigenous culture exemplified in the *Nailiyat* Dance. The chapter captures the essence of new thinking on postcolonial cultural identity and development. It emphasizes colonial culture imperialism and alienation with the case example of the Nailiyat cultural dance practices as a modality of cultural renaissance and resistance to colonial cultural imperialism and in particular, decolonization. The chapter challenges the contrasts of orthodox perception that vitiates the cultural and economic development relevance of the dance long venerated in precolonial Algeria. It further opposes contemporary postcolonial practices, which cast the legacies of such cultural dance in the shadows of retrogression and disdain, and argues in the alternative that there is a need to overcome cultural imperialism and alienation with a reverse to the cultural practices that existed decades before colonialism. This includes, "among other imperatives, not only ceasing to denigrate the dance but promoting the body's intelligence, specifying that the body (not the mind) always acts as a framework for non-fetishized and non-fetishizing dispositions."

In chapter 5, colonialism and destruction of the indigenous knowledge system are thrown up in an attempt to "push the epistemological frontiers for Africa's redevelopment paradigms." The authors provide critical approaches to understanding the epistemological relevance of Africa's indigenous knowledge systems (IKS). Thus, the chapter provides a critical theoretical model that could aid in decolonizing the knowledge system, namely African Critical Race Theory (AfriCrit) "as a potentially useful theory in reenergizing Africa's self-development." The argument is that AfriCrit can play a crucial role in rethinking the seeming dearth in viable self-development models in Africa.

Chapter 6 discusses the need to rethink "Africa's moral economy and social entrepreneurship for sustainable rural development in post-colonial Africa" as the basis for deconstructing colonial development models. The chapter substantially demonstrates that "development models in Africa must be home-grown and driven by the rural people themselves within the matrix of their own socioeconomic structures, which they are familiar with, over time."

Chapter 7 takes the argument on alternative development approaches to a new level. It demonstrates that while there have been debates on alternative development initiatives (ADIs) as a tool for Africa's decolonization and deconstruction of colonial development project, there have been less successful outcomes due to none implementation of the ADIs by postcolonial African leaders caused by inherent contentions and ideological conflicts between African leadership and its people over the meaning of development, its trajectories, outcome(s), and empowerment of the African people. Drawing on the Asian examples, the author argues that ADIs will only be successfully implemented if African leaders and the people build a common consensus.

In chapter 8, the author "challenges" the "colonial development model" and further argues for indigenous African models drawing on Ngugi wa Thiong'o's *Petals of Blood*. The chapter makes a case for indigenous knowledge and de-emphasizes capitalism for Africa's economic dependence and self-reliance.

Chapter 9 sheds new light on "nationalism and the decolonization of the ideology of development in Africa." The author explores "development ideology" from the viewpoint of colonial legacy, and raised concerns shared by development theorists who believe in "decolonizing development." In particular, the complexity of the relationship between the nationalist spirit, the decolonization process, and the development agenda in postcolonial African contexts is explored. In particular, the chapter builds on Franz Fanon's revolutionary decolonization theory and demonstrates the need to reexamine the complex linkages between nationalism and decolonization of the development ideology in Africa. It recommends indigenized socioeconomic transformation through a return to endogenous model of development for Africa.

Chapter 10 deals with what could be described as issues of colonial resistance to strengthen the normative space of the postcolonial renaissance. The chapter deepens the argument on colonial resistance with an additional emphasis on "women, resistance movements and colonialism in Africa." It draws on evidence from Egypt, Kenya, and Nigeria, and provides a comparative exploration of the dynamics of women's resistance to colonialism. The chapter shows that "colonial African women, like their male counterparts, were fighters who demonstrated a profound level of 'camaraderie' as they agitated and fought against the travesties of European imperialism." The chapter posits that these women bequeathed an enduring legacy of decolonization, political activism, and militancy to postcolonial African women. It argues that despite the efforts of women in the colonial era, postcolonial African women remain increasingly marginalized, which is a colonial legacy. An alternative inclusive development model to deconstruct colonial models and guarantee gender equality was suggested.

Chapter 11 reinforces the discussion on Africans' migration to Europe from a historical perspective, providing an appraisal of transcultural exchanges, and decolonization in the age of globalization. It examines how best to combine social interaction and resilience in an atmosphere of cultural imperialism. The authors argued that while globalization has created an avenue for "people to interact and relate across borders," issues of cultural exchange have accentuated "cultural imperialism" as African cultures are increasingly marginalized and subsumed. They put forward policy recommendations on culture reinstitution and resilience pointing to the need for decolonization in the age of globalization to strengthen African cultural heritage against postcolonial state inhibition policies.

In chapter 12, a range of reflections "beyond colonial development model and the quest for alternatives in Africa" as approaches for understanding colonialism's strategic instruments responsible for the destruction of indigenous knowledge system are critically examined. The chapter argues that until colonial perspectives and processes of development are de-emphasized, Africa's development aspirations will remain increasingly evasive.

Chapter 13 looks at "colonialism and misconception of development in Benin Province" and provides case examples from the oil palm industry. The chapter adopts a historical approach and demonstrates that in a bid to gain full access and control of the palm oil industry in Benin Province, all socioeconomic and political structures were ruthlessly transformed to fit "colonial development construct." The chapter demonstrates that despite the sector's contribution to the colonial economy, it has largely remained "comatose and neglected" in the postcolonial development policies of Nigeria. It argues for a reconsideration of the sector as colonial development was not only exogenous but also a case of development misconception, transposed on the postcolonial state with all its exploitative structures. This, as the chapter argues, points to the need for a radical break with colonial heritage.

In the same vein, chapter 14 deepens the argument on decolonization of state fragility and forced migration in postcolonial Nigeria and provides a desk review of the dynamics of state fragility and forced migration from colonial to postcolonial Nigeria. The chapter argued that state fragility and forced migration are colonial legacies. It went further to recommend alternative measures to decolonize state fragility.

Following this brief introduction, we focus discussions on a critical set of questions, which any critical approach to postcolonial study in the context of deconstructing the colonial development model would want to ask. First, how does the book make a distinct and coherent contribution in the field? What is colonial development model? What is a new postcolonial critique?

HOW DOES THE BOOK MAKE A DISTINCT AND COHERENT CONTRIBUTION IN THE FIELD?

The current debates in postcolonial studies are driven mainly by uncritical rhetoric. They are also without adequate theoretical insights into the idea of deconstructing colonial development assumptions and transformation of postcolonial African societies. There are few scholarly works on new postcolonial critique for students and scholars seeking to understand the recent development realities of postcolonial Africa. Essentially, decolonizing colonial development models remains one of the least studied or interrogated in the study of contemporary postcolonial Africa, as none of what could be seen as major works in recent postcolonial African studies, particularly since the post–Cold War era seem to have considered the concept important enough to be a tool for development analysis. Rather, development is canonized as a colonial invention, eurocentric phenomenon, and modernization, which has come to be taken as the obvious, casting indigenous development models and Afrocentric alternatives in the shadows of pessimism.

The development "imaginary" in colonial construction misplaces what should be considered development. Instead, it propagates the interest of the colonialists. This seems to have led to identity crisis and culture mutation in postcolonial Africa. What is understood as development often is different and disconnected from the needs of the populations in the postcolonial society. We must note the fact that only little is known about decolonization of colonial development in postcolonial studies, in theory and in practice. There is little debate on the conceptualization of colonial development. The effects of the depiction of development which has lingered for several decades within the postcolonial state include the unquestioned acceptance of colonial development models and taking for granted the desirability of real change as development.

This uncritical and naïve approach does not provide scholars with the needed depth of knowledge on indigenous development models. It also fails to deliver the knowledge necessary for alternative development in a globalizing world. The more recent critical turn in postcolonial critique has rightly questioned this decontextualized and contestable discourse. It has also critiqued its contradictory implications in the era of inclusive and sustainable development debate. Driven by Eurocentric assumptions, the colonial development model often ignores the existential realities shaping knowledge production and development (culture, race, norms, values, colonialism, identity, nationalism, imperialism, ecological/environmental implications, capitalist exploitation, inequality both in gender and class basis, and so on), and the concealed misconceptions such as "racism," "White supremacy," "modernization," "primitivity," "backwardness" that make colonial development model racialized and less inclusive.

Titles in the book range from critical, theoretical, conceptual, and case analysis. This is distinctive as particular attention is given to recent postcolonial trends. The chapters are written by experts in various subfields of postcolonial studies. The volume makes an original contribution. It argues that postcolonial understanding of development needs to be reexamined to radically deconstruct the dominant notion of development. It further sheds new light on historical and contemporary perspectives and provides a radical exploration of both the commemorative and pejorative strands of colonial development. It further rethinks issues of colonial legacy; the notion of institutionalized colonial practices constituting the dominant and ideal social order for legitimate practices. This in itself represents one of the core uncritical and naïve notions of postcolonial development theory and practice. These are critical viewpoints that provide in-depth conceptual and theoretical ideas that interrogate the assumptions of colonial development.

The alternative development models consider how inclusive development can contribute to a radical socioeconomic and cultural transformation of postcolonial societies, and promote participatory, and critical development. The focus on decolonizing colonial development is central in contemporary postcolonial studies. The book describes how alternative development approaches may be harnessed to address exploitation, underdevelopment, inequality, ecological, and environmental insecurity. In these contexts, decolonizing the colonial development model is not merely a subject of research but a research approach. The emerging alternative views about development contributes well to the deconstruction of colonial development models, and to indigenous development that considers sustainability, equitability, and inclusive well-being rather than economic notions, value augmentation, and exploitation as the key focus to measure progress. Research arising from these concerns puts ethics, equality, and sustainability first, rather than neocolonial exploitation.

The volume recognizes the turn toward deconstructing the colonial development agenda, while also understanding the opportunities and threats posed by colonialism and corresponding development crisis and how it has stimulated institutional development challenges among the postcolonial societies. With the emphasis on deconstructing the colonial development model, the book aims to critically explore the move toward "inclusive" development. It furnishes an existential idea of sociopolitical, cultural, and ecological nuances and complexities of the contexts within which alternative development agendas could be advanced, and move beyond the dominant colonial development assumptions that structure and determine development debates at the global and local policy levels.

The book fills important research and theoretical gap. It reexamines some of the ignored core development issues in cultural, epistemological, and ecological contexts, and in particular, focuses on theory and practice with case examples from Africa. It provides a conceptual, theoretical, and genealogical mapping of the contradictions and complexities of the colonial development mission. It offers new examples and an up-to-date framework for discussing the theme of decolonization. The volume has a sufficient global profile and local realities for the study of the problems and solutions to African development. Also, the book has an additional advantage of being theoretical and prescriptive, as each chapter provides some proposals on how to move Africa forward.

The specific benefits offered by its content, scope, and organization among others include the engagement with a series of key debates about how the new postcolonial critique and theoretical and conceptual approaches are contributing to postcolonial studies and in particular the deconstruction of colonial development model. It has a broad scope that covers themes such as alternative development, urbanization, ethical and moral economy, postcolonial development misconceptions, approaches to decolonization, hybridity, globalization, migration, modern slavery, IKS, nationalism, culture, and post-structuralism.

POSTCOLONIAL DEVELOPMENT WAVE

The recent decades have experienced a new type of "modernity," spreading through globalization, which some have linked to a new form of colonization. It is occurring in a period characterized by neoliberal trajectories of "disappearance of borders" and "openness" known as globalization.

To reexamine the real development purport of this recent "development wave," new postcolonial critique as alternative approach and an ideology has risen in response to ongoing rapid changes, notably the contemporary context of modernization, urbanization, globalization, and increasing interdependence. These changes are shaping postcolonial societies in different ways, including increasing dependency, ecological disruptions, environmental insecurity, and climate change.

Thus, over the past quarter-century, the term "development" has made an enormous contribution in virtually all spheres of study. The idea of "development" is vague and polemical as it is often used interchangeably with terms such as "change," "growth," "modernization," "progress," "industrialization," and so on. Development was originally theorized in the context of classical, neoclassical, neo-Marxist, and liberal ideas. This has become the standard for most debates in development studies (Seers, 1969; Todaro, 1979;

Sachs, 1992; Schuurman, 2000). Thus, development becomes the basis for constructing social reality. In that sense, the concept is used as a yardstick to gauge social progress. Poverty, inequality, unemployment, human development index, income, GDP, standard of living, sources of wealth of nations, and so on, are common indicators, implying development could be a process, and a progression that could be learned or adopted.

It is instructive that the UN declared 1960–1970 as the first development decade. Thus, development was seen in the light of economic growth with an emphasis on the attainment of a certain level of GDP. However, income alone does not sufficiently account for the development of a society.

The notion of development in postcolonial contexts particularly as it relates to the Third World is controversial and contestable, especially since the end of formal colonialism in the late 1970s, when most postcolonial societies started grappling with the challenges of nation-building and economic development (Seers, 1969; Todaro, 1979; Esteva, 1992; Escobar, 1995). The contention is partly because development is conceptualized more like a move from primitive lifestyle and savagery to modernity, as well as relief from diseases and chronic poverty. Samir Amin (1972:403) contends that the so-called "primitive" character was an invention of ideological necessity "born out of colonial racism." Hence, the West remained the model to pursue development.

Another strand of argument is the "development of underdevelopment" or the dependency sub school, where the development of the industrialized societies does not translate to the development of societies in the Third World. Instead, dependency ensues (Dos Santos, 1974). Again, development is largely seen as an intervention (Rist, 2008). This attracted criticisms pointing to the failure of development intervention (Esteva, 1992).

Development critiques had emphasized the misrepresentation of development from the above perspectives which ignored past historical depictions, Afrocentric realities, and sources of wealth of nations (Weinstein, 2008; Acemoglu, Johnson and Robinson, 2002). Development reality in postcolonial societies remains a less studied subject matter. Readily dominating discourses are poverty, modernization, primitivity, or backwardness, and so on. Esteva (1992:10) points out that, for two-thirds of the people on earth, the positive meaning of the word development, profoundly rooted after two centuries of its social construction "is a reminder of what they are not, rather it is a reminder of an undesirable, undignified condition."

In the same vein, Wolfang Sachs (1992) contends that the term development in the intellectual landscape stands like a ruin. This perspective, which forms part of the post-development school, argues that development is obsolete or bankrupt and that the practice of it has done more harm than good. Accordingly, William Easterly (2014) critiqued the Western notion of development, arguing that largely it has a narrow focus on the material well-being of beneficiaries.

By "development" in postcolonial perspective, we suggest all round institutional socioeconomic, political, and cultural transformation of previously colonized societies. And in particular, all those interactions and relationships in which the allocation of values and distribution of power is at stake between the imperial powers and the erstwhile colonies. It is the understanding of the condition of persistent progression toward positive socioeconomic change, including improved material and non-material well-being in postcolonial contexts. Well-being denotes steady improvement in individual and institutional capacities. It could be within socioeconomic, health, and cultural conditions. It entails absence of lack, impoverishment, diseases, exploitation, or deprivation. Thus, development should transcend material or economic well-being and encompass more substantial notions of freedom and radical absence of exploitation. The aim is to attain inclusive progress encompassing sociopolitical, ecological, cultural, and economic liberation as well as self-reliance among variety of development options or choices.

The thesis of "genuine or real wealth of nations" (Eisler, 2007; Henderson, 2018) holds that economic progress and its measurement should be based on "genuine efforts" of nations to attain economic progress. It should close inequality gaps and deploy equitable mechanisms. The exploitation of a nation by another should not be labeled economic progress. This error has left the notion of the "colonial development model" uncritical and superficial. For instance, how did Europe develop? Was there evidence of economic plunder of the colonies? How is development measured and how are the development deficits arising from such exploitation measured in the countries exploited? These are issues in the new postcolonial critique and salient gaps this volume seeks to fill. Besides, it seeks to address how the colonial state fostered economic development in the colonies.

Webster, Magdoff, and Nowell (2018) highlight Western colonialism as a political-economic phenomenon whereby various European nations explored, conquered, settled, and exploited large areas of the world. Similarly, Ashcroft, Griffiths, and Tiffin (1989) posit that the notion of "postcolonial," examines the study of the interactions among European nations and their former colonies. Rodney (1972) examined this scenario in the context of "colonial banditry." Similar accounts on "patterns of colonial penetration," as Amin (1972) pointed out, was informed by the economic interests of Europe. This was contradictory to the economic advancement of the colonies. There is evidence of coercive, repressive, and autocratic strands of the colonial state (Ake, 1996). Such agendas are rarely reviewed in discourses regarding colonial development backlash. Thus, the colonial legacy has stood as socially acceptable and central to the organization of everyday life in postcolonial societies. The postcolonial imaginary is deployed in a variety of social realities and assumptions—the notion that institutionalized assimilation of colonial "knowledge production" constitutes the standard for legitimate and prescriptive social existence—represents one of the cardinal premises of the postcolonial paradigm. In this context, the conception of the "conquered and colonized" informs, and defines the direction taken by the emergent postcolonial leadership that largely remain subservient and mere appendages of the European imperial powers.

A COLONIAL DEVELOPMENT MODEL?

The term "development," has emerged as one of the most well-known areas of inquiry in the discourse of transformation or change in postcolonial societies. The colonial state created an ideological state in which culture, knowledge production, law, education, religion, and media were geared toward what Althusser (1971:144) termed "ideological state apparatuses." Colonial ideology dominated much of the dynamics of colonialism. Gilbert Rist provides an influential counter-argument on colonial development. Rist (2008) locates the origins of the model to around 1870 to 1940 when the "great powers" put the then-dominant ideas into practice and, in a sense, opened the way to "development." He notes that "Western belief in 'development' has ancient roots. He argues that the late nineteenth century saw everything seemed in place, in terms of ideas, to embark upon the great adventure."

Was the aim of colonialism to develop or exploit the colonies? Western Europe colonized most of the developing countries. Henning Melber (2017:5) argued that "in the history of the expansion of Europe over the rest of the world in the name of 'development'—then often dubbed 'civilization'—the worst atrocities and crimes tantamount to genocide were committed. Development is at times a monstrous cloak or a cloak for monsters." Rist (2008:48) used the practice of slavery to critique the claim on colonial development when he argued that "Slavery in the ancient world or the Enlightenment, human sacrifice among the Aztecs, and European colonization belong to the same category. How could people have thought what has since become unthinkable, and legitimated what has become intolerable?"

In nearly over ten decades of postcolonialism, the need for deeper reflection on the development failures of colonialism has remained pertinent. Said (1978) suggests that to attend to postcolonial critique as an organizing conundrum is to deconstruct the social construction of colonialism canonized, venerated, and conceived largely as obvious. Similar studies tend to situate the colonial debate within the milieu of hybridity (Bhabha, 1994; Nyman, 2007). There is little or no debate over what the colonial development model means or modalities to deconstruct the elemental colonial legacy, which rather constitutes a way of life among the postcolonial societies. Spivak (1999:1) argued that colonial discourse if focused on issues of the colonized or colonies might often be a representation of present neocolonial knowledge by situating colonialism/imperialism in the past or through a linkage between past and our present.

Following the ongoing debates, is there a colonial development model? The notion of colonial development model remains contestable. It is also a major component of postcolonial studies often overlooked. Questioning the development assumptions and rationalities of colonialism, is clearly inevitable, for understanding how colonial administration was organized and operated. This is also important for gaining insights into the nature of colonial policies, power relations, and interactions linked to institutionalized dynamics of resource appropriation.

One such assumption is that all apparatuses of governance and institutions involved in colonial administration particularly in the reproduction of knowledge were certified by the colonial order through establishing structures that consign meanings based on the sphere of knowledge already in existence in colonial ideology. Weinstein (2008) takes considerable account of "specific historical, material, cultural, and social" contexts as necessary in any accurate analysis of postcolonial development. Beyond this, colonialism is cast in the shadow of pessimism (see Nandy, 1983).

Further, within the colonial order, what counts as normal and natural or as "fact" emerges from the existing ideological social order. Colonialism constricts the ability of the colonies to think otherwise. Any practice that is contrary to colonial ideology is deemed abnormal, deviant, or irrelevant. A major contradiction of this position is that colonial institutions that propagate European knowledge historically marginalize indigenous knowledge production. They emasculate the social construction of equality, alternatively, justified racism and slavery, legitimized White supremacy, and promoted arbitrary claims of colonialism through conquests and expedition. These arguments are consistent with several studies that have questioned the justification of colonialism, the verity of its claim to development, and the historical depictions to provide counter-narratives (Ake, 1996; Rist, 2008; Spivak, 2014).

Rather than preserve the traditional knowledge production, Spivak (1988) and Sharp (2009) argue that the subaltern, which can never express their reasoning, forms of knowledge, or logic, must form their knowledge based on Western knowledge systems, was created. Many "factual" knowledge concerning culture, artifacts, identity, and nationalism—the basis for development—are in crisis (Mercer, 1990). Presently, with the resurgence of the new nationalism, the rise of identity movements, protests, and similar activists interrogating the destruction of indigenous cultures and values have re-remerged, pushing for a return to indigenous knowledge production. The more these critiques challenge the taken-for-granted concern regarding indigenous knowledge production, the clearer it becomes that the current postcolonial order has no claim to economic development.

Relatedly, Hall (1992) has located the postcolonial identity within the purview of "crisis." Mercer (1990) reinforces the complexities of identity and diversity in postmodern politics. It is in a related perspective that Giddens (1992) identified similar contradictory consequences of modernity to self-identity and demonstrates that modernity is a post-traditional order which creates some institutional reflexivity. Thus, the colonial model did not account for the preservation of indigenous identity or economic development of the colonies. This argument leads to the critical construction of development questions regarding what interests colonialism served both in the discipline of development studies and in the practice of development and what social realities in development practice make the colonial development model evident.

The colonial development "imaginary," as it relates to colonies appears bereft of development in the real sense of the word. For instance, Escobar (2000:11) argues that against the earlier consensus on the imperatives of development, a major development contradiction is the inability of development to fulfill its promises in addition to the resurgence of several movements that questioned Western development rationality. In recent literature, Rahnema (1997:379) puts forward a basic understanding of development failure in the postcolonial context, stressing that development did not fail because governments, institutions, and people implemented it poorly, but rather because it is "the wrong answer to (its target populations') needs and aspirations."

These perspectives suggest that colonialism and development linkages remain contestable and contradictory. The insufficient analysis of this link provides enough grounds for a critical appraisal of development in colonial contexts as well as patterns of colonial development prejudice. This includes the universalization of European Enlightenment and the claims on formal government replicated in the civil service and similar category of colonial structure in the social construction of governance.

Development, as a colonial legacy, is framed within the realm of colonial construct even though it is "defined" or "framed" as a modality for economic progress. There is less evidence regarding how the colonial state provided a model for the development of the colonies. Since it was an interventionist, coercive, and absolutist state, the true meanings and practices such as equitable, participatory, and inclusiveness as significant indicators of development were missing in the colonial state. Development as a transformational category can never exist outside the people for whom the development is meant. It is this alienation of the people from the alleged "colonial development model" that renders it anti-development.

Instead, the colonial state remained coercive and wielded power in the business of administration and policy formulation. For instance, it legislated in the interest of the colonial office (Coleman, 1958). As a socially constructed category, the colonial model must be scrutinized concerning the interests and economic well-being of the colonies. That is, in development studies, we need to ask, what development ends were served by colonialism? Which development institution of colonial administration served the transformation of the colonies concerning economic advancement with far-reaching effects? It is one thing to assert that colonialism was pro-development and another to provide quantifiable evidence of such claims. What interacting variables overtime justify these claims to the development of the colonies? When we follow Seers (1968) the questions regarding poverty, inequality, and unemployment are pervasive in postcolonial societies. How, then, do we make sense of colonial plunder, brutal force, and criminality? (see Rodney, 1972). The notion of the "colonial development model" remains contestable.

In reality, the colonial "civilization mission" and "development" indicators such as improved social well-being, improved standard of living, freedom, equality, are rarely critiqued in the postcolonial development theory and analysis. Critique of institutionalized postcolonial exploitation, which had taken a complex and systemic form such as neocolonialism, imperialism, neo-imperialism, and more recently globalization, remains less revolutionary. If this depiction of development failure must change, new realities must emerge, alternative development models, new ways of thinking, and development practice must be pursued to question and deconstruct the postcolonial order. It is based on the illusory notions of the colonial "development model" that a new postcolonial critique becomes inevitable.

THE EVOLVING BASIS FOR NEW POSTCOLONIAL CRITIQUE

The past decade or so has seen an explosion of interest in the area of postcolonial studies (Spivak, 1999; Bongie, 2008; Hardt and Negri, 2001; Hallward, 2002). What links are being forged between the old and new debates in postcolonial studies? In particular, what critical conceptual and methodological common ground is re-established, including the challenges and prospects of new and ongoing interdisciplinary linkages? Emphasis here is laid on what has been termed the "new postcolonial critique" and the implications such thinking has for the way we understand the postcolonial societies in the era of globalization and the particular context of power, economics, and politics in relation to colonial hegemony and economic development of postcolonial societies.

So what does the new postcolonial critique emphasize? New postcolonial critique is that way of thinking in the neocolonial era, which examines both the laudatory claims and critical strands of colonialism and lays off any uncritical analysis. The effect of this depiction of reality is to rethink the notion of a colonial legacy that circulates as obvious; "a way of life," "a model to be pursued by all peoples of the colonized order," "unquestioned," "natural occurrence," while pristine and indigenous knowledge production is taken for granted, emasculated, marginalized, and branded "primitive."

Three interrelated themes stand out in debates on new postcolonial critique in the social sciences and humanities. First, the idea of shift from the notion of traditional nationalist struggles, anticolonial agitation, pan-Africanism, and anti-imperialism which championed the cause for decolonization and liberation struggles exemplified in the writings of W. E. B. Du Bois, Marcus Garvey, and Franz Fanon, leading to the independence movements of many formerly colonized societies. Space and time have led to works that have moved from the colonial exploitation to a wider exploration of complex dynamics of postmodernization and postcolonial dependency as colonialism has also led to the emergence of globalized system in postcolonial nation-states, in line with the Eurocentric capitalist modernity (Wallestein, 2002; Amadi, 2012). This has opened space for new research inquiry.

In particular, recent decades have seen new trends in postcolonial studies, particularly new forms of re-colonization—the view of colonialism, premised on assumptions about "colonial emancipation" or "transformation" of the colonies or what has been termed "colonial legacy"—the notion of universalization of colonial ideologies and practices among postcolonial societies. This has led to framing of issues that have tended to ignore questions of dynamics of exploitation, indigenous knowledge production, across time and space, often excluded from the analysis of the key themes of underdevelopment as well as past historical depictions of development reality such as the impact of slavery and slave trade on the postcolonial societies.

Such a selective view of development issues resulted in a seminal critique of colonial plunder, especially, *How Europe Underdeveloped Africa* (Rodney, 1972). This in turn gave rise to the emergence of certain perspectives on postcolonial debates that largely derived from alternative arguments regarding postcolonial studies in development theory (Said, 1978). This has both theoretical and practical implications, as aspects of postcolonial underdevelopment strands become evident in development studies (Sachs,

2017). A greater attention to the debates surrounding the new postcolonial critique, and an exploration of its divergent implications, resulted in a more critical stance on postcolonial studies, one which explores a diverse range of new development perspectives, prospects and challenges in the globalization era such as post-modernization, post-structuralism, post-culturalism, post-developmentalism, feminism, and so on (Shiva, 1988; Giddens, 2001; Ferguson, 2006).

Second, the "development decade" and "development politics" of the global south framed around Western assumptions and understanding of the new turn neocolonialism and neo-imperialism have taken leading to structural adjustment policies, the rise of multinationals, or global corporatism of the erstwhile colonialists led to works on new forms of imperialism as well as rise of Western multinationals controlling the economic realities of the postcolonial societies (Said, 1994; Walestein, 2002; Calinicox, 2009; Bakan, 1995; Amadi, 2012).

In the 1970s, Edward Said's book *Orientalism* popularized postcolonial studies in academic debates. The postcolonial critique seeks to interrogate some of the assumptions of colonialism. In its broad field of inquiry, it aims to understand the colonial ideology and refutes the universalization of European Enlightenment both in cultural studies, power, knowledge production, gender, information, and dissemination. As Ingraham (1994:7) points out, it is a "mode of inquiry which makes use of what is and what is not said in any social text and theorizes the disjuncture between the two." Ingraham (1994:7) emphasizes that critique is "a 'decoding' practice which exposes textual boundaries and the ideologies which manage them, revealing the taken-for-granted order they perpetuate and opening up possibilities for changing it."

Postcolonial critique has both political and epistemological relevance in postcolonial theory and development discourse. It espouses indigenous culture reinstitution and identity restoration against colonial imposition, exploitation, gender inequality, cultural dislodgement, and imperialism (Amadi, 2018). It also denotes resistance to European knowledge production. For instance, Said (1978) critiqued the nineteenth-century European imaginaries of oriental cultures. This takes account of a wide range of research inquiries such as geography, history, anthropology, literary works, and social discourses to buttress their linkages with European colonial history and knowledge system. Orientalism constituted an academic field of inquiry to explore the Orient, also an exploration of the interconnections of knowledge production with political power, and in how such knowledge is administered and in the process results in the subjugation of the Orient. Young (2001) revisited some of the earlier assumptions of postcolonial critique including the anticolonial struggle movements and revival of indigenous knowledge. Thus, the

European hegemonic knowledge system was built around the oriental notion, in which dominant postcolonial critiques draw to pursue their arguments on European colonialism and modernization project (Said, 1978; Foucault, 1980a; Chakrabarty, 1992; Giddens, 1992; Ferguson, 2006; Quijano, 2007). Essentially, there is evidence of juxtaposition of colonialism with modernization as Aníbal Quijano (2007:171) points out that the era of European colonial domination was furthered with European modernity.

Critique of the Modernization School first arose in Latin America as a response to the bankruptcy of the program of the United Nations Economic Commission for Latin America (ECLA) (Amadi, 2012). In short, the ECLA promoted protectionist policies together with industrialization through import subsidies, which, in practice, resulted in a brief economic expansion in the 1950s followed by economic stagnation (unemployment, inflation, declining terms of trade, etc.) (Amadi, 2012). Relatedly, Escobar (2007:184) links colonialism to modernity pointing out that there is no modernity without colonialism.

Under these conditions, postcolonial inquiry investigates the implicit aftermath of the colonial knowledge production and overall social order, looking at the struggles to overcome the contradictions of colonial exploitation and related asymmetries. As a mode of inquiry that begins in postcolonial contexts, the postcolonial thesis explains and emphasizes how individual and collective social relations of the colonized societies were organized and exploited through systemic social arrangements. How this contact became institutionalized and undermined or enhanced the economic development of the colonized societies is central to postcolonial studies. Critical analysis of institutionalized postcolonial analysis reveals its linkages to the colonial labor force, mode of material wealth acquisition, mode of production, the economic interest of the colonial state, dynamics of production of social and economic hierarchies, and so on. An elaborated new postcolonial critique emphasizes that colonialism was bereft of elements of development; accountability, transparency, equality, and so on for its policies and practices within the colonies, rather an all interventionist and all-powerful colonial state existed alongside exploitation. It adopted coercion rather than dialogue. This has acerbated rather than reduced all forms of oppression in its practices. Propagating the legacy of colonialism not only provides ground for critical assessment to advance the theoretical reach of colonial exploitation and inquiry but equally provides the emancipatory orientation for postcolonial societies.

Third, since the turn of the millennium, postcolonial criticism has experienced growing concern regarding resurgent "post-postcolonial" turn or moment and the (in)adequacy of postcolonial models of critique to confront new power structures in a globalizing era (Simek, 2014). Thus, despite the surge of writings (Spivak, 1999; Bongie, 2008; Hardt and Negri, 2001;

Hallward, 2002; Simek, 2014), it appears postcolonial critique has been less transformative in Africa.

The exploitation, alienation, fear, and frustration that shaped decades of colonial exploitation gave rise to new thinking in the post-1990 era following the end of the Cold War as there was an increasing need to focus on dynamics that could contend with neocolonialism, neo-imperialism, new dependency and decolonization, to foster economic liberation as postcolonial Africa remains the poorest region. This accounted for the emergence of the new postcolonial critique and alternative development models. As this era marked possible end to the leviathan's legislative and executive domination over what should count in knowledge production, regulation, and dissemination— the so-called coloniality of power, knowledge and being (Ndlovu-Gatsheni, 2015). Essentially, the works of Botswanan feminist and postcolonial critic, Bagele Chilisa who consistently critiques Western knowledge production that undermines localized knowledge and gender inequality have been relevant in recent debates on decolonization of education and knowledge production.

How decoloniality could revolutionize global power, politics, social relations, and knowledge production remains a perennial problem in postcolonial societies. A recognition of the emergence of the network society, new nationalism, rise of racism and new identity, populism across Europe and America, current patterns and processes of modern slavery, immigration, and in particular, globalization has led to a wide body of new works in re-colonization and decolonization, including new forms of culture imperialism, evolutionary ecology, and climate change (LaCapra, 1991; Castels, 2000; Tomlinson, 2009; Gidens, 2001; Harvey, 2005; Amadi and Agena, 2014). These themes have cast new light on some perennial postcolonial problems such as issues of hybridity, globalization, environmental security, ecological injustice, environmental racism, gender inequality, and distributive justice. Thus, new perspectives in postcolonial studies have challenged modern slavery, immigration, new forms of racism, ecological breakdown, and environmental insecurity. The new postcolonial critique in a variety of ways challenges the deeply embedded conceptions of globalization, inequality, and increasing global chaos (Cerny and Prichard, 2017) and suggests new ways of thinking about postcolonial societies in the late twenty-first century and beyond.

Thus, new postcolonial critique examines the interrelations and interconnections, which, when viewed generally, provide a useful way of theorizing patterns and dynamics of production, distribution, and exchange inherent in the postcolonial societies. This sheds light on the understanding of inequality, power, and domination integral to colonialism and points to the basis for the exploration of the features of development in colonial contexts. Thus, all forms of anticolonial and recently anti-globalization movements and colonial resilience today can be referred to as new postcolonial critique. The rise of varieties of new postcolonial critique such as anti-racist movements, environmental rights movements, gender rights groups, anti-genetically modified foods (GMFs)movements, ecological justice, and social rights movements, and their implications on alternative development requires scholarly attention to attain a more lucid understanding in relation to new postcolonial critique.

Based on growing concern regarding the complex effects and challenges of colonial legacies in postcolonial societies, new postcolonial critique emerged to further critique colonialism and modalities for alternatives and in particular, broaden the scope of postcolonial studies. Easterly (2014) has suggested that Africa's postcoloniality is marked by rising poverty, hunger, and malnutrition. In the same vein, Driessen (2003) argues that European colonialism introduced chronic diseases that were alien to the colonies and had long ceased to exist in the developed societies.

In several decades of postcolonialism, the social apparatus of economic and political liberation remains enervated in the postcolonial order (Rist, 2008). Sen (1999) sums up development as the removal of obstacles and enlargement of choices and capabilities. Thus, new postcolonial critique is a new impetus to the original forms of decolonization such as nationalism. It extends to increasing concerns with post-structuralism, postmodernity, feminism, and recently post-development debates.

New postcolonial critique revisits post–Cold War underdevelopment as well as development failures of the postcolonial societies. It reexamines such failures and in particular the ways recent "modernity trends" manifest and structure the rise of indigenous development. Sociologist Manuel Castells had argued that new society had emerged following globalization, this society is built on what he called the "information hypertext" which has changed the notion of social relations. What has remained increasingly contradictory is how the poor postcolonial societies are catching up with trends associated with these changes.

The increasing failure of the postcolonial state to provide alternative routes to new frontiers of power in a globalizing order resulted in the emergence of new development thinking (Spivak, 1999, 2014; Hardt and Negri, 2001; Hallward, 2002; Rist, 2008; Simek, 2014; Stiglitz, 2019). The rise of new postcolonial critique in the late 2000s provoked radical scholarship to further interrogate postcolonial legacies of the late twenty-first century largely linked to globalization, ecological breakdown, modern slavery, racism, feminism, and knowledge production. In particular, postcolonial debates have been an offshoot of postcolonial literary studies in the 1960s following the works of writers such as Chinua Achebe, Peter Abrahams, Charles Nnolim, and Ayi Kwei Armah.

Against this backdrop, how can new postcolonial critique provide a model of alternative development taking into consideration the persistence of poverty, neocolonial influence, neo-imperialism, exploitation, and global power asymmetry? In particular, what are the potential ramifications of new postcolonial critique in the transformation of postcolonial societies of Africa? These are some of the cutting edge debates in the present volume. This volume adopts a multi-disciplinary approach including theoretical, conceptual, and case examples in critiquing the universalist assumptions of the colonial development model in the context of capitalism's bogus claim of universal expansion from Europe to the rest of the world. Besides, the chapters connect colonialism and vested colonial economic interests to the problem of non-institutionalization of development among the postcolonial societies. This entails an analysis of power relations to unravel the illusions of the development assumptions of colonialism. As Acemoglu, Johnson, and Robinson (2002), and Sokoloff and Engerman (2000) have argued, that colonialism affected the institutional environment differently, which had varying institutional impacts on the economic performance of the postcolonial societies. This volume critiques the notion of "colonial development" as a tool that legitimizes capitalist exploitation and control. Furthermore, the chapters acknowledge the continued theoretical relevance of dependency, neocolonialism, neo-imperialism, and globalization in postcolonial development studies and see as crucial such conceptual frameworks, in understanding the state, economy, and the international capitalist system in the analysis of the development of the developing societies.

Above all, the volume seeks to demonstrate that colonialism in the first place was not intended to develop the colonies; rather it was an invention to further the economic interests of Europe. Therefore, an attempt is made to explain the gaps in the new postcolonial theory by demonstrating the dearth of postcolonial development critique of contemporary Western globalization, knowledge production, and underrepresentation and marginalization of the Third World societies such as Africa, and in particular, demonstrate how alternative development paths could be fostered.

As a result, the book calls for a reconsideration of the notion of colonial development model as the key organizing concept of postcolonial societies, to deconstruct the prevailing practice, in which institutionalized colonial vestiges undermine indigenous knowledge production and values. This requires a new engagement with new postcolonial critique. If such notions are institutionalized in Africa's development paradigm, the aim of this volume may have been served.

CONCLUSION

The volume reflects how development policy and practice can lead to more inclusive, equitable, and fairer global development systems among the poor societies with Africa in perspective. Chapters of this volume draw on theoretical and conceptual perspectives from a range of disciplines (e.g., history, politics, communication, economics, sociology, ecology). Central to the book is an investigation of how postcolonial development research can lead to practice and action, especially when set against the increasing development crises of African societies, through alternative approaches involving inclusive, equitable, fair, and people-based models. The book aims to explore multiple perspectives across postcolonial studies, incorporating case studies from across Africa in particular, exploring nuanced theoretical debates on postcolonial discourse identifying what worked and what did not work, drawing from historical, comparative, and contemporary perspectives to explore the decolonization of colonial development models by providing alternative approaches.

The book particularly offers innovative research agenda that explores the changing contexts, emerging potentials, and challenges to postcolonial studies. Recent development trends following globalization suggest that postcolonial studies in the global south are in a period of transition and innovation. The book draws attention to emerging development contradictions and changing contexts of postcolonial research.

REFERENCES

Acemoglu, D., Johnson, S. & Robbinson, J. (2002). Reversal of fortunes: Geography, and institutions in the making of the modern world income distribution. *Quarterly Journal of Economics* 118, 1231–1294.

Agger, B. (1992). *Cultural Studies as Critical Theory*. London: Falmer.

Agozino, B. (2019). Humanifesto of the decolonization of criminology and justice. *Decolonization of Criminology and Justice* 1(1), 5–28.

Ake, C. (1996). *Democracy and Development in Africa*. Washington, DC: Brookings Institution.

Allen, F. (2016) Decolonizing African Political Science and the Question of the Relevance of the Discipline for Developmet (181–192), In Sabelo J. Ndlov-Gatsheni and Siphomandla Zondi (eds). Decolonizing the Univesity Knowledge Systems and Development in Africa, North Carolina: Carolina University Press

Alesina, A., Easterly, W. & Matuszeski, J. (2011). Artificial states. *Journal of the European Economic Association* 9(2): 246–277.

Althusser, L. (1971). Ideology and ideological state apparatuses. In L. Althusser (Ed.), *Lenin and Philosophy and Other Essays*, pp. 127–186. London: New Left Books.

Amadi, L. (2018). Reinventing global ethics, globalization and inequality: Africa in perspective (354–1377). In M. Masaeli, S. Yaya, & R. Sneller (Eds.), *African Perspectives on Global Development*. UK: Cambridge Scholars Publishing.

Amadi, L. & Ekekwe, E. (2014). Corruption and development administration in Africa institutional approach. *African Journal of Political Science and International Relations* 8(6): 163–174.

Amin, S. (1972). Underdevelopment and dependence in black Africa origins and contemporary forms. *The Journal of Modern African Studies* 10(4): 503–524.

Appadurai, A. (1996). *Modernity at Large: Cultural Dimensions of Globalization.* Minneapolis, MN: University of Minnesota Press.

Ashcroft, B., Griffiths, G. & Tiffin, H. (1989). *The Empire Writes Back: Theory and Practice in PostColonial Literatures.* London: Routledge.

Bhabba, H. (1994). *The Location of Culture.* New York: Routledge.

Birdsall, N. (2006). The World is not Flat: Inequality and Injustice in our Global Economy UNU World Institute for Development Economics Research (UNU-WIDER) WIDER Annual Lecture 9.

Branko, M. (2006). Global income inequality: A review. *World Economics* 7(1): 131–157.

Bruce. C .(1999). Webs with no spiders, spiders with no webs: The genealogy of the developmental state. In Meredith Woo-Cummings (Ed.), *The Developmental State,* pp. 61–92. Ithaca, NY: Cornell University Press.

Chakrabarty, D. (1992). Provincializing Europe: Postcoloniality and the critique of history. *Cultural Studies* 6(3): 337–357.

Chakrabarty, D. (2000). *Provincializing Europe: Postcolonial Thought and Historical Difference.* Princeton, NJ: Princeton University Press.

Chang, H. (1999). The economic theory of the developmental state. In Meredith Woo-Cumings (Ed.), *The Developmental State,* pp. 182–199. Ithaca, NY: Cornell University Press.

Clapham, C. (1996). *Africa and the International System. The Politics of State Survival.* Cambridge Press.

Coleman, J. (1958). *Nigeria Background to Nationalism.* University of California Press.

Driessen, P. (2003). *Eco-Imperialism: Green Power, Black Death.* Belleview, WA: Free Enterprise Press.

Easterly, W. (2007). Was development assistance a mistake? William easterly. *The American Economic Review* 97(2): 328–332.

Easterly, W. (2014). *The Tyranny of Experts: Economists, Dictators, and the Forgotten Rights of the Poor.* Basic Books.

Eisler, R. (2007). *The Real Wealth of Nations.* San Francisco, CA: Berrett-Koehler Publishers.

Engerman, S. & Sokoloff, K. (2000). History lessons: Institutions, factor endowments, and paths of development in the new world. *Journal of Economic Perspectives* 14(3): 217–232.

Escobar, A. (1995). *Encountering Development: The Making and Unmaking of the Third World.* Princeton, NJ: Princeton University Press.

Escobar, A. (2000). Beyond the search for a paradigm? Post-development and beyond. *Development* 43(4): 11–14. The Society for International Development. London: SAGE Publications.

Escobar, A. (2007). Worlds and knowledges otherwise. *Cultural Studies* 21(2): 179–210.

Esteva, G. (1992). Development. In Wolfgang Sachs (Ed.), *The Development Dictionary: A Guide to Knowledge as Power,* pp. 6–25. London: Zed Books Ltd.

Etounga-Manguelle, D. (2000). Does Africa need a cultural adjustment programme? In S.P. Huntington & L.E. Harrison (Eds.), *Culture Matters: How Values Shape Human Progress.* New York: Basic Books.

Ferguson, J. (2006). *Decomposing Modernity: History and Hierarchy after Development.* Irvine, CA: Department of Anthropology, University of California, Irvine.

Foucault, M. (1980a). *Power/Knowledge: Selected Interviews and Other Writings 1972–1977.* Hertfordshire: Harvester Press.

Foucault, M. (1980b). Power and strategies. In C. Gordon (Ed.), *Power/Knowledge,* pp. 134–145. New York: Pantheon.

Giddens, A. (1991). *Modernity and Self-identity: Self and Society in the Late Modern Age.* Stanford University Press.

Hall, S. (1992). *The West and the Rest: Discourse and Power.* Oxford: Polity.

Hallward, P. (2002). *Absolutely Postcolonial: Writing between the Singular and the Specific.* Manchester University Press.

Hardt, M. & Negri, A. (2000). *Empire.* Cambridge, MA: Harvard University Press.

Henderson, D. (2018). The genuine wealth of nations. *Hoover Digest,* No. 2, Spring Hoover Institution.

Ingraham, C. (1994). The heterosexual imaginary: Feminist sociology and theories of gender. *Sociological Theory* 12(2): 203–219.

Johnson, C. (1982). *MITI and the Japanese Miracle.* Stanford, CA: Stanford University Press.

Kraidy, M. (2002). Hybridity in cultural globalization. *Communication Theory* 12(3): 316–339.

Matthews, S. (2004). Post-development theory and the question of alternatives: A view from Africa. *Third World Quarterly* 25(2): 373–384.

Melber, H. (2017). *Development Studies and the SDGs - Mapping an Agenda.* EADI Policy Paper Series.pp1–13

Milanovic, B. (2012). *Globalization and Inequality.* Cheltenham: Edward Elgar Publishing Limited.

Mercer, K. (1990) *Welcome to the Jungle: Identity and Diversity in Postmodern Politics.* London: Lawrence & Wishart.

Nandy, A. (1983). *The Intimate Enemy: Loss and Recovery of Self Under Colonialism.* Oxford: Oxford University Press.

Nelson, S. (2013). Koh-I noor diamond will not be returned to India, David Cameron insists. Huffington Post UK. https://www.huffingtonpost.co.uk/2013/02/21/koh-i-noordiamond-not-returned-india-david-cameron-insistspictures_n_2732342.html?guccoun

Ndlovu-Gatsheni, S. (2015). Decoloniality as the future of Africa. *History Compass* 13(10): 485–496.

Nustad, K. (2001). Development: The devil we know? *Third World Quarterly* 22(4): 479–489.

Nyman, J. (2007). The hybridity of the Asian American subject in Cynthia Kadohata's floating world. In K. Nyman (Ed.), *Reconstructing Hybridity: Post-colonial Studies in Transition*, pp. 195–230. Amsterdam and New York: Rodopi.

Ohmae, K. (1995). *The End of the Nation State*. New York: Free Press.

Okowa, W. (1996). *How the Negro Underdeveloped the Tropics: A Questioning Theory of Development*. Diobu: Port Harcourt Paragraphics.

Onimode, B. (1983). *The Political Economy of the African Crisis*. London: Zed Books and Institute for African Alternatives.

Pempel, T. (1999). The developmental regime in a changing world economy. In Meredith Woo Cummings (Ed.), *The Developmental State*, pp. 137–181. Ithaca, NY: Cornell University Press.

Pieterse, J. (1991). Dilemmas of development discourse: The crisis of developmentalism and the comparative method. *Development and Change* 22(1): 5–29.

Pieterse, J. (2000). After post-development, *Third World Quarterly* 21(2): 175–191.

Pieterse, J. (2010). *Development Theory: Deconstructions/Reconstructions*, 2nd edition. London: Sage Publications Ltd.

Quijano, A. (2007). Coloniality and modernity/rationality. *Cultural Studies* 21(2): 168–178.

Rahnema, M. (1997). Towards post-development: searching for signposts, a new language and new paradigms. In M. Rahnema & V. Bawntree (Eds.), *The Post-Development Reader*, pp. 377–403. Cape Town: David Philip.

Rahnema, M. & Bawtree, V. (Eds.) (1997). *The Post-Development Reader*. Cape Town: David Philip.

Rist, G. (2008). *The History of Development: From Western Origins to Global Faith*. Translated by Patrick Camiller, 3rd edition. London: Zed Books Ltd.

Rodney, W. (1972). *How Europe Underdeveloped Africa*. Washington, DC: Howard University Press.

Sachs, W. (1992). *The Development Dictionary: A Guide to Knowledge as Power*. London: Zed Books.

Said, E. (1978). *Orientalism*. New York: Vintage Books.

Santos, B. (1995). *Toward a New Common Sense: Law, Science and Politics in the Paradigmatic Transition*. London and New York: Routledge.

Schuurman, F .(2000). Paradigms lost, paradigms regained? Development studies in the twenty-first century. *Third World Quarterly* 21(1): 7–20.

Seers, D. (1969). The meaning of development. *International Development Review* 11(4): 1–6.

Sen, A. (1999). *Development as Freedom*. Oxford: Oxford University Press.

Sharp, J. (2009). *Geographies of Post Colonialism: Spaces of Power and Representation*. Thousand Oaks, CA: Sage Publications.

Simek, N. (2014).The criticism of postcolonial critique. In J.R. Di Leo (Eds.), *Criticism after Critique*. New York: Palgrave Macmillan.

Spivak, G. (1985). Feminism and critical theory. In P. Treichler, C. Kramarae, & B. Stafford (Eds.), *For Alma Mater*, pp. 119–142. Chicago: University of Illinois Press.

Spivak G. (1988). Can the subaltern Speak? In G. Nelson & L. Grossberg (Eds.), *Marxism and the Interpretation of Culture*. Urbana, IL: University of Illinois Press.

Spivak, G. (1999). *A Critique of Postcolonial Reason: Toward A History of the Vanishing Present* Harvard University Press.

Spivak, G. (2014). *The Post-Colonial Critic: Interviews, Strategies, Dialogues*. New York: Routledge.

Todaro, M. (1979). *Economics for a Developing World*. London: Longman.

Wallerstein, I. (1979). *The Capitalist World-Economy*. Cambridge: Cambridge University Press.

Webster, R., Magdoff, H. & Nowell, C. (2018). *Western Colonialism.* Encyclopædia Britannica, Inc.

Weinstein, B. (2008). Developing inequality. *The American Historical Review* 113(1): 1–18.

Young, C. (1988). The African colonial state and its political legacy. In D. Rothchild & N. Chazan (Eds.), *The Precarious Balance State and Society in Africa.* West View Press.

Young, C. (1994). *The Nature and Genesis of the Colonial State in the African Colonial State in Comparative Perspective*, pp. 43–76. Yale University Press.

Young, R. (2001). *Postcolonialism: An Historical Introduction*. Wiley-Blackwell.

Chapter 1

Development Paradigms and the Framing of Postcolonial Identity

Urbanization, Waterfront Development, and the Eko o ni baje *Ethos/Slogan in Lagos*

Adebisi Alade

This chapter examines the politics of waterfront development in postcolonial Lagos within the context of *Eko o ni baje* (which means, Lagos shall never decline, Lagos shall keep soaring, or Lagos will not spoil) ethos. Following its coinage between 1999 and 2007, successive administrations have deployed the slogan as a participatory ideology to mobilize grassroots support for neoliberal development programs to transform Lagos into a world-class city. While some scholars view such development as "urban fantasies," this chapter shows how the identities and voices of people in marginal communities across Lagos waterfronts have been attacked and silenced under the exercise of state power. It argues that, though the ethos nurtures opportunity for citizens' participation in urban transformation, its distortion as a legitimizing discourse for elitist/modernist development renders poor Lagosians in informal settlements as invisible urban workforce, and as a "threat" to the city's progress. By showing how globally circulating development models interact with and are reshaped by local context, the chapter challenges the Lagos government's rhetoric of *Eko o ni baje*, which correlates neoliberal projects with good governance. It recommends that postcolonial waterfront development projects, as a model of industrial modernity, should be pursued with respect for people's right to basic amenities.

INTRODUCTION

In the early 1980s, it was estimated that about 1.4 million new buildings would be required to mitigate the growing deficiency of inclusive housing infrastructure in Lagos before the year 2000 (Lagos State Ministry of Economic Planning and Land Matters, 1980). However, successive military regimes that managed the state from 1983 to 1999 failed to make adequate provision for the new housing units as only 10% of the projected figure was completed by 2000 (Lagos State Ministry of Economic Planning and Budget, 2013, pp. 48–49). Under the influence of rapid urbanization and poverty, street trading and squatter/informal settlements increased, both on land and on waterfronts. In a bid to transform Lagos after he assumed office in 1999, the civilian administration of Asiwaju Bola Tinubu, which ended the fifteen years of military rule in Lagos, adopted a participatory governance approach to managing the city's development crisis as well as to legitimize his policy interventions.

Tinubu's government invented the city's participatory development ethos/slogan: *Eko o ni baje* to engage residents in the process of urban transformation that his administration planned to implement. By giving every Lagosian a sense of belonging and responsibility in the development of the city, the ethos enhanced civic participation and acceptance of state-led social programs. As the regime rolled out its development projects, this slogan quickly evoked a vision of a "new city," especially when the administration initiated, among others, a New/Satellite Town Development Scheme that was to provide low-cost housing units for Lagosians (Nwanna, 2015, pp. 311–312). The overwhelming support he enjoyed at the end of his tenure encouraged successive administrations to constantly deploy *Eko o ni baje* as a development discourse to unite Lagosians against the status quo, to transform the physical appearance of the city, and unintentionally, to exclude poor working-class residents from access to land and social services as the city strives for international competitiveness.

Although the ethos/slogan was initially coined to gain residents' support for continuous renewal of the city toward achieving a world-class status, its unintended consequences have however been gentrification and forced evictions of poor Lagosians from informal settlements as a result of the government's uncritical adoption of foreign development models. For instance, despite the creation of the Lagos Megacity Development Authority (LMDA) by the Federal Government in July 2006 with an accompanying World Bank loan of $200 million for slum upgrade, the acceleration of property and infrastructural development in Lagos still resulted in the forced eviction of Otodo-Gbame, Ilubirin, and Makoko/Iwaya waterfront residents to make way for neoliberal "world-class" property development (Obono, 2007, p. 36; Ojo & Meynen, 2012). As Governor Babatunde Fashola (2007–2015) used the "Eko o ni baje" slogan to legitimize the launching of the Eko Atlantic City project in 2003, houses of people living on the fringes of Bar Beach were burned down by the Nigerian police force in 2008 to create space for construction equipment (Oyelowo, 2013).

While some scholars have considered the role of waterfronts in increasing government revenue via job creation and tourism (Minca, 1995; Hurley, 2006), others have demonstrated its usefulness for city boosting (Clarke, 2006; Forward, 1970). Also, much has been written on neoliberal urban renewal and its effect on a slum in developing countries (Frederick, 1983; Myers, 2003). However, local sociopolitical ideologies that cast these processes and phenomena as "development" are yet to be examined in detail as works investigating cities' development ethos/slogans as a conduit for critiquing public policy legitimization in Africa are still lacking. Since Lagos presents a striking case of the crisis of urbanization in West Africa (Olukoju, 2004), this chapter discusses the forceful dislocation of poor Lagosians on Makoko waterfront and assesses the political purpose that *Eko o ni baje* ethos serves, especially regarding how it fosters marginalization and favoritism across the different strata of postcolonial Lagos.

On the one hand, the chapter examines the living condition in the Makoko waterfront community in the context of Lagos's development and how the state government has been instrumentalizing *Eko o ni baje* ethos to deflect the problem of urbanization to poor people in the city. On the other hand, it explores the tension between globally circulating urban development models, their uncritical importation, as well as the local experiences in Lagos. Drawing on a broad range of sources (published and archival), the chapter demonstrates how the government's urban fantasies in Lagos advance our understanding of city transformation and waterfront development in the African context. It does not only reveal the plight of the poor urban working class in Lagos, it also attempts to liberate *Eko o ni baje* ethos from the government's distortion as a legitimizing discourse for forced eviction. The chapter recommends that in addition to capital investment in slum upgrade (instead of demolition), the Lagos state government should adopt a genuine participatory development structure that would instrumentalize grassroots contribution to urban renewal policy articulation and implementation.

IMAGINED CITIES: THEORIZING EXOGENOUS AFRICAN URBAN DEVELOPMENT FANTASIES

Since independence, urban development has been a major problem in most African states given their significance as nodes of ideas, sociopolitical development, and local economic growth. As politicians strive to transform and make their cities more internationally competitive, scholars have identified several barriers which appear to be legacies of colonialism in these cities (Falola & Salm, 2005; Mendelsohn, 2018). While most colonial capital in Africa is port cities with far-reaching impact on their spatial organization and growth (Olukoju, 1993; Gleave, 1997), other patterns and structures include the centralization of administrative power, state control of land, segregation, and increasing slum settlements (Fox, 2014). According to postcolonial theorists, these features survived decolonization and prevail in many African independent states (Ake, 1996; Mbembe, 2001).

Theorizing these features as what remained colonial in postcolonial African cities, Rakodi (1995) and Mamdani (1996) situate their persistence within the broader analysis of African decolonization, which occurred under conditions that allowed the maximal incorporation rather than a repudiation of colonial state's residues into the "new" postcolonial state. By analyzing the recolonization of African cities by postcolonial political and capitalist elites, urban theorists show that the most profound legacy of colonialism in Africa is the retention of colonial urban planning ideas and laws as the inherited structure turns cities into battlegrounds of power interplay (Njoh, 2003; Ndi, 2007). In this battleground, the state retains exclusive right to land while deploying collectivist ideologies as tools of social control in a bid to produce "better cities" (Pile et al., 1999; Murray & Myers, 2006). In this sense, ownership, control, and uses of urban space are not only contested, but actions/inactions of (state/non-state) actors go a long way to determine inclusion/exclusion (Cooper, 1987; Myers, 2003).

Henri Lefebvre's article particularly indicates that even though "there are no longer colonies in the old sense of the word, but there already is a [metropolitan] semi-colonization which subjects immigrants from the rural areas . . . to a concentrated exploitation through the methods and system of spatial segregation" (Lefebvre, 1976, p. 36). This perspective depicts the top-down pattern of most postcolonial town planning as a colonial legacy that is helping to create contrasting walled/gated highbrow neighborhoods and ghettos in cities (Pile et al., 1999: Chapter 4). Also, it is this "policy of economic and cultural marginalization [which] the West had imposed in the colonial era and adopted by postcolonial epochs, that caused African labor to relocate within what is now imperialistically termed as the 'informal' economies" (Ndi, 2007, p. 28). In most former colonial capitals in Africa, these informal settings are found in slums and on waterfronts. With the size of the urban middle class increasing alongside the inherited inequalities in these slum and informal communities on waterfronts, a range of other theoretical perspectives have emerged on how African city planners and politicians are trying to challenge and transform urban informalities and disorder.

Marcinkoski (2017) suggests that the desired models for developing African cities are often those found outside the continent in form of tourist/luxury enclaves. Others connect the increasing fancy architecture in many postcolonial African cities to statist economic agenda and competition for investment, which pushes politicians toward neoliberal projects (Cain, 2014; Nwanna, 2015). Using the transformation of Baltimore as a case study, Harvey (2001) theorizes waterfront renovations as part of urban development, which travels alongside neoliberal development. Noting the unintended gentrification that such policy mobility usually provokes in cities, he joins other critics to argue that distributive issues and social costs are often neglected when implementing these fancy capitalist urban transformation projects.

Despite the persistent problem of housing in postcolonial African cities, Vanessa Watson (2014) observes that African politicians prefer the globally circulating elitist and enclavist models, which she theorizes as "urban fantasies." According to the author, the alienating models are preferable because African elites believe that the "new cities and developments will be 'self-contained' and able to insulate them[selves] from the 'disorder' and 'chaos' of the existing cities" (Watson, 2014, p. 229). Thus, foreign property developers are hired to map out cities for the new visions. In his critique of the neoliberal urban renewal, Murray (2017: chapter 8) argues that informal settlements of poor urban working class are targeted as a disorder that must be removed to pave the way for a world-class megacity. While politicians continue to present this exclusionary model of development as positive transformation, the author's framework casts their *modus operandi* as the "suspension of the rule of law and the 'unexceptional' relaxation of conventional regulatory regimes, where the use of the rhetoric of emergency, necessity, and the 'common good' typically serve as the grounds for legitimation" (Murray, 2017, p. 307).

Theorists have further shown that African politicians and city planners have shifted their desired artistic style of the imagined cities away from mimicking former imperial metropoles such as Paris and London to the twenty-first-century architectural designs in Dubai, Shanghai, Singapore, and Tokyo (Watson, 2009, 2017). With little care for context, these models often ignore local particularities, including culture, economies, climate, and history (Murray, 2017, p. 27). Examples of such tourist/luxury enclaves include the Eko Atlantic city in Lagos, the proposed Konza Techno City in Nairobi, the Moroccan Green City of Mohammed IV, Hope City in Accra, and the proposed Zenata Eco City in Casablanca. For Watson, the moral "Trojan horse" that politicians usually deploy in advancing these revanchist programs is the prospective reliable infrastructure, economic opportunities, and crime-free environment that such modernist projects promise to engender. However, given the failure of government to leverage the assets of African cities in establishing new development paradigms, most imported urban development models have largely exacerbated the living condition of Africans they are supposed to improve as the limited resources in cities are shifted away from the majority poor (Watson, 2009, pp. 176–178).

Given the economic and social disruption caused by these anti-poor urban fantasies, scholars have linked the neoliberal model to urban place marketing and entrepreneurialism, which engender social polarization (Harvey, 1989; Marcinkoski, 2017). While these imagined tourist cities sometimes attract capital investments to African cities, the jobs they create are usually for a particular group of people with a particular qualification that is unlikely to benefit the majority of urban lower-class residents who constitute the subaltern class (Watson, 2017). In other words, the development projects that claim to be undertaken explicitly in service of poor urban working-class Africans remain inaccessible to them. Worse still, the latter's "informal" settlements are summarily removed from African commercial hubs to accommodate luxury enclaves that conform to postcolonial politicians' idea of rational order.

Yet, theories of modernity and neoliberalism do not often capture the politics of urban transformation (Parnell & Robinson, 2012). Thus, postcolonial theorists have rejected the simplistic understanding of African urban fantasies by proposing that we examine the complex relationship between the rulers and the ruled (Mbembe, 2001: chapter 3). Building on Sylvia Croese's study of Luanda's waterfront development, which views the politics of city boosting and rebranding in postcolonial Africa as an undemocratic quest of weak postcolonial states to achieve domestic legitimacy and stability (Croese, 2018), this chapter contributes to the bourgeoning literature on urban transformation by suggesting that we study how African politicians and city planners correlate anti-poor development models with good governance and improvement, especially through their mobilization of participatory development ethos/slogans like *Eko o ni baje*.

Lagos development scholars are yet to fully explore the unconventional uses and impact of *Eko o ni baje* as a development discourse in the recent transformation of the city. Few who have examined the purpose that the ideology serves only do within the context of its normative stance—for uplifting Lagosians and expressing their tenacity as they make collective effort to develop the city (Opeibi, 2007, p. 238; Akinsete et al., 2014, p. 238; Gant, 2017, pp. 5–6). To Agbetiloye (2020), it means "that all hands are on deck to ensure the progress and development of the state." Adegoju (2013, p. 282) tilts toward this conventional understanding of *Eko o ni baje* by arguing that "when people are adequately mobilized in their languages, the results can be quite impressive." Taking the ideology at face value like many Lagosians, the author pays less attention to the exclusionary tendencies of the ethos/slogan as he submits that residents sometimes turned themselves into watchdogs of the Lagos "megacity dream." Albeit, he makes an important contribution by noting that Lagos political elites strategically adopted the mantra for political expediency. By showing the legitimizing function of *Eko o ni baje* ethos within the context of postcolonial development in Lagos, the chapter agrees with Edward Said that "neither imperialism nor colonialism is a simple act of accumulation and acquisition. Both are supported and perhaps even impelled by impressive ideological formations" (Said, 1993, p. 8).

HISTORICAL CONTEXT (LATE COLONIAL POLICY) OF URBAN REGENERATION IN LAGOS

It was estimated in 2014 that about 1 billion people live in urban informal settlement globally (UN-Habitat, 2014; Collier et al., 2019, p. 3). Even before this time in sub-Saharan Africa, 71.9% of urban population had been living in slums and waterfront settlements by 2001 where basic amenities and social services are non-existent (UN-Habitat, 2003, p. 13). This is because urban development and revitalization that should be rooted in the interpretation of African cities' history and cultural tradition continue to toe the path of the European urban revitalization model, often without the human security component of the latter. From the forced removal of the autochthonous from the Ikoyi area of Lagos in 1919 to pave the way for a European Reservation Area to the establishment of the Lagos Executive Development Board (LEDB) in 1928 as a response to the 1924–1930 Bubonic plague in the colonial capital (Olukoju, 2013, p. 24; Bigon, 2016), redlining, gentrification, and demolition of informal settlements had been part of the unintended consequences of colonial town planning before 1960.

Of these urban renewal attempts by the colonial government in Lagos, the most controversial was implemented in the late 1940s and early 1950s. This was due to two major reasons. The first is the population increase from 98,303 in 1921 to 267,407 in 1952, and the rate of urbanization that increased from 10 to 48.2% in Lagos from 1951 (Sada, 1969, pp. 117–133; Gandy, 1996, p. 386). Second, following the forced removal of Lagosians from the Victoria Island and Ikoyi areas to Mushin and Ikeja parts of the commercial city to establish among others, a race course, a Marina, and a Supreme Court building in the 1930s, the economic impact of World War II worsened the living condition of poor colonized Africans (Olukoju, 1993). Perceiving the urban poor as a threat to its desired "modern" city, the LEDB declared a slum clearance scheme in March 1951, which targeted low-income communities in Broad Street, Balogun, Idumota, Isale-Agbede, Aroloya, and Victoria Street (*Daily Times*, March 29 1951). While ignoring the postwar poverty and high cost of living in the city, city officials couched their ill-timed urban renewal program, which gentrified residential neighborhoods in the language of humanitarianism, civic/social responsibility, and improvement.

The city's development board emphasized that the revitalization across the city "aims at re-planning Lagos on a more scientific basis . . . [and] one of the boldest adventures in human engineering to be devised throughout the continent of Africa" (*West African Pilot*, April 5 1951). This generated polarized responses from Africans. For instance, the Nigerian Youth Movement who though supported the re-planning of Lagos critiqued the urban renewal scheme based on its method and timing. The youth group argued in the *Daily Service* of April 5, 1951, that:

> Building materials now cost five times their worth in 1946. The acute housing condition in Lagos today is such as makes the scheme right at the outset almost prohibitive. The rehousing scheme planned at Suru Lere [Lagos Mainland] is far from being satisfactory. It will mean a very high increase in the budget of those who may be lucky to find room in Suru Lere. Through no fault of theirs, people whose children school in Lagos would be compelled to waste money on transport . . . a lot of inconveniences will be experienced by workers whose offices are in Lagos.

Indeed, the colonial government in Lagos could not control the abnormally high prices and scarcity of building materials in the postwar era. Although a resettlement plan that would provide victims of the slum clearance with alternative housing had not been constructed, the city planners were more interested in clearing the business districts at all cost. Even if this unsound LEDB urban renewal project, which aimed at destroying over 1,400 houses, was justified by the state's rhetoric of sanitation and public health, the 913 proposed housing schemes in Surulere only provided for 5,000 persons (*Daily Service*, April 6 1951; *Daily Service*, April 19 1951).

To further display their insensitivity to the plight of the "unsophisticated" urban poor and "fanatical" public defenders, Lagos urban managers issued a strongly worded public warning to the city's perceived enemies of progress who objected to the "real road to salvation" (*West African Pilot* April 7 1951). For most Lagosians, however, the urban renewal scheme was far from being their road to salvation. Instead, it was nothing short of a disguise for land grabbing. Convinced that the re-planned Lagos Island area was not intended for the habitation of low-income Africans that were evicted, Lagos civil society representatives responded to the colonial government's public warning by dissociating themselves from the Lagos Legislative Council which supported the initiative (*Daily Service*, April 10, 1951, and July 14, 1954). In particular, all parties against the urban renewal scheme, including the Lagos Market Women Guild, the Lagos Advisory Council, the Lagos Aborigines Central Council, and the Egbe Ilu of Lagos (the Lagos Town Council), adopted a joint resolution demanding that the colonial governor John Macpherson suspend the slum clearance to allow civil society study the scheme (*Daily Service*, April 10, 1951).

This colonial essentialist vision of cities as well as the state hidden normative theories of governance extended into the postcolonial period, where in urban Lagos, similar ambitious urban renewal programs would colonize the city's social reality—the failure of government. The case of neglect in the Makoko waterfront community offers a useful example, not only of urban stratification and forced eviction in most developing countries but also that globally circulating urban development policies and models are not implemented uniformly but rather interact with and are reshaped by local context.

POSTCOLONIAL URBAN RENEWAL: *EKO O NI BAJE* ETHOS AND MAKOKO WATERFRONT SETTLEMENT

After the city of Lagos became a state in 1967, the state government established the Lagos State Development and Property Corporation (LSDPC) to replace the LEDB. Given the severe economic recession and the consequent lack of funds for infrastructural development in the late 1970s and 1980s (Zeleza, 1999), many rural and peri-urban dwellers migrated to Lagos in search of employment opportunities. The local causes of these problems were the massive post-civil war exodus from Eastern Nigeria to Lagos and the mismanagement of the huge oil wealth of the previous years. The resultant population explosion and housing deficit increased the number of residents in Lagos's informal waterfront communities, including Agboyin, Iwaya, Ilaje, Oworonshoki, Makoko, and Moba. During the military regime of the late 1980s and early 1900s, efforts to impose rational order on the city culminated in the displacement of poor working-class residents from some of the slum settlements (Agboola & Jinadu, 1997). Among others, about 300,000 low-income families were forcefully evicted from the Makoko waterfront in southeast Lagos in July 1990 (Nwanna, 2015). The "slum" is now Victoria Island Extension and Lekki Phase I—a mega-expensive plot of land with multi-million-naira properties such as the Oniru Private Housing Estate, which evicted Lagosians could not afford.

Without any doubt, the developed properties beautified Lagos, but they also served other purposes. The displacement they engendered made the poor poorer as people lost their properties and also faced housing, health, and employment problems. Out of about 42,000 residents with proof of ownership in the community, just 2,933 landlords who had received their proof of ownership before 1972 were rhetorically resettled as the apartments allocated to them were not habitable (Folarin, 2010, pp. 70–71). On the other hand, the socially connected capitalist and political elites who had not necessarily owned properties in the community successfully secured new homes. Following other waterfront evictions in Ilubinrin, Ijora-Badiya, and Ijora Oloye in 1996, many of those rendered homeless moved to Makoko waterfront (Folarin, 2010, p. 59; Centre on Housing Rights & Evictions, 2006, p. 4), an informal settlement built with stilt-supported shacks, bounded on the east by a lagoon and on the south by the Third Mainland Bridge.

The displaced people could hardly contest their eviction as the 1978 Land Use Act states that "all land comprised in the territory of each State in the Federation are hereby vested in the Governor of that State and such land shall be held in trust and administered for the use and common benefit of all Nigerians following the provisions of this Act" (Laws of the Federation of Nigeria, 1990, Part I). This exclusive right to land would be mobilized continuously to alienate informal waterfront residents in the quest for a megacity. Being the largest slum settlement in Lagos with six districts and about 40,000 to 85,000 residents (Akinsete et al., 2014, p. 239; Adama, 2020, p. 8), the informal community would later become a target of neoliberal development in the early twenty-first century since most of the poor residents lacked the financial power or social connection to obtain government-sanctioned land tenure security.

Between Nigeria's independence in October 1960 and her transition to democratic rule in May 1999, Lagos had not only become an industrial city, but the incoming civilian government also had to grapple with the social decay left behind by military dictators. Significantly, the city's population had skyrocketed from 3.5 million in 1985 to 7.3 million in 2000 (UN-Habitat, 2014), creating massive housing and crime problem. From May 1999 to May 2007, Lagos experienced relative transformation under the Government of Bola Tinubu. During this period, the statist agenda of Lagos as the "center of excellence" was promoted by engaging residents in the city's development process. He solicited people's support, initially through the political ethos/slogan "Jeun s'oke" (originally coined by commercial bus drivers, meaning "Let's move on" or "have your fill and move up") in an age of brazen money politics. Later, he adopted *Eko o ni baje*, and based on the overwhelming acceptance garnered, Tinubu declared his megacity ambition for the city in 2000 (Omoegun, 2015, p. 102).

Given his technocratic approach to governance, which resulted in the expansion of the state service sectors, Tinubu's policies were judged people-centered (Olokesusi & Wapwera, 2017, p. 263). Among others, the Lagos State Economic Empowerment and Development Strategy (LASEEDS) that was created in 2004 targeted "cohesive coordination of the development process through the adoption of a bottom-up approach and inclusiveness of stakeholders" (cited in Filani, 2012, p. 18). Some scholars argue that his focus on poverty alleviation among the subaltern class of Lagos earned him the name "Area Boy Governor" as he channeled the energies of youth gangs (known as Area Boys) into productive activities by employing them in traffic and sanitation offices

(Whiteman, 2012, p. 207). These laudable achievements conveyed the idea that the Lagos, which must never decline or spoil, is not only the urban architecture but also the marginalized urban poor who are struggling to survive.

Though LASEEDS also aimed at depopulating high-density areas by providing new satellite towns, existing forty-three "blighted" areas however remained outside this urban renewal project as poor residents of slums such as the Makoko waterfront community were stripped of their citizenship, including their rights to housing and social amenities. While Tinubu's "Area Boys" who proved to be politically instrumental during elections and electioneering campaigns in the state were quickly de-radicalized on the assumption of office, the poor working-class residents of informal communities served little to no purpose in Lagos's politics, hence, their exclusion from the city's development programs. The forced eviction of more than 5,000 people from the Ijora-Badiya area in October 2003 and another 3,000 from Makoko waterfront in April 2005 (Amnesty International, 2003, 2006, p. 8), does not only capture the exclusionary development which the political slogan *Eko o ni baje* masked in postcolonial Lagos, it also shows the reinvention of colonial urban planning which proceeded based on political and economic objectives without genuine consultation of or compensation to residents.

The case of Makoko particularly stands out for two major reasons. First, the demolition of the houses, churches, and medical clinics of this urban poor was neither carried out legitimately nor for public good. Rather, it was implemented in order to help "execute a court judgment from 2000 which granted ownership of the area to a private landowner" (Amnesty International, 2006, p. 1). The absence of alternative housing for this subaltern class suggests the state violation of the United Nations criteria for legitimate eviction as well as of the human rights Resolution 1993/77, which protects people's right to adequate housing. Second, Makoko residents rejected the rhetoric of participatory development couched in *Eko o ni baje* slogan because of the agency displayed by the subaltern class in the face of state-sanctioned violation of their human rights. The residents' positive action, which temporarily stopped the demolition and eviction, materialized in form of mass protest, supported by nongovernmental organizations like the Social and Economic Rights Action Center (Amnesty International, 2006, p. 9).

Officially, the area is known as Makoko-Iwaya Waterfront. It falls under the jurisdiction of Yaba Local Government Authority, but because the community is considered "illegal," six *Baale* (local chiefs) are appointed to maintain law and order within the six villages that make up the settlement (Ogunlesi, 2016). Of these six, Oko Agbon, Adogbo, Migbewhe, and Yanshiwhe float on the lagoon, while Sogunro and Apollo are on land. The only medium of transportation within the floating villages is a canoe and their economic activities revolve around water—mostly fishing, sand dredging, boat-making, and sawmill. Lagos government neither recognizes the settlement nor provides them with basic sanitation infrastructure. One of the problems confronting Makoko before 2015 was the poor management of domestic waste. Many residents engaged in open defecation into the lagoon and about nine families shared one makeshift toilet and bathroom (Lagos State Government, 2002, p. 134). Solid wastes were also discharged directly into the lagoon where they practice fishing. During heavy downpour in the neighborhood, rain leaves solid waste and sewage on the entrance of many floating shops and houses (Aderibigbe, 2012).

The lack of potable water further complicates the poor sanitation in the settlement as residents rely on a shallow public well dug by Yaba Local Government Authority outside the community. However, a retail water kiosk within the community, as well as retail polythene pouches (sachet water), provided potable water for drinking. As retail water from the kiosk is extremely expensive (USD 12 = N4000 NGN before 2020), the problem that salinity poses to the quality of groundwater in Lagos makes sachet water the best option for drinking (Muraya, 2014). As noted in the introduction, the LMDA was created by the Federal Government in July 2006 to manage the improvement of the Makoko waterfront alongside other eight slums in Lagos using the World Bank loan of $200 million allocated to Nigeria. However, the funds remained unavailable till Mr. Tinubu left office in 2007 (Mabogunje, 2011, pp. 618–619).

By 2007, the popular acceptance of Tinubu's ethos/slogan, *Eko o ni baje*, which called for a united effort to develop Lagos, had legitimized the digitization of the state's tax collection system; the creation of the Lagos State Waste Management Authority (LAWMA) to improve sanitation; the introduction of Lagos State Bus Services to ease urban transportation, while the 260MW of electricity generated through the new Independent Power Project boosted the city's economy (Filani, 2012; De Gramont, 2015). Indeed, *Eko o ni baje* had become a tool of urban governmentality and, in this context, it also legitimized the removal of markets categorized as "informal" as well as to prosecute street traders through the Kick Against Indiscipline (KAI) brigades that were introduced to curb urban incivility. If Tinubu coined *Eko o ni baje*, his successor, Babatunde Raji Fashola popularized the participatory development ethos/slogan as a legitimizing discourse for statist political and economic agenda.

After Tinubu's chief of staff Mr. Fashola succeeded him in May 2007, the protégé quickly complimented the work of his boss. The lawyer-cum-politician did not only share Mr. Tinubu's vision of megacity, he also subscribed to the opinion of Napoleon Bonaparte (1823, p. 212) that "under a good administration, the Nile gains on the desert; [but] under a bad one, the desert gains on the Nile." In June 2007, one month after his inauguration, Fashola replaced the defunct Lagos State Waterfront and Tourism Development Corporation with the Ministry of Waterfront Infrastructure Development. The new agency was to transform Lagos waterfronts into a modern world-class tourist center to draw foreign investment into the city (Basinski, 2009; Adama, 2020, p. 6). Like his predecessor, Fashola adopted *Eko o ni baje* as a rallying cry for urban renewal, following closely the top-bottom technocratic approach he had helped his boss put in place. By 2008, substantial square meters of land had been reclaimed from the Lagos lagoon for the construction of Eko Atlantic—an island labeled the "Manhattan of Africa." Fashola's business model led to an increase in the Internally Generated Revenue (IGR) of the state, which permitted fancy transportation projects such as the Bus Rapid Transit (BRT) and the launching of a light rail project in 2010.

When the Federal government finally disbursed part of the World Bank loan to Lagos, Fashola's administration allocated USD 3.2 million for the Makoko upgrade (Adama, 2020, p. 9). Similar to how the former governor associated himself with Area Boys in Lagos, Fashola made a similar effort to present his administration as people-centered and participatory. Between 2007 and 2011 when he contested for second term, Fashola's government facilitated small-scale window-dressing deliberative exercise in the Makoko community where residents and their leaders met with World Bank and government representatives to discuss the redevelopment of the area (Ambe-Uva, 2017). Indeed, this discussion resulted in the facelift of three elementary schools, a market, and the road leading to the market, but little was done to improve the condition of water and sanitation in the settlement. By 2013, "drainage was still a problem and the compound had not been paved. Electricity and water had not been provided. The borehole and overhead water tank had been constructed but was not functioning because the contractor claimed he had not been paid the full amount" (Adama, 2020, p. 11). This affirms Pateman's (2012, p. 9) claim that such window-dressing deliberative exercises are just "useful legitimating devices for an already-decided policy." The poor upgrade also illustrates that social improvement, which was the goal of the prior meetings, would only become a reality when the conveners' objective result in social justice.

Similar to the way Angolan national government used the redevelopment of Luanda Bay in the nation's capital to hold onto political power (Croese, 2018), Mr. Fashola and his political party, Action Congress (now the All Progressives Congress), believed that their political survival and re-election in the richest state of Nigeria depend on the number of modernist projects their administration can execute before the next election. This perhaps attests to why Fashola asserts that "it is practically impossible to survive without infrastructure" (cited in Adama, 2020, pp. 6–7). As in Angola where attractive images of the Luanda waterfront were used as campaign materials by the ruling party (Croese, 2018, p. 8), the rhetoric of inclusion that was couched in *Eko o ni baje* as well as the neoliberal projects it engendered won Mr. Fashola and his party a second term in office after the 2011 gubernatorial election in Lagos. If the rhetoric of "dirty Africans" necessitated official segregation and social stratification, which was a part of British modernism in colonial Lagos, the rhetoric of *Eko o ni baje* expresses the continuity of European material civilization. Ideologically, the ethos/slogan became a development discourse and style of thought in the city, which politicians deploy regularly to colonize the social reality in many poor working-class communities, as well as for legitimizing elitist development programs that would position their administration as progressive and developmental.

Upon his re-election, Mr. Fashola continued his top-bottom urban renewal project (Bradlow, 2012). Although most modernist projects of his administration were practically effective in attracting foreign investments to Lagos, some of his urban renewal projects were anti-poor and repressive (World Bank, 2011; Olusina, 2013; De Gramont, 2015). Worried that "capital will not come into a 'dirty economy'" (Whiteman, 2012, p. 252), Fashola's administration abandoned the rhetoric of participatory development he once facilitated in Makoko settlement before his re-election as another forced eviction from the waterfront was attempted on July 12, 2012. With short notice of 72 hours, Makoko residents were ordered by the state Ministry of Waterfront Infrastructure Development to vacate the slum (Nossiter, 2013). Diverse reasons were given by the Lagos state government for the decision to demolish Makoko waterfronts that year, including the need to remove settlements shrinking the lagoon, the need to improve human security and rid the state of criminals, as well as, the need to remove all impediments to economic and gainful utilization of the waterfront (Ibiwoye, 2014; Alabi, 2018). In the context of the latter, Fashola was reported to have declared that his government was "battle-ready to wipe away small communities whose residents are mainly low-income earners" (Sessou & Adingupu, 2012). If Makoko is indeed shrinking the coastline of the lagoon, one, therefore, wonders whether Eko Atlantic is not doing the same thing.

During the forced eviction, about 300,000 were rendered homeless while one fatality was recorded (Bradlow, 2012). Non-compliance by Makoko residents was due to rumors in some quarters about a deal between some government officials and an influential estate developer regarding the value of the waterfront to real estate and the megacity ambition. Part of the weapons of resistance deployed by NGOs and residents of the waterfront were propaganda and mass protest. One Mr. Felix Morka of the Social and Economic Rights Action Center (SERAC) was reported to have maintained that the slum demolition was an attempt by Fashola to rid the state of those perceived to be non-indigene (Alabi, 2018). Although this propaganda forced the government to stop demolition and forced eviction from the waterfront, it however could not prevent the successive regime from executing similar unpopular urban renewal projects.

Given the persistence of housing problem in Lagos, blighted communities continue to emerge across the city. By 2014, the state Ministry of Physical Planning and Urban Development (2016) estimated that over 100 informal settlements exist in the state. Rather than provide shelter for this urban poor, the Lagos government continues to pursue its urban fantasy under the umbrella of *Eko o ni baje*. Despite the backlash received by the Fashola administration for its economic valuation of waterfronts at the expense of human security, his successor, Mr. Akinwunmi Ambode (2015–2019) toed the same path of neoliberal development, which ignores the economy and history of the city. At the inauguration of Epe-Marina lagoon reclamation by Mr. Ambode on July 26, 2016, the governor unreservedly announced that his administration would work to replicate Dubai Marina in Lagos. Triumphantly, the governor declared that "we want to duplicate what you see in Dubai Marina. This is a whole stretch of two kilometers of real estate and new tourist centers that we are putting in Epe and Badagry at the same time" (Akinsanmi, 2016; Lagos State Ministry of Waterfront Infrastructure Development, 2016). His idea of urban renewal makes one wonder why a project meant for Lagosians must be a replica of the Emirati's despite the differences in geography, history, culture, population, and economy. The governor's intention reflects the uncompromising posture of Lagos politicians in their quest for a competitive megacity which they plan to achieve through elitist projects such as sky-high buildings and fancy waterfronts for recreation and tourism.

In pursuit of this imagined future for Lagos, Ambode's government, like his predecessor, clamped down on and destroyed informal waterfront communities across the city. Legitimizing the inhuman treatment of urban poor, the governor stated that "most of the issues we have with kidnapping are perpetrated by illegal settlers by the waterfront" and to remove these "illegal" settlers from Lagos waterfronts, the "demolition of all the shanties" around the creeks and waterways must commence (Daniel, 2016). Subsequently, from November 9 to 11, 2016, the Otodo-Gbame waterfront community in the Lekki Phase I area of Lagos was attacked, leaving over 25,000 people homeless (Amnesty International, 2017, p. 23).

Those who had no place to go stayed back to rebuild the settlement, but whatever was left of their shacks were destroyed by the Lagos government in another demolition exercise in March and April 2017. This time, the governor ignored the court injunction which forbad his administration from displacing the people. Instead, another waterfront settlement, the Ilubirin fishing community was attacked in March, September, and October 2016, and again in April 2017. At the end of the entire demolition exercise, about

10,000 to 30,000 residents became homeless and four people killed (Amnesty International, 2017, pp. 31–35). When some residents of the slum marched in protest to the Governor's office, his new participatory initiative —Office of Civic Engagement—could not initiate a dialogue. The Lagos government's use of coercive force depicts Anderson's (1964) "bulldozer" approach to urban regeneration. Furthermore, where the economist De Soto (2000, p. 14) sees "heroic entrepreneurs," the Lagos government sees informalities, and where urbanist Rem Koolhaas sees inventive urban residents with "ingenious, critical alternative systems" in the face of failed governance (Koolhaas, 2000, p. 653), the Lagos government sees criminals who pose threat to the development of the competitive world-class city.

CONCLUSION

This chapter has demonstrated how the global model of urban transformation interacts with the social reality in Lagos as the state government makes effort to create a specific form of urban development in the city. It argues that postcolonial urban renewal experience under civilian administration since 1999 resonates with the elitist/modernist approach of the LEDB in the early 1950s. Without any doubt, the neoliberal projects are laudable, but their imposition and impact on poor neighborhoods call for a rethink of urban development programs in postcolonial African cities. This is because Lagos politicians and planners often premise their urban transformative programs on the participatory ethos/slogan *Eko o ni baje*, which in theory, associates all residents with the policy-making process of government, but in reality, the development discourse helps politicians in labeling marginalized people and their communities as "illegal" and "non-compliant" with the state's imagined vision of world-class megacity. In this context, *Eko o bi baje* becomes one of the postcolonial rhetoric of participatory governance, which political elites mobilize as an instrument of urban governmentality, particularly for legitimizing statist political and economic agenda with minimal resistance from the unsuspecting public.

In respect to the neoliberal development projects which *Eko o ni baje* ethos/slogan promotes, the chapter argues that Lagos politicians and urban planners often fail to acknowledge how the anti-poor projects destroy the livelihood of poor working-class residents. In other words, by mobilizing *Eko o ni baje* as a participatory development discourse, Lagos politicians do not only give Lagosians the impression that all hands are on deck to ensure the progress of the state, and that their perspectives matter in public decision-making processes, but that successive administration also confers legitimacy on their political and economic policies through the ethos/slogan. In this context, whatever space opened by the "participatory" development ethos/slogan, they remained tightly controlled by the capitalist and political elites, who through their unpopular modernist urban renewal projects, continue to deflect the burden of urban "improvement" to marginal communities and groups. Even though development experts in the state may argue (in a superficial level) that the economic value of urban revitalization through forceful eviction from waterfronts is reasonable for the greater good, such argument would hardly endure constructive scrutiny within the context of human rights discourses.

The chapter thus recommends that while the economic value of urban waterfronts and their financial worth for a megacity like Lagos is enormous, sanitation, housing, and by extension, human security of poor citizens in marginal communities should not be compromised for neoliberal development agenda. In a bid to ensure this, Claude Ake's "residual option" for sustainable development should guide African urban planners and politicians. The theorist argues that in postcolonial Africa, development is erroneously taken to be a project rather than a process, and to correct this contradiction, he suggests that African states should embrace genuine participatory governance structure (Ake, 1996, chapter 5). For him, development must not be imposed but rather it should be understood as something that people must do for themselves under an inclusive political administration. In fact, the UN's Right to Development (RtD) support this approach. In other words, a government with participatory institutions would not only respect/protect civil and political rights, which Amartya Sen (1999) calls the foundation of immanent development, but would also provide a veritable avenue for enhanced citizen inclusion in development policy articulation and implementation. In the context of Lagos, and by extension, African cities, this approach would guide what Warren (2009) calls a "rebirth of strongly democratic ideals" in policymaking. Finally, it would facilitate sustainable and inclusive urban renewal while stimulating people-centered urban transformation.

REFERENCES

Adama, O. (2020). Slum upgrading in the era of world-class city construction: The case of Lagos, Nigeria. *International Journal of Urban Sustainable Development*. 12(2):219–235.

Adegoju, A. (2013) Indigenous language orientation for effective citizenship education in 21st century Africa: Reflections on the Nigerian experience. *Sociolingusitic Studies*, 7(3):273–292.

Aderibigbe, D. (2012, March 5). Makoko: The wasted Venice of Lagos! *Nigeria Tribune*.

Agbetiloye, A. (2020, February 19). Can we still say "Eko oni baje oo"? *Campus Reporter*.

Agboola T. & Jinadu, A. M. (1997). Forced eviction and forced relocation in Nigeria, the experience of Maroko in 1990. *Environment and Urbanization*, 9(2):271–288.

Ake, C. (1996). *Democracy and Development in Africa*. Washington, DC: The Brookings Institution.

Akinsanmi, G. (2016, July 27). Ambode: We are already replicating Dubai in Lagos. *ThisDay*.

Akinsete, E., Hoelzel, F. & Oshodi, L. (2014). Delivering sustainable urban regeneration in emerging nations: Introducing neighbourhood hotspots. *Journal of Architectural Education*, 68(2): 238–245.

Alabi, B. O. (2018). Urban renewal schemes and the plight of internally displaced persons in Nigeria. In T. Falola & B. Falola (Eds.), *Struggles Over Urban Space, Citizenship, and Rights to the City*. New York: Routledge.

Ambe-Uva, T. (2017, September 23) The Makoko sustainable regeneration plan. *Participedia*. Retrieved from https://participedia.net/case/5006

Amnesty International. (2003, October 21). Nigeria: Mass forced evictions in Lagos must stop. AFR 44/034/2003.

———. (2006, January 24). Making the destitute homeless: Forced evictions in Makoko, Lagos State. AI Index No AFR 44/001/2006.

———. (2017, November 14). Nigeria, the human cost of a megacity: Forced evictions of the urban poor in Lagos, Nigeria. AI Index AFR 44/7389/2017.

Anderson, M. (1964). *The Federal Bulldozer: A Critical Analysis of Urban Renewal, 1942-1962*. Cambridge, MA: MIT Press.

Basinski, S. (2009). *All Fingers Are Not Equal: A Report on Street Vendors in Lagos*. Nigeria, Lagos: Cleen Foundation.

Bigon, B. (2016). Bubonic plague, colonial ideologies, and urban planning policies: Dakar, Lagos, and Kumasi. *Planning Perspectives*, 31(2):205–226.

Bradlow, B. (2020, February 12). Reflecting on evictions in Makoko, Lagos: Moving from reactive to proactive decision-making. Shack/Slum Dwellers International. Retrieved from https://knowyourcity.info/contact/

Cain, A. (2014). African urban fantasies: Past lessons and emerging realities. *Environment & Urbanization,* 26(2): 561–567.

Centre on Housing Rights and Evictions. (2006 December). Forced Evictions Violations of Human Rights 2003–2006, *Eviction Monitor*, 1(2): 27–30.

Clarke, C. G. (2006). *Decolonizing the Colonial City: Urbanization and Stratification in Kingston*. Oxford: Oxford University Press.

Collier, P., Glaeser, E., Venables, T., Blake, M. & Manwaring, P. (2019). *Informal Settlements and Housing Markets*. London: International Growth Centre.

Cooper, F. (1983). *Struggle for the city: Migrant Labour, Capital, and the State in Urban Africa*. Beverly Hills: Sage.

———. (1987). *On the African Waterfront: Urban Disorders and the Transformation of Work in Colonial Mombasa*. New Haven, CT: Yale University Press.

———. (1996). *Decolonization and African Society: The Labour Question in French and British Africa*. New York: Cambridge University Press.

Croese, S. (2018). Global urban policymaking in Africa: A view from Angola through the redevelopment of the Bay of Luanda. *International Journal of Urban and Regional Research,* 42(2): 198–209.

Daniel. (2016, October 9). Kidnapping: All shanties along Lagos waterfront must go, says Ambode. *Metro News*. Retrieved from www.informationng.com/2016/10/kidnapping-shanties-alonglagos-waterfront-must-go-says-ambode.html#.

De Gramont, D. (2015). *Governing Lagos: Unlocking the Politics of Reform*. Washington, DC: Carnegie Endowment for International Peace.

De Soto, H. (2000). *The Mystery of Capital: Why Capitalism Triumphs in the West and Fails*. New York: Basic Book.

Falola, T. & Salm, S. J. (2005). *Urbanization and African Cultures*. Durham: Carolina Academic Press.

Filani, M. O. (2012). *The Changing Face of Lagos: From Vision to Reform and Transformation*. Brussels: The Cities Alliance.

Folarin, S. (2010). The spatial economy of abjection: The evacuation of Maroko slum in Nigeria. In W. Adebanwi & E. Obadare (Eds.), *Encountering the Nigerian State*. New York: Palgrave Macmillan.

Forward, C. N. (1970). Waterfront land use in the six Australian state capitals. *Annals of the Association of American Geographers*, 60(3): 409–614.

Fox, S. (2014). The political economy of slums: Theory and evidence from sub-Saharan Africa. *World Development*, 54: 191–203.

Gandy, M. (2006). Planning, anti-planning and the infrastructure crisis facing metropolitan Lagos. *Urban Studies*, 43(2): 371–396.

Gant, K. (2017). Eko o ni Baje (May Lagos Be Indestructible): Lens-based representations of transformation in Lagos, Nigeria, 1990-2001. Ph.D. Dissertation Presented to the Faculty of the Graduate School, University of Texas at Austin.

Gleave, M. B. (1997). Port activities and the spatial structure of cities: The case of Freetown, Sierra Leone. *Journal of Transport Geography*, 5(4): 257–275.

Harvey, D. (1989). From managerialism to entrepreneurialism: The transformation in urban governance in late capitalism. Geografiska Annaler Series B, *Human Geography*, 71(1): 3–17.

———. (2001). *Spaces of Capital: Towards a Critical Geography*. New York: Routledge.

Hurley, A. (2006). Narrating the urban waterfront: The role of public history in community revitalization. *The Public Historian*, 28(4):19–50.

Ibiwoye, D. (2014, May 20). Makoko: A slum that refuses to dissolve. *Vanguard*. Retrieved from *https://www.vanguardngr.com/2014/05/makoko-slum-refuses-dissolve/*.

Koolhaas, R., Belanger, P., Chung, C., Comaroff, J., Cosmas, M., Gandhi, S., Hamilton, A., Ip, L., Kim, J., Shepard, G., Singh, R., Slayton, N., Stone, J. & Wahba, S. (2000). Lagos, Harvard project on the city. In R. Koolhaas et al. (eds), *Mutations, événement culturel sur la ville contemporaine*. Bordeaux: Arc en Rêve, Centre d'architecture.

Lagos State Government. (2002). *Lagos Metropolitan Development Project*. Kristiansand: Stoveland Consult.

Lagos State Ministry of Economic Planning and Budget. (2013). *Lagos State Development Plan 2012-2025*. Lagos: Lagos State Government.

Lagos State Ministry of Economic Planning and Land Matters. (1980). *Lagos State Interim Regional Plan 1980-2000*. Lagos: Lagos State Government.

Laws of the Federation of Nigeria. (1990). Land Use Act, 1978: Chapter 202. Federal Government of Nigeria.

Lefebvre, H. (1976). Reflections on the politics of space. *Antipode*, 8(2): 30–37.

Mabogunje, A. L. (2011). *A Measure of Grace: The Autobiography of Akinlawon Ladipo Mabogunje*. Ibadan: Bookbuilders.

Magaji, A. (2016, September 30). Now that Ambode has arrived. *The Guardian*. Retrieved from *https://guardian.ng/opinion/now-that-ambode-has-arrived/*.

Mamdani, M. (1996). *Citizen and Subject: Contemporary Africa and the Legacy of Late Colonialism*. Princeton, NJ: Princeton University Press.

Marcinkoski, C. (2017, February 10). Africa's speculative urban future. UrbanNext. Retrieved from https://urbannext.net/africas-speculative-urban-future/.

Mbembe, A. (2001). *On the Postcolony*. Berkeley, CA: University of California Press.

Mendelsohn, B. (2018). Making the urban coast a geosocial reading of land, sand, and water in Lagos, Nigeria. *Comparative Studies of South Asia, Africa, and the Middle East*, 38(3): 118.

Minca, C. (1995). Urban waterfront evolution. The case of trieste. *Geography*, 10(3): 225–234.

Ministry of Physical Planning and Urban Development. (2016). Lagos State Urban Renewal Agency: Introduction. Retrieved from www.physicalplanning.lg.gov.ng/index.php/policiesdirectives/urban-regeneration/.

Muraya, J. W. (2014, February 7). Water, water everywhere: Life and death inside Nigeria's floating village. *Daily Nation*.

Murray, M. J. (2017). *The Urbanism of Exception: The Dynamics of Global City Building in the Twenty First Century*. New York: Cambridge University Press.

Murray, M. J. & Myers, G. A. (2006). *Cities in Contemporary Africa*. New York: Palgrave Macmillan.

Myers, G. A. (2003). *Verandahs of Power: Colonialism and Space in Urban Africa*. New York: Syracuse University Press.

Napoleon, B. (1823), *Memoirs of the History of France During the Reign of Napoleon: Vol. II*. London: H. Colburn and Company.

National Archives Ibadan. (1912, January 16). CSO 1/19/45, Despatch 28 - Egerton to Harcourt: Comments on the census, 1911.

———. (1931). Comcol 1/739, Vol. II, Census 1931: Lagos Colony Population and Statistics.

———. (1951, March 29). L.E.D.B. slum clearance scheme for Lagos. *Daily Times*.

———. (1951, April 5). A breach of faith. *Daily Service*.

———. (1951, April 5). Slum clearance scheme for Lagos. *West African Pilot*.

———. (1951, April 6). 1,500 houses affected by slum clearance scheme: Surulere housing scheme provides for 5,000 persons. *Daily Service*.

———. (1951, April 7). To build and not destroy. *West African Pilot*.

———. (1951, April 10). Land acquisition. *Daily Service*.

———. (1951, April 19). We oppose this scheme. *The Daily Service*.

———. (1954, July 14). Lagos chiefs oppose slum clearance scheme: Fasinro cites British slum. *Daily Service*.

Ndi, A. (2007). Metropolitanism, capital, and patrimony: Theorizing the postcolonial West Africa. In F. Demissie (Ed.), *Postcolonial African Cities: Imperial Legacies and Postcolonial Predicament.* London: Routledge.

Njoh, A. J. (2007). *Planning Power: Town Planning and Social Control in Colonial Africa.* London: University College London Press.

Nossiter, A. (2013, March 1). In Nigeria's largest city, homeless are paying the price of progress. *The New York Times.* Retrieved from https://nyti.ms/XfVTjg

Nwanna, C. (2015). Gentrification in Nigeria: The case of two housing estates in Lagos. In L. Lees, H. B. Shin, & E. L. Morales (Eds.), *Global Gentrifications: Uneven Development and Displacement.* Bristol: Policy Press.

Obono, O. (2007). A Lagos thing: Rules and realities in the Nigerian megacity. *Georgetown Journal of International Affairs*, 8(2): 31–37.

Ogunlesi, T. (2016, February 23). Inside Makoko: Danger and ingenuity in the world's biggest floating slum. *The Guardian.*

Ojo, G. & Meynen, N. (2012, August 30). Destroying Africa's oldest and best-known slum: Makoko. Environmental Justice Organizations.

Olokesusi, F. & Wapwera, S. D. (2017). Political stability, metropolitan governance, and transformation in Lagos. In D. Gómez-Álvarez et al. (Eds.), *Steering the Metropolis: Metropolitan Governance for Sustainable Urban Development.* Washington, DC: Inter-American Development Bank.

Olukoju, A. (1993). Population pressure, housing and sanitation in West Africa's premier port-city: Lagos, 1900-1939. *The Great Circle*, 15(2): 91–106.

———. (2013). Infrastructure development and urban facilities in Lagos, 1861-2000. Ibadan: Institut français de recherche en Afrique, Institut français de recherche en Afrique.

———. (2004). *The "Liverpool" of West Africa: The Dynamics and Impact of Maritime Trade in Lagos, 1900-1950.* Trenton, NJ: Africa World Press.

Olusina, O. (2013, May 12). LASG's alleviating poverty with transport infrastructure. *This Day Newspaper.*

Omoegun, A. O. (2015). Street trader displacements and the relevance of the right to the city concept in a rapidly urbanising African city: Lagos, Nigeria. PhD dissertation, Cardiff University

Opeibi, T. O. (2007). One message, many tongues: An exploration of media multilingualism in Nigerian political discourse. *Journal of Language and Politics*, 6(2): 223–248.

Oyelowo, A. (2013, August 20). A safer waterfront in Lagos, if you can afford it. *The New Yorker.* Retrieved from https://www.newyorker.com/business/currency/a-safer-waterfront-in lagos-if-you-can-afford-it.

Parnell, S. & Robinson, J. (2012). (Re)theorizing cities from the global south: Looking beyond neoliberalism. *Urban Geography*, 33(4): 593–617.

Pateman, C. (2012). Participatory democracy revisited. *Perspectives on Politics*, 10 (1):7–19.

Pile, S., Brook, C., & Mooney, G. (1999*). Unruly Cities? Order/Disorder.* London: Routledge.

Rakodi, C. (1995). *Harare: Inheriting a Settler-Colonial City: Change or Continuity?* Chichester: John Wiley & Sons Ltd.

Sada, P. O. (1969). Differential population distribution and growth in metropolitan Lagos. *Journal of Business and Social Studies,* 1(2): 117–133.

Said, E. W. (1993). *Culture and Imperialism.* London, Chatto and Windus.

Sen, A. (1999). *Development as Freedom.* Oxford: Oxford University Press.

Sessou, E. & Adingupu, C. (2012, July 21). Makoko people abandoned in misery. *Vanguard Newspaper.*

UN-Habitat. (2003). *The Challenge of Slums: Global Report on Human Settlements 2003.* Nairobi: United Nations Human Settlements Program.

———. (2014). *Background Paper: World Habitat Day 2014, Voices from the Slums.* Nairobi: United Nations Human Settlements Program.

Warren, M. E, (2009). Governance-driven democratization. *Critical Policy Studies,* 3(1): 3–13.

Watson, V. (2009). 'The planned city sweeps the poor away...': Urban planning and 21st century urbanization. *Progress in Planning,* 72(3): 151–193.

———. (2014). African urban fantasies: Dreams or nightmares? *Environment and Urbanization,* 26: 213–229.

———. (2017). New African city plans: Local urban form and the escalation of urban inequalities. In A. Datta & A. Shaban (Eds.), *Mega-Urbanization in the Global South: Fast Cities and New Urban Utopias of the Postcolonial State.* Abingdon: Routledge.

Whiteman, K. (2012). *Lagos: A cultural and historical companion.* Oxford: Signal Books.

World Bank. (2011). Lagos urban transport project implementation completion and results report. No. ICR00001848. Washington, DC: World Bank.

Zeleza, P. T. (1999). The spatial economy of structural adjustment in African cities. In P. Zeleza & E. Kalipeni (Eds.), *Sacred Spaces and Public Quarrels: African Cultural and Economic Landscapes.* Trenton: Africa World Press.

Chapter 2

Nationalism in Postcolonial Studies
A Case for Hybridity
Nick T. C. Lu

This chapter discusses the problems of nationalism in the postcolonial world. It has been observed that in adopting nation-building as the main path toward liberation, political class in the post-colonies created new minorities, marginalized non-dominant social groups, and further entrenched the political order of the nation-state throughout the world. Moreover, with capitalist mode of production now assuming a truly global dominance, there is not yet any commensurate political and legal institution to contain the economic consequences. Hence, thinking and acting beyond nationalism, whether in forms of regionalism, cosmopolitanism, or internationalism, has been central to postcolonial studies. This chapter offers an overview of the debate on nationalism in postcolonial studies. It suggests that the common practice of pitting nationalism against cosmopolitanism obscures the humanist vision implied in both concepts and there is a need to refocus public discourse on the thematic of humanism. Finally, the chapter makes a case for promoting hybridity to change the political status quo and suggests that we see hybridity not as exclusively a postmodern condition but as coextensive with nationalism in modernity and construct a robust counterculture around it.

INTRODUCTION

In critiquing the rise of nativism in contemporary African cultures, noted Ghanaian philosopher Kwame Anthony Appiah (1992) argued that the proliferation of cultural nationalism on the African continent, both accompanying and following decolonization, is a direct result of European imperialism and its imposed modernity on the African peoples which has profoundly shaped the way they viewed themselves and their cultures. As he wrote, "Nativism organizes its vaunted particularities into a 'culture' that is, in fact, an artifact of Western modernity. While Western criteria of evaluation are challenged, the way in which the contest is framed is not" (p. 60). Appiah's incisive comment reflects a larger problem concerning the role of nationalism in much of the non-Western, postcolonial world. It is, moreover, a fundamental problem that plays out not just in culture and philosophy but also in politics.

Since the nineteenth century, most Asian, Latin American, and African peoples who were historically on the receiving end of imperialist aggression invariably resorted to some forms of nationalism to achieve political autonomy, assert cultural sovereignty, and organize national economy in order to offset decades of epistemic and material violence inflicted by imperialism and, hopefully, to negotiate with Western nation-states on a more equal footing. While anti-imperialist and anticolonial nationalism undeniably played a decisive role in the independence movements of many formerly colonized and semi-colonized peoples, it has also led to the realization of a truly globalized system of the nation-state, a system that has its roots in the Eurocentric capitalist modernity. It was in view of this history that Appiah (1992) asserted that anti-imperialist (cultural) nationalism, rather than challenging the terms of competition laid down by imperial powers, reinforces them insofar as it basic remains a reactive ideology whose goal is essentially to "catch up." A further consequence of anti-imperialist nationalism is that it quite literally created "new minorities" in the postcolonial nation-state (Amin, 1997, p. 62). The double bind of nationalism in the postcolonial context—the conflicting imperatives of following the Western model of development to catch up and of charting one's unique path toward modernity—gives rise to a host of complex questions that have been taken up frequently by postcolonial scholars. Is nationalism still a useful ideology or is it rather an impediment to the overall progress of postcolonial countries, given the continued and widespread uneven development in the South? Can development only be carried out on a national-territorial basis and organized by a nation-state? Does postcolonial nationalism, by making genuine regional solidarity difficult, if not impossible, lend itself to imperialism's old trick of divide-and-conquer? Is it realistic, or even desirable, to think of post-nationalist alternatives to the current system of the nation-state? This chapter does not have definitive answers to all these questions, but it hopes to provide some productive ways to rethink them in the following pages.

Before proceeding to the main discussion, a brief history of nationalism is in order. Though various scholars have ventured different theories to explain the rise of the nation, it is commonly accepted that the nation is a modern phenomenon whose emergence coincided with capitalist mode of production and the gradual ascension of the bourgeoisie to become the sole ruling class in Western Europe. Benedict Anderson (1983), Ernest Gellner (1983), Karl

Deutsch (1966), to mention the most influential scholars, all tied the rise of the nation as the dominant political order to the social changes brought about by capitalist modernity in different ways: print capitalism, industrialism, and communication technology. Indeed, in Marxian historiography, it was through the kind of large-scale division of labor necessitated by capitalist mode of production and sharply increased intercourse between town and country that the first bourgeois states in Western Europe—Britain, France, the Netherlands, most importantly—were able to organize the culturally and linguistically diverse productive forces within their territories to form nation-states. And as the intense competition among European bourgeois nation-states increasingly took on a global character, national boundaries worldwide began to be redrawn and eventually eroded. Such are the historical roots of our lived reality of globalization and the nation-state. A few key points can be extrapolated from the above synopsis. First, the nation and, subsequently, the nation-state are products of capitalism, as Amin (1997) put it unambiguously (p. 65). Second, nationalism is a consent-manufacturing ideology that, by "sometimes [taking] pre-existing cultures and [turning] them into nations, sometimes [inventing] them, and often [obliterating] pre-existing cultures," naturalizes the existence of the nation and legitimizes the authority of the nation-state, which is essential in the maintenance of global capitalism (Gellner, 1983, p. 49). Finally, the nation is an immanent contradiction of capitalism whose functioning requires simultaneously the existence and destruction of the nation.

This chapter takes as its theoretical framework the Marxist humanism as developed by the New Left critics and several anticolonial thinkers such as Frantz Fanon and Ngũgĩ wa Thiong'o. It is a theoretical outlook that recognizes the transformative power of human agency while being aware of human society as a totality. In the following, the chapter will first provide an overview of the debate on nationalism in postcolonial studies. It will not be realistic to attempt an exhaustive account in the limited space of a chapter. The purpose, rather, is to discuss important texts that indicate representative arguments and trends.

As is the case in most fields of study, postcolonial scholars occupy a spectrum of positions on the topics of nation and nationalism. Perhaps due to the so-called linguistic turn where Foucauldian and Derridean theories, for example, became wildly popular in Western academia in the 1970s and 1980s, earlier critical writings tended to express a general mistrust of nationalism on grounds of its being a totalizing ideology and its well-documented, notorious tendency to marginalize non-dominant social groups. At the turn of the century, however, scholars have attempted a corrective to this earlier tendency. Timothy Brennan and Pheng Cheah, for instance, have both voiced unequivocal support for nationalism in the global south because, as they observed, in the absence of a world-state, the nation-state remains the only effective protection of people's economic interest, cultural integrity, and general well-being under the current regime of neoliberal globalization. Viewed in a broader historical perspective, the ongoing debate on nationalism in postcolonial studies reflects the fundamentally contradictory role of the nation in capitalist modernity. Nonetheless, where there is difference, there is also continuity. Postcolonialist debate on nationalism, despite individual scholars' differences, has continued to revolve around and expand on the theme of humanism of the Leftist tradition and move toward a common goal, that is, to theorize a future world order that puts human values first, with or without the nation.

In the latter part of this chapter, in the spirit of James Clifford's (1997) phrase—"mak[ing] the best of a bad situation"—a case will be made for the popularization of hybridity consciousness and—which amounts to the same thing—for the gradual unlearning of exclusionary nationalist interpellation (p. 257). The argument is that the liberal nation-state that we have inherited from post-Enlightenment Europe has proved time and again it is unable to protect the interest of the poor and only mitigates the sharply widening wealth gap domestically and internationally, because it has been historically set up in such a way as to accommodate and maintain the hegemony of the capitalist class or national bourgeoise. While duly heeding previous arguments for the necessary existence of the nation-state in the South, the chapter also contends that being politically responsible for one's immediate community does not necessarily come into conflict with cultivating an egalitarian mindset conducive to forging transnational grassroots solidarities.

NATIONALISM IN POSTCOLONIAL STUDIES: FROM KANT AND MARX TO THE POSTCOLONIAL PRESENT

Central to the contemporary discussion of the nation is a recurrent conceptual antagonism that pits the nation against cosmopolitanism or internationalism, with the former associated with backwardness and the latter progress in our time. Traditionally, for intellectuals on the Left, the nation is seen as more or less an anachronism that should meet its death at some point in the natural course of history, as this is, arguably, the logical outcome of an unprecedented level of economic integration of all nationalities and the rapid advancement of human intellect and social organization reflecting such a world-historic change. This teleological belief in the inevitable end of the nation can be attributed to two foundational thinkers, Kant and Marx, who set the tone for contemporary progressive attitude toward the nation. In his seminal ethico-political work, *Perpetual Peace*, written as a future constitution for all states, Kant (1795/1903) envisaged a future where human beings will finally transcend state boundaries and achieve perpetual peace by establishing a "federation of free states" governed by law, republicanism, and the public rights of humanity because, as he saw it, our innate qualities of reason and moral duty would eventually prevail over self-conceit and compel all states to form a cosmopolitan politico-economic union in which people of all nationalities can thrive in peaceful coexistence (p. 120).

Kant's rational-moral narrative of the purposive movement of world history was later met with a materialist revision in Marx's writing where division of labor and commercial intercourse serve as the driving forces of history rather than universal reason.

In German Ideology, Marx (1846/1998) wrote that it was through division of labor and intercourse that the first European bourgeois states were able to systemize the productive forces of various nationalities within their territories and then proceed to compete, as unified nation-states, for monopolies in the colonial market through tariffs, prohibitions, and treaties. And later in *The Communist Manifesto* (1848/2008), he further indicated that it was because of the competition among these bourgeois nation-states that national boundaries in the rest of the world became increasingly irrelevant, as they have "through exploitation of the world market given a cosmopolitan character to production and consumption in every country" and have "drawn from under the feet of industry the national ground" (p. 38). In the end, because the bourgeois exploitation of the market and labor has encompassed the entire world, it follows that workers across the globe must act "world-historically" as an international force to counter this unprecedented scale of exploitation (Marx, 1846/1998, p. 57). Hence, the enshrined Marxist doctrine, internationalism. It was also in Marx's analysis that the contradictory tendency of capitalism to simultaneously give birth to and destroy the nation was brought into relief.

Clearly, whether considering from an idealist or a materialist standpoint, the historical trend is for human community to progressively grow and move toward the end state of a universal politico-economic union. Following this logic, the current reign of the nation-state can only be understood as a transitional stage that must eventually be overcome and substituted with cosmopolitan and internationalist principles, if humankind is to attain a higher state of happiness and a non-exploitative world economy. Not surprisingly, against this long-established intellectual tradition, a concept like the nation which entails immediate territorial commitment of a smaller scale is sometimes dismissed as nostalgic and regressive.

Founding intellectuals of postcolonial studies spoke of the nation in a language that often belied the teleological assumptions underlying the very concept, and in a tone marked by general disagreement with archaism. In an interview, for example, Gayatri Spivak (2008) proclaimed categorically that anticolonial and national struggles are "a thing of the past [emphasis added]" (p. 248). Although her insights that anti-colonialism sanctions "the kind of national identity politics that can lead to fascism" and can "work in the interest of terrible cultural conservatism, which is generally bad for women" are indisputable, she rejected the continued relevance of anticolonial national struggle by alluding to the thinking discussed above to highlight its outmodedness (p. 248). Staying true to her Marxist lineage defined in part by a futuristic penchant for larger units of solidarity, Spivak (2007) proposed the idea of "critical regionalism," which stresses grassroots cooperation that goes "under and over nationalisms" (p. 94).

In Edward Said's commentary on anticolonial nationalism in *Culture and Imperialism*, a similar language of forward-looking, pragmatic dismissal of old paradigms is hard to miss. Building on Frantz Fanon's critique of national consciousness in *The Wretched of the Earth*, Said (1993) asserted that anticolonial nationalism was no more than a foil for Western imperialism, not only because it was born out of a dialectical relation with the latter but also because of early nationalist thinkers' dependency on Western epistemology (his example was Afghani's debt to Renan) (p. 263). Said's peculiar characterization of this early brand of Third World nationalism revealed his intent to compartmentalize anticolonial history and apply a closure to a period in which nationalist struggles belonged: "orthodox nationalism," a term that exaggerates its rigid and archaic nature (p. 273). Although Said's criticism of nationalism was driven by a suspicion of grand narratives typical of poststructuralism, he nevertheless rehearsed the teleological belief in the necessary death of the nation in history and its inevitable replacement by a better formation yet to come which, in his case, was a spontaneous, non-doctrinal coalition of resistance groups. As he wrote, "Nationalist culture has been sometimes dramatically outpaced [emphasis added] by a fertile culture of resistance whose core is energetic insurgency, a 'technique of trouble,' directed against the authority and the discourse of imperialism" (p. 267). Still, for someone who valued intellectual eclecticism throughout his career, it would be mistaken, as Brennan (2013) reminded us, to simply consider Said an opponent of nationalism.

Criticism of nationalism and theorization of viable alternatives have been important undertakings in postcolonial studies since the onset, as more and more thinkers affiliated with poststructuralism and Western Marxism in one way or another have continued to offer theoretically informed arguments and propositions. Nevertheless, a closer examination of the ideals of cosmopolitanism and internationalism as they were first envisioned by Kant and Marx suggests that much of the earlier progressive suspicion of the nation might not be entirely justified, and that the difference between nationalism, cosmopolitanism, and internationalism in their original senses might not be as significant in spirit as it is in form.

First, it is crucial to understand that Kant's and Marx's critiques are not directed at the nation as such, but the absolutist states (for Kant) and the bourgeois states (for Marx). As Pheng Cheah (1998a) reminded us, Kant could not have made European nations his target of reform when he penned Perpetual Peace, because "the phenomenon and concept of 'the nation' [was] still at an embryonic stage" in his time (p. 26). On the other hand, for Marx, the principal actors in exploiting the world market and labor were the European bourgeois states. Hence, despite the ascent of nationalism in the mid-nineteenth century Marx was apparently "more concerned about abolishing the state-apparatus than its epiphenomenon, the nation-form" (Cheah, p. 28). By re-dividing the nation and state and making the nation an empty vessel ready to be refilled with a new content, Cheah was then able to make an argument for popular nationalism as a way to retighten the hyphen between the nation and state in the postcolonial world, meaning, to make the state work for the people through popular struggle.

It would be appropriate to pause briefly to offer a criticism of Cheah's arguments. While his archaeological reading of Marx is extremely valuable in correcting the confusion of nation and state and revealing Marx's true intent, the way nationalism is invoked in practice today more often than not corresponds to what he regarded as Marx's analytical error. Specifically, mainstream understanding of nationalism today is similarly characterized by an inextricable entanglement and a hierarchical relation of the two concepts: namely, state (essentially consisting of representatives of the ruling class) and nation. Thus, his call for re-tightening the hyphen between nation and state and reclaiming state power through the demonstration of popular will is, frankly, easier said than done. Worse, his fear that "the exclusionary dimension of popular nationalism can always be manipulated by state elites and captured by official nationalism" appears the norm rather than exception around the world (p. 313). Discussions of bottom-up nationalism and cosmopolitanism have been around for a long time. The crux of the problem remains that the state apparatus working in tandem with capital interest continues to define the terms and parameters of nationalism and cosmopolitanism. For now, it is worthwhile to dwell a bit on the Marxian legacy of "collapsing of the nation into the state" in the historical unfolding of anti-imperialist struggles and discuss the intervention made from a non-European standpoint by Fanon and Ngũgĩ, two of the most perspicacious theoreticians of Third World nationalism.

From Marx onward, the nation has been conceived as more or less organically linked to the state, especially because nationalism has since become one of the hegemonic lenses through which most modern subjects view the world. Accordingly, several attempts have been made to formulate larger networks of solidarity to bypass the national level in both conceptual and institutional senses. The earlier supranational alliances based on common race (Pan-Africanism) and common religious culture (Pan-Arabism) and, more recently, the postmodern celebration of an uprooted, exilic existence, and the poststructuralist insistence on a spontaneous, non-doctrinal coalition of interest groups all attest to this development. Amid this broader intellectual current, there were still voices insisting on the priority and relevance of national liberation. Fanon (1963/2004), for instance, has shown us in his criticism of Pan-Africanism, specifically its cultural form, Negritude, that what matters most is not the size or scope of solidarity, but whether such solidarity has a humanist content which draws directly from the actual histories of people's struggles for freedom, democracy, and justice, that is, from praxis. Fanon argued that Negritude is a reactive construct invented to disprove Europe's sweeping denial of the existence of a precolonial African culture: it is "a glorification of cultural phenomena that become continental instead of national, and singularly racialized" (p. 154).

As he further explained, since there is little empirical ground other than a reified category of Blackness or Africanness on which to base its claims, Negritude is "increasingly cut off from reality," from people's continual struggle for self-determination and liberation (p. 154). Fanon's insistence on historicizing the liberation struggle of various African peoples led him to proclaim that "every culture is first and foremost national" and that "to emphasize an African culture rather than a national culture leads the African intellectuals into a dead end" (pp. 152, 154). For Fanon, the correct path toward achieving African unity should resemble an outwardly expanding circle with the priority being for individual African peoples to take control of their own nations and attain national consciousness through continuous struggles against imperialism. Only then is it possible for a progressive international union to emerge, because "it is at the heart of national consciousness that international consciousness establishes itself and thrive" (p.180).

Echoing Fanon's thought on African unity, Ngũgĩ (1986) elaborated on the idea of national consciousness by providing it with a psycho-linguistic underpinning and, in doing so, reasserted the primacy of national liberation over international unity. In Ngũgĩ's anthropological account, a national language is a natural product of a people's needs to communicate in the common struggle to produce wealth within their immediate natural and social environments and, therefore, carries cultural values of the community handed down from one generation to the next. As such, the native tongue of a people is an "image-forming agent" that has everything to do with how a people perceive themselves in relation to other peoples in the universe, that is to say, with their self-understanding, self-positioning, and self-esteem (pp. 15-16). After centuries of "self-mutilation of the mind, the enslavement of our being to Western imperialism," one of the most urgent tasks for Africans, Ngũgĩ argued (n.d.), is to decolonize the mind by reclaiming and revitalizing the national language (p. 29). It is only after the mind is decolonized and self-esteem reestablished in this way that a colonized people can appreciate "the humanistic, democratic and revolutionary elements in other people's literatures and cultures without any complexes about his own language, his own self, his own environment" (pp. 28–29). Once again, like Fanon, Ngũgĩ proposed a process whereby liberation starts from the nation and gradually expands outward. Such is what he meant by a "quest for relevance": "A person must know where they stand in order to know in what directions they must proceed" (Ngũgĩ, n.d. p. 32). The only question here, however, is that Ngũgĩ analogy can be misleading, as a nation should not be personified too hastily because the problem with the nation is precisely that it sometimes works against group interest and individual will.

For Fanon and Ngũgĩ, an internationalist concept like African unity would be an empty slogan if individual African peoples did not first undergo a revolutionary process of material and psychological decolonization as well as a democratic process of reclaiming their nations from the hands of both the imperialist state and the national bourgeoisie it cultivates at home. Their intention was to set the priority right rather than opposing nationalism with internationalist and cosmopolitan ideals. In other words, theirs was "not a call for isolationism but a recognition that national liberation is the basis of an internationalism of all the democratic and social struggles for human equality, justice, peace and progress" (Ngũgĩ, 1986, p. 103). Nations, in both thinkers' minds, are not obstacles to internationalism or cosmopolitanism but quite the opposite. They are the precondition or building blocks of it. It is through a common effort to redress inequities between nations and states and the skewed social relations the lopsided international structure engenders at home that one nation connects with another and, in this way, fills any internationalist concept that might arise afterward with a humanist meaning.

The above discussion should make clear that the common thread that ran through Kantian cosmopolitanism, Marxian internationalism, and Fanon and Ngũgĩ's conceptions of the nation was the same humanist intention to set humanity free from the vicious cycle of militaristic and economic competition among states and their perennial collusion with multinational capital. Other than Kant who is infamous for being anti-democratic, all call for genuine democracy that allows for people's direct participation in public affairs. The goal is the same, but the means to achieve it are different. In this respect, it can be argued that beneath the different shapes and sizes of the various imagined communities that have been proposed or realized in the past, what truly makes a difference is the existence or non-existence of a humanist kernel, a genuine intention to promote democracy, to redefine social relations, and to realize a fairer redistribution of wealth. Whether it is nationalism, critical regionalism, pan-nationalism, or any supranational alliance based on race, class, gender, religion, culture, or social agenda, none of them is inherently more progressive than the other. From the European history of fascism, Nazism to the recent resurgence of White nationalism in many parts of the North as a response to recurring global economic crises, the devastating effects of nationalism is too well known to require a full tally. But, on the other hand, supranational blocs are not in themselves a guarantor of peace and progress. Sometimes they bring the exact opposite consequences; witness Imperial Japan's Greater Asian Co-Prosperity Sphere, the Soviet example of class-warfare-turned totalitarianism, the irrational nuclear arms race during the two-bloc era, and finally the complete disregard for human lives by ISIS in the present time. Without democratic and humanist content, any larger union can be just as oppressive as some of the most narrow-minded varieties of nationalism. Even in a quasi-cosmopolitan world, which not all but some of us live in today thanks to increased physical mobility and improved information technology, the marginalization of humanism by multinational business interest and egoistic state policies predisposes such a fledging cosmopolitanism to amount to no more than a travesty of Kant's vision.

Timothy Brennen's discriminate critique of the distortion of cosmopolitanism since the late twentieth century onward and his attempt to redirect scholarly attention to the legacy of anticolonial nationalism help illuminate this line of thinking. Seeing that the term "cosmopolitanism" has been regularly coopted by some unscrupulous metropolitan commentators to cover up and sugarcoat an American-led cultural imperialism, Brennen (1997) proclaimed, in a Fanonian voice, "Nationalism is not dead. And it is good that it is not" (p. 317). Using Latin American ex-colonies as an example, he contended that nationalism remains the only viable means for these countries to assert autonomy against an overwhelming tidal wave of Americanization that will not stop until "a dead level of uniformity" is achieved (p. 30). Thus, terms such as "liberation," "the people," and "the indigenous," Brennan continued, while much ridiculed by metropolitan theory due to their rootedness in nationalism, "remain vital today because there is simply nowhere else to go [than turning nationalist]" (p. 317). Brennen's assessment, it bears repeating, should not be read in binary terms as a romantic celebration of nationalism and a repudiation of the post-Enlightenment cosmopolitan project. Rather, it is meant to underscore the fact that the humanist vision which constitutes the core of Kant's and Marx's cosmopolitanism is on the verge of being swept away in today's capitalist cosmopolitanism. Yet the same vision is kept alive, however tenuously, in the tradition of anticolonial nationalism.

In retrospect, postcolonial debate on nationalism, like most intellectual discussions, has been caught in the broader dialectic of nation and anti-nation peculiar to the contradictory nature of capitalist modernity. The dilemma of nationalism, or the national question if you will, first rose to prominence at the time of the Second International and is still relevant in our time. Like their socialist predecessors, some postcolonialists worked on theorizing alternatives to the current political order, while others tried to find better ways to work within the existing framework of the nation-state. Regardless, in carrying on the Leftist tradition of human emancipation, postcolonialism sets its eye on a clear goal: to contain, if not defeat, the practices of inhumane capitalist profit-making and the ever-lurking threat of state violence, especially for the sake of world populations who are most vulnerable to these forces. Over the past decades and through constant back-and-forth, this debate has made more clearly both the relevance and dangers of nationalism in the postcolonial world. Will nationalism become a thing of the past one day? No one can answer that question now. However, in line with Brennen's position, this chapter also argues that, while the vision of cosmopolitanism must be kept alive as a common goal of humanity, one should take seriously Fanon and Ngũgĩ's contention that as long as there are people remaining culturally, economically, and politically subjugated by their own or other states and multinational corporations, it is premature to speak of true cosmopolitanism.

As various global crises continue to exert incredible pressures on the world's poor communities—crises including, not least, issues related to climate change, worsening income inequality, and heightened border policing—the stakes are perhaps higher than ever to carefully reconsider the efficacy of national resistance. Insofar as nationalism, as a political doctrine, demands every nation to act on its own interest, the global political landscape and the existing hierarchy in the international division of labor will never be truly challenged and, as a result, humans will only end up in the same place again and again. Thus, it is a never-ending task for postcolonial studies to propose ways to forge transnational solidarity, to construct social and political forces larger than the nation-state to contain the ambition and aggressiveness of global capitalism and imperialism. This leads to the second topic of the chapter, hybridity as a counterculture.

HYBRIDITY AND THE UNLEARNING OF NATIONALISM

Hybridity is a theoretical concept developed by several postcolonial thinkers to challenge discourses of racial and cultural purism historically underpinning colonialism, both Eurocentric and internal. The concept, in recent decades, is often invoked interchangeably with or alongside terms such as syncretism, plurality, diaspora, and bricolage. It has also been characterized variously and dismissively as a postmodern cliché, a mere language play, or even a downright ideology of global capitalism. While these criticisms possess validity to different degrees, what this chapter wishes to underscore is a conception of hybridity from a more pragmatic standpoint. In other words, the sense of hybridity stressed here is not the kind of wishful thinking that one finds, for example, in Homi Bhabha's (1994) high theory in which hybridity is said to disturb the stable self-representation of the West and accordingly arouse the colonizer's guilt. Though it is agreeable, with Bhabha, that if nationalism is an ideology that promotes unity by invoking notions of common race, culture, history, religion, and inhabitation, hybridity is its natural antithesis that questions precisely what commonality even means and on whose terms by highlighting the arbitrary nature of all commonalities.

This, however, does not mean that hybridity should be understood narrowly as a "postmodern" phenomenon of late capitalism as many critics have asserted. Rather, hybridity is something that has always existed alongside nationalism. Although there is value in the argument that the nation-state remains the only viable political formation for the time being and one must not give up nationalism as a strategic instrument to inspire collective actions, the chapter maintains that the gradual unlearning of nationalist thinking holds the key to changing the status quo of North-South inequality in the long run and postcolonial studies remain well-positioned to do the important work of bridging cultural and national divides.

In recent years, the idea of regional integration has received strong support from influential scholars such as Samir Amin (2006), Walter Mignolo (2000), and Kuan-Hsing Chen (2010). The reason is easy to understand; there is an urgent need for Southern countries to construct transnational, multifaceted frameworks of cooperation to counterbalance U.S. global hegemony. While this proposition seems perfectly reasonable on paper, the realities are much more complicated and cannot be easily resolved by invoking similar patterns and histories of colonial experiences in previously colonized regions (Mignolo, p. 741). What about the present moment where U.S. foreign policy still actively bifurcates all regions? Take East Asia, for example. The historical feuds between Japan and the two Koreas, South and North Korea, Japan and China, China and Taiwan, and to a lesser extent, China and South Korea seem impossible to reach a sustainable reconciliation in the current state of affairs, not to mention that three out of these five states are currently U.S. client states. Japanese right-winged politicians' visits to the Yasukuni Shrine irrespective of Korea's and China's protests, South Korea's deployment of THAAD missile system in compliance with U.S. global military scheme, Taiwan's constant exclusion from international bodies as a result of Beijing's political pressures all had rekindled long-held mutual hostilities between these countries and triggered widespread tensions in the past. What can be added to these highly publicized events are the less told but not infrequent occurrences of insensitive xenophobia and discrimination against migrant works and minorities in all these societies. Events like these simply do not bode well for the prospect of regional integration. Such is the reason why it is necessary and urgent to start the difficult work of unlearning nationalist thinking and complementing it with an acknowledgment that all cultures and societies are, by necessity, historically and inherently hybrid.

One of the earliest critiques of hybridity is that it arises out of a linguistic reduction of imperialism and thus is an insubstantial form of resistance. In his essay "Given Culture," Pheng Cheah (1998b) attempted a materialist critique of what seemed to him a purely culturalist and idealist theorization of cosmopolitanism, specifically Homi Bhabha and James Clifford's hybridity theory. His main charge against Bhabha and Clifford was that both placed an uncritical faith in the transformative power of cultural signification and representation; that they repeated the "commonplace assertion that discourse produces the real" and thereby "obscure the material dynamics of nationalism" (p. 292). In particular, he saw Bhabha's hybridity theory as having limited political efficacy because it is premised upon "a reductive understanding of colonial rule as the establishment of cultural authority through the deployment of symbols" while overlooking a whole spectrum of material forms of domination such as politics and economics (p. 294). Cheah further concluded that hybridity is a politically irresponsible and ineffective concept, as it offers little for us to consider "our responsibility to the given" and mainly attempts to theorize "our freedom from the given" by replacing the actual reality with a discursive one (p. 292). To him, nationalism was "the most progressive form of postcolonial transformative agency in contemporary globalization" (p. 301). Robert Young (1990) similarly critiqued Bhabha's revisionist account of Indian colonial history and claimed that the latter constructed a voluntarist site of resistance by "[reading] between the lines" to locate moments of textual indeterminacy, that is, moments when colonial power appeared unsure of itself (p. 149).

Hybridity, to be sure, is mainly an ideological product abstracted from the concrete social relations created by the increasingly globalized economy in the past two centuries. However, this does not mean that it exists only in the discursive space. Rather, hybridity is also corporeally lived, experienced, and repeatedly reproduced by human action in the actual postcolonial space. Henri Lefebvre's theory of space is relevant here. As he (1974/1992) wrote, "(Social) space is not a thing among other things, nor a product among other products; rather, it subsumes things produced, and encompasses their interrelationships . . . there is nothing imagined, unreal, or 'ideal' about it compared, for example, with science, representations, ideas or dreams" (p. 73). A strict separation of the material and ideational dimensions of imperialism and anti-imperialism will then be tantamount to denying the transformative power of culture and human creativity.

Although it should be fully acknowledged that capitalist interest and state power control popular access to most information and objects in today's world and, as such, hybridity remains more directly experienced in the urban space, the truth remains that what constitutes our "given" are the unalterable histories of colonization, forced economic integration, and imposed cultural mixture. Under these circumstances, it may not be as productive to adopt a nationalist view that strictly defines ours and theirs, indigenous and foreign, as to creatively and strategically mobilize and become affiliated with decolonial ideas and forces of various cultural origins. In responding to Cheah's critique of his conception of hybridity, this is what Clifford (1998) had to say: "Whatever 'freedom' is asserted [with the concept of hybridity] is not inherent in discourse . . . but is, rather, a pragmatic response, making the best of given (often bad) situations. The cultural inventiveness at stake is a matter of specific juxtapositions, selections, and overlays offered and imposed in limited historical junctures" (p. 366).

What seems to be a stronger criticism is that hybridity often applies only to the relatively privileged populations who enjoy a certain degree of physical mobility. As Cheah (1998b) rightly reminded us that, for the majority living in the global south, to become hybrid through physical migration is simply not an option in the current neoliberal reality of exacerbated uneven development. And, as seen above, Timothy Brennan's legitimate concern about the gradual erosion of peripheral cultures in the South by American cultural hegemony attending globalization similarly led him to insist on the necessity of defensive nationalism. Is hybridity, then, merely an uncritical celebration of a rootless identity informed by a postmodern and poststructuralist sensibility which mainly reflects university postcolonialists' privileged enunciative position, as Arif Dirlik (1997) asserted?

As the chapter showed earlier, postcolonial intellectuals have been well informed of the histories and cultures of global capitalism and anti-colonialism and have produced a literature about nationalism that is more complex than simply taking sides. As such, the polemic that habitually equates postcolonialism with postmodernism or poststructuralism no longer holds. The more fundamental question remains this: Is hybridity an ideology or cultural reflection of global capitalism which functions to naturalize the latter? Yes, for the most part, but it also forms with nationalism an immanent contradiction of capitalist modernity.

It is certainly true that collective actions are urgently needed to demand changes in the existing hierarchy of production between the North and South and reverse the unrelenting global trends of cultural homogenization and commodification. However, one should be extremely cautious when making an argument for nationalism in any shape and form. An exclusionary and essentialist identity politics by nature, nationalism can, and often did, easily turn from an emphasis on responsibility to one's nation to one of irresponsibility and even hostility to the less national or the non-national. Without a truly democratic political structure in place, nationalism can easily be used as a gatekeeper of global capital for whose sake it manages existing social relations and eliminates cultural diversity more forcibly and directly than the latter. In times of economic crises, as we often see, nationalism channels popular discontent toward the presence of immigrants—thereby further blocking the international movement of labor—and places blame on political dissidents and minorities for threatening national unity. In order to turn the nation into an economically competitive unit, it justifies the imposition of a dominant language and culture and does so sometimes under the deluding banner of multiculturalism (as if all differences were equally valued) while in effect punishing those it deems unable, unwilling, or unworthy to assimilate. When speaking of Chinese nationalist language policy, Rey Chow (2013) explained how Beijing's privileging of Mandarin reinforced orientalist reduction of cultures and worked in synergy with capitalist modernity which preferred to work with relatively homogenized nation-states free of complexity: "Mandarin is properly speaking, also the white man's Chinese . . . the enforcement of Mandarin in China and the West is rather a sign of the systematic codification and management of ethnicity that is typical of modernity" (p. 48).

To return to the initial question: Is hybridity an ideological product of global capitalism? Certainly, but no more than nationalism. Both have the potentials to aid and undermine the smooth functioning of global capitalism. Nationalism has in the past inspired and continues to inspire anticolonial movements to defend the interest of the popular classes, assert native cultural value, and establish popular sovereignty and self-determination. Still, it has not gotten us very far. How else did we go from a three-world system to a fully-fledged globalized economy? It is as Said argued anticolonial nationalism is a foil for imperialism. The knee-jerk response of fighting imperialism with nationalism risks, culturally, challenging orientalism by way of self-orientalization and, with the manipulation of the political elite, turning the state into a facilitator of global capital flow under the permanent, and sometimes paramount, imperative of development. On the other hand, global capitalism has since the heyday of imperialism spawned a huge international class of hybrid functionaries. However, it has also given us people like Ho Chi Minh, Aimé Césaire, Frantz Fanon, and C. L. R. James who embodied the archetypical organic intellectuals of the globally oppressed in modernity; who set their eyes on the goal of writing "a new history of men" and forging a different kind of international community based on the principles of humanism and socialism (Fanon, 1963/2004, p. 238).

Taking hybridity, a historical knowledge of mutual enrichment among cultures, as a starting point, there are two ways in which we may proceed to build an alternative world order to the current capitalist globalization sustained by the interstate system. One of these is epistemological and the other is ontological or experiential. Epistemologically, this involves avoiding and contesting methodological nationalism in the production of knowledge. In rebuilding our knowledge of the past in a non-nationalist way, some scholars proposed taking a network conception of society that documents to links not just between nations but also cities, regions, and organizations of different sorts (Delanty, 2015), while others suggested fully accounting for the historical influences of both foreign and domestic actors (Storm, 2015). These strategies readily lend themselves to constructing region-based and region-specific knowledge that uncovers and promotes the historical connectedness and cultural affinity among peoples of the same region. Such a body of knowledge will then serve as the foundation of regional reconciliation and collaboration and inform development without taking the West as a "universal" model or inevitable frame of reference. Jeremiah O. Arowasegbe (2016), in his discussion of the work of Claude Ake, also recognized the need to construct an endogenous body of knowledge to serve as the "material condition of autonomous development of Africa" by developing a scholarship that "takes its local existential, intellectual, and political contexts seriously while also seeking to be globally reputable" (pp. 611, 627).

The retrieval and retelling of the past are far from enough to build a transnational counter-hegemonic framework. Praxis is another key factor that will substantiate and add an experiential dimension to such a framework. Recent researchers have consulted long-term data and confirmed that the "multiple, interconnected crises" or "systemic crises" engendered and continually exacerbated by global capitalism have created the material condition for transnational, counter-hegemonic movements (Smith et al., 2018, p. 373). In other words, global capitalism, while causing various forms of human suffering and environmental deterioration, carries the seeds of its own demise, not least in the forms of technical connectivity and communication infrastructure in our current conjuncture. Recent examples of transnational counter-hegemonic movements include the transnational labor movements in the Philippines and Pakistan (Brookes, 2018), the mutual projection between Taiwan and Hong Kong's democratic movements (Lin and Haack, 2020), and most remarkably, the string of internationalist feminist strikes that influenced each other swept through much of Europe and the Americas since October 2016 under various slogans such as "Nosotras Paramos," "We Strike," "Viva Nos Queremos," "Ni Una Menos," and "Feminism for the 99 per cent" (Fraser, Bhattachrya & Arruzza, 2018). All these encouraging movements give us reasons to believe that through grassroots, spontaneous, and democratically organized movements, people of various national origins can work together to take back their power, redefine issues, and create new values.

Hybridity is, of course, nothing new. It has been for the most part relegated to a residual or latent status by the dominant nationalist culture worldwide but also sporadically made palpable as a structure of feelings at different points in modernity. As Amin (1997) wrote, it is historically a norm rather than an exception before the advent of nationalism. For over two centuries, nationalism has conditioned human mind to perceive the current political order of the nation-state as natural and inevitable and demanded the ruling class around the world to organize social relations and political and cultural institutions according to its logic. Though today's ideal national society equipped with a proper mechanism of political representation may offer protection to its citizens through an array of legal and political institutions premised upon the bourgeois social-contract model, internationally each nation remains first and foremost for itself, which leads to the current world situation where the wealthy and powerful nations dictate the terms of negotiation and survival for all. In a sense, hybridity is both pre-nationalist and post-nationalist. In many colonial literatures of the early twentieth century, there were already writers who explored and articulated abundantly the possibilities and consequences of multiple cultural identifications. It is post-nationalist, not in the sense of replacing nationalism but in the sense of modifying it. Postcolonial studies have traditionally contributed to the bridging of boundaries in several ways. The (intellectually or physically) hybrid practitioners in the field have built an international epistemology that drew inspiration and knowledge from various cultural locations to address local and global problems, uncovered marginalized histories of transnational connectedness, and redefined cultures traditionally grouped in national terms by studying the historical trajectories of populational and cultural contacts.

CONCLUSION

At ACLA's 2019 conference in Georgetown, a paradoxical panel titled "Internalization of Nationalism" caught my attention. I thought to myself, if this is where we are headed, it would not be a bad synthesis; it would be a much-needed adjustment to the existing political and economic arrangements on both national and international levels. Internationalization of nationalism might very well anticipate a global landscape consisting of regional federations.

In this chapter, I have attempted an overview of how nationalism has been debated in postcolonial studies. Building upon the legacy of anticolonial struggles and incorporating Marxist, deconstruction, psychoanalysis, and poststructuralist theories, as well as individual scholars' unique cultural knowledge, postcolonialism has contributed to a better understanding and theorization of the role of nationalism in the permanent struggle of world anti-imperialism. I have also argued that nationalism or no nationalism has never been the most important issue. At the core of the discussion is a continual search for ways to preserve and realize humanist ideals against the constant threats of capitalist exploitation, state violence, and cultural extinction in the global south.

Of course, no one can say with any certainty if nationalism and its political realization, the nation-state, would in the future give way to regionalism and, eventually, cosmopolitanism. However, the current system of nation-states increasingly appears unsustainable. As Amin (1997, 2006) indicated, the predicament that we are facing today lies in the fact that while capitalist economy assumes a truly global dominance, there is no commensurate international political and legal bodies to regulate its far-reaching social, cultural, and environmental consequences. This is why unlearning nationalist indoctrination and balancing it with a historical knowledge of human and cultural interconnectedness is important. Most, if not all, modern individuals spend their formative years being molded into a national subject but only some have the intent, wherewithal, or leisure time to unlearn that education. This is the major obstacle ahead and the building of a counter-hegemony against nationalism needs to take place. In my view, the way forward cannot continue to be an antagonism between imperialism and postcolonial nationalism because the latter, much like the earlier transnational Negritude, remains a reactive ideology. What is required is a collective unlearning, both in the center and periphery, of nationalism along with its various malaises, ethnocentrism, self-interest, and extreme cultural pride.

REFERENCES

Amin, S. (1997). *Capitalism in the Age of Globalization: The Management of Contemporary Society.* Zed Books.

Amin, S. (2006). *Beyond US Hegemony? Assessing the Prospects for a Multipolar World.* Zed Books.

Anderson, B. (1983). *Imagined Communities: Reflections on the Origin and Spread of Nationalism.* Verso.

Appiah, K. A. (1992). *In My Father's House: Africa in the Philosophy of Culture.* Oxford University Press.

Arowosegbe, J. O. (2016). Endogenous knowledge and the development question in Africa. *Cambridge Review of International Affairs* 29(2), 611–635.

Bhabha, H. K. (1994). *The Location of Culture.* Routledge.

Brennan, T. (1997). *At Home in the World: Cosmopolitanism Now*. Harvard University Press.

Brennan, T. (2013). Edward Said as a Lukácsian critic: Modernism and empire. *College Literature* 40(4), 14–32.

Breuilly, J. (1994). *Nationalism and the State*. Chicago University Press.

Brookes, M. (2017). Labour as a transnational actor: Alliances, activism and the protection of labourrights in the Philippines and Pakistan. *Development and Change* 48(5), 922–941.

Cheah, P. (1998a). Introduction part II: The cosmopolitical—today. In P. Cheah & B. Robbins (Eds.), *Cosmopolitics: Thinking and Feeling Beyond the Nation* (pp. 20–41). Minnesota University Press.

Cheah, P. (1998b). Given culture: Rethinking cosmopolitical freedom in transnationalism. In P. Cheah & B. Robbins (Eds.), *Cosmopolitics: Thinking and Feeling Beyond the Nation* (pp. 290–328. Minnesota University Press.

Chen, K. H. (2010). *Asia as Method: Toward Deimperialization*. Duke University Press.

Chow, R. (2013). On Chineseness as a theoretical problem. In S. M. Shih, C. H. Tsai & B. Bernards (Eds.), *Sinophone Studies* (pp. 43–56). Columbia University Press.

Clifford, J. (1997). *Routes: Travel and Translation in the Late Twentieth Century*. Harvard University Press.

Clifford, J. (1998). Mixed feelings. In P. Cheah & B. Robbins (Eds.), *Cosmopolitics: Thinking and Feeling Beyond the Nation* (pp. 362–370). Minnesota University Press.

Delanty, G. (2016). The making of European society: contesting methodological nationalism. *Innovations: The European Journal of Social Science Research* 29(1), 3–15.

Deutsch, K. (1966). *Nationalism and Social Communication: An Inquiry Into the Foundation of Nationality*. M.I.T. Press.

Dirlik, A. (1997). *The Postcolonial Aura: Third World Criticism in the Age of Global Capitalism*. Westview.

Fanon, F. (2004). *The Wretched of the Earth*. Gove (Original work published 1963).

Fraser, N., Bhattacharya, T., & Arruzza, C. (2018). Notes for a feminist manifesto. *New Left Review* 114, 113–134.

Gellner, E. (1983). *Nations and Nationalism*. Cornell University Press.

Kant, I. (1903). *Perpetual Peace: A Philosophical Essay,* M. C. Smith (Trans.). Swan Sonnenschein & Co. (Original work published 1795).

Lefebvre, H. (1992). *The Production of Space*. Blackwell.

Lin, K., & Haack, M. (2020, October 1). Viewing Taiwan from the Left. Jacobin. Retrieved from https://jacobinmag.com/2020/01/taiwan-elections-hong-kong-protests-china-dpp-kmt

Marx, K. (2008). *The Communist Manifesto*. Pluto (Original work published 1848).

Marx, K. & Friedrich E. (1998). *The German Ideology. Prometheus* (Original work published 1846).

Mignolo, W. (2000). The many faces of cosmo-polis: Border thinking and critical cosmopolitanism. *Public Culture* 12(3), 721–748.

Ngũgĩ, W. T. (1986). *Decolonising the Mind: The Politics of Language in African Literature*. Boydell & Brewer.
Said, E. (1993). *Culture and Imperialism*. Vintage.
Smith, J., Gemici B., Samantha P. & Hughes M. M. (2018). Transnational social movement organization and counter-hegemonic struggle today. *Journal of World-System Research* 24(2), 373–402.
Spivak, G. (2008). *Other Asias*. Blackwell.
Spivak, G. & Judith, B. (2007). *Who Sings the Nation-states*. Seagull.
Wood, A. (1998). Kant's project for perpetual peace. In P. Cheah & B. Robbins (Eds.), *Cosmopolitics: Thinking and Feeling Beyond the Nation* (pp. 59–76). Minnesota University Press.
Young, R. (1990). *White Mythologies: Writing History and the West*. Routledge.

Chapter 3

Maintaining Law and Order or Maintaining Conditions Ideal for the Exploitation of Africa?

A Counter-Colonial Critique of Colonial Development Assumptions

Biko Agozino

Walter Rodney theorized that under the colonial situation, the maintenance of law and order is a cynical way of talking about the maintenance of conditions favorable for the exploitation of Africans and the expropriation of the surpluses produced by African labor for the benefit of Europe. This chapter will explore whether this statement still holds in postcolonial Africa following the restoration of political independence. Concerning the genocidal wars, massive corruption, underdevelopment of infrastructures, repressive policing of dissent, crises of unemployment, inflation, and poor health facing Africans, a critique of the sustainable development goals in Africa will be offered with special reference to the assumption that the colonial boundaries drawn by imperialism to divide and weaken Africans would be sustained along with the bureaucratic structures of the militarized police, genocidal militarism, and feudal anachronism in a developing Africa. The theory of Pan Africanism will be revisited to evaluate its applicability to the People's Republic of Africa or the United Republic of African States proposal. Early parts of this chapter summarize Rodney's arguments. Finally, The closing part focuses on the mobilization of Africans towards addressing their problems.

INTRODUCTION

This chapter offers a close reading of *How Europe Underdeveloped Africa* by Walter Rodney to show that it remains a relevant theoretical framework for the analysis of the politics of law and order and the advancement of decolonization in Africa. The chapter argues that the expropriation of surpluses from Africa by colonizers that Rodney theorized is an ongoing process that is protected by the neocolonial regimes through what they cynically call the maintenance of law and order, according to Rodney.

What has changed from the colonial years is the extent to which the phantom bourgeoisie identified by Frantz Fanon in *The Wretched of the Earth* has joined their class allies to continue looting resources from Africa and stashing them in Europe to dialectically continue developing Europe at the expense of underdeveloped Africa. The background theory that informs the chapter is the framework offered by Kwame Nkrumah in *Neo-Colonialism: The Last Stage of Imperialism*. The logical conclusion from this theoretical framework is that the complete erasure of the colonial boundaries and the restructuration of Africa as the United Republic of the African States or the People's Republic of Africa will be the missing intervention for the redevelopment of Africa. The international community and African rulers miss this point when they assume that Africa will remain atomized as 55 countries that were carved out to benefit Europe instead of continuing the struggle to decolonize Africa by coming together as a united political economy of scale.

"The colonies have been created for the metropole by the metropole," Rodney (1972: 149) started in chapter 5 of his classic by quoting this French saying. The background to this discussion is the enslavement of Africans by Europeans for more than 400 years to which Rodney devoted his earlier chapters. The history of the Trans-Atlantic Slavery is assumed to be so well-known to readers that it does not need to be rehashed in this chapter with a focus on the colonial and postcolonial epochs. The exploitation of labor and natural resources could be beneficial for the development of a culture if the surpluses are reinvested in the society. But in the case of Africa, it was forced to play the role of a place from which raw materials were extracted with African labor and expatriated to Europe for the development of Europeans. Rodney uses the word, exploitation, to describe the process of extraction by oppressed workers. Can you think of a better word for this common phrase in extractive industries? Rodney suggests that exploitation is an accurate description because the dialectical process resulted in the development of Europe at the same time that it dialectically resulted in the underdevelopment of Africa.

The 2019 UN Report on Sustainable Development Goals (SDG) paid pathological attention to Africa by almost always emphasizing that all the goals are desperately needed in "Sub-Saharan Africa" (UN, 2019). Concerning the pejorative term, "Sub-Saharan Africa," Ekwe-Ekwe (2019) warned that the international community and Africans should stop applying it exclusively to

Black Africans (presumably, excluding White South Africans) since such a prefix is not applied to people from any other region of the world, suggesting that Africans may still be regarded as sub-human. The UN report diplomatically avoided mentioning that the reasons why Africa remains desperately in need of all the 17 SDG despite being the richest continent (in terms of natural resources) include the fact that Africa went through a peculiar experience of enslavement, colonization, apartheid, and neocolonialism unlike the experiences of any other continent as documented by Rodney and others (Agozino, 2019; Nehusi, 2019; Davis, 2018; Hirji, 2017). Under the postcolonial conditions of today, surplus value continues to be expropriated from the labor of Africans by the international community in alliance with the African phantom bourgeoisie identified by Fanon (1963).

Surplus value is defined as the portion of the productivity of the work that was not paid as salary but retained as a profit. Given that colonial administrators and companies paid a pittance to their African workers, the rate of surplus value was very high because wages were very low in Africa compared to Europe. Those who worked on colonial plantations, in mines or in cities under colonialism were heavily exploited. Many Africans resisted working for the Europeans because they saw such workers as slaves to the White men, having experienced hundreds of years of the hunting of tens of millions of labor in black skin during slavery. Africans were forced to seek paid employment to pay the taxes that the colonial system imposed on them. But most continued to rely on farming on their shambas and or on petty trading to sustain their families under colonialism. This contrasted with Europe where the serfs lost their access to land after feudalism ended and depended completely on wage labor in factories for survival for which they had to be paid "living wages" that were still low but much higher than what African workers earned (Rodney, 1972: 150).

African workers were poorly paid because 1) colonial authorities monopolized political power after crushing African resistance militarily, 2) African workers were too dispersed and too small in number to organize collective bargaining, and 3) colonial authorities were racist and believed that the White European working class deserved better pay. Even the lighter-skinned Arabs and Berbers of North Africa were treated as "Blacks" by the racist French colonizers while racist apartheid South Africa classified East Indians as non-White but gave them some privileges above the African majority. In England, this colorism led to collective struggles by immigrants under a political Blackness that said that you are Black if you are not White (Hall, 2017). Recently, Oxford University used this strategy to make it seem that they were admitting 15% of their students as Black (including Asian students) whereas the breakdown of the admissions proved that only 1.5% of Black British students were offered admissions in recent years.

If all the working class (including White, Black, Asian) had come together to demand better wages and improved working conditions, the employers could have been forced to offer them a better deal even in the colonies and internal colonies. But the workers were divided by race, education, and gender and were thereby weakened in their struggles for better pay. White working people in Europe were often very racist against Black working people both in Europe and in the colonies without knowing that their wages would be depressed so long as the Black working classes were forced to labor under stiff exploitation just as was the case during slavery, despite what Du Bois (1935) theorized as the psychological wages of Whiteness. The Welfare state in Europe came about when the working people united to elect pro-labor progressive administrations but the irony is that the same labor-prone administrations also refused to decolonize Africa and restore independence to Africans. Instead, obstacles were placed in the paths of African workers who tried to form trade unions under colonialism.

"The Nigerian coalminer at Enugu earned one shilling per day for working underground and nine pence per day for jobs on the surface," stated Rodney (1972: 150). Compare this to the wages of the poor coal miners in Wales, Scotland, or Germany who earned in one hour what the Enugu miner earned in a week. The American shipping line, Farrell, paid U.S. workers five out of six the total costs of loading in Africa and offloading the same amount of cargo in the United States in 1955. The European and U.S. employers who paid better wages in Europe and North America still made a profit but the peanuts paid to African workers demonstrate how much more intense the exploitation of African workers was. Do you think that it was necessary to pay European workers better because of the higher costs of living in Europe compared to colonized Africa? If so, remember that the standard of living was better in Europe partly because of the exploitation of African workers.

Moreover, if costs of living in Africa determined lower wages, how come the European staff employed in the colonies always earned a lot more than the Africans at all levels? In Gold Coast (Ghana), British employees earned an average of 40 pounds a month while the Africans earned an average of 4 pounds a month before World War II. In 1934, forty-one gold miners were killed in an accident and the colonial government offered only 3 pounds as compensation to each family. Moroccans and Algerians earned about 16% of what was paid to French colonial employees. Lord Delamere controlled 100,000 acres of Kenyan land while the Kenyans were forced to carry a Kipande pass to be able to travel around begging for jobs that paid 15–20/ per month. In Southern Rhodesia (Zimbabwe) Africans were paid no more than 15/ a month and in Northern Rhodesia, Africans earned 3 pounds monthly as skilled drivers while Europeans did the same job for 30 pounds a month. The situation was even worse under apartheid and the African wages were even cut during the Great Depression of 1930s (Rodney, 1972: 151).

The media presented Africa as an investment opportunity with huge returns. British investment in the gold mines of South African ran into over 800 million pounds in the 1950s and yielded an annual profit of over 100 million pounds. In the Congo, King Leopold did not even bother paying wages to Africans but used slave labor to extract rubber and worked millions of Africans to death in the process. Liberia was nominally independent but the U.S. company, Firestones, owned 1 million acres of a huge rubber plantation acquired at 6 cents per acre and used poorly paid African labor to work the plantation for huge profits returned to the United States to make the company one of the top 25 most profitable with a royalty of only 1% offered to Liberia (Rodney, 1972: 154).

Some apologists may argue that colonialism benefited African peasants by allowing them to harvest or grow cash crops like cocoa, palm oil, or rubber independently without having their labor exploited by the colonizers. Rodney rejected such an argument given that the peasants were exploited by middle men who were sometimes Europeans but more often lighter-skinned Syrians, Lebanese, Indians, and other Arabs who took a small cut of the profits from the peasants and marketed in bulk to the European trading companies that were initially set up as slave trading companies.

When there was a bad harvest, they advance loans to the African peasants so that they could pay their taxes and if they failed to repay with future harvests, their farmland could be foreclosed on. During the depression after World War I, the Europeans tried to reconstruct their economies by intensifying the exploitation of the peasants through a double-squeeze system of determining the prices of imported manufactures and determining the prices of raw materials:

> For example, prices of palm products were severely reduced by the UAC and other trading companies in Nigeria in 1929, while the cost of living was rising due to increased charges for imported goods. In 1924, the price for palm oil had been 14/- per gallon. This fell to 7/- in 1928 and to 1/2d in the following year. (Rodney, 1972: 156)

As a result, Nigerian women declared war against colonialism and burned down the offices of the trading companies and the homes of the colonial chiefs who had attempted to tax the women. The women won by forcing the British to abolish the offices of the colonial chiefs among the Igbo who were proud to say that they knew no kings. Also, up till today, market women do not pay taxes unless they were also civil servants or company workers who paid as they earned, though they paid to rent their shopfronts.

The United African Company still made a profit of more than 6 million pounds in 1935 (Rodney, 1972; Agozino, 2014).

As soon as the European economies recovered, they launched into the second European tribal World War over who should control the larger colonies in Africa. The European companies took advantage of this to offer African farmers even less for the raw materials and cash crops they harvested. There were strikes by workers to protest the low wages and rising costs of goods in the markets across Africa.

Shipping companies were exploitative of the peasants who harvested cash crops. They charged more for cargo from West Africa and the charges were passed down to the peasants. Also, the banks did not extend any loans to African farmers and workers for investment. Banque de Senegal and the British Bank of West Africa monopolized banking in West Africa, while Barclays Bank and Lloyds Bank were financial giants that started trading by investing in the human trafficking of Africans during slavery. When Azikiwe set up the African Continental Bank as an indigenous bank, he was investigated for fraud simply because his party, the National Council of Nigeria and the Cameroons, resolved to deposit the revenues of the Eastern Nigeria government with the only indigenous bank in the country while he was the Premiere of the Eastern Region. The Foster-Sutton Commission of Inquiry found that he did not do any wrong but that he should have resigned from the board of the bank to avoid a conflict of interest (Hansard, July 25, 1956). He agreed and handed the bank over to the government of the Eastern region under self-rule. By comparison, in 1960 the Standard Bank of South Africa made a profit of over 1 million pounds and paid a dividend of 14% to shareholders (Rodney, 1973: 163–164).

COLONIAL GOVERNMENT AS ECONOMIC EXPLOITER

The roles of the colonial administration were (1) to protect the companies from their countries against competition with companies from other countries, (2) to arbitrate conflict between companies from their own country and, (3) to maintain conditions favorable for the maximum exploitation of Africans. According to Rodney (1972: 158),

The last-mentioned objective was the most crucial. That is why colonial governments were repeatedly speaking about "the maintenance of law and order," by which they meant the maintenance of conditions most favorable to the expansion of capitalism and the plunder of Africa. This led the colonial governments to impose taxes.

The system of taxation was used to finance the administration that exploited Africans and also to force Africans to become laborers in order to earn money for the taxes. In addition, the army, the police, and the civil service were set up to force Africans to give up their land for capitalist farmers. Marketing Boards were set up to regulate the prices that peasants were paid for harvesting produce for export but they became monopolies that paid Africans less and less. During the imperialist tribal World Wars, African surpluses helped to transfer tens of billions of dollars to the European countries to support their war efforts. The colonial administrations also used forced labor to construct roads and railway lines for the evacuation of harvests. The French forced Africans to be conscripted into the military and used them to subdue other Africans but also used them to perform public works without pay. In Kenya, the Mau Mau land and freedom army was led by Dedan Kimathi to fight the British to recover their land and thousands of Kenyans were killed or tortured. Some of the survivors won an out of court settlement with the British government in 2013. Do you think that the colonial administrations should pay reparations to people of Africa descent for slavery and for colonial exploitation as suggested by Fanon (1963) and by Agozino (2004), among others, and as demanded by Caribbean countries in recent court litigation? Stuart Hall reminds us that although few of the people who received reparations after the abolition of slavery were those born to enslaved African women who were raped by plantation owners, reparations have never been offered to the enslaved and colonized people of African descent (Hall, 2017).

Bourgeois propagandists still say that colonialism did not benefit Europe financially and some claim that the enslavement of Africans was not profitable for Europe (Thornton, 2015; Fieldhouse, 1966; Clark, 1936). What do you think of the suggestion that "rational" and "enlightened" Europeans would continue a relationship with Africa for hundreds of years and wage bitter struggles to continue the relationship if it was not profitable for Europe? During Memorial Day, do you remember the sacrifices by people of African descent in defense of Europe during the World Wars as Sembene Ousmane demanded in the film, *Camp de Thiaroye* as reported by the *Guardian*, London, Nov. 10, 2017? (See also Agozino, 1995)

Science and technology helped Europe to develop capitalism and so no one should say that it was colonialism or slavery alone that produced capitalist development. However, slavery and colonialism did contribute an indispensable link to the development of science and technology in Europe. Profits and surpluses from 400 years of slavery and decades of exploitation in the colonies were reinvested in Europe to fund research and development activities as Eric Williams (1945) documented in his doctoral dissertation at Oxford University.

Technology was developed to crush palm kernels and produce oil for the soap and cosmetic industries. The same technology was adapted to crush coffee beans and produce instant coffee to make the product more widely consumed. New rubber plants were bred to produce more rubber for the car industries. Yet, no investment was made to industrialize agriculture in Africa with the result that the African went into colonialism with the hoe and emerged with the hoe, while losing all the independent craft industries that were emerging before contact with Europe. Have you imagined why Africans went from making the delicate roped pot of Igbo Ukwu in the tenth century to a situation where they import everything from toothpicks and match sticks to pens, pencils and even food in the twenty-first century? We were robbed.

Shipping was developed by Europeans during the monopoly of the criminal trafficking of millions of Africans for hundreds of years. During colonialism, ships were refrigerated to carry perishable goods and new types of ships were developed to serve as palm oil tankers that later became crucial for the transportation of petroleum products.

In the military field, the protection of monopoly interests in the colonies required technological developments in the military to avoid losing colonies to competing European countries or to African freedom fighters. The rivalry over colonies in Africa led to the tribal World War I and World War II and resulted in huge leaps in military technology research and development. The military was the major site of science and technological development in Europe.

The growth of monopoly capital was recognized by Du Bois as a consequence of colonialism. This was analyzed in detail by Lenin (1917) who regarded monopoly capitalism as a feature of imperialism or finance capital which he saw as the highest stage of capitalism. Nkrumah (1965) defined *Neocolonialism* as the last stage of Imperialism. The danger in monopoly capitalism is that it tends to kill competition and so laws were later passed to prevent one company from monopolizing activities in any industry. Yet powerful companies continue to buy over smaller start-ups and strip them to have little or no competition while Africa remained the source of raw materials and dumping ground for manufactures as well.

Colonialism also led to the development of multinational corporations that were often more wealthy than many countries in Africa and Asia. It was, therefore, difficult to hold multinationals accountable given that they did not have diplomatic relations with the countries where they operated. The United States tries to check multinational companies by making it illegal for them to use bribery to get business contracts abroad while the U.S. military is used to invade and control foreign countries to make it easy for U.S. companies to operate. In South Africa, the apartheid regime benefited from foreign direct investment from Europe and North America before students and the wider communities started campaigning for divestment from the racist country that relied on poorly paid Black labor to extract natural resources from many miles below the earth.

J.S. Mill stated that the West Indian (slave) trade was like trade between European town and country. The exception is that under colonialism, African countries were forced into an international division of labor that confined them to the production of raw materials while the European countries monopolized the production of manufactured goods. Iron ore was extracted from Africa and mixed with chrome and columbite to make steel in Europe and North America with no steel plants sited in Africa. Copper was also mined in Africa but the technical processing was done in Europe to produce cables essential for the development of electricity, cars, telephone, and electronics that were virtually absent in Africa.

The uranium necessary for the development of nuclear bombs and nuclear power plants came from Africa but the processing was monopolized by Europeans and North Americans. France tested its atomic bombs in the Sahara Desert in the 1960s and may have contributed to increased desertification in the region. The United States used the propaganda that Iraq bought some uranium from Africa as a justification for the invasion of the country after 9/11.

William Lever started Lever Brothers in 1885 while Europeans were scrambling for Africa at the Berlin Conference. Within ten years, its brand of Sunlight Soap was selling 40,000 tons in England and more in the colonies. The factory rose from its swamp location to become a multinational company with factories in the United States, South Africa, Switzerland, Germany, and Belgium but none in Black Africa where the bulk of the raw materials came from. Within another ten years, its sales rose to 60,000 tons a year. Rodney suggests that the contributions of African colonies can be traced through the rising fortunes of the Lever Brothers company. Do you agree that this is a valid and reliable method?

Lever Brothers got concessions from Belgium to extract palm oil from hundreds of acres in the Congo. It later bought an Austrian firm that specialized in crushing palm kernels to extract oil. Lever Brothers was active across West Africa and tried to buy out competing firms or go into partnership with them to form the subsidiary, United African Company which made 300 million pounds turnover per year during World War I. Scientific research was also supported by the need to produce higher-quality margarine with vitamins and test them on laboratory animals to establish that they were safe for human beings. When Germany lost access to natural oils, the scientists tried to experiment with "soapless detergents" by trying to make detergents from coal tar. By 1960, Unilever had four laboratories—two in Britain, one in Holland, and one in the United States—together employing 3,000 research workers. None in Africa!

These profitable activities resulted in developments in transportation and marketing through chain stores. But the by-product of soap, glycerin, was also used to make explosives with which Europeans blew each other up during World War I while others applied the explosives to mining. The surpluses that produce large monopoly capital do not fall from heaven or arise from savings; they are acquired through the primitive accumulation or initial methods of force, slavery, robbery, exploitation, colonialism, and oppression of millions of people for years, according to Marx (1954). Do you agree with this Marxist conclusion of Rodney?

LAW, ORDER, AND EXPLOITATION

France and Portugal regarded their colonies as extensions of their national territories and fought brutal wars against the demand for the restoration of independence to keep those colonies under their domination and exploitation. Britain and Belgium did not have theories of external territories in Africa but they encouraged settler colonialism and also waged bitter wars of repression against the natives who demanded to have their land back. For example, in Kenya thousands were killed during the Mau Mau Land and Freedom Army uprising. Also in Southern Rhodesia (Zimbabwe) the White minority farmers declared unilateral independence from Britain rather than grant political independence to the majority African population who fought the Chimurenga war of national liberation that Bob Marley sang about. In the case of Portugal, being a poor European country that depended on the exploited colonies for its very existence, the war of repression was particularly brutal in Guinea, Angola, and Mozambique (Cabral, 1979). In South West Africa (Namibia), the Germans nearly exterminated the Herero and the Nama ethnic groups to steal their land in a rehearsal for the holocaust but were yet to offer any reparations to the survivors (Drechsler, 1980). Germany recently offered development aid to Namibia for the Heroro genocide but no reparations yet.

During the conquest of Africa by European countries, they relied on African troops often conscripted and subjected to the command of a few European officers. Also during both the World War I and World War II and European tribal wars, hundreds of thousands of Africans were conscripted to go and fight for the European countries that colonized them. Germany had 11,000 Africans fighting on her side in Tanganyika (Tanzania), while the British relied on the King's African Rifles to defeat the Germans there. France had 200,000 African troops on its side during World War II and 25,000 of them were killed in action (Rodney, 1973). West Indian troops, African Americans, and East Indians were also conscripted into the British army to help in the defeat of Germany, Japan, and Italy. After the war, France continued to use its colonized African troops to suppress nationalist uprisings in other French colonies, including Vietnam, up to 1954.

There was an economic partition of Africa that did not follow the political partition of the continent. Even after Germany was defeated and the colonies it controlled were assigned to France, Britain, and South Africa to administer as trusts, German capitalists were allowed to invest in business opportunities in the colonies through banking and finance and shipping, insurance, and transportation. When Salazar seized power in a 1932 coup in Portugal he proclaimed that he was going to build a new state based on the labor of "inferior people," meaning Africans. After World War II, the United States offered the Marshall Plan for Europe to help their economies to recover quicker lest the workers' revolution in the Soviet Union became more attractive to European workers. The benefit to U.S. capitalists was that they were able to invest in businesses in Africa under the colonies controlled by Europeans but also in Liberia which was practically a U.S. colony.

The European countries used their higher rates of profits from the African colonies to offer bribes to European workers to soften their exploitation by capitalism. Thus, the European countries were able to offer social welfare programs such as free education up to high school level, national health insurance for all, old-age pensions, and unemployment benefits. None of that was offered to the colonized Africans

Europe also suffered from colonialism because some of the techniques used to repress Africans were introduced in Europe to help to control the workers. For instance, the colonel who commanded the German colonial war in East Africa returned to Germany and was promoted as a General who led the brutal massacre of protesting workers in Hamburg. Also, Mussolini experimented with concentration camps in Africa in the 1930s before trying the same in Italy during World War II.

The involvement of the United States in the Vietnam War led to counter-intelligence warfare in the United States itself and troops opened fire against students at a couple of campuses while Black Panthers like Fred Hampton were executed after the assassination of President Kennedy and the Attorney General, Robby Kennedy along with Malcolm X and Martin Luther Jr. France implemented the tactics used against the nationalists in Algeria in France itself and resulted in the death of many French citizens of North African descent. Britain used colonial strategies to control the Northern Ireland region where the Irish Republican Army wanted the British to leave and allow the North to reunite with the mainly Catholic South but the mostly Protestant North preferred to remain in the United Kingdom. A military junta took power in Portugal and waged colonial war along with repression at home. Colonialism may have been profitable for the ruling class but the working class also paid a price for it in terms of lost liberties in Europe.

Africa needs a democratic revolution led by the working people. For that to happen, the united peoples of Africa must start their socialist party whose primary goal is to take over state power from the neocolonial bourgeoisie and their imperialist allies. Once in power, the party must embark on a revolutionary program of actualizing Africa's unfinished liberation. The SDGs document expressed support for the 2063 plan of the African Union to form a confederation but Africans yearn for a federation immediately.

The revolutionary situation in Africa today can be analyzed concretely and strategically under the following themes and categories as a guide to the resolution of activists committed to launching a platform for a social-democratic revolution across Africa under the ideological leadership of the working people and revolutionary intellectuals in alliance with the peasantry, following Lenin closely (Lenin, 1963):

The old neocolonial regimes across Africa have been thoroughly discredited and have lost the hegemonic struggles for legitimacy before the people. They represent less than 1% of the class of phantom bourgeoisie, a parasitic class that lacks any of the productive capacities usually associated with a capitalist ruling class, according to Fanon. The rulers use clientelism to buy the services of the workers in the state machinery of the army, police, and the bureaucracy as the state apparatuses for oppressive and exploitative rule over the masses. They are in alignment with archaic monarchical rulers who should have been abolished throughout Africa and replaced with elected Town Mayors checked by Town Councils. The African comprador bourgeoisie is maintained in the office with the support of the foreign bourgeoisie who are only interested in the expropriation of surpluses from our hard-working people and in the extraction of natural resources.

In some African states, power has shifted to reformist regimes that frequently prove incapable of transforming the structural contradictions that condemn more than 1 billion talented Africans to a life of insecurity amid abundance. Some of these neoliberal regimes try to legitimate themselves in office by obsessing about the recovery of public funds stolen by past regimes while the elements in the current regimes rarely get caught until they are out from the office and their bourgeois rivals try to recover stolen loots from them, only to be stolen by the incumbents in turn (Agozino, 2003).

None of the neoliberal reformist regimes in Africa has shown interest in convening the constitutional conference of all Africans to chart a new course of state formation that would benefit all Africans at home and in the Diaspora with emphasis on class-race-ethnic-gender justice articulation or intersectionality. All the ministerial appointments are given to lackeys of the bourgeoisie and the vast majority of them are masculinists and ethnic triumphalists without room for gender parity despite the immense talents of African women and their enormous contributions to decolonization struggles and despite the symbolic gender parity in the African Union parliament.

Given the above conditions, no bourgeois regime deserves the loyalty of African activists, workers, and peasants. It is up to us as scholar-activists to ally with workers and peasants and build an alternative platform for the masses and boldly campaign to win power democratically and thereby end the misrule of our people by a parasitic gang of exploiters and oppressors.

The Africana Mass Party must avoid being boxed into the colonial boundaries imposed on Africans by imperialists. Already, opportunist groups are laying claim to the name of parties circumscribed by the boundaries of individual neocolonial states in Africa. Let us leave them with their discredited ideologies of bourgeois nationalism and let us avoid what Fanon identified as the pitfalls of national consciousness.

Let us boldly call our party the Africana Mass Party with a manifesto to organize in every African state. Instead of regarding Africa as the center of our foreign policy, let us smash the colonial boundaries that the masses have disdainfully disregarded. Africa should be the center of our domestic policy and the working people should be mobilized to erase the crippling colonial boundaries and allow our mighty people to rise and be counted as citizens of the twenty-first century.

In alliance with imperialism, the ruling classes across African states have intensified what Gramsci (1971) called the war of maneuvers and war of positions against our people by colluding to arm terrorist groups and the genocidal states as the excuse for foreign aggression in Africa. The reformist regimes run around the imperialist countries begging for more arms with which to wage war against our people and simply hide the huge military aid funding that they receive annually from imperialists in foreign bank accounts while committing genocide against our people with crude fetishes of militarism. They divide the masses by inciting the lumpen proletariat to rise and attack fellow Africans whose languages are mocked as incomprehensible Makwerekwere (Matsinhe, 2016).

The Africana Mass Party in Africa will abolish the importation of arms from any foreign suppliers and will concentrate on building social security by investing in agricultural, educational, health, scientific, and technological revolutions that will also enable Africans to develop and produce all the means necessary for the defense of our people. Since the armies, police, and bureaucracies across the states in Africa have shown no interest in fighting against the enemies of Africans but only specialize in committing genocide against our people, let us commit ourselves to the abolition of the armies of occupation and the repressive police forces that the imperialists imposed to keep our people under oppression eternally.

The Africana Mass Party must organize a dual power now even before we win any state office. We must have organs for the education of our people, for health research, for agricultural experiments and outreach for cooperative economics, for media and cultural work and for the security of the workers and peasants without waiting for the discredited phantom bourgeoisie to offer leadership to Africans. This will enable the Africana Mass Party to counter the dictatorship of the phantom bourgeoisie with the democracy of the working people across Africa.

Let us plan our local party branches in every ward and every state across Africa and in every diaspora African majority state that commits to our program to enable us to hold our annual congresses as soon as possible. With the trust that we are bound to enjoy among the majority of Africans at home and abroad, if only one-third of Africans can sign up as card-carrying members of our party it will be one of the biggest mass parties in history.

As a revolutionary party, the masses of our people will be attracted to our party and will rapidly swell our ranks. We had better be ready to lead this massive awakening in our people lest petty bourgeois ideologues hijack them and deceitfully use them to shore up the discredited system of neocolonialism. Let the bourgeois parties go to the people against the Africana Mass Party and let us see who would more quickly organize and mobilize our people across the ridiculous colonial boundaries that our people have always transgressed in their search for survival.

We must concern ourselves with objective conditions and not with any ideas in the heads of any individuals. Our work is carved out for us by Azikiwe (1937), Frantz Fanon (1963), Kwame Nkrumah (1965), Claudia Jones (2008), W. E. B. Du Bois (1995), Pierre Mulele (1973), Amilcar Cabral (1979), Walter Rodney (1973), C. L. R. James (1969), Samora and Justina Machel (1988), Ruth First (1970), Joe Slovo (1988), Kwame Ture (2003), Chris Hani (1991), A.M. Babu (1981), Samir Amin (2010), Ifi Amadiume (2000), Viviane Saleh-Hanna (2008), Edwin Madunagu (1982), and Bene Madunagu (2007), to mention but a few, like that of the merciless practical critique of the pitfalls of national consciousness with which the phantom bourgeoisie of Fanon has been dividing and dominating our people.

As Steve Biko (1987) observed, the most potent weapon in the hands of the oppressors is the minds of the oppressed. If we allow our people to be seduced permanently by the ideology of nationalism, sexism, and ethnicity, they will continue to refer to the comprador bourgeois dictatorships across Africa as 'our national leaders' whereas the working people have no nations yet, all we have is Africa full of oppressed and exploited working people yearning to be mobilized and united to free ourselves from oppression and exploitation democratically.

The bourgeoisie maintains its domination over the masses in Africa through the exercise of hegemony or intellectual and moral leadership sold to the people, not by force but not without force or the threat of force, but through coerced consent (Gramsci, 1971) engineered through "deception, flattery, fine phrases, promises by the million, petty sops, and concessions of the unessential while retaining the essential," as Lenin put it (1963), followed by Slovo (1988) and by Madunagu (1982) in the defense of national democratic revolution strategy as a step toward revolutionary internationalism.

To counter the bourgeois propaganda and threat or use of force, we need to launch our newspaper as an essential tool in the mobilization and re-education of our people across Africa. The availability of Internet and information technologies means that we have no reason to postpone this crucial decision any further except the lethargy that Eskor Toyo railed against. Even before the party is launched, let us constitute the party organ and start reaching out to the people daily (Toyo, 1989).

Given the threat of wars and terrorism across Africa today, it is common to observe petty-bourgeois intellectuals calling for the defense of the fatherland by all patriots. This is a way to deceive the masses by making them believe that their interests are the same as those of the bourgeois dictatorship and their imperialist partners. The defeat of terrorism is sold to the masses as a task for all the people but the propagandists have never offered any example where terrorism was ever defeated militarily even by the mighty militaries of imperialism. Instead, wherever the imperialist forces have intervened militarily to defeat terrorism, they have managed to make matters worse for the poor masses that are routinely destroyed by the imperialists as collateral damage while being simultaneously targeted by the terrorists for kidnapping and suicide bombing (Onwudiwe, 2001; Oriola, 2013; Ezeonu, 2018).

Down with militarism and up with the education of the masses as a way to eliminate the oppressive conditions of mass impoverishment that breed terrorism. Down with national consciousness that seeks to divide and weaken Africans and up with internationalism among African states to leverage our immense resources for the peaceful and democratic development of our societies. Down with sexism and sectarianism!

The wars raging across African communities cannot be ended with mere slogans. The wars cannot be ended merely by appealing to the working people of Africa to declare their will and preference for peace. The wars are raging across Africa not because the bourgeoisie is an evil class bent on the destruction of the people, although bourgeois war-mongers benefit from the wars (Ekwe-Ekwe, 2006; Achebe, 2012; Soyinka, 1996).

The wars raging across African communities are the result of 1,000 years of underdevelopment that stripped Africans of our indigenous philosophy of non-violence and imposed the rapacious ideology of capitalist greed as the means of achieving societal goals via selfish profits. To end the tendency to wage wars across Africa, we must overthrow the system of capitalism and replace it with socialism.

When the working people take over control of state power across Africa, there will no longer be any need for the workers' state to wage war against the working people. The People's Republic of Africa will be too busy providing the social security needs of Africans and will not have the time or resources to devote to war-mongering internally or externally. With the unity of the working people across Africa as citizens of democracy of scale, no internal or external ants would ever be tempted to attempt to swallow the African elephant again by force or by fraud.

The dual power structures built by the party now will lay the foundation for a new type of state across Africa through which the people shall govern their own lives. The bourgeois states imposed on Africans by imperialism and retained by the comprador classes rely on the monopoly over legitimate force to keep the people under domination.

The Africana Mass Party will abolish the capitalist state of militarism as soon as we achieve state power, the proletarian state would cease to be a bourgeois state for the oppression of other classes by the bourgeoisie. The standing army and the police state would be abolished and replaced by the masses of the people armed with knowledge and technologies of the self to defend their rights and maintain their wellness democratically and non-violently.

The Africana Mass Party is not an anarchist party because we recognize the need to win state power and use the power to smash the exploitative structures of capitalism before allowing the state to wither away when there is no longer any need for the state to be an instrument for the oppression of other classes by the ruling classes. We will prevent the restoration of the police force by organizing community watch committees across Africa and by relying on restorative justice models as opposed to retributive justice.

THE AGRARIAN AND NATIONAL PROGRAM OF THE AFRICANA MASS PARTY

Currently, there are agrarian and nationalist crises all over Africa. Nomadic cattle herders are frequently in conflict with sedentary peasant farmers because somebody's cattle ate somebody's crops and somebody is always trying to steal somebody's cattle, resulting in armed conflict in which massacres are common.

The cattle herders should be commended for single-handedly supplying the beef that has fed our people for more than 100 years and the peasant farmers must be commended for growing most of our staple food items. The current crises arose from the fact that the mode of production lags behind the means of production and we must revolutionize both the mode of production and the ownership of the means of production in the agrarian sector and in the industrial sector.

Instead of relying on the archaic medieval methods of herding cattle for hundreds of miles in search of pasture and water, we must develop cattle ranches where the cattle must be kept and feeds are brought to them instead. This will create sources of livelihood for the youth who may specialize in cutting grass and supplying to the ranches while the ranches would help to improve nutrition by supplying milk to school children.

Moreover, the youth who are employed by wealthy absentee owners of the herds would finally have the ample opportunity to go to school with their peers. Some of the peasant farmers may team up and start their cooperative ranches too with the support of grants from the People's Republic of Africa.

With the threat of desertification intensifying and forcing ethnic nationalities to encroach on the land of their neighbors, the Africana Mass Party will nationalize all land in Africa and allocate land to all who need it to avoid a situation where a few capitalist farmers own all the fertile land while the masses of the people are reduced to unemployed landless farm workers. We will support the conservation of forests by developing wind and solar power generators for cooking and electricity across Africa. We will launch a program of planting trees for each African citizen every year to help us to sequester the carbon emission in the atmosphere.

The Africana Mass Party seeks to defeat those who are bent on dividing the people along ethnic lines. We will build a larger state to encompass the whole of Africa as an alternative to the unviable multiplication of sovereign state structures that imperialism mushroomed across Africa for the obvious purpose of underdeveloping the divided and weakened Africa, as Rodney observed.

However, the unification of Africa will not be attempted by the Africana Mass Party through militarism and violence but the democratic unification of the people. The more democratic the People's Republic of Africa, the more confident the Africana Mass Party will be in guaranteeing the right to self-determination for all ethnic nationalities, and the right to secession from the People's Republic of Africa.

The Africana Mass Party recognizes the undeniable contributions of African women to the liberation struggle. As Samora Machel stated, we do not regard the liberation of women as an act of charity for which the men expect to be patted on the back (Agozino, 1997). Rather, we regard the liberation of women from sexism as inextricably intersected or articulated with the struggle against imperialism and racism; it is the precondition for the revolution. Accordingly, all elected or appointed offices of the Africana Mass Party, all offices of the People's Republic of Africa, and all employment opportunities in industries will be filled based on gender parity.

We will enforce compulsory education for all our people, including women and men. We will enforce equal pay for equal work. We will legalize the right of women to choose abortion and we will legalize sex work (Sudbury, 2005).

We will legalize same-sex relationships and provide comprehensive health coverage for all Africans. Women and men will have equal access to land and equal human rights in the People's Republic of Africa where oppressive widowhood practices will be outlawed (Oyewunmi, 1997; Amadiume, 2000; Nzegwu, 2006).

CONCLUSION

Socialists are not nationalists. They are internationalists. Thus, the People's Republic of Africa will offer citizenship to the African Diaspora internationally and to working people globally who wish to join us in building the People's Republic. As the crises of late imperialism force poor people to risk their lives in their attempts to migrate, the people's republic of Africa will be welcoming poor refugees and migrants who seek to come to Africa in search of peaceful coexistence, irrespective of race, class, and gender.

This requires partnership with socialist parties in other parts of the world and collaboration in the innovation of policies that will advance socialism worldwide for the benefit of the working people of the world. For this purpose, the Africana Mass Party will convene an international conference of all socialist parties in the world to be held in Africa for the first time. We must declare to the world that the Africana Mass Party is active in the new Socialist International without waiting for an international congress and that we are ready to advocate for all oppressed nationalities anywhere in the world.

Our internationalism starts right here in Africa by abolishing the ridiculous colonial boundaries that imperialism imposed on us. Our internationalism is extended to the African Diaspora all over the world who have a right to return as citizens of the People's Republic of Africa united democratically, while Diaspora states that wish to join the People's Republic of Africa will be welcomed with open arms.

The party can simply be called the Africana Mass Party without limiting the organization to the colonial boundaries of any African state or continental Africa, excluding the Diaspora. We must reach out and organize branches of our party across Africa and the African Diaspora and avoid the lethargy of nationalist parties. As Tajudeen Abdul-Raheem (1996) used to scream: Do Not Agonize! Organize!

REFERENCES

Abdul-Raheem, T. (1996). *Pan-Africanism: Politics, Economy, and Social Change in the Twenty-First Century.* New York: New York University Press.

Achebe, C. (2012). *There Was a Country: A Personal History of Biafra*. New York: Penguin.
Agozino, B. (2019). Rethinking education for underdevelopment and education for development in Africa. *Africa Update* XXVI(3), Summer. https://www2.ccsu.edu/africaupdate/?article=414#_ednref1
Agozino, B. (2014). Revolutionary African women: A review essay of the women's war of 1929: A history of anti-colonial resistance in eastern Nigeria. *The Journal of Pan African Studies* 7(3):3–19.
Agozino, B. (2004). Reparative justice: A pan African criminology primer. In Anita Kalunte Crumpton and Biko Agozino (eds.), *Pan African Issues in Crime and Justice*. Aldershot: Ashgate.
Agozino, B. (2003). *Counter-Colonial Criminology: A Critique of Imperialist Reason*. London: Pluto Press.
Agozino, B. (1997). *Black Women and the Criminal Justice System: Towards the Decolonisation of Victimisation*. Aldershot: Ashgate.
Agozino, B. (1995). The third debt to the third world: The representation of the politics of law and order in Camp de Thiaroye. *Third Text* 36: 3–13.
Amadiume, I. (2000). *Daughters of the Goddess, Daughters of Imperialism: African Women, Culture, Power and Democracy*. London: Zed Press.
Amin, S. (2010). *Ending the Crisis of Capitalism or Ending Capitalism?* Oxford: Pambazuka Press.
Azikiwe, N. (1937). *Renascent Africa*. New York: Negro Universities Press.
Babu, A.M. (1981). *African Socialism or Socialist Africa?* London: Zed Press.
Biko, S. (1987). *I Write What I Like: A Selection from His Speeches and Writings*. London: Heinemann.
Cabral, A. (1979). *Unity and Struggle: Speeches and Writings of Amilcar Cabral*. New York: Monthly Review Press.
Clark, G. (1936). *The Balance Sheets of Imperialism: Facts and Figures on Colonies*. New York: Columbia University Press.
Davis, A. (2018). 'Foreword' in Walter Rodney, *How Europe Underdeveloped Africa*. London: Verso.
Du Bois, W.E.B. (1995). The Pan-African congresses: The story of a growing movement. In David L. Lewis (ed.), *W.E.B. Du Bois: A Reader*. New York: Owl Books.
Du Bois, W.E.B. (1935) *Black Reconstruction: An Essay Towards the History of the Role that Black People Played in the Attempt to Reconstruct Democracy in America, 1860-1880*. New York: Harcourt, Brace and Company.
Drechsler, H. (1980). *Let Us Die Fighting: The Struggle of the Heroro and the Nama*. London: Zed Books.
Ekwe-Ekwe, H. (2019). *The Longest Genocide – Since May 29 1966: Essays*. Darkar: African Renaissance.
Ekwe-Ekwe, H. (2006). *Biafra Revisited*. Dakar: African Renaissance.
Ezeonu, I. (2018). *Market Criminology: State-Corporate Crime in the Petroleum Extraction Industry*. New York: Routledge.
Fanon, F. (1963). *The Wretched of the Earth*. New York: Grove Press.
Fieldhouse, D.K. (1966). *Colonial Empires*. New York: Weldenfeld and Nicolson.

First, R. (1970). *The Barrel of a Gun: Political Power in Africa and the Coup d'Etat.* London: Allen Lane.

Gramsci, A. (1971). *Selections From the Prison Notebooks.* London: Lawrence and Wishart.

Hall, S. (2017). *Familiar Stranger: A Life Between Two Islands.* Durham: Duke University Press.

Hani, C. (1991). *My Life: An Autobiography Written in 1991.* Johannesburg: SACP.

Hirji, K.F. (2017). *The Enduring Relevance of How Europe Underdeveloped Africa.* Montreal: Daraja Press.

James, C.L.R. (1969). *A History of Pan-African Revolt.* Washington, DC: Drum and Spear Press.

Lenin, V.I. (1963). *The Tasks of the Proletariat in Our Revolution: Draft Platform for the Revolutionary Party.* Selected Works, Vol. 2, Moscow: Progress Publishers.

Lenin, V.I. (1917). *Imperialism: The Highest Stage of Capitalism.* Petrograd: Iskra, republished, Selected Works, vol.1, Moscow: Progress Publishers, 1963.

Madunagu, B. (2007). *Women's Health and Empowerment: Speeches, Essays and Lectures, 1995–2006.* Calabar: Clear Lines Publications.

Madunagu, E. (1982). *Problems of Socialism: The Nigerian Example.* London: Bogle l'Ouverture.

Marx, K. (1954) *Capital,* Vol. 1. Moscow: Progress Publishers.

Matsinhe, D. (2016). *Apartheid Vertigo: Discrimination Against Africans in South Africa.* Aldershot: Ashgate.

Nehusi, K. (2019). Forty-seven years after: Understanding and updating Walter Rodney. *Africa Update* XXVI(3), Summer. https://www2.ccsu.edu/africaupdate/?article=414#_ednref1

Nkrumah, K. (1965). *Neocolonialism: The Last Stage of Imperialism.* London: Thomas Nelson.

Nzegwu, N. (2006). *Family Matters: Feminist Concepts in African Philosophy of Culture.* Albany, NY: SUNY Press.

Onwudiwe, I.D. (2001). *The Globalization of Terrorism.* Aldershot: Ashgate, republished by Routledge, 2018.

Oriola, T. (2013). *Criminal Resistance? The Politics of the Kidnapping of Oil Workers in Nigeria.* Aldershot: Ashgate.

Oyewunmi, O. (1997). *The Invention of Women: Making an African Sense of Western Gender Discourses.* Bloomington, IN: University of Minnesota Press.

Rodney, W. (1972). *How Europe Underdeveloped Africa.* London: Bogle l'Ouverture.

Saleh-Hanna, V. (2008). *Colonial Systems of Control: Criminal Justice in Nigeria.* Ottawa: University of Ottawa Press.

Slovo, J. (1988). *The South African Working Class and the National Democratic Revolution.* Pretoria: SACP.

Soyinka, W. (1996). *The Open Sore of a Continent: A Personal Narrative of the Nigerian Crisis.* Oxford: Oxford University Press.

Sudbury, J. (2005). *Global Lockdown: Race, Gender and the Prison-Industrial Complex.* New York: Routledge.

Thornton, B. (1915). The Truth About Western "Colonialism". Accessed from https://www.hoover.org/research/truth-about-western-colonialism,

Toyo, E. (1989). *The Working Class and the Third Republic*. Calabar: Directorate for Literacy.

Ture, K. (2003). *Ready for the Revolution: The Life and Struggles of Stokely Carmichael*. London: Simon & Schuster.

United Nations. (2019). *Report of the Sustainable Development Goals*. New York: United Nations.

Williams, E. (1945). *Capitalism and Slavery*. Chapel Hill, NC: University of North Carolina Press.

Chapter 4

Postcolonial Development and Nailiyat Dance of Algeria
An Unorthodox Approach
Fouad Mami

Contemporary Algerians rarely, if ever, approve of women dancers from the wider Ouled Nail region. This chapter challenges orthodox perceptions, which vary between those who view the dancers as "whores-by-nature" and those tolerating them only as a weekend or holiday distraction. Tracing their art to the Sufi legacy of North Africa, these dancers are enmeshed in a much older tradition that was dominant even before the Neolithic revolution. What such a legacy involves is a state of being that categorically defies capitalism. Hence, before the colonial annexation (i.e., before the 1860s), Algerians used to venerate the Nailiyat and come to their performances guilt-free. Indeed, the dance had been, until the colonial takeover, synchronous with Ouled Nail's seasonal migration: trekking southward to the *beni m'zab* oasis in the fall and northward to their homelands in the spring. Such a pastoral-nomadic order as the Nailiyat embodies recreates the movements of the graceful pigeon; hence, the name of the dance, the *fezāai* or "the shuddering bird." Consequently, the chapter finds that, in order to shed alienation (colonial or otherwise), postcolonial Algerian development planners have little alternative but to reverse what their colonial predecessors set in motion a little over a century and half ago. This involves, among other imperatives, not only ceasing to denigrate the dance but promoting the body's intelligence, specifying that the body (not the mind) always acts as a framework for non-fetishized and non-fetishizing dispositions. Nevertheless, the Nailiyat's tendency to manifest being in becoming leads to a stateless and moneyless order, antagonizing thereby the stalemate facing the postcolonial planner.

you don't decolonize with weapons, but with the soul. Decolonization isn't triumphing over the colonists, but over the demons inside yourself. (Daoud, 2017, p. 165)

INTRODUCTION

Over half a century since its political independence, Algeria still defaults to a colonial model of development, which largely explains the country's present impasse. In its economy profile listing for Algeria, *index mundi* estimates that more than 95% of export earnings come from the hydrocarbon sector (*Index Mundi*, 2019). Surprisingly, the country's postcolonial planners have executed developmental schemes congruent with those set by their predecessors, the French colonial administrators, despite the country's pronounced anticolonialist rhetoric and policies (Boukhobza, 1991, p. 15). Postcolonial policies reproduce colonial plans of development because they trust in the same knowledge paradigm. Cartesian dualism—known as the body-mind dualism—allowed the presumed qualities of the mind, synthetic *a posteriori* knowledge, to predominance, severing any significant role for sensations[1] (Kant, 1998, p. 156). The Orientalist gaze, with which French conquerors encountered defeated Algerians in 1830, not only attributes no agency to the body; it objectifies it.

Eugène Delacroix's painting, *Femmes d'Alger dans leur appartement* (1834), exemplifies the Orientalist innuendoes typical of the colonial project in the then newly prized colony. Finished only four years after the fall of Algiers, it forces the viewer to overlook any traces of embodied interiority and concentrate instead on the immaculate flesh. The three ladies are supposedly grieving over how life stales inside a *harem*, implicitly suggesting how they would welcome "relief" from the inertia of idleness. With the French occupation advertised as the spreading of civilization, little doubt remains as to who will relieve the "tormented" ladies and who would like to keep them "enslaved." Paul Cezanne pertinently notes that the predominant yellow in the painting suggests how the displayed ladies are meant to be delighted in, like whisky (Prodger, 2016). The voyeuristic gaping at the picture of the beautiful, painted women manifests as the consumption of the body as mere flesh in the service of carnal desire. With the painting, the French occupiers clearly could not "integrate modes of thought and feeling so different from their own" (Dunwoodie, 2005, p. 301), and their mind-biased knowledge with respect to the desired but scorned Algerians, or *indigènes* (in the jargon of the time), amounts to little more than a premeditated and entrenched stereotype, justifying occupation. With the Oriental gaze, the colony becomes economically subservient to the metropole's drive for capital accumulation in the name of *la mission civilisatrice*. Considered historically, the development of the metropole translates precisely into the development of capital for the mother country and underdevelopment for Algerians.

This chapter explores how Algeria could be developed if her successive developmental planners were to become more appreciative of body thinking. Not only does such a paradigm no longer exist, but it has been systematically crushed. Postcolonials carry "a body not aware of itself as a body, a body 'off the radar'—even to itself" (Russel and Gardner, 2018, p. 380). In considering the dance performed by the women of Ouled Nail, or Nailiyat, we can locate instances of thinking in terms of the body. This "embodied knowledge," as proposed by Maurice Merleau-Ponty (1908–1961), and "ecological affordances" by James Gibson (1904–1979), and as performed by Nailiyat dancers, are deemed capable of generating a model of development that is fundamentally antagonistic to underdevelopment, as it redistributes wealth fairly because it organically connects with the body. When carefully observed, through the body mode of knowing, one can trace a development model that does not end in an impasse. Toward this end, the studied dance proposes a mode of knowing rooted in decolonial thinking, bypassing the postcolonial. Contrary to postcolonial thinking, which has been determined to undo Orientalism, decoloniality celebrates the body and expects it to succeed where the mind falls short. But in order for the body to instantiate developmental plans, preliminary work has to clear away the sedimented biases of the mind.

Aware of Karl Marx's charge of "closed temporalities" regarding Oriental societies (Marx, 1882, p. 242),[2] the chapter pursues a dialectical-historical and materialist reading as outlined by Hegel, Marx, Engels, and Rosa Luxemburg. If anything, the Nailiyat illustrates how her dance cannot be just a dance, a fetishizing spectacle entertaining alienated audiences for the purpose of endlessly perpetuating the generation of profit. With the Nailiyat, one notes an immanence which specifies how development is possible outside the usual prerequisites: state regulation and money. Studying the socioeconomics of Ouled Nail, one cannot fail to locate multiple instances of Paleolithic and Mesolithic modes of production, flowing harmoniously with the Neolithic one in a rare symbiosis.

While such a mode of production does not necessarily lift the Marxian verdict (at least not in this chapter), it nevertheless points at viable structures to abrogate total collapse. Transitioning toward the communism of the future can be effected without the dramatic floundering of the present. Besides, vestiges of the primordial order which the Nailiyat dance brings into motion facilitate that smooth transition. Indeed, the dwindling of the oil revenues obliges the postcolonial Algerian development planners to consider alternatives. Because it never had to struggle with concepts such as unemployment and crisis until the firm sealing of borders and options toward the 1850s and 1860s—that is, the tightening of colonial control—such a reciprocal economy is deemed affluent (Sahlin, 1972, p. 9). Whenever they become serious about finding a safe outlet away from the dictatorship of commodity fetishism, postcolonial development planners will be humbled by learning all about the Nailiyat dance.

In five sections, the study makes an argument in favor of a developmental model rooted in what I call "body thinking," as mediated via the Nailiyat dance. The first section of the chapter explains why developmental plans in Algeria grounded in the mind have ended literally in an impasse, spelling underdevelopment. The second expounds how, in being mind-induced knowledge, Orientalism delegitimizes the dance, reducing it to a combination of the exotic and the spectacle. Orientalism does so by deliberately encouraging audiences not to scratch the dance's sociopolitical surface, overlooking important distinctions between the erotic and pornographic on the one hand, along with the sacral and sacred on the other. The third specifies certain movements, such as those that pertain to the pelvic region and how, on the whole, choreography embodies a decolonial approach to development. The fourth traces the sublime in the phenomenological interactions of music, body movement, and attire. The fifth accounts how, in scolding the body's mode of knowing, postcolonial players in Algeria keep reproducing colonial development, the one bent on leaving Algerians in apathy and servitude.

DANCE AND DEVELOPMENT CONTRAPUNTALLY APPROACHED

One impediment to extoling the body in Algeria is Islamism. Unlike Sufi mystics, who embrace dance and take it as one path leading to the divine, Islamists inhibit cults of the body, conceiving the body as inherently sinful. For reasons not foreign to postcolonial development (furthering capitalist global expansion), French colonialism, as the chapter evolves, only intensifies such an alienation from the primordial tradition honoring the body. Differently put, the colonial development planner prizes open a crack that preexisted the entrance of colonialism to the scene. The crack bears on the confusion between the sacral and the sacred, to be expanded on in the second section. Meanwhile, it is useful to keep in mind how the Sufi stands in line with the sacral, that component which thrives on the spiritual, away from orthodox dictations. Islamism, however, issues from preoccupations with the sacred and testifies to the jurisprudential aspects of the faith. Hence it becomes necessary to trace how the controversy between the Sufis and Islamists is located.

Indeed, scorning the body outlines the two parties' inability to negotiate the heavily charged concept of pantheism or *waḥdat al-wujud*. For the Sufis, the divine essence of God permeates everything, nature and Man, where literally everything is divine. For orthodox Muslim theologians, especially those who have shaped Islamist dogma, pantheism contradicts the essence of the faith (Mamed Oglu, 1988, p. 246). Being the twin social actor with anticolonial nationalism in colonial and postcolonial times, Islamism emphasizes the primacy of the mind, while approaching the body as a site of passive inscriptions, always supplied by the mind. The patriarchal bias stipulates the mind as Godly; the body, however, is seen as ungodly. Obviously, the Sufis deride such understanding as too simplistic to distinguish between the Manifest and non-Manifest of Being (Chittick, 1989, pp. 89–90). Of relevance in such a discussion is the cultural impasse ensuing from the ontological divide dominating the postcolonial scene. Kamel Daoud—as the epigraph reads—notes how the Algerian body has a long way to go before it can be decolonized; differently put, before genealogically instilled stifling and entrapment are lifted.

In wearing either the *hijab* or *burqa*, apparently harmless acts of excessive covering of the female body, the Muslim jurisprudent registers an implicit dread before a presumed active female sexuality (approached as *la femme fatale*) (Mernissi, 1985, p. 45). If left to its own devices, that dreaded sexuality, which is nothing but the sensuality of the body in its bloom, ushers in chaos, social disorder. The *hijab* or *burqa,* then, formalizes the androcentric bias in jurisprudent terms; a fictive outlook against the body's possible instantiation. For any consummation—one possible manifestation of a body —of desire becomes socially destructive if it is not religiously sanctioned; hence the delusional twist in the logic of *hijab*. The same unspecified and imagined threats were extended to a hysterical level during colonial violence, ending in the objectification of the body (Hannoum, 2010, p. 9). Postcolonial practices accelerate such hysteria leading now to advanced scales of alienation, and even decomposition, namely, the ontological kind that brands the body as a site of negation (Macey, 1999, p. 8). Cruel as it is, physical violence is nevertheless the translation of ontological violence, stemming from the untenable terror of the body, set in process well before the colonial encounter. In the Sufi, that is, sacral framework, equal deployment of both masculine and feminine attributes of the divine works toward validating spaces of the divine (Shaikh, 2012, p. 127). For God can be shrouded in equally masculine and feminine bodies. Hence, constructed hierarchies such as mind over body, or man over woman, remain categorically erroneous.

In overlooking the ontological divide between body and mind—and amplifying thereby superficial differences between nationalists and Islamists, the postcolonial developmental impasse assumes a tragic scale. The impasse, as Addi claims, issues from falsely conceptualizing the developmental lag in terms of the need to catch up technologically with the developed world. What the postcolonial state thinks it has achieved rather subscribes to the capitalistic mode of production through a state-owned and controlled capitalistic economy.

The socialist ideology has been sold for populist consumption. Like Frantz Fanon's call for imaginative emancipation in terms of a conceptual breakthrough for development (1968, p. 157), Addi equally emphasizes how the technological lag is a trap wherein the real lag is, rather, conceptual. In actively seeking to reverse colonial objectification with the same epistemic presuppositions with regard to development, nationalists and Islamists seek to win what is basically their opponents' battle.

With every school built, hospital inaugurated, or major infrastructure delivered, colonial and postcolonial planners, both Nationalist and Islamist, in spite of their presumed ideological differences, only increase inequality and alienation. Eventually, they start competing against their very own achievements, which, due to the alienation of the Algerians' senses—given the planners' bias against the body—only infuriates expectations for more material acquisitions. When rooted in mind-based thinking, development becomes doomed to multiply its own negation in an insane loop. It can be insightful to consider how Algerians lived well before the colonial encounter (Boukhobza, 1991, p. 35). Because it is rooted in a pastoral-nomadic order, defining a socioeconomic reality at odds with capitalism, the following chapter specifies that the Nailiyat's dance (dancing approached as thinking in terms of body) is endowed with the capacity to generate and execute a decolonial development model.

Overlooking taints of impurity as colonial constructions, the Nailiyat's dance underlines how to think through the body. The spontaneous and enticing body movements indicate a precognitive and complex sensory structure engaging creativity geared toward wealth generation, along with its equal distribution.

And it is not the dancer's fault that she cannot reflect back and articulate the complexity of her sensory structure. It is the multiplicity of the body's forms and positions, translating the movements in the dance, which parodies rigid identities. The parody lifts the classical Marxian objection against "primitive communisms," opening the door for future studies regarding the mode of being and economy outlined in the dance.

Alternatively, what the mind tags as little but entertainment, often imbued with indecency, is a later codification in the history of the dance with the aim of scorning the agency of the body to maintain alienation and enlistment in the capitalist camp. James Gibson's approach to perception, being always susceptible to action and where the "individual sensory units have to function vicariously" (1966, pp. 4–5) ensures that the Nailiyat dance cannot be just a dance. It is, rather, a worldview with a solid developmental vision and practice.

As the Nailiyat dances, her audience experiences a move from passive sensation toward active perception or proprioception. The audience becomes engaged in an intricate process of sense recomposition. As such, the dancer positively influences what otherwise would remain alienated admirers. Eventually, one learns how the pastoral-nomadic social fabric constantly generates solid economic opportunities. The same order even has the capacity to limit the soulless accumulation of capital by limiting monopoly.

However, celebrating the dance as folklore has ultimately succeeded in shutting off the dancers' threat to global capitalism. Given the current closure, the dance offers a meticulous antidote that invalidates conceptual restrictions which can decolonize development. With a decolonial approach, patronage of Algerian women exercised by successive development planners—colonial administrators, postcolonial nationalists, or Islamists—can be upset. The movements that the dancers perform reflect the complexity of the inner being, the one deemed capable of reversing alienation. The sensations emit a logic independent of the mind, and, as such, that logic is deemed capable of neutralizing the arrogance of the intellect and readying Algerians to appreciate the wealth of being and the economic opportunity therein.

Equally, the socioeconomic context of the dance underlies a pastoral-nomadic arrangement that allowed members of the Ouled Nail community to coexist in relative harmony until the colonial conquest of their territory in 1852. One wonders how postcolonial development planners could overlook such an arrangement. The deterministic tone marking classical Marxist discourse, spanning from Marx and Engels to Rosa Luxemburg, and which considered modes of production in "primitive communist societies" such as Algeria, India, or China as doomed before the machine of capitalistic accumulation, has been inhibitive for researchers to consider alternative models for development with proven records of success (Luxemburg, 2003, p. 350).

Since the ruling elites in postcolonial Algeria sought to reproduce the Soviet model of development, the Marxist bias persists and precolonial economies, no matter how organic or egalitarian, are deemed too archaic in an overall campaign to even compare and later compete with capitalism. But what if that pastoral-nomadic organization is indeed subversive? And what if Marx's anxiety over bringing forth a scheme for a full-scale revolution is part of the problem, not the solution? Such a bias explains how the transcendental dimension that the dance incorporates is often found derisory and counterproductive. I find it insightful to explore how the body culture, as enfolded in the dance, would have evolved into the present had colonialism not interrupted that culture's organic order and flow. This may read like nostalgia, but the crisis currently facing global capitalism begs consideration of alternative development models, namely the combination of pastoralism and nomadism where unemployment, for example, is never heard of.

A MULTILAYERED BIAS AGAINST THE DANCE

Smothering the Nailiyat dance's artistic and economic vigor has been possible through confusing two concepts: the erotic with the pornographic and the sacral with the sacred. When the pastoral-nomadic arrangement, such as that of Ouled Nail, becomes synonymous with the shallowly sensual, and subsumed under the pejorative gaze of Orientalism through Belly Dancing, it becomes understandable how postcolonial Algerians remain insensitive to dance and bodily thinking. Context is everything; consuming a derogatory narrative as history ends in an advanced state of decomposition.

With more than $1,000 billion in oil revenues spent over two decades (2000-20), Algeria still lacks basic infrastructure. Little wonder that postcolonial development planners revert to a reactionary mood in the form of a double negation, through both nationalism and Islamism. Reprehending the dance explains the nationalists' and Islamists' narcissistic drive to be and act as the Other, the imperialist subject. Given the inflated sense of self-pertaining to the Other, the latter cannot tolerate the nationalist-Islamist's desire for an improved status. The postcolonial lives now are in an ontological limbo (Fuss, 1994, p. 23). Internalizing colonial knowledge, postcolonial planners fall prey to the vilification of the dance and overlook its subversive and dismantling potential.

Studying multiple dance traditions, scholars find that for reasons pertaining to the maintenance of a favorable *status quo*, "colonial administrations perceived indigenous dance practices as both a political and a moral threat to colonial regimes" (Reed, 1998, p. 506). Without vilification, and armed with her body, the Nailiyat not only neutralizes the colonial army or uncovers the shaky foundation behind the postcolonial setup, but helps to inculcate a more egalitarian arrangement.

Indeed, the dance was systematically vilified through the writings of the Arab Bureau, a colonial institution charged with the annihilation of functional sociopolitical orders, setting the stage for the capitalistic take over. If ever brought to light during the postcolonial period, the Nailiyat dance is introduced as either folklore or spectacle. The dance's chance of revolutionizing Algerians' understanding of themselves and decolonizing erroneous perceptions of their body, in what can be called an ontological championing of a colonially free development, remains closed. Folklore emboldens counterproductive discourses of exoticization and auto-exoticization (Reed, 1998, p. 515). Insisting on viewing dance as a sullied or spectacular undertaking perpetuates an economy that demeans the body-type of thinking. That same mindset besets and haunts the postcolonial Algerian subject, sabotaging any chances for truly breaking with the colonial paradigm.

Perhaps the first step toward ontological decolonization of the sort outlined above comes with saving the erotic from the voyeuristic or pornographic. Recalling Fanon's emphasis on the battle for concept and the need to imaginatively kill the colonized—that state of being Fanon qualifies as "the blackness of the black" in the postcolonial or decoloniality— "decolonization" means *epistemic reconstitution* (Mignolo, 2018, p. 382, emphasis added).

Postcolonial puritanical iconoclasm becomes fixated with the same alienating logic, spelling out the present closure. Here, Orientalism becomes a structure of corrupting sense-making mechanisms, accelerating thereby political, literary, or historical seizure of non-European societies and their varied ways of life (Hallaq, 2018, p. 7). Classifying the dance as folklore speaks of the ever-present *"geopolitics of knowing*, sensing and believing; the *coloniality of knowledge* and *colonial difference"* (Mignolo, 2018, p. 363, emphasis in the original). Interestingly, the dance's demotion to either spectacle or folklore underscores the colonial administrators,' postcolonial nationalists,' and Islamists' geopolitical bent on perpetuating the Orientalist objectification of non-European epistemic variables.

With a critical eye less on the dance performed by the women of Ouled Nail and more on the institution of prostitution, since the former Regency of Algiers became known a haven for whoredom during the second half of the nineteenth century, two scholars' insights mark a critical transition from the cult of the erotic and sublime to the pornographic and voyeuristic. The first stimulates the animal instinct for the purpose of "inspiring devout meditation"; the second merely arouses the same instinct with the objective of release (Levinson, 2012, p. 89). The colonial administration's decisions to found *bordels militaires de campagne* (BMCs)—or military whorehouses— resulted in a rupture from courtesanry, or the age-old practice known as *harem* girls (Taraud, 2009, p. 245).

Taking a pronounced feminist approach, a second study finds the survival of the entire colonial adventure would not have been possible without subsuming native women under the category of "whores-by-nature" (Limoncelli, 2010, pp. 124–125). By restricting Nailiyat art to a single place—the cafes— colonial administrations stifled the sublime, bearing on the sense-orienting and corrective encounter between the performer and the entertained audience.

Differently stated, colonial administrators took precautions not to sabotage the colonial project by carefully brainwashing their soldiers lest they fall prey to the subversive influence of sublime performances. In considering how

Algerian women continue to be disparaged and scorned, even decades after regaining political independence, a third study demarcates the role played by skepticism between the sexes in the postcolonial impasse (Ferhati, 2010, p. 261). Brilliant as they are, these studies illustrate how dance has been mobilized to keep either the colonial or postcolonial trapped in ontological fixations, sabotaging his or her chances of ever emerging from the colonial trap.

Regarding the second confusion, the sacred takeover of the realm of the sacral, one sociological analysis enumerates how precolonial life was open to differences and receptive to multiplicities.[3] By recalling the example of precolonial Nailiyat, one wonders how postcolonial Algerians have become equally estranged from both themselves and each other by perpetuating rationalizations of the body as a site of sinful inscriptions on a par with prostitution, a sensibility hardly experienced during precolonial times.

On any Algerian beach, visitors will be struck by the increase in *burqini*-wearing women. In their conservative outlook to what constitutes public decency on the beach, postcolonial development planners gloss over the developmental model that the body can inspire. Everyone notes a hypervisibility of that body through a "reversed nudity" in *burqinis* and *burqas*.

Instead of cheaply relishing the sensual, the dance revels in it for the purpose of active engagement in the wonders of ever-creative existence. The transition from docility and alienation to embodied knowledge is coordinated through a spontaneous and carefree choreography. The Nailiyat dance reads as ontological contentment with the world, a delight that leads to a value-adding economy. Hyper- or pathological sensuality, which Orientalism expresses through either Belly Dancing or its categorical opposite, the *burqa*, can be viewed as facets of the same coin. Representations of the religious/sacred stand at odds with the sacral; they stifle the body. That is, they refuse to locate a veiled manifestation of the divine (LaMothe, 2005, pp. 244–245).

Saturated by commentaries inspired by Orientalism, the dance, however, remains, at best, underestimated in its "social functions, symbolic systems, philosophical meanings or political implications" (Cohen Bull, 1997, p. 270). Little wonder how, in seeking decolonial development, the essay processes Nailiyat dance in terms of the sacral, bent on relocating divinity nowhere but in the dancer's moving body. The religious and the sacred—nevertheless—barely tolerate such a move, explaining, thereby, continued alienation, domestication, and servitude of man.

It comes as no surprise, then, that the present analysis builds around the image of the dancer as she recreates the Sufi, flowing and melting in the divine. Contrary to the imposed meaning of a sign through representation, a symbol is more open to multiple and even contradictory interpretations. In other words, a single meaning of the dance cannot be maintained, except through an *a priori* or preselection that violently (because unjustifiably) removes the dancer's image from the capacity to evoke other plausible meanings than the one preselected. The dancer-as-image presupposes a "transparent, immanent, present without mediation" (Verstegen, 2016, p. 215).

Dismantling the "commodification" of the body, its degradation to the level of "passive, inert . . . and rarely that which provokes, incites or promotes" (Grosz, 2002, p. 78) remains achievable through the dance. Limiting the perception of the dancer to the sensual signals a conscious choice, translating the bias of the mind as it subsides into what Orientalism seeks to denigrate.

With Orientalist portrayals, one often notes the Platonian understanding of how an image traces the chronological emergence of reality but fails to ontologically account for that reality (Kaza, 2018, p. 204). Through the dancer's free flow, the audience's imagination intensifies through the process known as "thickness": the image of the dancer assumes a dynamic liveliness, through which the iconicity of the image escapes the radar of immediate perception.

READING BODILY MOVEMENTS

Uncovering the Orientalist layers of coding does not necessarily subscribe to a campaign for authenticity and cultural purity. My analysis of the Nailiyat's dance refers to Kimberly Larkspur's 2017 performance for a company based at Houston, Texas, The *Orientalis*, entitled: "Nailia Dance,"[4] a recreation of an 1893 show by a troupe from Boussada, Algeria (the heart of Ouled Nail). I am aware of critical views regarding the capacity to ever break free from the Orientalist gaze. The following analysis does not strive to find an imagined purity of the dance. Indeed, the risk of an imagined purity lies in what one Indian traditional dancer terms, the "paradox that ensures [the fact that] dancers reproduce the very assumptions they claim to want to challenge" (Thobani, 2019, p. 180). Resolving the paradox may only be possible by lifting the identarian layers of the dance and highlighting the dance's "embeddedness" in a socioeconomic reality at odds with capitalism, as with the Nailiyat. Hence, the choice of performance analyzed here: a reproduction of the Nailiyat dance by a professional dancer at an American university. Correspondence with Larkspur outlines her efforts at recreating the movements' details from the abundant anthropological literature. In terms of non-objective problems related to the Orientalist gaze and colonial setting, the feedback from online viewers asserts that active dance troupes from Ouled Nail in Algeria do not substantially differ from that received by Larksur's performance. Given the amount of distortion that touches the art, it has become common to find viewers from the Ouled Nail region scorning the dance: an example of the alienation underlying the politics of identification outlined earlier.

The dance follows a high-pitched—even piercing—accompaniment on the *zerna*, a woodwind instrument common in North Africa and elsewhere. The dancer puts down a cigarette she has been smoking, shoots the audience a clueless look and, with a solemn face, entranced by the unfolding high-pitched bursts from the *zerna*, starts her sense-recomposing performance. Rhythm is ensured by drumbeats supplied in the background. The audience notes the performer's rippling of the chest, rolling of the belly, waving of the hips, and streaming of the feet. The body movements are uncontrolled, instantiating how the body steers itself. The dancer's body exerts pulsations of outward energy. These pulsations are creative, non-cognitive translations of sensations pulling through and cascading out of the arms, upper chest, and abdomen. Depending on the degree of immersion with the *zerna,* in both the dancer and her audience, sometimes even the gums start crawling. In short, the audience notes the dancer's electrified body-in-motion, a complete surrender to the high-pitched *zerna* and the breathless anticipations of successive moves modulated via the drumbeats.

The anticipation of an exalting experience, triggered from memory, is certainly a challenge for spontaneous experience and the healthy recomposition of the senses. Therefore, whenever the setting and context accentuate the element of either the exotic or the folkloric, the audience is denied access to the richness of being ushered in by the dance and the music. North American and European, even postcolonial audiences, often come for confirmation of their own biases. The fetishization of that which is otherwise deemed a liberating dynamic, ushered in by the dance and the music, is underway, leaving little, for a sublime encounter.

Put differently, the predominantly structural perception of the dance-as-entertainment, representation or recreation (or the three altogether) explains that which stays largely shut: the possibility of conceiving development in non-alienating dynamics. In short, the dance as a privileged window into a richer interiority, free from commodification, remains inaccessible; that wealth of being can be traced in fleeting moments (fractions of seconds when measured against chronological time), where the dancer performs the customary pelvic circle, closing her eyes as she experiences a sweet musing. Musing here equals the capacity to be rooted in the earth, confident of bringing forth a scenario that dictates one's own response to challenging situations. As in figure 4.1

> [T]he circle is the most perfect movement. The great circle knows no beginning or end, no nostalgia, no separation; it is all-encompassing, all-receiving . . . [Soon] comes an impulse, a vibration, and the pelvis gives in and starts circling, slowly shaping the round, full strength into a circle, circling quietly and carefully at first, like intuition being born . . . The source of all [. . .] strength grows

Figure 4.1

over and beyond the limits of your body ... your hips circle and take in all your surroundings, the trees, the houses, the streets, over and away from the city. (Al-Rawi, 1983, 2012 Kindle Location)

Indeed, the dance facilitates an understanding of the dictation of one's own terms in life as the norm, not the exception. From the start, such dictation specifies how fallacious it is to presume the primacy of the mind. Instead, one learns the spontaneous emergence of opportunity (ontological and economic) from the body: vibrations, corrugations, and sometimes little fluctuations. Such emergence is confirmed from ecological research, where "the vestibular apparatus provides information about both linear and rotary components of physical movement. A passive movement elicits perception; an active movement is accompanied by proprioception" (Gibson, 1966, p. 67). Even in situations where one can be visually impaired, sequestered, or even detained, active participation in the pursuit of the target—be it economic opportunity or otherwise—will necessarily land concrete results.

Central to proprioception and the vestibular apparatus lies the Nailiyat's clothing. In comparison with Belly Dancing, the Nailiyat's overclothing cannot be a mere formality dictated by a normative morality. This mode of dress participates in the Sufi preoccupation with attaining the state of fanā. It cannot be farfetched to think of this state as evaporation or annihilation in Being, God. Indeed, what distinguishes the Nailiyat's attire from "Belly Dancing" is the way in which she comes fully clothed. As such, the audience does not capitalize on the pornographic. One misses the vibrations of intimate parts of the body, but one's imagination is engaged in the dismantling of alienation and commodification.

Uplifting the senses begins with synthesizing the materiality of the body, its fleshiness, into the dormant economic opportunity safeguarded therein. The synthesis begins with raising questions as to how and where opportunities can be availed. The absence of a script, indicated through impulsive acting, sabotages the tyranny of the mind, its persistent urge to stay constantly in command. Through the setting, or what Gibson calls the "environment," that which is immediately affordable, the vestibular apparatus measures the dancer's distances and administers the movements. The same absence of script distinguishes the ronggeng dancers in Indonesia; formal instruction comes only later to refine a preexisting talent (Tohari, 2012, p. 8). Instead of nursing the opaque and the implicit, Belly Dancing thrives on the explicit and the obscene. Sufi categories of veiling and unveiling are still at work here; the veiling being solicited. Elements like a wrapping hip scarf, with gold coins to emphasize the belly or chest movements, are a cheap way of winning the audience. As it lifts opacity, Belly Dancing flips toward fetishism, whose effect is the blocking of the body's capacity to raise questions. Audiences of Belly Dancing remain passive; they know they are there for a recreative night, wherein the alienating order goes uninterrupted. Staying transfixed in the contractions, the sweet physiological happenings in the dancer's semi-nudity unmoors the audience; the Nailiyat, unlike the Belly Dancer, solicits, through her bashful attire, a free range of imagination to recompose the obvious and the status quo. She encourages the audience not to accept the obvious and the immediate. In other words, she constantly pushes toward a revolutionary approach.

With the Nailiyat, one is there for a sublime encounter, a revolutionary moment par excellence, even if it comes in the form of an entertainment. The morning after, one is ever ready to beat up one's alienation. The revolutionary aspect of the Nailiyat's dance manifests in her overdressing, which actively encourages the constant creation of spun images of what stays hidden: the dancer's moving-inquisitive body. In order to overlook the flesh (as distinct from the body), clothing has to be decent, midway between unrevealing and bashful. To tap into the revolutionary character of the dance, the Nailiyat's attire actively participates in the "essencing" of the desired state of being, along with its material reality. Her clothing participates in transcending the fixation against the phenomenological manifestation of the present, be it precarity or abundance. The Nailiyat operates with the idea that that which is presently lacking or absent from existence cannot just be ignored, as it is not nonexistent. Commenting on Ibn 'Arabi, Chittick finds:

> Most Sufis take the position that the outward form (ṣūra) is a deceptive veil, even though it reveals the Divine Reality in some manner . . . That which

appears is, in fact, Being, the Divine Reality Itself. The phenomena are fundamentally nonexistent, and even if one can refer to their "coming into existence," this is in fact a metaphor. What appears to us is the One Being, but colored by the properties of nonexistent possible things. (1989, p. 89)

Two notes stand here. First, the veil or hijab is a metaphor which one has to be too superficial to mobilize into an identity, the way it has been upheld in the post-colony. Second, the veil is a call to school the senses in registering the ephemeral presence of the manifest. Hence, the affluent or oppressive instantiation of the material world (as with the toughest episodes during colonial or postcolonial times) should not deceive the passive observer to despise the economically disenfranchised dancer. The Nailiyat's attire is probably the surest way of reminding the audience that what is publicly displayed cannot decide the dancer's dasein; how else can the audience learn the difference between "appearance" and "self-showing" (Heidegger, 1927, p. 28) without verbal explanation or articulation?

Likewise, the rolling of two scarfs near the end of the performance (figure 4.2) reminds anyone seeking a literal reproduction of the movements that the attempt is doomed to failure. One has to step away from a passive posture to an active one. That is, one has to be a dancer or actively try to be one. As no script exists, everyone "enact[s] the consciousness of the body [as] it invades the body, the soul spreads over all its parts" (Merleau-Ponty, 1958, p. 75 quoted in: Gallaher 1986, p. 143). The scarves come at a critical stage, called

Figure 4.2

fanā, or self-annihilation, in Sufi rituals; exactly when the audience members desire to melt into the performer. But the accelerating pace of the choreography is meant to emphasize the parable, recalling that the desired union should focus on that which essentially lies beyond, hidden in the isthmus (*barzākh*). Importantly, the denied gratification is a reminder that the economic question (the hunt for profit) must not spin out of control.

The experienced lightness is nothing but a relief from the tyranny of the "I," when ego-smashing ends in chasing the fantasy of piling up capital. The experienced lightness proves that dis-alienation is possible. Dis-alienation is the expansion toward the well-being of the collective, of the "we." The accelerating pace of the music confronts the audience with its pre-individual components. Fleshing, made explicit through an overtly revealing costume, fires back as it dwells on the illusory consummation of the desired sensation. Consummation, in this context, does not even start to resemble the climaxing hunger for a transcendental union.

THE OPEN TEMPORALITY OF THE DANCE AND DECOLONIAL DEVELOPMENT

Unlike other woodwind instruments, the sensations emitted from the *zerna* come as an interruption from the quotidian, which is none but "that aspect of the forgotten in the everyday" (Russel and Gardner, 2018, p. 388). The piercing sound stimulates the audience members to engage with the sensation that the sublime experience has already started some time earlier, and its echoes will continue to affect the audience for some time after it ceases.

Differently put, the beginning of the playing on the instrument is not exactly a beginning; it is a replay—though not exactly—of that which lies pulsating inside some interior, that is, spiritual dimension, and will continue ringing in the air for a while after its material cessation. The actual commencement of the *zerna* is always from some middle point, emphasizing an ontological spatiality.[5] Time is neither chronic nor linear. One senses a constant supply of infinite beginnings; that is, bursts of energy in the midst of the exhilaration going on, "a worlding of the world" (Heidegger, 1927, p. 99); hence, the logic of interruptions that do not end in syncopation.

The *zerna* is so loud that it cannot announce itself in low or shy terms. Still, it is so evocative and captivating that one cannot engage in reflective thinking, as one is forced to experience without exactly noticing what Gille Deleuze calls, "the presentness of the present" (1994, pp. 76–77). Through the unfolding revelry, one is literally freed from the hiatus caused by rivaling sensations, ranging from recalling to anticipation. Instead, one learns through the *zerna* the art of alertness, staying active in the immersion and immediacy of the thereness; that is, concentrating fully with the player and, as the dance commences, with the dancer.[6]

Through its piercing emissions, the *zerna* evinces the immediacy of the thereness, celebrating one's pre-individuality where one is free from all nostalgia and all anticipation. The proof of a successful staging of "the presentness of the present'" is how qualifiers like adversity or merriness started to portend inauthentic impositions from the mind. As the performance ends, audiences report the ease and lightness of starting all over because they have both learned and practiced momentary relief from rigid impositions.

Transitioning from rigid identities to pre-individuality by shutting off rivaling sensations is paralleled in the performer's synthesized answer with the emitted sound which is her dance. As the *zerna* heats, the dancer puts down a cigarette and creatively merges with the choreography. Her embodiment is her non-reflective translation of melody through the dance. She synthesizes the notes into an entirely novel instantiation. But the move from passive attendance to creative performance through the dance needs to be underlined. As well as exoticization via displaying unfeminine manners, smoking a cigarette indicates the extent to which one is engrossed with the fetish, drifted by reflective thinking, and bypassed by the ideal. That ability to leave the seductive call of the pipe behind exhibits the capacity to leave the world of cogitation, the choice to dictate one's terms and deride reflective rationality. That "leaving behind" is never formal. The door ushers in the vehicle of being, which is processed via one's body. The transition is radically deep, so that every movement—no, every vibration—speaks of a disconnect, a liberation from the equally enticing world of the mind.

The genre of the dance is evidence of that transition. In the region of Ouled Nail, it is called *fezāai*, signifying the involuntary shudder characteristic of orgasmic pleasure. The dance recreates the movements of the shivering pigeon as it migrates, like members of the Ouled Nail tribe, to warmer climates during the winter and cooler ones during the summer. Members of Ouled Nail community are constantly on the move, looking for spots of greenery where their animals can graze. After tending their fields by readying the soil and planting wheat, they leave in early November southward to the *M'zab* Valley, where they tend to sheep grazing over little pastures.

Meanwhile, they exchange goods with the inhabitants of the nearby oases; with the harvesting of wool (from sheep shearing), they buy dates. Returning north to their homeland in May, they sell the dates in the *tell* (Mèdèa and Algiers) and reap the wheat soon afterward. They store the wheat in secret underground granaries that last up to seven years of draught. Once the harvesting is over, they leave their animals to graze on the leftover of the pasture.

By the end of the summer, they decamp for the south and start all over, a cycle that used to go uninterrupted from time immemorial until the coming of the colonial conquest in 1852 (Brower, 2009, p. 110). That shuddering bird is part of a pastoral-nomadic experience, which explains why Nailiyat dances in the first place. In flapping her hands along with the ostrich feather on the meticulous head embellishments, she is pointing at that which animates her people's spirit. Here, the shuddering pigeon ceases to be a soulless object. It comes to life, less as a concept and more as a being with whom "one shares a corporeal situation" (Gardner, 2019, p. 161). The pigeon again begs consideration of the chances enfolded in a non-stationary lifestyle.

Drawing on the pigeon's symbolism (not representation), with its consortium of qualities, such as grace and energy, emphasized through the light leaps and skips, the choreography recreates the same energy and grace in non-alienated audiences. The early movements are soon mutated into the shaking of the arms and other body parts. Inspiration from avian life reproduces the vitalism of the pigeon's economy: no paucity and no senseless accumulation. This balance is regulated by accessing the sublime experience. In a trance, the dancer neither smiles nor cries; she is well engrossed before the unraveling readjustment: sense restructuring away from the static and centering (any center), to a rhizome in Deleuzian terms. As the audience, we have glimpses into a world foreign to the one established by the market economy, an immersion in the figure of the animated pigeon.

Paucity of resources, in precolonial times obliging Ouled Nail girls to travel to lands outside their native home, becomes no reason to either demean or insult the dancer. The golden coins she collects at the end of the performance are expressions of fetishization-free appreciation. If an attendee does not throw a coin, it is detrimental to his self-image and worth. But the exchange is not capitalistic. One wonders how such an economy cannot set the foundation for the communism of the future.

Even with the coming of the Orientalizing gaze of the colonials, appropriation is a breach from, not the norm of, the dance (Limoncelli, 2010, p. 127).[7] It is not irrelevant to add that no consummation of the erotic energies used to take place, but the Nailiyat sleeps with whomever she chooses and fancies, not whoever pays the highest.[8] Objectification comes later as a colonial codification of the art. Additionally, the Nailiyat never rejects or abandons any offspring from the encounter (Lazreg, 1994, p. 30). The criteria for her fancying underline the sharing of her body with whomever displays the promise of a richer and equally respectful interiority.[9] What matters is that, through her body art, the Nailiyat is able to smooth and attune the senses of whomever manifests preeminence of mind, proving how fundamentally wrong he or she is.

ALLEGATIONS OF PROSTITUTION CONTEXTUALIZED

Because the Nailiyat had a proven record in breaking alienation, the colonial authorities were keen to underline the imminent danger they had to address. If casual pleasure-seeking soldiers were to come under the hypnotic and subversive influence of the Nailiyat on their own, that is, "unshielded" with the Orientalist objectifying umbrella, the colonial expansionist plans of total (territorial as well as ontological) control would come to naught. That is why colonial administrators were quick to have recourse to the strictest ban in orthodox Islam to condemn the dance. It becomes understandable how the propaganda machine of colonialism emphasized pejorative references in order to ensure the constant supply of non-subversive pleasure-giving, particularly after the crushing of popular resistance from the 1860s onward.

The change from moderate attire to overtly revealing costumes (fitted tops, hip belts, and harem pants) started to appear increasingly during the last decades of the nineteenth century, subscribing to the colonial fetishizing schemes. The Nailiyat dancers have, by now, become literally banned for dancing outside in the open air. Slowly, the dancer is labeled a café woman or *bent l'qāhwa,* with an ID restricting her movements as an instituted prostitute (Ferhati, 2010, p. 261). Still, it is useful to note that all Algerians, as early as 1830s onward, were tagged as a collection of communities plagued with "vice," showcasing alarming rates of prostitution (MacDougall, 2017, p. 91). Delacroix's recreation of Algerian women ushered in a brave new world for colonial Algerians. His painted rendering of flesh confirms the objectification of the Algerian territory (the body) to the colonial scheme of things (the mind), articulated in grandiose terms, such as *la mission civilisatrice* and sold as development.

With the end of the colonial episode, decolonizing development was the sensible target to achieve. What is worrisome, however, is how postcolonial nationalism that followed suit continued to function with the same epistemic tools that left "bird-animated" Algerians outside the equation of development. Worse yet, oil—and very little outside geostrategic calculations of oil—has been univocally trusted as the surest way to the egalitarian utopia. Little, if anything, is said in respect to how the pastoral-nomadic way of life—evoked in the dance—can develop the country and its people simultaneously.

Meanwhile, postcolonial nationalism, just like Islamism, has vehemently condemned the Nailiyat dance and deemed it a desacralization of Muslim honor. If tolerated, the dance is presented as nothing but folklore, a weekend or occasional spectacle meant for diversion or ego-boosting heritage and little else.

The present chapter has elucidated the ways that dance can be an instrument for engendering a postcolonial economic model, processed in non-capitalistic and egalitarian terms. What the Islamists and nationalists overlook is the fact that "whether voluptuous dances are lascivious or not depends less on anything inherent in the dances themselves than on the individual dancer and the tastes of the audience for whom they are performed" (Wood and Shay, 1976, p. 22). Part of the answer to the question why nationalists skip the chance of considering non-objectifying elements of the dance for purposes of alternative development is that, during critical moments in negotiating Algeria's independence, zealots for "a French Algeria" developed a fixation on nurturing their image of the women-liberator from the "misogyny and backwardness" of indigenous culture through veil-lifting campaigns (Shepard, 2006, p. 189).

Here, one registers the effect of that fixation on veiling, less as a symbol and more as a representation geared toward short-term political ends. Thus, it becomes understandable that, in consequence of the complicated body politics inherited from the Orientalizing gaze—pertaining to the ways in which colonial administrators, nationalists, and Islamists alike shun the body (represented by dancing), the dance's developmental promise has not yet been unearthed.

Neither the nationalists nor the Islamists have scratched beyond the surface to spot the dance's socioeconomic underpinnings that could usher in a non-capitalistic development model. Instead, the puritanical iconoclasm prevailing during the postcolonial era has had to project the presupposed stigma onto others, as the Ouled Nail are thought to be "too clean and pure" to undergo the humiliation of cigarette smoking and body parts shaking before gaping audiences with open-mouthed desire. As one scholar notes in the Iranian context, the charge of the "dancer-as-degenerate" (Meftahi, 2016, p. 152) becomes an effective way of projecting one's inferiority complex onto other peoples: either the Jews or *beni aadas*, a pejorative term reserved for a gipsy tribe known for its unabashed manners (Ait Khadash, 2015).

Consequently, one wonders how, without a decolonial approach to the heavily fetishized body, Algerians could come up with a meaningful development. Both as a protection from lascivious gazes or as freedom from patriarchal control, veiling in postcolonial Algeria infuriates these pathological inscriptions and fixations. Veiling becomes an intensification of the mirage of undoing the colonial. That phantasmal undoing impairs the addressing of a stigma-free approach to the Algerian body, together with that body's capacity to undermine the capitalistic dynamic with its pastoral-nomadic order.

CONCLUSION

Decolonizing the Algerian body for purposes of an enduring development can be inspired by reflecting how that body used to constructively engage with both itself and its reality before the colonial encounter. When dissected, the epistemic violence that underlines that encounter, which has been further encroached upon during postcolonial times, involves the exclusion of nearly all non-cognitive tools of transcendence. A promising example of such a non-cognitive tool is the dance of the women of Ouled Nail in Algeria. The dance is rooted in a culture where inhabitants have traditionally been organically attached to their means of production. Indeed, the synergy of that socioeconomic approach to reality may have been rarely matched.

Through a phenomeno-ecological reading of one dance performance in the Nailiyat genre, we can discern how Nailiyat choreography can be mediated toward an easy-going and unfetishized body, as it echoes the pigeon. The dance could have been deployed for a decolonial model of development, inspiring state planners today to challenge the ascending pressures of the market economy. In opening up the body's mode of thinking, as unfolded in the Nailiyat dance, postcolonial Algerians can bring the hidden potential to conscious awareness, thereby avoiding traps, closures, and fixations. Breaking the dictatorship of oil can be made possible by looking at it as an alienating device. Instead, Algerians will embrace a reservoir of meaning mediated via the body, rich in mutual trust and economic potential.

Unless postcolonial Algerians decolonize unmitigated perceptions of the trap that thrive on alienation from the body, development will likely stay foreign and enigmatic. Research on the dancing body demonstrates how the body is equipped with a decolonizing potential. Furthermore, the discussion aims to encourage future research on why the *hijab* (Islamic covering) dampens the complexity of both visible and invisible phenomena. Feminists misjudge the *hijab* as a form of mental slavery. Without being apologetic, the fixation on *hijab* denotes an image that hides a more pertinent discussion that could move postcolonial Algerians out of their impasse. Alternatively, introducing the dance as part of an intricate socioeconomic activity, known as the pastoral-nomadic order, will hopefully become valued for the decolonial approach to development.

NOTES

1. Early on in the First Critique, Kant notes the following distinctions:

"I call that in the appearance which corresponds to sensations its *matter*, but that which allows the manifold of appearance to be intuited as ordered in certain relations, I call the *form* of appearance. Since that within which the sensations can alone be ordered and placed in a certain form cannot itself be in turn sensation, the matter of all appearance is only given to us *a posteriori*, but in form must all lie ready for it in the mind *a priori*, and can therefore be considered from all sensation." pp. 155-6. (Emphasis in the original) While acknowledging the existence of the body's capacity for maneuver through sensation, accounting for that capacity has to be processed through the mind negates that capacity.

2. "To his daughter, Laura, he [Marx] wrote, 'Moslems in fact recognize no subordination; they are neither subjects nor administrative objects, recognizing no authority.' But he didn't fail to also note: 'Nevertheless, they will go to the devil without a revolutionary movement.' "Karl Marx to Laura Lafargue, April 13, 1882, *Collected Works*, vol. 46, 242; Hudis, "Marx Among the Muslims," 67 Quoted in: Dunayevskaya 1991, 191).

3. In the region of Ouled Nail, Lazreg specifies how "the practice of marrying a prostitute would persist in Algeria into the 1960s. This denotes a non-misogynist conception of prostitution often seen as a reproved act performed under duress. Therefore, helping the person who commits it was tantamount to bringing the person back to faith." (1994, 14).

4. The Dougherty Theatre, Austin TX November 20th, 2015 https://www.youtube.com/watch?v=Kt1g75xKouM&list=RDKt1g75xKouM&start_radio=1

5. A note on ontological spatiality can be traced in this technical detail:

"In a sense, the melody, which is the arrangement of space, is fixed, for each *maqam* carries with it a typical pattern of melodic movement and emphasized notes. To get a better sense of this form, compare the maqam to the waltz. A waltz is characterized first and foremost by a fixed arrangement, not of space, but of time: the time signature never strays from ¾. A composer creates a melody and sets it to this time signature. The melody is subject to no rules; every waltz has a different one. But the rhythm, the arrangement of time, never varies.36 In a *maqam*, on the other hand, it is time rather than space that is not subject to rules—there is no constant meter, no fixed beats regularly repeated. This creates a feeling of eternity, without beginning or end." (Al-Rawi 2012, Kindle Location 1451)

6. Note how in Sufi music, and in contrast to the drum, the flute/*zerna* evokes the needed leveling effect:

"The drum announces the arrival and presence of the all-powerful king. It is the sign of transcendence, of the discontinuity which separates us, the impoverished, the dependent, from Him, the Highest, subsisting in Himself, while the human voice and the flute sing of the Immanence, the inexhaustible Wealth (*al-ghanā*) that no human imagination will ever be able to comprehend but whose every manifestation, mode or station (*maqām*) is capable of becoming a grace and a blessing for the believer." (Michon 2006, 166)

7. Mernia Lazreg reports on how the Nailiyat used to deride French admirers seeking carnal pleasure.

8. In a similar context, LaMothe reads Nietzsche's dance imagery in *The Birth of Tragedy*. Interestingly, I find the mother-figure in Nietzsche's work and as specified by LaMothe corresponding with the Nailiyat as the latter too is "… neither a virginal fantasy nor a consuming void. "She [the dancer] appears as a symbol, and then as a symbol of internal contradiction. She appears in the form of a kinetic image, as a process of her own bodily becoming, a creative and destructive power alive within each human, within which every human lives." (LaMothe 2005, 252)

9. Reflecting on the theory of aesthetic evolution as proposed by Richard O. Prum (2017, 54 Kindle Location), one concludes that the Nailiyat being an embodied pigeon underlines how she instinctively fights for her survival.

REFERENCES

Addi, L. (2006). The political contradictions of Algerian economic reforms. *Review of African Political Economy 108*: 207–217.

———. (2012). Sociologie politique d'un populism autoritaire. *Confluences Méditerannés*, 2(81): 27–40.

———. (2017). *Radical Arab Nationalism and Political Islam*. (A. Roberts. Trans.). Georgetown University Press.

Ait Khadash, R. (2015, September). beni aadas, gadjar al-djazair al-manboudine" al-bayan. Retrieved from https://www.albayan.ae/editors-choice/varity/2015-09-15-1.2459623

Al-Rawi, R. (2012). *Grandmother's Secrets: The Ancient Rituals and Healing Power of Belly Dance* (M. Arav. Tans.). Northampton, MA: Interlink Books.

Boukhobza, M. (1991). *Octobre 1988: évolution ou rupture?* Alger: Édition Bouchène.

Chittick, C. W. (1989). *The Sufi Path of Knowledge*. New York: State University of New York Press.

Cohen. B. & Cynthia, J. (1997). Sense, meaning, and perception in three dance cultures. In Desmond, C. (Ed.), *Meaning in Motion: New Cultural Studies of Dance*. Duke University Press, pp. 269–288.

Daoud, K. (2017). *Chroniques: Selected Columns, 2010-2016* (Zerofsky E. Trans.). New York: Other Press.

Deleuze, G. (1994) *Difference and Repetition* (1968) (Patton P. Trans.). New York: Columbia University Press.

Dunayevskaya, R. (1991). *Rosa Luxemburg, Women's Liberation, and Marx's Philosophy of Revolution*. Urbana, IL: University of Illinois Press.

Dunwoodie, P. (2005). *Francophone Writing in Transition: Algeria 1900-1945*. Bern : PeterLang, AG European Academic Publishers.

Ferhati, B. (2010). Enquêter sur la prostitution en Algérie. Souvenir de Bou-Saâda. *L'Année de Maghreb VI*, 253–268.

Fuss, D. (1994). Frantz fanon and the politics of identification. *Diacritics* 24(2/3):19–42.

Gallagher, S. (1986). Lived Body and Environment. *Research in Phenomenology* 16(1): 139–170.

Gardner, S. (2019). How Seudati put me in touch with birds. In Bond, K. (Ed.), *Dance and the Quality of Life*. Springer International Publishing, pp. 167–176.

Gibson, J. J. (1966). *The Senses Considered as Perceptual Systems*. London: George Allen & Unwin Ltd.

Grosz, E. (2002). Notes on the thing. *Perspecta 33*:78–79.

Gurminder K. B. (2014) Postcolonial and decolonial dialogues. *Postcolonial Studies* *17*(2):115–121. doi: 10.1080/13688790.2014.966414

Hannoum, A. (2010). *Violent Modernity: France in Algeria.* Cambridge, MA: Harvard Center for Middle Eastern Studies.

Hallaq, W. B. (2018). *Restating Orientalism: A Critique of Modern Knowledge.* Columbia University Press.

Heidegger, M. (1927). *Being and Time* (Stambaugh J. Trans.). Albany: State University of New York.

Index, Mundi. (2019). "Algeria Economy Profile" https://www.indexmundi.com/algeria/economy_profile.html

Kant, I. (1998). *Critique of Pure Reason* (Guyer, P. & Wood A. Trans.). Cambridge University Press.

Kaza, A. (2018). *Al-Ṣūrah bayna al-Khafā' wa al-Tajallī 'inda Muḥyī al-Dīn Bin 'Arabī.* Mominoun Without Borders for Publishing and Distribution, Lebanon.

LaMothe, L. (2005). "A god dances through me": Isadora Duncan on Friedrich Nietzsche's revaluation of values. *The Journal of Religion 85*(2): 241–266.

Lazreg, M. (1990, Summer). Gender and politics in Algeria. Unravelling the religious paradigm. *Signs* 15(4): 755–786.

———. (1994). *The Eloquence of Silence: Algerian Women in Question.* New York and London: Routledge.

Levinson, J. (2012). Is pornographic art comparable to religious art? Reply to Davies. In Maes, H. & Levinson, J. (Eds.), *Art and Pornography Philosophical Essays.* Oxford University Press.

Limoncelli, A. (2010). *The Politics of Trafficking: The First International Movement to Combat the Sexual Exploitation of Women.* Stanford, CA: Stanford University Press.

Luxemburg, R. (2003). *The Accumulation of Capital* (Schwarzschild A. Trans.). London and New York: Routledge.

Macey, D. (1999). Fanon, phenomenology, race. *Radical Philosophy* 95: 8–14.

Mamed, O. & Kerimov, G. (1988). Basic principles distinguishing orthodox Islam from Sufism. *Institute of Muslim Minority Affairs Journal* 9(2): 245–250.

McDougall, J. (2017). *A History of Algeria.* Cambridge University Press.

Meftahi, I. (2016). The Sounds and Moves of *ibtiẓāl* in 20th-century Iran. International Journal of Middle East Studies, Vol. 48.

Merleau-Ponty, M. (1958). *Phenomenology of Perception* (Colin S. Trans.). London and New York: Routledge.

Mernissi, F. (1985). *Beyond the Veil: Male-Female Dynamics in Muslim Society.* London: Saqi Books.

Michon, J. (2006). Sacred music and dance in Islam. In Michon J. & Gaetani. R. (Eds.), *Sufism: Love and Wisdom.* Bloomington, IN: World Wisdom, Inc.

Mignolo, W. (2018). Decoloniality and phenomenology: The geopolitics of knowing and epistemic/ontological colonial differences. *The Journal of Speculative Philosophy* 32(3): 360–387.

Prodger, M. (2016). Damnation, Dante and decadence: Why Eugène Delacroix is making a hero's return? *The Guardian*, Feb. 5. https://www.theguardian.com/artanddesign/2016/feb/05/damned-souls-decadence-eugene-delacroix-hero

Prum, R. (2017). *The Evolution of Beauty*. London and New York: Doubleday.
Reed, S. (1998). The politics and poetics of dance. *Annual Review of Anthropology* 27: 503–532.
Russell, D. & Gardner, S. (2018) ... dance for the time being: Russell Dumas in conversation with Sally Gardner. *Postcolonial Studies* 21(3): 379–390.
Sahlin, M. (1973). *Stone Age Economics*. London and New York: Routledge Classics.
Saikh, S. (2012). *Sufi Narratives of Intimacy: Ibn 'Arabī, Gender, and Sexuality*. Chapel Hill, NC: University of North Carolina Press.
Shepard, T. (2006). *The Invention of Decolonization: The Algerian War and the Remaking of France*. Ithaca and London: Cornell University Press.
Taraud, C. (2009). *La prostitution coloniale – Algérie, Tunisie, Maroc (1830-1962)*. Éditions Payot & Rivages.
Thobani, S. (2019). Decolonising Indian classical dance? Projects of reform, classical to contemporary. *South Asian Diaspora* 11(2): 179–192.
Tohari, A. (2012). *The Dancer* (Lysloff R. Trans.). Lontar: Jakarta.
Verstegen, I. (2016). The anti-sign: Anti-representationalism in contemporary art theory. *Culture, Theory and Critique* 57(2): 215–227.
Wood, L. & Shay, A. (1976). Dance du ventre: A fresh appraisal. *Dance Research Journal* 8(2): 18–30.

Chapter 5

Colonialism and the Destruction of Indigenous Knowledge Systems

Daring to Push the Epistemological Frontiers for African Re-development Paradigms

Nathan Moyo and Jairos Gonye

This chapter critiques the dynamics of Africa's crisis of development which has pervaded the continent despite numerous developmental initiatives undertaken since the 1960s. The chapter re-examines how European intrusion, through slavery and later colonialism, resulted in the willful and symbolic destruction of the indigenous knowledges that had set the African continent on its own developmental trajectory. African indigenous histories and dances are drawn on to exemplify the epistemicide of colonialism that was aimed at the destruction of the African people's being. This chapter argues that indigenous knowledges that are grounded in the people's being could be harnessed for rethinking Africa's self-development on its own terms. Thus, the chapter foregrounds these extant knowledges to suggest African Critical Race Theory (AfriCrit) as a potentially useful theory in reenergizing Africa's self-development. The argument is that AfriCrit can play a crucial role in rethinking the seeming dearth in viable self-development models in Africa. As a theory of critical self-introspection, *AfriCrit* impels Africans to reimagine what developmental milestones various African empires could have achieved had they been spared the devastating encounter with Europe. The theory suggests that viable developmental models should be homegrown, informed by the knowledges and understandings found in the local socio-ecological environment.

INTRODUCTION

This chapter critiques the dynamics of Africa's crisis of development which has pervaded discourses about the continent. Eurocentric critics have deliberately located the reasons for Africa's stagnated development in African people's perceived obsession with the so-called backward traditions in order to justify their replacement by the modern standards of Western Europe and America at colonization (Metzler, 2009). However, despite the postcolonial African leaders' adoption and adaptation of the Western-initiated development models, modernity has remained a mirage for Africa. The euphoria of independence and the certainty of development that characterized most African countries as they emerged from colonialism, beginning with Ghana in 1957, and buoyed by formal education, fizzled with the successive failed attempts to "take-off."

Nevertheless, committed critical African theorists and scholars such as the writers of this chapter believe there could be an alternative path to African development. The urgency of our chapter's undertaking arises because, as the world is poised to enter the third decade of the second millennium, the African continent, alongside Latin America and parts of Asia, finds itself trapped in a seemingly unending quagmire of underdevelopment that Ali Mazrui (1980) sadly describes as the "African condition."

The central problem that frames the chapter is that development in Africa is defined along Eurocentric paradigms with Africa pushed to play "catch-up" with the West (Matunhu, 2011; Rodney, 1981). The touted "catch-up" premised on the Eurocentric and American mantra of modernization has not materialized. The question is, whether it was inherent in Africa's biophysical nature that Africa suffers ceaselessly or that it was a political and economic ruse by the Western European intruders so that they continue to have access to the continent's resources. It is important to mention that Africans were, prior to the violent intrusion of their continent, making significant developmental milestones as exemplified by Asante's apprenticeship system, the rural Malawians' indigenous agricultural methods, and the people of Zambia's, Zululand's, and Zimbabwe's indigenous food preservation methods and local plant medicinal innovations (Mashoko, 2018; Matunhu, 2011; Rodney, 1972). Indeed, it could be ascertained that certain African empires could have experienced levels of development almost equivalent to those of the West or even greater in some aspects prior to the arrival of Europeans (Boon & Eyong, 2005; Rodney, 1981). Momoh (2020) credits precolonial African societies for posting enduring development milestones of a scientific and technological nature that were anchored on Indigenous Knowledge Systems (IKS). In his wide-ranging review of literature on African artistic and technological contributions to human civilization he singles out boat-making technology of Benin, Nigeria; iron smelting of Meroe; architectural physicists of Sumeria /Egypt) and Zimbabwe; art and poetry of Mali; gold smelting of Ghana; and money minting of Ethiopia and Eriteria (Momoh, 2020). Most of these encouraging advancements which promoted easy agricultural production or trade, for instance, had been achieved hundreds of years before the encounter with the colonialists.

It is thus a matter of historical conjecture that Africa's self-development trajectory would have been vastly different had Africans been encouraged to develop within their contexts, and on the basis of the IKS that they had evolved over time. This conjecture invites us to rethink the underpinning epistemological assumptions that have been fore-fronted in the African continent's quest for re-development. It also offers us an opportunity to advance and imbricate the epistemological frontiers through generating new insights. As Mpofu and Ndlovu-Gatsheni, (2019:2) argue, theoretical interventions on the part of African intellectuals are required to "rethink and unthink" colonially designed notions of development in order to rid the continent of the exotic and toxic Eurocentric paradigms which have been responsible for Africa's perpetual misery. For example, the Rostowian five-stage model of development, which gained popularity in the 1960s and was premised on the notion of a "take-off" in which newly independent African states were presented as being on the precipice of this "take-off," has since become ahistorical and discredited (Matunhu, 2011; Rodney, 1972; Rostow, 1960). Similarly, the Bretton Woods inspired models of development premised on the structural adjustment programs (SAPS) that were in vogue in the 1980s and early 1990s have been discarded as they failed to lead to any meaningful development in Africa (Mhone, 1995). Such attempts at development are best described as a more subtle attempt at keeping Africa under the Euro-American imperial shadow. Ndlovu-Gatsheni (2014:185) opines that the models are rooted in "modernist artefacts of Euro-North American-centric modernity such as capitalism, globalization, and neoliberalism." The failure of such models is because of their cynicism and "total disregard of the cultural, social, political and traditional values of the recipient countries" (Matunhu, 2011:67). Thus, the contribution this chapter makes is to dare and push the epistemological frontiers of criticality by positing African Critical Race Theory (AfriCrit) (Gonye & Moyo, 2018) as a more robust postcolonial critique that could enhance an understanding of the dynamics of Africa's crisis of development. It is hoped that such understanding will lay the foundations for Africa's re-development.

The entry point to the chapter is the realization that, to this day, the African continent is unable to chart its own developmental strategy as the tentacles of colonialism have seemingly entrenched themselves on the African psyche, with development being conceptualized through a Eurocentric prism. The existing postcolonial theorizing has not succeeded in deconstructing the dominance of the Eurocentric epistemology in the production of knowledge. Such pitfalls of postcolonial theories and development could be gleaned, though with varying degrees of failure, in the reorganization of the rural populace into productive and trading communities undertaken in Amilcar Cabral's Guinea during the liberation struggle against the Portuguese, the social humanism and production units in Kenneth Kaunda's new Zambia, and the African socialism or Ujamaa in Tanzania under Julius Nyerere.

The foregoing examples from postcolonial Africa's 1970s political doyens suggest that though these African leaders dreamed of developing their countries, they still somehow drew theoretical and development models from outside Africa, whether it was China/Russia (Nyerere) or Israel (Zambia). The same cannot however be said for Cabral who had a deep respect for Guinean African culture and development. What is evident, however, is that the formal end of imperialism and "the rise of so-called post-colonial states" (Funez-Flores & Phillion, 2019:2) has not brought about that anticipated rupture with colonial knowledge constructs that marginalized IKS in the school curriculum. It is most pertinent to refer to the school curriculum since modern development was obsessively linked to the Western style of education at the expense of IKS that had however seen the rise in artistic exploits in West African communities, architectural exploits in Egypt and Zimbabwe, agricultural innovations and weather/climate pattern forecasts in Malawi and many rural communities of Africa south of the Sahara, and the bracelet and iron tool making in Ghana and other places (Momoh, 2020; Mafongoya & Ajayi, 2017; Green, 2015). Thus, the research question that the chapter addresses is: How may the ontologies and epistemologies embedded in IKS be reimagined as the basis for decolonizing knowledges for Africa's re-development?

The chapter is organized as follows: The preceding section above has introduced the problem and the aim of the chapter. The next section maps the key conceptual issues that frame this chapter. A brief methodological account that is used to generate the data and the rationale follow. This is followed by a critique of colonialism and its denial of IKS. History and dance as examples of embodied knowledges are used as illustrations, with a bias to Zimbabwe. The section that follows then presents AfriCrit as the theoretical framework that deepens criticality beyond the limitations of postcolonial theory per se. The concluding section revisits the nexus of knowledge and power in the context of a new re-development paradigm for Africa south of the Sahara. The key terms are explained in the section immediately below.

Africa's self-developmental trajectory was "premised on the Indigenous knowledges and technologies that were valid, legitimate and useful knowledge systems" (Ndlovu-Gatsheni, 2018:2). The descriptor "Indigenous" denotes that the knowledge therein is unique to the inhabitants of the place and as such is "bound to place, to the environment and deep knowledge of the environment, and is absolutely necessary for human survival" (Smith, Maxwell, Puke & Temari, 2016:138). IKS are thus all encompassing and include "stories and songs, [as] visions, prophesies, teachings and original instructions, [as] genealogies and memories" (Smith, Maxwell, Puke & Temari, 2016:138). For instance, the Maori of New Zealand and the Aboriginal Australians both developed holistic systems of knowledge well before the arrival of Europeans (Smith, Maxwell, Puke & Temari, 2016:138). Africans in North, East, West, and Southern Africa also developed their own indigenous knowledges. For example, the Egyptians are associated with what is known as Egyptian civilization, while Zimbabwe hosts the Great Zimbabwe monuments, arguably one of the most revered architectural marvels of the modern age (Rodney, 1981). Such achievements disprove colonial self-fulfilling prophecies that claim indigenous peoples were unimaginative, had no organization, could not even travel long distances across their own land, let alone across oceans as explorers or traders (Smith, Maxwell, Puke & Temari, 2016). Indigenous knowledges are embedded in practices such as dances, ceremonial rituals, folklores, and ways of production for survival. It was therefore inevitable that both history and dance as the embodiment of the ontologies of indigenous people would be targeted for annihilation and outright distortion by the colonial educators alongside missionaries, who wittingly and unwittingly became willing accomplices in the colonial enterprise. Indigenous histories and dances may be viewed as being at the center of a peoples' identity. Dance and history help remember and glorify the cultural achievements and historical milestones of a people. As such they have potential to be rallying points for unity and mobilization of Africans against colonial cultural invasion. In this regard, history and dance were perceived as threatening to Eurocentric norms and values and had to be diluted and made safe for the new colonial order.

METHODOLOGY

This chapter employed the indigenous and decolonizing research paradigm (Smith, 1999) in order to highlight sensitivity to the cultural construction of ontologies, and hence, what counts as knowledge. The paradigm, in foregrounding all knowledges as valid and legitimate makes possible an understanding of what John (2019:52) calls the "material, the embodied, and the visceral lived realities through which colonization persists, but more importantly, it gives space to center (sic) the embodied realities through which Indigenous peoples resist." The historical method (Cohen, Manion & Morrison, 2007) was therefore adopted to reconstruct and reinterpret the past with regard to its ramifications that continue to be felt even today. Such an approach enabled the researchers to reformulate the significance of African IKS as most evidently represented in African history and dance and exhorted in AfriCrit.

The chapter builds on the works of eminent postcolonial scholars such as Mignolo (2000), Freire (2000/1968), Chakrabarty (1992), Spivak, (1988), Said (1979), and Fanon (1965), among others, who have pioneered a critique of colonialism as a not so benevolent ushering of the colonized into history, civilization, and modernity. However, more recent scholarship inspired by the works of Mignolo (2009, 2013, 2018), Santos (2009), and Ndlovu-Gatsheni (2015, 2014) among others, privileges decoloniality as a heuristic that is more adept at deepening criticality and addressing the perceived limitations of the early generation of postcolonial scholars. The African historian Toyin Falola's question "To what extent can Africa self-develop?" (Falola, 2005:4) remains pertinent to both postcolonial critics and their African critics, respectively. The response to that question, however, is you never can tell. While some postcolonial African leaders and their theorists swallowed the bait that African development and "progress" could only come through adopting Western European development pathways, ensured through expanding formal education (Metzler, 2009), Dei and Simmons (2009) view development as relating to how people use their own creativity and resourcefulness to respond to major economic and ecological stressors. It could thus be argued that Africa was clearly self-developing before colonial intrusion (Falola, 2005) forcibly disrupted her trajectory. As Ndlovu-Gatsheni (2015:4) points out, colonialism amounted to a "theft of history for Africa," and that "translated into theft of its future." The root of Africa's crisis has to be understood from that historical aberration. Africa's crisis of development as articulated above is thus an urgent matter, also requiring more theorizing and re-theorizing. For instance, Matunhu (2011:67) posits that "Africa needs to outgrow poverty and underdevelopment but this may not be possible as long as we still believe in the power and strength of modernity at the expense of promoting new theories for Africa's development."

COLONIALISM AND THE DESTRUCTION OF IKS: THE POWER/KNOWLEDGE NEXUS

An historical critique of colonialism that is deployed herein seeks to explore the nexus between knowledge production and power in the colonial context, and hence, show how the willful destruction, intellectual plunder, and silencing of IKS during colonization was part of a grand strategy to subdue the South. The colonization of the South succeeded to the extent that it did because it fore-fronted the axiom "Knowledge is Power." Embedded in this logic of power in the colonial context was the denial of the humanity of the indigenous people as well as the indigenous knowledges that existed prior to colonialism. Their "being," which made them knowing subjects, was abrogated in order to justify the classification of indigenous people as the "Other" (Said, 1979) and therefore incapable of knowing. Such denial of "knowing" and of having knowledges of the indigenous people implied that, for the colonizers, indigenous people were not "rational" beings and, therefore, had no institutions, culture, or beliefs worthy of respect. Leonardo (2018:12) explains that "knowledge production has always been part of the colonial project for it was not only a material imposition of a foreign or external power but a concerted effort internally to supplant an existing way of life with another." Hugh Trevor-Roper, professor of History at Oxford, for instance, is on record as claiming, "there is only the history of Europeans in Africa. The rest is largely . . . darkness. And darkness is not a subject of history." He stated further that all there was were "the unrewarding gyrations of barbarous tribes in picturesque but irrelevant corners of the globe." This was a complete perversion of history and cultural creativity and heritage, which was employed to justify colonization.

Colonialism as the violent disruption of the historical progression of the African continent drew on Euro-North American-centric modernity as a broad discursive terrain through which to justify the looting, annihilation, and marginalization of the material and human resources of the continent. The local industries which had developed were supplanted by capitalist production, which was characteristically extractive (Metzler, 2009; Rodney, 1981). For instance, African knowledges to perform traditional healing procedures, "African-scientifically" tested means to ensure spouse, food, or crop security and so on were repressed through the Witchcraft Suppression Acts that affected the uptake of indigenous medicines in colonial South Africa, Zimbabwe, Malawi, and others. Breidlid (2013:16) puts it graphically thus, "through epistemological colonization the West imposed its authority to authenticate or invalidate knowledge systems other than its own, which implied invalidation and resulted in epistemic genocide across the globe."

Santos (2009) coined the descriptor "epistemicide" in an attempt to draw parallels with genocide—in order to convey the symbolic "mass murder" of the indigenous knowledges. The net result of the epistemicide was the imposition of cultural imperialism on the colonized. Another component of this cultural imperialism is what is now termed "linguicide" (wa Thiong'o, 2009); the linguistic equivalent of genocide. In all African countries colonized by Belgium, Portugal, France, or England, the colonial language automatically became the language of power, hence the language of knowledge, culture, and instruction. The primary aim of the colonizers was to domesticate or transform indigenous populations from what they perceived to be their [Africans] "primitive" ways by alienating them from their culturally embodied knowledges. The success of the colonial epistemicide of IKS as valid knowledge is expressed succinctly in the words of Chakrabarthy (1992:94) where he remarks that:

> Virtually all branches of European knowledge and science have grown with the confident conviction that the world is knowable only through those categories of knowledge that have been developed in Europe—indeed that the world may even exist only in and through such categories of European modernity.

Epistemicide against IKS is manifest in the ways in which the colonizers sought to "distort people's history; demean their ancestors; despise their culture, their language and their philosophy" (Moyana, 1989:1). Destroying African philosophy, particularly virtues of Ubuntu, would entail weakening the African indigene's personhood and societal responsibility. The hallmark of epistemicide was the engendering of a monolithic worldview premised on Eurocentric modernity, as the Africans were made to reinterpret their outlook on life in accordance with an arbitrary developmental scale (Moyana, 1989). The following section, for want of space, only explores how the cognate fields of history and dance were targeted by the epistemological imperialism that was central to the colonial education curriculum, with specific reference to Zimbabwe.

AFRICAN TRADITIONAL DANCES AND HISTORIES AS TARGETS OF COLONIAL EPISTEMICIDE: THE CASE OF ZIMBABWE

The colonial school curriculum was premised on what Spivak (1990) describes as Western academic canonization and historiography which was intended to alienate the Indian subalterns, including Africa's, from their cultures. Moyana (1989:2) observes that the idea is to make the oppressed feel ashamed of themselves and admire the oppressors so much that they emulate their ways, their language, and their behavior, and thus submissively accept their right to rule.

Missionaries were at the forefront of the epistemic onslaught on traditional dances which they perceived as pagan and as superstition (Gonye & Moyo, 2015; Hapanyengwi-Chemhuru & Makuvaza, 2014:1). The robust bodily movements and energetic stamping of the ground characteristic of many traditional dance practices across Africa were misunderstood by both colonial administrators and missionaries for distractive licentiousness. Such vibrant energy and attendant celebration in traditional dances such as Jerusarema/ Mbende performed by the Shona people in Central and Northern Zimbabwe and Isitshikitsha performed by the Ndebele of Western Zimbabwe were regarded as a political and moral threat to Western values, as they constituted an alternative worldview to the Eurocentric representations of reality as well as sites of political resistance. Dance as a site of social mobilization has also been evident in Ghana, South Africa, Angola, and elsewhere. Trapped within the prism of their Eurocentric worldview, the missionaries and colonizers failed to appreciate the valid and legitimate knowledge and cultures that are extant in such dances to the extent of banning their social performance (Gonye & Moyo, 2018). Instead, what was foisted on the learners were Eurocentric dances such as ballet which alienated the indigenous learners (Gonye & Moyo, 2018). Instead of drawing from the riches of cultural diversity, the colonialists considered traditional African and European dances as irreconcilable, which resulted in the "dirty" indigenous ones being denied space in the curriculum. Such willful exclusion and marginalization of traditional dances from the school curriculum resonates with Asante's (2003:37) argument that "African cultural interests have been consistently undermined by a determined Eurocentric intellectual conspiracy that began in the 15th century." The unfortunate reality is that in the present postcolonial period such valid knowledges as are embodied in traditional dances are struggling to find space in the postcolonial school curriculum. In Zimbabwe, it is only in the Zimbabwe Curriculum Framework, 2015–2022, revised recently, that a dance curriculum that foregrounds traditional dances has been developed. This development is a stark reminder that epistemicide has not ended with the juridical independence of the African state and that cultural dependency on the West persists.

An illustration of epistemicide was the attempt to alienate Africans from their history through the teaching of an alien European history to the indigenous learners. Mungwini (2017:30) explains this attempt at annihilation of Zimbabwe's indigenous history as follows:

> Not only has the West denied history to the African but they have also attempted to plant their race at every significant symbol of civilization even in pre-colonial Africa. We are here reminded of colonial theories about the construction of the Great Zimbabwe monuments together with the sustained efforts to sever and disinherit ancient Egyptian civilization from the rest of Africa.

The ahistorical attempt to attribute the construction of Great Zimbabwe monument to any other people except the indigenous is a startling attempt at the theft of indigenous history by colonial historiography. Denying the indigenous people a historic achievement at the height of their power was a cynical and yet well-calculated move aimed at dismissing the levels of development that the continent had achieved prior to the arrival of the Europeans. Thus, the colonizers intended to achieve mental subjugation of the Africans through such deliberate falsification and distortion of history. Moyana (1989:52) notes as regards the Rhodesian syllabus that: "The history which is taught him (colonized) is not his own. Everything seems to have taken place out of his country." Colonial Zimbabwe was named Rhodesia, after Cecil John Rhodes, the colonial architect. This eponymous christening of a country was another attempt to deny Zimbabwe her history of origin by assuming that anything of interest in this part of Africa only began after the arrival of Rhodes. While epistemicide refers to the destruction of IKS, broadly imagined, the above examples make apparent that a new term "historicide" is necessary to capture the enormity of the theft of African history. "Historicide" is an attempt to push the boundaries of theorizing in order to understand the nuanced ways in which colonialism sought to destroy IKS. The following section presents AfriCrit as a potentially useful heuristic for deepening criticality on the issue of Africa's basis for development.

TOWARD AN AFRICAN CRITICAL RACE THEORY (AFRICRIT) FOR AFRICA'S SELF-DEVELOPMENT

In an earlier work, Gonye and Moyo (2018:159) developed African Critical Race Theory (AfriCrit), a theory that they deemed "a necessary step toward an epistemic insurrection against the taken-for-granted notion of whiteness as normative" in the arts curriculum. In that chapter, the authors employ the theory to appreciate and challenge the continued influence of Western European legacies in the postcolonial African curriculum. This current chapter draws on and extends those earlier ideas. Such a move might open up the envisaged theory to a wider application, especially as Gonye and Moyo theorize how the indigenous knowledge embodied subjects such as History and Dance could still be drawn upon to illustrate how the cultural strength embedded in them could illuminate the way to Africa's development despite being pushed to the margins during the entrenchment of European colonialism in Africa. AfriCrit specifically emerges from the writers' analysis of Critical Race Theory (CRT) as a theory which broadly counteracts "persistent Whiteness" that has occasioned the permeation of White supremacy in all aspects of American experience including education (Yosso, 2005:72). According to Yosso, CRT is also an effective tool in interpreting and interrupting other power-mediated manifestations that include "classism, ethnocentrism, and neocolonialism" (Yosso, 2005: 72). The writers here similarly submit that AfriCrit could be useful in objectively critiquing development models from outside Africa, be they from capitalist Western Europe or communist Russia or China. Our earlier formulation of AfriCrit is that:

> AfriCrit would generally enable an interrogation and reclamation of African arts and practices that range from wood carving, pottery, sculpture, theater, dance, song, to literature and architecture. Here, we posit that AfriCrit could offer the disadvantaged people of the African continent a heuristic for interrogating and understanding how they are positioned in the global world. AfriCrit becomes a hankering toward pan Africanism, which is etched in the traditions of resistance and reclamation of what is African. It [AfriCrit] might, for example, help tease Africans on what they make of the fact that European colonialists doubted that the Zimbabwean people built the Great Zimbabwe monuments, preferring to ascribe this architectural marvel to "'white,' foreign" people (Fontein, 2006:772) and referring dismissively to the monuments as the "Zimbabwe ruins." (Gonye & Moyo, 2018:165)

It is clear from the above quotation that the writers believe that AfriCrit may enable many Africans from the African continent to appreciate that they have been framed negatively by the so-called dominant European races because of the latter's desire to appropriate and harvest Africa's resources. AfriCrit could thus enable Africans to comprehend the economic reasons why African innovations, cultures, and IKS, epitomized in their arts and celebrated in different practices, have been racially pulverized and belittled, hence the urgency to resurrect and re-embody them. This should awaken them to the ruse of the touted Eurocentric development agenda in Africa. The agenda had never been neutral but economic; it was a calculated capitalist disempowerment of a whole continent through a forestalling and replacement of African creativity and history.

The ideas of social and developmental theorists such as Lewis, Karl Marx, and Rostow provided fertile ground even for postcolonial theorists to link development and modernity to Western typologies of economic transformation. For Karl Marx, the British railway line in India was a precursor to the unavoidable development of India. Karl Marx envisaged a natural, linear uptake of development by the yet-to-be-developed nations, where he declared: "the country that is more developed industrially only shows, to the less developed, the image of its own future" (Marx, 2015 [1867:7]). Western Europe was not only seen as a model for industrial development but for science and education as well. Informed by the Hegelian stereotypical reductionism, colonial administrators and missionaries frowned upon all the traditional forms of education existing in Africa, taking them as primitive and lacking of any standard or philosophical basis. The condition of the completely "wild and untamed being" could possibly be ameliorated if he or she was exposed to the standards of Western European missionary education or, at least, Islamic ones (Funteh, 2015:141) that would rinse him or her of primitiveness.

Resultantly, for any innovation, Africa would look up to Europe for models. For any material requirement Africa would depend on Europe for deliveries, a perfect way to thwart traditional African inventiveness and production. AfriCrit could thus nudge Africans to realize that by offering developmental models and assistance to Africa, Europe, and America might not necessarily be granting economic freedom to Africa. Further, the theory thus anticipates an analogous questioning of why bring into the African curriculum lopsided Eurocentric history and European dances at the expense of African history and dance.

This chapter reiterates that it was not only the Eurocentric scholar who was impressed by the so-called developmental philosophy (Funteh, 2015) but the latter-day postcolonial elite as well, particularly those who took charge of government and curriculum at independence. By adopting the colonial administrative institutions and colonial education curriculum intact, and again by either accepting the Euro-American models of development or opting for those of Russia or China—their supporters during the anticolonial struggles—the leaders of postcolonial Africa have demonstrated little trust in home-grown examples of development that are extant in IKS. We therefore find AfriCrit useful in interrupting that postcolonial condition. AfriCrit promises to go beyond postcolonial theory's obsession with Eurocentric representation of the other (Ziai, 2012) to theorize the material value to the African, of that which is represented, including IKS. It also interrogates whether Russia's and China' intentions were economically disinterested when they offered alternative models of development to the African leaders. AfriCrit could, indeed, help Africans to argue for the acknowledgment of the practical value of their indigenous forms of education, forms which are not limited to the four walls of the "modern" classroom, but actually seek to address the material needs of the African. AfriCrit desires to escape the tag associated with "postcolonial studies," that, "[It] does not tend to concern itself with whether the subaltern is eating" (Sylvester, 1999:703). This literal substantial limitation in the postcolonial theory suggests the need for its extension. This is especially so in contemporary African nations such as Zimbabwe, Angola, Burkina Faso, or Kenya, where the postcolonial state has overall control over the economy, yet still fails to adequately provide "the promised' development, food and social amenities to the citizens" (Sylvester, 1999).

Nonetheless, like postcolonial theory, AfriCrit also locates the problems of the contemporary African individual not only in the "White" European imperial character but also in the psyche of some postcolonial African elite. But AfriCrit criticizes the postcolonial African elite for seeming to glibly believe that the poverty or stunted development of Africa is caused by its primitive traditions and practices and that this poverty could be solved by Africa retracing the Western European stages of development. Also important is to recognize the inherence of the Ubuntu philosophy, an African-centered philosophy which advocates humanness, cordiality, and reciprocity in African lifestyle and personality, as well as the learning and training that take place informally or under traditional smiths- or griot-type apprenticeships, among others. In the African traditional training scenario, a youth would be attached to an expert elder for a certain period and receive home-based practical instruction on a preferred knowledge area such as metalwork or history recording and narration (griot), among others. All these advances had been trashed by the European colonialists who needed Africans to lose self-confidence for easier manipulation.

Unlike other forms of postcolonial theory, AfriCrit exhorts the total rejection of the unilinearist developmental view to modernity for its self-seeking character and blinkering of some of the co-opted, self-abnegating African elite. AfriCrit also endeavors to look beyond the identity politics of postcolonial theory as it bemoans the fact that, sometimes, people of African descent actively participated in misleading fellow Africans to shirk their own established IKS in exchange for European formulas. AfriCrit appeals boldly to ideas of African scholars who trust African authenticity in its diversity; not to apologists who wave the wand of hybridity to hide their hesitancy to confess that African traditions and culture impede African modernization. The theory would thus do well to consider how Araeen (2010) despises some of the ways in which African artists and scholars have attained the so-called modern status through self-alienation. Araeen (2010:278) exposes Africa's folly of looking up to Europe for models of progress through a criticism of how, by such looking up to European techniques at the expense of African originality, these seemingly progressive African mimics ended up concocting adulterated "modern" African art thus:

> Was it a benign creative force that led to this beginning, or was it meant to trap the imagination to serve a specific purpose? The answer to this lies within the new social forces that emerged in Nigeria at the end of the nineteenth century, resulting from the colonially imposed Western ideas of human progress and advancement—and they actually produced Onabolu. The realism of his work is a product of colonialism, not an opposition to it as some believe. To understand this, it is necessary to acknowledge that colonialism was not a monolithic regime under which everything was carried out by force of stick or gun. The success of a colonial regime depended not only on its violence but also on liberal means by which it successfully enticed the natives to participate in its consolidation and administration. This produced an educated class in Africa, as in other parts

of the colonial world, which accepted the modernity of a Western system and, by adopting it, not only took part in the colonial regime but ultimately took over its very administration in the name of postcolonial independence and self-determination. [Emphasis ours] (Araeen, 2010:278)

The above quotation gives an insight into some of the limitations of the postcolonial theory as espoused by some African elites. Such neo-colonized African scholars miss the underlying Eurocentric assumption that the African ways and practices were inferior therefore unsuitable, irrational therefore unscientifically tenable, and traditional therefore unlikely to result in a modern nation. Therefore, genuine African creativity evident in the Nigerian, Songhai, or the Shona arts, pottery, masks, weaving, sculpture, and suchlike would be evaluated not as essentially good art but as interesting relics whose value is in their exoticism or esotericism. Such actions worked to disconnect potential African innovators from their beckoning indigenous sources of inspiration.

Colonial education, in cahoots with Christianity and policies by the political administration, ensured that some of the educated Africans despise their own cultures in favor of Western European ways of life and outlook (Chinweizu & Madubuike, 1980). This could be why AfriCrit sees sense in going Cabral's route, back to the source, to seek a resurgence of the "indestructive" culture of the African people. For Cabral (1973:41–43), there is an inherent link among culture, history, and the development of productive forces, hence the impatience of the imperialists to "liquidate" African people's cultures. Cultural annihilation would negate the historical development and progression of Africa. From his experience under Portuguese colonialism, Cabral became convinced that all these "retrograde" colonial powers had always been keen to exploit the resources of their colonies, directly as colonial masters or indirectly through a co-opted African neocolonial class. They could, therefore, not be trusted nor expected to offer altruistically any exemplary development path. Rather, Cabral exhorts all freedom and progress loving Africans to trust the potential of their diverse African cultures in order for them to be completely liberated and poised for progress. AfriCrit borrows from Cabral's conviction that a people's progress is hinged upon the culture of the people; no nation can develop and triumph outside of her culture. AfriCrit further exhorts those interested in Africa's economic transformation to reconsider how culture should be the bedrock of that development. The theory encourages all Africans to reflect on the reasons why real development has eluded the continent, one of which has been the relentless "underestimation of the cultural values of African peoples, based upon racist feelings and upon the intention of perpetuating foreign exploitation of Africans, [which] has done much harm to Africa" (Cabral, 1973:51).

AfriCrit endeavors to theoretically exorcise the bane of African progress, which has been the glib belief that Africa could still develop through copying the ways of her erstwhile racist under-developers. From an AfriCrit standpoint such a scenario suggests a denial of Africa's history, and a rejection of the lessons drawn from the exploitative relations between the White imperialists and the colonies over centuries. The skewed relations were also promoted in Africa through the introduction and enforcement of a fawning curriculum where subjects such as African History and Dance were misrepresented and suppressed. Regrettably, the influential African elites hesitated to challenge this educational aberration as they gloried in the semblance of sophistication the Eurocentric history and dances afforded them. However, for AfriCrit, the Africans could mentally liberate themselves if they dumped the habit of aping the race that despises them and would seek to exterminate their culture and IKS. It is Cabral who offers solace to Africans by reassuring them of the defiant survivalist nature of African culture:

> the culture of African peoples is an undeniable reality: in works of art as well as in oral and written traditions, in cosmological conceptions as well as in music and dance, in religions and belief as well as in the dynamic balance of economic political and social structures created by African man. (Cabral, 1973:50)

It is implied in the above quotation that African culture abides in practices such as the oral renditions and written records of African History as well as in the performance and learning of African dances, among others, hence the importance of encouraging them in African curricula. Both these IKS, like the others, are the bedrock of African cultural pride, identity, and creative vision. AfriCrit believes that a belief in the history of African developmental focus and achievement could encourage present-day Africans to also believe that it could be possible for Africa to develop on her own terms. This is so since in its original sense AfriCrit was framed as a heuristic "to conceptualize and reframe the continent's experiences dating back to the days of slavery, through colonialism to post-independence. It posits that African artists use the arts [as historians use the past and present] to express our political, economic, and cultural struggles, all of which point to a history of racist colonial domination and anti-colonial resistance" (Gonye & Moyo, 2018:166).

WITH SELF-INTERESTED MODELS EVERYWHERE, WHEREFORE AFRICA?

Our argument has been that AfriCrit could play a crucial role in rethinking the dearth in viable self-reliant development models in Africa. While the chapter has consistently emphasized the African predicament of being coerced to take up the IMF- or World Bank-funded Euro-Americentric models through the carrot and stick tactic, it has also recognized the existence of competing models from the Soviet Union and China. As Keita (2016) opines, the postcolonial African leaders had to choose between the Euro-American free market capitalism and the communists' state capitalism. We, too, acknowledge the fact that African leaders seemed like pawns in a game of chess. We contend that since the Cold War was essentially about the political and economic control of the world after the Second World War, African leaders ought to have realized that neither the West nor the East could really present to a less developed country a development model that would free that country from the "donor" clutch. The same critical introspection we accord to AfriCrit should therefore assist postcolonial citizens to fathom that it was not enough to realize that neither the Rostowan, the Lewisian, the authoritarian state capitalism, the Lagos Plan, nor the NEPAD had the key to unlock Africa's development. Indeed, non-indigenous models had not only been self-serving, being informed by the global political economy, but had all along funded the racist subterfuge that African indigenous knowledge and techno-how were too backward to support any development project. The notion that your own homestead's embers could not provide the spark to a flaming development needs to be rejected.

AfriCrit redirects postcolonial African citizens toward a re-evaluation of the several African self-initiated development models, focusing on their theoretical and processual flaws. Such models include Cabral's reorganization of liberated rural Guineans for development, Kaunda's humanist developmental programs in Zambia, Nyerere's Ujamaa, or African socialism in Tanzania, and even the current Rwandan model under Kagame. For want of space, we argue here that despite the weaknesses in these initiatives, their African initiators had realized the possibilities of involving local communities in development. However, it remains clear that even these efforts were largely inspired by foreign models. No gainsaying that Nyerere's Ujamaa flopped because the Russians did not fully agree with his improvisations. Inadequate foreign funding could have affected all these earlier initiatives. Another problem self-introspection could unmask is that despite certain postindependent African nations having adopted either the communist/socialist philosophies of Russia and China after the 1917 and 1948 revolutions, respectively, or the mixed or free market economy styles, the Africans could still not realize development. In the former case, while Russia's and China's stranglehold on state economy seemed to have achieved industrial and technological development for them, their African imitators did not experience significant development (Keita, 2016). Instead, corruption and cartelism proliferated at the expense of the expectant ordinary citizen. AfriCrit argues that corruption might not have happened to current levels had African leaders anchored their development strategies in the indigenous philosophy of Ubuntu, which favors communalism and not individualism, cooperation and not competition. We argue that the emergence of cartelism in many African countries such as Zimbabwe, South Africa, and Nigeria is because development projects are imposed from above and not arising from what the people on the ground really need or on how they think what they need could be really achieved. Taking a miniscule example from rural contexts, we submit that communities do not need development projects to be either donated or imposed on them. They need to initiate them, plan for, and undertake them, with of course support from government and well-wishers.

To hunker for a modernizing socioeconomic development full of prospects for prosperity is not wrong; what is wrong is to do it for purposes other than the satisfaction of all citizens. We therefore propose a model that is informed by a desire to satisfy the needs of all, especially the ordinary African. We propose that Africa move away from the situation that if one wants to see an industry one has to travel to the city. That arrangement was one brought about by the colonizers who had never imagined developing the rest of the colony but the capital city only, where most of them resided. Yet, in precolonial Africa, development was context-based, informed by the needs of the local community, available resources, and human labor; be it boat making along fishing and trading waterscapes, iron toolmaking around mining settlements to help improve land preparations, or for defensive purposes for surrounding communities. The same can be said about how innovations in basic art, pottery, and bracelet, copper or gold minting, architecture, herbal medicine, agriculture, and science were all intended to ensure that local people had enough to eat and for development and trade.

What we recommend above seems to resonate with Keita's (2016:43) recommendation where he suggests "efficient and people-oriented government policies as a necessary step for development." Development "can be achieved only when the various populaces are boldly involved through direct action" (Keita, 2016:44). It is crucial that Keita mentions the need for the various citizens to be boldly and directly involved in the process. This communal involvement is what we believe could have happened during the precolonial breakthroughs. However, we refute his premise that there is need for regional integration, including currencies. We are hesitant of any regional integration which precedes local solutions to inhibitive disparities such as rural-urban dichotomies, gender and ethnic inequalities as well as political and geographic barriers that favor the cities. Rather, we believe that it is important to move development projects away from the symbolic centers of power and initiate these developments in our local communities first. When our local regions are fully developed and producing surpluses, it would be natural for them to seek trade and partnerships with other places or regional zones. Hence the importance of ensuring that our own currencies attain stability and firmness first before integration. This move might avoid the possibility of the marginalization of certain local zones.

We thus, go further to suggest that African scholars actually need to invent more critical and self-reflective locally inspired theories. We have hereby initiated that project by proposing AfriCrit. AfriCrit could enable curriculum stakeholders to critique the postcolonial curriculum in Africa as being weighed down by residues of a colonial curriculum that have to be dumped for they were essentially antithetical to the social and economic advancement of the colonized majority.

Ultimately, while we acknowledge the link between knowledge and development, we would rather prefer African educational institutions produce graduates who cherish their cultural values and who are not ashamed to draw from useful examples from IKS. We think that encouraging the study and discussion of subjects such as African History and Dance could assist learners to appreciate the embodied knowledges that led our ancestors to confidently undertake novel innovations. We believe the epistemological value of Dance as a learning subject to be that in it resides the itchiest of our diverse African identities and cultural traits; what we value and revere most, what excites and moves us as an African people in a competing global space are all embedded therein. Further, the study of History acquaints our youth to the most treasured aspects of our lives, the enduring African achievements etched in architectural structures such as the Great Zimbabwe monuments, Egyptian pyramids. and Yoruba artifacts, among others. History records and suggests that Africans can muster their indigenous knowledges and come up with self-initiated cultural achievements, entrepreneurial achievements, and scientific breakthroughs marking the historical trajectories of our African nations as reported by Momoh (2020). AfriCrit argues that modernity does not lie in discarding the marrow of one's cultural attributes, values, and worldviews, but in harnessing these in fruitful ways as did the Chinese, the Koreans, and the Japanese when they developed their nations largely on their own terms. AfriCrit contends that the cure to the debilitating legacies of colonial curriculum lie in adopting a curriculum with a philosophy that is rooted in the IKS peculiar to each African country. Overall, Africans need to align their indigenous knowledges with their development purposes.

CONCLUSION

The chapter has demonstrated that colonialism in Africa has been responsible for the destruction and supplanting of IKS that characterized different African communities that were also at various stages of contextually based development. Following attainment of independence beginning in the mid-twentieth century, many postindependent African countries were persuaded to adopt foreign-framed models of development that would possibly lead to economic and social development. The chapter has argued that this strategy was premised on the global architecture of education, which privileged Eurocentric modernity. African IKS were conceived as irrational, unscientific, and therefore incapable of charting Africa's developmental path. This Eurocentric worldview was also facilitated by the actions of the postcolonial elites who were unwittingly coerced into thinking that there was nothing to look back to in the IKS of their motherland. The chapter proposed the AfriCrit theory as a means to appreciate better the politics at play. It argued that the theory could embolden Africans to ask questions not about why development seemed to have eluded the continent despite Western European and American developmentalist interventions but about why development in Africa ceased precisely at the point of first contact with colonialists. Hence, Africans should reimagine what developmental milestones various African nations could have achieved had they been left to develop at their own pace and in relation to their environmental demand factors. Africa's encounter with Europe, beginning with the sixteenth-century slave trade era, proceeding through the nineteenth-century colonial years, and cynically being ameliorated in the 1950s Truman declamations and development mantra, actually consigned African nations to stalled development, instead of the so-called pathway to development. The chapter further argued that AfriCrit as a critique and extension of postcolonial theory could encourage Africans to realize that the various indigenous learning systems and homegrown technological innovations among the indigenes have played a role in the earlier development of sprawling African empires. Finally, as a theory, AfriCrit recognizes the partiality of knowledge and can only get stronger when it is subjected to further critique by concerned Africans, other international postcolonial subjects, as well as those of an unlike disposition.

REFERENCES

Araeen, R. (2010). Modernity, modernism and Africa's authentic voice. *Third Text* 24(2): 277–286. doi: 10.1080/09528821003722272.

Asante, M.K. (2003). The Afrocentric idea. In A. Mazama (Ed.), *The Afrocentric Paradigm, Asmara*, pp. 36–53. Eretria: Africa World Press.

Boon, K., & Eyong, T.C. (2005). *History and Civilizations: Impacts on Sustainable Development in Africa., in Regional Sustainable Development Review*. Africa, Oxford, UK: Eolss Publishers.

Breidlid, A. (2013). *Education, Indigenous Knowledges, and Development in the Global South, Contesting Knowledges for a Sustainable Future*. London: Routledge.
Cabral, A. (1973). *National Liberation and Culture. Return to the Source: Selected Speeches by Amilcar Cabral*, pp. 39–56. New York and London: Monthly Review Press.
Chakrabarthy, D. (1992). Postcoloniality and the artifice of history: Who speaks for "Indian" pasts? *Representations* 37: 1–26.
Chemhuru-Hapanyengwi, O., & Makuvaza, N. (2014) Hunhu: In search of an indigenous philosophy for the Zimbabwean education system. *Journal of Indigenous Social Development* 3(1): 1–15.
Chinweizu, J. O.,& Madubuike, I. (1980). *Toward the Decolonization of African Literature: African Fiction and Poetry and Their Critics*. London: Routledge and Kegan Paul.
Cohen, L., Manion, L., & Morrison, K. (2007). *Research Methods in Education*. London: Routledge.
Dei, G.J.S. (2014). Indigenizing the curriculum: The case of the African university. In G. Emeagwali and G. S. Dei (Eds), *African Indigenous Knowledge and the Disciplines*, pp. 165–180. Rotterdam, Netherlands: Sense publishers.
Falola, T. (2005). Writing and teaching national history in an era of global history. *Africa Spectrum* 40(3): 499–519.
Funteh, M.B. (2015). Dimensioning indigenous African educational system: A critical theory divide discourse. *International Journal of Humanities and Social Science* 5(4): 139–150.
Gonye, J., & Moyo, N. (2015). Traditional African dance education as curriculum reimagination in Zimbabwe: A rethink of policy and practice of dance education in the primary schools. *Research in Dance Education* 16(3): 259–275.
Gonye, J., & Moyo, N. (2018). African dance as an epistemic insurrection in postcolonial Zimbabwean arts education curriculum. In A. M. Kraehe et al. (Eds.), *The Palgrave Handbook of Race and the Arts in Education*, pp. 157–174. Palgrave Macmillan, Cham. https://doi.org/10.1007/978-3-319-65256-6_9.
Green, E. (2015). Production systems in pre-colonial Africa. In E., Frankema & E. Hillborn (Eds.), *The History of African Development*, pp. 1–13. African Economic History Network. www.aehnetwork.org/textbook/.
John, K. D. (2019). Rez ponies and confronting sacred junctures in decolonizing and indigenous. In L. T. Smith, E. Tuck & K. W. Yang (Eds.), *Indigenous and Decolonizing Studies in Education: Mapping the Long View*, pp. 50–61. New York: Routledge.
Keita, L. (2016). Models of economic growth and development in the context of human capital investment – The way forward for Africa. *Africa Development* 41(1): 23–48.
Leonardo, Z. (2018). Dis-orienting western knowledge coloniality, curriculum and crisis. *The Cambridge Journal of Anthropology* 36(2): 7–20. doi:10.3167/cja.2018.360203.
Lomawaima, K. T., & McCarty T.L. (2006). When tribal sovereignty challenges democracy: American Indian education and the democratic ideal. *American Educational Research Journal* 39(2): 279–305.

Mafongoya P.L., & Ajayi, C.C. (Eds.) (2017). *Indigenous Knowledge Systems and Climate Change Management in Africa*. Wageningen, Netherlands: CTA.

Marx, K. (2015 [1867]). *Capital a Critique of Political Economy. Volume I Book One. The Process of Production of Capital*. Moscow, Russia: Progress Publishers.

Mashoko, D. (2018). Integrating indigenous knowledge of food preservation with school science in Zimbabwe. Unpublished PhD. Dissertation submitted to Wits University. South Africa.

Matunhu, J. (2011). A critique of modernization and dependency theories in Africa: Critical assessment. *African Journal of History and Culture* 3(5): 65–72.

Mazrui, A. A. (1980). *The African Condition: A Political Diagnosis*. London: Heinemann.

Melchior, E. (2011). Culturally responsive dance pedagogy in the primary classroom. *Research in Dance Education* 12(2): 119–135. doi: 10.1080/14647893.2011.575223.

Metzler, J. (2009). The developing state and education: Africa. In R., Cowen & A. M. Kazamias (Eds.), *International Handbook of Comparative Education*, pp. 277–294. Springer Science + Business Media B.V.

Mhone, G. (1995). Dependency and underdevelopment: The limits of structural adjustment programmes and towards a pro-active state-led development strategy. *African Development Review:* 7(2): 51–85. doi: 10.1111/j.1467-8268.1995.tb00071.x.

Mignolo, W. (2009). Epistemic disobedience, independent thought and decolonial freedom. *Theory, Culture & Society* 26(7–8): 159–181.

Mignolo, W. (2012). *Local Histories/Global Designs: Coloniality, Subaltern Knowledges and Border Thinking*. Princeton, NJ: Princeton University Press.

Mignolo, W. (2013). Introduction. Coloniality of power and decolonial thinking. In W. Mignolo & A. Escobar. (Eds.), *Globalization and the Decolonial Turn*, pp. 1–21. New York: Routledge.

Ministry of Primary and Secondary Education. (2015). *The Curriculum Framework for Primary and Secondary Education 2015-2022*. Harare, Zimbabwe: Curriculum Development and Technical Services Unit.

Momoh, M.M. (2020). Colonialism and the destruction of indigenous knowledge systems: Reflection on African arts, science and technology. *International Journal of Research and Scientific Innovation* 7(3):10–18.

Moyana, T.T. (1989). *Education, Liberation and the Creative Act*. Harare, Zimbabwe: Zimbabwe Publishing House.

Mungwini, P. (2017). *Indigenous Shona Philosophy: Reconstructive Insights*. Pretoria, SA: UNISA Press.

Ndlovu-Gatsheni, S.J. (2014). Global coloniality and the challenges of creating African futures. *Strategic Review for Southern Africa* 36(2): 181–202.

Ndlovu-Gatsheni, S.J. (2015). Genealogies of coloniality and implications for Africa's development. *Africa Development* XL(3): 13–40.

Rodney, W. (1981). *How Europe Underdeveloped Africa*. Howard, Washington, DC: Howard University Press.

Rostow, W. (1960). *The Stages of Economic Growth – A Non-communist Manifesto*. Cambridge: Cambridge University Press.

Santos, B. S. (2009). *Epistemologias do Sul*. Coimbra: Almedina.

Santos, B. de Sousa, Nunes, J.A., & Meneses, M.P. (2008). Introduction. opening up the canon of knowledge and recognition of difference. In B. de Sousa Santos, (Ed.). *Another Knowledge Is Possible: Beyond Northern Epistemologies*, pp. ix–lxii. London: Verso.

Shizha, E. (2013). Reclaiming our indigenous voices: The problem with sub-Saharan African school curriculum. *Journal of Indigenous Social Development* 2(1): 1–18.

Smith, L. T. (1999). *Decolonizing methodologies: Research and indigenous peoples*. London: Zed Books.

Smith, L. T., Maxwell, T. K., Puke, H., & Temar, P (2016). Indigenous knowledge, methodology and mayhem: What is the role of methodology in producing indigenous insights? A discussion from mātauranga māori. *Knowledge Cultures* 4(3): 131–156.

Sylvester, C. (1999). Development studies and postcolonial studies: Disparate tales of the third world. *Third World Quarterly* 20(4): 703–772.

Trevor-Roper, H. (1969). The past and present: History and sociology. *Past and Present* 42: 3–17.

wa Thiong' o, N. (2009). *Something Torn and New: An African Renaissance*. New York: Basic Civitas Books.

Yosso, T. J. (2005). Whose culture has capital? A critical race theory discussion of community cultural wealth. *Race Ethnicity and Education* 8(1): 69–91.

Ziai, A. (2012). Postcolonial perspectives on 'development'. ZEF Working Paper Series, No. 103. University of Bonn: Center for Development Research (ZEF).

Chapter 6

Deconstructing Colonial Development Models

Rethinking Africa's Moral Economy and Social Entrepreneurship for Sustainable Rural Development in Postcolonial Africa

Mike O. Odey

This chapter adopted a historical methodology to analyze theoretical and empirical evidence on the trajectory of African development under colonial rule and goes further to deconstruct the development models used by different colonial powers, which largely benefited the European powers and had very little positive impact on Africa. The central problem of investigation in the chapter centers on the need for a radical rethinking of *African moral economy* and *social entrepreneurship* to articulate an indigenous alternative model of development for postcolonial Africa as colonial rule bequeathed legacies of backwardness rather than development on the continent. Four objectives are used to address this problem: The first is to review literature on colonial rule in Africa as background for understanding the nature and character of colonial rule in Africa. The second objective is to provide conceptual framework from different perspectives on the concepts of *development*, *African moral economy*, and *social entrepreneurship*. The third objective is to deconstruct the colonial development models in Africa, which involves a critique of literary and philosophical views on the European claims that African colonization was meant to civilize/develop the continent. Set against the limits of the colonial models of development, the fourth objective is to propose an alternative indigenous model for postcolonial African development, using the concepts of African moral economy and social entrepreneurship. The main thesis of the chapter is that development models in Africa must be homegrown and driven by the rural people themselves within the matrix of their own socioeconomic structures, which they are familiar with over time. The chapter provides links between Africa's moral economy and social entrepreneurship for sustainable rural development in postcolonial Africa, which is a new contribution to knowledge in the overall argument.

INTRODUCTION

There are two broad lines of debate on African development strategies: The first is in favor of external approaches, which are generally in tandem with the colonial development paradigm. The second is oriented toward internal/ indigenous knowledge systems, which continue to gain popularity and wider acceptance (Amin as cited in Ahooja et al., 1986). Ideas and theories of development are not new. However, contemporary development thinking keeps shifting and it is currently assuming a more global character in response to global changes of actors, policies, and issues (Scholte & Soderbuam, 2017).

There is enough evidence to demonstrate the absolute necessity for theorists and practitioners of postcolonial African development to set aside the mantra of the existing development theories and models that are in favor of colonial powers because they are unable to resolve the problematic of African development *impasse* over time, which has been accentuated by the huge gap in the level of development between the global North and South, and human suffering in Sub-Saharan Africa (SSA).

The emerging perspectives on postcolonial African development are encapsulated in concepts such as "another development agenda" (Scholte & Soderbaum, 2017), "endogenous development" (Amin, 1986; Slee, 1993), and "sustainable development" (Brundtland Report, 1987). The central argument in the chapter is directed toward providing a viable "endogenous" alternative model to drive the postcolonial African development agenda. In the chapter, the word "indigenous" is used interchangeably to mean the same thing as "endogenous," which is the opposite of "exogenous" as something that originated from outside, such as development model under colonial rule.

Endogenous development is increasingly becoming a powerful idea in development thinking, but still lacks a thorough theoretical underpinning, especially in Africa, according to Slee (1993) and as adopted in this chapter. In Slee's (1993) formulation, endogenous development is characterized by local people's ideas controlling development processes, unlike exogenous development, which relegates local people's ideas to the background. Under the endogenous category, development options are locally determined, unlike in the exogenous development, which are externally determined. In endogenous development, the benefits of development are retained locally and there is regard for local customs and traditions. Exogenous development exports the benefits of development rather than retaining them (Slee, 1993).

Against this backdrop, this chapter argues that postcolonial development models in Africa must be homegrown and be driven by the rural people themselves within the matrix of their own socioeconomic structures, which they are familiar with, over time. The chapter is divided into four main parts: Part one is introduction. Part two is literature review on colonial rule in Africa. Part three is conceptual framework. Part four is deconstructing the colonial model of development in Africa. Part five is a rethinking African moral economy and social entrepreneurship for endogenous alternative model of development in postcolonial Africa.

LITERATURE REVIEW ON COLONIAL RULE IN AFRICA

Reliance on the works of other intellectuals on the subject articulated in this chapter is unavoidable and a matter of deliberate choice because of the convergence of opinions on the dominant variables running through the chapter. Be that as it may, the literature review here is focused on colonial rule in Africa, and later constituted the basis for deconstructing the colonial models of development in the continent.

The entrenchment of colonial rule and models of development by different colonial powers in Africa began in the later part of the nineteenth century, following the 1844/1885 Berlin conference, which partitioned Africa into different colonial territories (Crowder, 1976). The French, British, German, and Portuguese colonial powers occupied the West African sub-region; through military conquest and signing of treaties between local chiefs and the colonial powers for protection against other colonial powers.

Between the 1950s and 1960s, colonial rule gradually came to an end, in most parts of Africa, except the South African Apartheid regime, the longest and most cruel history of colonial domination in Africa. Each colonial power had its administrative policy and different development models. Falola's (2002) edited volume represents different views from the African perspectives on different aspects of colonial rule in Africa. Most of the contributors discussed colonial political systems, their economic and educational impact, rather than development models. Falola (2002) saw colonialism as a decisive agency of African modernization, which reshaped many African institutions and the way they perceive others. However, as Falola (2002) argued, colonialism was fraught with strong elements of racism, relegation of African culture, imposition of European values on Africa, and economic exploitation, which was why in the European imperialist ideology Africans were seen as *inferior humans*. Thus, colonialism was agency of European domination, with little or no regard for African development.

Crowder's (1976) volume is a synthesis and comparative analysis of African responses to French and British colonial rule, and the impact of their administrative policies in West Africa. The volume is a good representation of the nature of colonial subjugation in Africa as a whole. Crowder (1976) observed that colonial rule had little positive impact on the daily lives of West Africans, beside the appointment of new African rulers as agents of colonial administration to collect taxes used for running the colonial administration, construction of roads, bridges, and railways, and provision of health services. According to him, colonial rule facilitated the introduction of new cash crops, such as cocoa and coffee as well as provision of security system to pave the way for Missionary activities and establishment of schools, which later served the colonial administration very useful purposes (Crowder, 1976).

In the same volume, Crowder (1976) maintained that colonial models of development in West Africa were based on the European ignorance about Africa and the culture of the people, whom they regarded as a *lost race in primitive barbarism* and in *a dark continent* and can only be *enlightened by the European civilization*. Some colonial officials even put it more crudely thus: "West African races should be treated as immature and under-developed children and should be controlled and directed by his white brother" (as cited in Crowder, 1976, p.20). Most European narratives are almost the same about Africa during the colonial period; as African primitivism, a continent without history, and people who are more than fortunate to come under colonial rule. For example, as Lugard (1965, p.3) put it, "as a barbaric race, Africa must first be colonized before they can be civilized by the White race." However, colonial powers were not benevolent agents of development as they portrayed themselves in the colonial literature (Crowder, 1965; Easterly, 2007). Rather, they were more interested in establishing colonial territories to get raw materials for the European manufacturing industries, establish markets, maximize profit through cheap labor, and put in place colonial infrastructure to tax and exploit African territories (Austin, 2015; Amin, 1974).

Finally, it is significant to note from Crowder's (1965) volume, three crucial questions for the deconstruction of colonial model of development in Africa, later in the chapter: One, to what extent did colonial administration radically change the indigenous systems of government for the good of the people. Two, how far did colonial rule produce a social and economic revolution in West Africa and the rest of the continent? Three, to what extent did the so-called *colonial revolution* bring Africa to the orbit of the modern world? Davidson (2005) analyzed the African experiences during and after the colonial rule and observed that as slave trade was assuaging in the early nineteenth-century colonial rule began to set in along the West African coast.

And how, under colonial rule, "the developed world, has continued to take its cut of Africa's dwindling wealth and transferring it to the developed countries of Europe and America," (2005, p.26) despite Africa's numerous miseries, crises, slow growth, and self-development. Davidson's book has some of the worst derogatory remarks about Africa during the colonial period. For instance, he saw "Africans coming ashore in nakedness and hungry, but were lucky to be alive, and people without history," when Freetown, Sierra Leone was the earliest colony of modernizing literacy and the most influential; that, "Africans can only be transformed into nation-states on the British, or another European model, or become civilized at least, because civilization must come from abroad" (2005, p.39). Davidson (2005) further reiterated that new nation-states, emerging from imperial or colonial oppression, have to modernize their institutions, their modes of government, and their political and economic structures, but in doing so, why should they adopt models from those very countries or systems that had oppressed and despised them, why not modernize from the models of their own history or invent new models. This explains why Davidson (2005) portrayed the early years of postcolonial independence Africa as the era of "Black man's burden," drifting from the optimism of "Africa for the Africans" to the era of "disappointment" or "disillusionment" (2005, p.40).

Similarly, as Fanon (1967, p.16) argued, "it is very true that we need a model, and that we want blueprints and examples, but Africa does not have to imitate European models of development to succeed, because the European model of development can only give us mortifying set-backs, spiritual degeneration and throw us off-balance." Easterly (2007) sees postindependence Africa as an era of the *White Man's Burden* for two reasons: first, the misery and extreme poverty in Africa and second, why foreign aid has not facilitated African development over time. Thus, Easterly (2007) re-echoed the covenant of the League of Nations that European powers should not renege from, "the promise for peoples not yet able to stand by themselves" and "the well-being and development of such peoples form a sacred trust of civilization," because "the tutelage of such peoples should be entrusted to advanced nations" and "aim at instructing the natives and bringing home to them the blessing of 'civilization'" (Easterly, 2007). According to Easterly (2007), it was the tutelage of the so-called *uncivilized* and *underdeveloped Africa,* also classified as *the third world*, that turned out to be *the White Man's Burden* in form of foreign aid, which has "done so much ill and so little good," instead of developing Africa.

Calderisi (2007) also addressed "why aid is not working" in the development of postcolonial Africa. He attributed Africa's backwardness to internal factors such as bad governance and the culture of corruption, rather than the failure of the colonial powers, and suggested ten alternative ways by which to regain "the lost decade of African development," such as, recovery of public funds from individual accounts, exposure of bank accounts of government officials to public scrutiny, limiting foreign aids to a few countries who are serious with poverty reduction, and integrated rural development.

"Analyzing the costs and benefits of colonialism," Manning (1974, p.5) observed that as much as it is becoming increasingly fashionable to assess the impact of colonial rule on Africa development, the first thing to do is to lay the ground rules for doing so: These include, commerce, government expenditure, monetization of the economy, technical advancement, taxation, European investment opportunities in Africa, regulatory action, law and order, opportunity costs, education, and political coercion. The most relevant questions in his analysis include whether colonialism in Africa was a "good or bad thing" and "whether the benefits exceeded the costs, and to who?" (Manning, 1974, p.7). He also stretched the analysis beyond economic spheres and used "economic historical-hypothesis" to answer the questions: "Was colonialism beneficial to Africa, and compared to what?" (Manning, 1974). For a correct assessment of the impact of colonial rule and their models of development in Africa, Manning (1974) suggested that each scholar should adopt his own hypothetical position, because, as Austin (2015) observed, most European scholars and foreign powers in Africa see their roles from two perspectives: either as a modernization of static African economies or retardation to Africa's development processes.

CONCEPTUAL FRAMEWORK

This section provides a conceptual framework of three basic concepts to complement the literature review in the previous section. These include the concept of *development*, which is linked to rural development in the analysis, *African moral economy*, and *social entrepreneurship*.

To begin with the concept of *development*, there has been no generally acceptable definition, conceptualization, or theory that fully explains what development really means despite the overwhelming attention it has received all over the world since the post–World War II period. Since then, development is defined from different disciplinary, theoretical, and overlapping perspectives, without any consensus. For instance, many scholars perceive development as economic growth, which is just an aspect, though easier to measure than development due to the complexity of the latter (Todaro & Smith, 2002). Apart from that, the concept of development has continued to assume global dimensions than ever before, with focus on the African predicament.

Between the 1940s and 1970s, the conventional definition of *development* was generally accepted as growth of GDP in national income and sustained increase in the total output of goods and services. Development was also seen as shift from subsistence level to more dynamic and complex levels of growth (Todaro & Smith, 2002). Also, in the traditional sense, for any nation to be considered as economically developed, its growth rate was considered to be at least 5 to 7% annually (Todaro & Smith, 2002). However, in popular economic thought, the conceptualization of development in terms of growth in GDP is considered too narrow and insufficient because the idea of growth in GDP does not always translate into meaningful changes in the living standards of the majority of people concerned (Todaro & Smith, 2002). To Rostow (1960), development is seen as *stages of economic growth*, beginning from the traditional stage to the last stage of high mass consumption of goods and services, which he regarded as *modernization* as well as "the logic," "continuity," and "a sweep of modern history" or "modern society." Sachs (2005) conceived development in terms of the provisioning of economic possibilities such as investment opportunities and helping the poor to engage in grassroots solutions to their problems instead of looking for foreign aids as the best way to end poverty. He also gave instances how ex-colonial territories such as Bangladesh and India achieved prosperity like the developed world by adopting the right strategies and approaches (Sachs, 2005).

In the *Asian Drama*, Myrdal (1968) analyzed the political economy and poverty of Southeast Asian countries in their struggles for political independence, and the gaps between their expectations and possibilities of growth. Of particular relevance for the analysis in this chapter is Myrdal's (1968) suggestion, that there are *always alternative routes* to achieve development; first, by demolishing conventional approaches to development and second, by going further to plan achievable development programs to suit local needs.

At this juncture, it is important to link the concept of rural development to development in general. However, there are still arguments and broad comparative distinctions between rural and urban centers and what constitutes *rurality* between the advanced global North and the less developed countries. Although there is no precision in the definition of what constitutes a rural place, according to David Smallbone et al. (1993) (as cited in, Curran, 1993), the classification of rural areas in Europe is generally applicable to African rural communities, as village settlements with large populations of poor people experiencing different forms of deprivation, and high levels of vulnerability and hunger.

Klugman (2002) further suggested that African rural communities are characterized by overdependence on land and subsistence agricultural production with sparse demographic composition living in small scattered villages and aged parents without electricity, reliable means of transport, pipe-borne water, and absence of non-farm business opportunities and youth migration to cities. In African rural communities, risk evasion and the need to diversify one's sources of income are common, which lead to migrations and dependence on the goodwill of others for general self-provisioning. Despite intensive agricultural activities in rural communities, food security is precarious and largely driven by weather conditions and one's purchasing power. Furthermore, most rural areas are remote from major markets, and limited to supply of farm produce and items that are used for survival strategies of disadvantaged people. These are the views of Nandes (2008) and Margarian (2011) in analyzing the role of entrepreneurship in terms of rural development through job and wealth creation, and raising the living standards of rural people. To Sen (1999, p.5), development is not an end in itself, but the enhancement of "human capacity to function" and "the ability to meet one's basic needs and having a sense of self-worth, to raise people's living standards, remove poverty and promote longevity." Now, it is imperative to ask, "What extent did the colonial models of development in Africa achieve all these characteristics of development?"

AFRICAN MORAL ECONOMY

According to Hyden (2007), the origins of the concept of *moral economy* can be traced to three possible sources: First, to Scott (1976) on anthropological research on Southeast Asian subsistence peasant culture. The next is Polanyi (2001), who differentiated political economy from moral economy and showed how the European industrial economy was transformed from social-cultural structures to a more complex society. The third source on the origin of moral economy, according to Hyden (2007), is from the French neo-Marxist scholars who used the concept of mode of production to explain the African production systems from the perspective of economic and social anthropology. Berry (1975), Tosh (1980), and others later joined the debate and provided a more accurate perspective on the African ingenuity and adaptability to invent new ways of dealing with challenges of their daily lives. Over time, the conceptualization of moral economy has transcended the arguments of Goran Hyden as already presented.

In the African context, the concept is surrounded by several misgivings and not yet popular in rigorous research, except in Economic Anthropology and a counterrevolution to neo-liberal and neoclassical economic thought. But that was in the past. Africa's moral economy is synonymous with Africa's indigenous/subsistence rural economic system and brings together moral and economic issues as a lifelong phenomenon before colonial rule in Africa. But outside Africa, the closest parallel of the concept may be found in Edward Thompson's (1971) original formulation on the plights of the *English working class*, and another parallel from Scott's (1976), *The Moral Economy of the Peasant in South East Asia.* Both instances are prototypes of the experiences of Africa's rural agricultural economy.

One of the latest works on the concept of moral economy is by Carrier (2018), who observed that the concept is used more frequently in the social sciences with too many confusing definitions, which according to him hinders reflection and careful thinking. Like Hyden (2007), Carrier (2018) drew much inspiration from Thompson (1971) and Scott (1976) to elucidate the meaning of moral economy with a caveat for a more precise definition. He encouraged those using the concept of *moral economy* to think more carefully about it in terms of clear intellectual substance (p.20). Carrier (2018, p. 18) maintained that, despite the inherent confusion in the use of the terminology, "time has come for *moral economy* to serve as the organizing narrative for the revival of progressive ideas." To him, the word, *moral* is a "contrast to the self-serving materialism that characterizes modern market societies and how many anthropologists see neoliberals and neoclassical economics as the intellectual foundation of moral economy" (Carrier, 2018, p.19). Although Carrier (2018) was unable to forge out a new and more precise definition of moral economy as he anticipated, he concluded by emphasizing that, people must recognize the fact that they have moral obligation toward others, as much as the value and utility of their engagements in every economic activity demands.

In addition to Carrier's (2018) submission, Götze (2015) provided a robust conceptual history and analytical prospect of moral economy. The thrust of his argument was to challenge Thompson's (1971) ideas by bringing several issues into the debate. He traced the etymology of the two words separately, "moral" and "economy" to classical intellectual history, which were derived from two Greek words for "house" and "manage," respectively (Götze, 2015). Putting the two words together, moral economy is rendered as household manager, to signify *leadership, administration, order, and arrangement.* Götze (2015) further observed that before the publication of Thompson's essay, the concept of moral economy was used long before his time during the Middle Ages, but in a rather restrictive sense with emphasis on economy.

In modern era, agrarian connotation in the use of moral economy has become more apparent when "land as an economic factor is seen from a domestic and moral perspective, rather than in terms of profitability or macro-economic linkage." As Götze (2015, p.5) further noted, "the compound phrase was first used in a sermon preached before an audience in the University of Cambridge in 1729 with reference to *the moral Economy of Things.*" Ever since then, it has become increasingly imperative to update the divergent views on the concept of moral economy like other dynamic concepts in contemporary academic research.

The second word, "economy," in the composite terminology of *moral economy*, is linked to the first, "moral," and refers to the production, and distribution of goods and services as well as the moral justice of the elite toward the less privileged. As Thompson (1971) and Scott (1976) clearly argued, what this means is that the morality of economic production is the hue and cry of the poor for fairness, equity, and distributive justice from the privileged ruling class to the rural agricultural population. This also explains why the rural sector should be the focus of the application of the concept of moral economy as an alternative model of development as demonstrated in this chapter.

Sugimura (2004) observed that the concept of moral economy is universal, complicated, and analyzed from different disciplinary perspectives. He explained African moral economy in the context of its cultural peculiarity, and how rural commodity production of the African peasantry functions through a network of kinship, friendship, and neighborliness based on the norms of "generalized reciprocity," in which counter-obligations to pay back or reciprocate goodwill to relations and neighbors are not necessarily anticipated (Sugimura, 2004). According to him, African moral economy is not an obstacle to development because it is geared toward social production and consumption of available resources for everyone's survival (p.7).

Kumiko (2005) examined the meaning and relevance of different forms of moral economy in East Africa, with focus on productive and reproductive activities among rural household communities. He argued that in African moral economy, agrarian economic activities and social life overlap and complement each other, and never work at cross purposes. Furthermore, in African moral economy, "family reproduction is given priority over profit maximization, and wealth is not accumulated for productive purposes, but for social benefits" (Kumiko, 2005, p.5). In other words, under African moral economy, interpersonal relationship is meant to enhance reproductive purposes. Apart from that, in rural Africa, small informal institutions constitute the basis of strength for everyone working for the survival and growth of others without necessarily looking for reciprocal reward. Africa's rural economy is basically set within the rhythm of indigenous subsistence agriculture, which all rural dwellers are familiar with and free to be part.

Against this background, the inherent self-sustaining mechanism in Africa's moral economy as so far shown makes it about the most viable alternative for the transformation of Africa's rural subsistence economy in ways that have not been critically contemplated before now.

Some have argued that Africa's moral economy does not promote development because it is characterized by dissipation through reciprocal redistribution of available resources (Hyden, 1980; Tosh, 1980). But such an argument is by those who are not familiar with African precolonial economies, which before the advent of colonial rule were for the most part geared toward self-sufficiency (Austin, 2010); although under colonial rule, African societies were wrongly regarded as, "consumer," rather than "production communities," and "archaic" because, they were "economies of affection," "uniform," "wasteful," "unchanging," and "consumption societies by nature" (Kumiko, 2005, p.18; Hopkins, 1973). However, most of the misgivings surrounding Africa's moral economy have been debunked as demonstrated by the African resilience and initiative to generate, not only what Scott (1976) referred to as, the principle of *mutual reciprocity, safety first*, and subsistence insurance, but also wealth generation through household commodity production for export under the harsh circumstances of colonial rule.

CONCEPTUAL FRAMEWORK ON SOCIAL ENTREPRENEURSHIP

The conceptual underpinning of Social Entrepreneurship for the analysis of this chapter first requires a clear understanding of the conventional meaning of entrepreneurship from which the concept of social entrepreneurship derives. *Entrepreneur* or *entrepreneurship* is a conventional word derived from a French word *entreprendre* which literally means "to undertake" or, be a "go-between" or "a manager" (Hisrich et al., 2009; Schumpeter, [1934] 2008). Both concepts are complex with several definitions due to diverse approaches and interests in them from different disciplines.

The origin of the concept of *entrepreneurship* is usually traced to Say (1803) (as cited in, Dees, 2001), who perceived an entrepreneur as one who undertakes risk to for purposes value creation, with the capacity to shift economic resources from an area of lower productivity to a higher one. According to Say (1803), the role of a traditional entrepreneur is inelastic and goes beyond making financial profit to include general managerial competence. About a century later, Schumpeter ([1934] 2008) and other entrepreneurs agreed that *entrepreneurial spirit* is the main engine of economic growth "when an entrepreneur begins to dream, if he has the will to conquer, the impulse to succeed and the joy of creating." Schumpeter also stressed that entrepreneurial profit is a direct consequence of innovation, or what constitutes the productive factor.

From the foregoing, an entrepreneur is one who ventures into creating and distributing new products to maximize economic profits, by recognizing new opportunities and the ability to take action, manages risks, and uses resources prudently. According to Swedberg (2007) (as cited in Croitoru, 2012, p.138) "from all the existing theories of entrepreneurship, that of Schumpeter remains the most fascinating, with an indelible influence on the theory of interest on capital investments, entrepreneurial activities and profits and economic development." Filion (2011), one of the later generations of entrepreneurship researchers, asserted that traditional entrepreneurship is a complex phenomenon with several definitions and characteristics from which to draw inspiration and conceptualize social entrepreneurship. According to him, social entrepreneur is a leader of social groups and an owner of an enterprise who engages in several non-profit, social activities, and safety nets to bring about transformation in society. Filion (2011) further shows that "financial/market profit" is to the conventional entrepreneurs while "social profit" is to social entrepreneurs who use social and economic resources to transform society and social well-being.

Drawing from these broad perspectives on the concept of entrepreneurship from which social entrepreneurship is derived, we can now proceed to engage in more concrete terms, the conceptual framework of *social entrepreneurship*. The emergence of social entrepreneurship in entrepreneurial research is relatively new and has shorter history than the parent word, *entrepreneurship* and *moral economy*. It is one of the latest branches in the lexicon of conventional entrepreneurship. There are several suggestions about when it first appeared in academic literature: Thompson (2002) claimed that the concept first appeared in academic literature in 1960. However, Carrier (2018) and El Brashi (2013) noted that the concept was coined later by Joseph Banks in 1972, and even later by Drayton in 1980. According to El Brashi (2013, p.189), it was Joseph Bank who first invented the concept of social entrepreneurship in 1972 in a seminar on *the sociology of social movements* in which he argued about how to use managerial skills to solve social problems. In the 1980s, the idea of social entrepreneurship was directed toward sustainable public wealth rather that of private individual. On the other hand, Thompson (2002) has shown that, in the last two decades, there is a fluid line between research in the traditional entrepreneurship and the emerging social entrepreneurship, and that the former emphasizes economic features, while the latter emphasizes social responsibility toward the achievement of social change and creates social value to meet social needs. Social entrepreneurs are mostly involved in community work to transform rural life and may be regarded as non-profit executives who are more concerned about helping the poor to solve their social problems.

DECONSTRUCTING THE COLONIAL MODEL OF DEVELOPMENT IN AFRICA

The conquest and effective occupation of the African continent by different colonial powers was followed by the realization that they had huge problems of how to control and exploit the people and the available resources in the colonies to their advantages. There was also the issue of what would be the most suitable development model for each territory. The choice of European development model in Africa was moderated by the method with which each colonial power occupied their territories; whether by treaty or conquest. And this problem was quite different from the problem of the nature of the occupied territory, whether the area was a centralized, homogenous, or heterogeneous society. Apart from all these, the choice of the colonial official on the spot moderated the choice of the model of development used by each colonial power.

By 1930, the stage for European economic imperialism, characterized by Emmanuel's (1972) *Unequal Exchange* was set in most colonial territories. This required each colonial power to choose a development model that would fit the above-mentioned circumstances and make their plans a reality. The general rule was that colonial development models were focused on how to secure raw materials, markets, cheap labor, and investment opportunities in Africa.

This section critically examines the various development models used by each colonial power in different colonial territories in Africa, as well as their impact and the extent of their successes and failures. Without prejudice to any particular theoretical underpinning, the effort here is an extraction of the hidden truths from colonial historiography, highlighted above in the literature review to deconstruct the colonial model of development in Africa.

As already observed, different colonial powers used different policies of administration and models of development in Africa to suit their purposes. Arising from the foregoing, it is necessary here to deconstruct each of them in turn, by examining the extent to which they facilitated the development of the continent. Manning's (1974) analysis of "the costs and benefits of colonialism in Africa" is one of the best approaches toward the deconstruction of colonial models of development in Africa presented under three schools of thought: The first is the liberal school, represented by Crowder (1976) and Adeyeri and Adejuwon (2018), who argued that colonial rule had *bad and good effects* on the African development. They added that colonial rule discouraged indigenous industrialization and was export-oriented, and that colonial territories were established to supply cheap raw materials, and become trading posts for European merchants, and markets for European manufactured goods. But on the other hand, according to this school of thought, Africans benefited as well from the colonial infrastructure, in terms of communication network, monetization of the economy, the banking system and credit facilities, as attributes of the development of the colonial economy.

The second school of thought is championed by *colonial apologists*, who believed that colonial rule in Africa was *implicitly a good thing* because, as they argued, it laid colonial infrastructure such as telecommunication system, road network and the railways, built schools, open commercial activities, monetized the economy, and established colonial administrative institutions. Some of those in this category include Michael Crowder (1976) and Gann and Duignan (1967) as cited in Manning (1974).

The third school of thought is the most radical and a priori position, championed by Rodney (1972), Fanon (1967), Suret-Canale (1988), and Manning (1974). According to this view, the impact of European colonialism in Africa was a bad thing, "which is a statement of fact, rather than moral judgment," because, it was meant to satisfy European interests of colonizing and exploiting Africa rather than developing the continent.

This is further illustrated in the colonial policies of administration and models adopted to suit the peculiarities of their development needs in different parts of Africa. Between the two World Wars, three dominant models of development were used; in West Africa, around the Congo basin, East Africa and French Algeria in North Africa. These include *assimilation, indirect rule, and paternalism*. The French model of development called *assimilation* advocated for common identity between her colonial territories in West and North Africa, and the mother country. The French colonial policy was more of association between the colonies and France. In particular, Assimilation had two aspects of development, known as personal and non-personal: including administrative, political, and economic assimilation. Personal assimilation involved subsuming African culture into French culture. This was mere assumption, which did not take long to discard because it was unachievable. As Jan (2019) argued (as cited in, Kamalu, 2019), French colonial designs as "cultural imperialism" fell short of its objectives in light of the fact that "only about 15% of the people of Francophone Africa speak French while the rest of the population gives preference to local and indigenous languages" (p. 18). *Non-personal assimilation* was taken to great lengths with the assumption that all men are equal, whether African or European. Thus, attempts were put forward to assimilate African into French culture, either immediately, gradually, or through selection. But due to the inherent problems in non-personal assimilation model of development and the difficulties of integrating the African economies with that of France, the model came under heavy criticism and ended in fiasco. Apart from that, the French colonialists considered African traditional institutions unsuitable to administer and exploit colonial territories for the mutual benefits of the indigenous population and European powers. The French colonialists also thought that to use the existing African institutions at all would require reorganizations to fit into their scheme of things. Had any of the two core aspects of assimilation policy worked, it would have meant that the French colonial model of development also thrived in Africa. But that was far from being the case.

The second is the British model of development, known as *indirect rule*, which is based on colonial theory that African and Europeans are culturally distinct, and that European powers should rule Africans through their institutions. *Indirect rule* as a model of development emphasized the role of chiefs in local government administration after their modifications in two ways; either where such institutions were diametrically opposed to European rule, or whenever it was necessary to modify them to enhance colonial exploitation of the territories such as introduction of taxes, development of cash crop production, establishment of colonial infrastructures such as railways, road networks, communication system. Lugard the brainchild of the British *indirect rule* conceived the idea as a dynamic model of development and expected that it would respond simultaneously, to the challenges of the colonial-cum-indigenous administration, and to every other emerging need, which may necessitate the modification of the model as often as necessary.

The third is the Portuguese and Belgium theory/model of development called *paternalistic or association*. This model emerged as a result of the dilemma and criticisms surrounding the fact that the French could not assimilate African culture because it is alien and racially distinct from African culture, which the French considered biologically inferior. As to whether the *Paternalism/Association* facilitated the development of Africa under colonial rule, Kamalu (2019), observed that "Belgian and Portuguese colonial territories experienced the worst form of exploitation, and they were the least educated and least developed in Africa" (p.18). Under this policy, the colonial model of development created a scenario of desperation for cash to pay taxes. For instance, it led to the emergence of colonial migrant cheap laborers who moved from place to place in search of unskilled jobs for the building of the colonial infrastructure such as railways, roads, government offices, plantations, and mining, which were meant to facilitate the running of the colonial government, rather than the development of the territories. According to Nwachukwu and Abuoma (2016), the colonial transport system was a major instrument in the hands of the colonial government to attain their objective of making the colony an export-based economy, through the evacuation of raw materials to the coast for exportation, administrative control, and enhancement of internally generated revenue.

The deconstruction of the colonial model of development in Africa also requires an examination of the various sectors of the colonial economy, including the agricultural, commercial, industrial, as well as communication and monetization of the colonial economy.

The model of development in the agricultural economy in all colonial territories was primarily to produce cash and food crops simultaneously, which Watts (1983) referred to as "double squeeze." First, to produce cash crop for export and as raw materials to enable farmers pay their taxes on the one hand and, and second to produce food crop for local domestic consumption, internal trade, and those in the mines.

Even long after colonial rule, African agricultural economy remains as traditional as it ever was, which is to say that the colonial model of development did not develop the sector. But strangely, it can be argued that, from the perspective of the colonial powers, the model of development succeeded because, it left the African agricultural economy untransformed, because, that was the hidden intention: As Macamo (2005) has argued, this was a contradiction and, "from the African perspective, development does not even exist: Better still, development is an argument, and a fallacious one at that"(p.3).

The colonial agricultural sector had several manifestations: For example, in Kenya, South Africa, Zimbabwe, and French *Algeria*, there were *plantation economy, settler* economy, and peasant economy in West Africa. In the *settler agricultural economy*, the real owners were French commercial agricultural farmers who used unskilled African workers and cheap migrant-laborers or forced labor. According to Fanon (1967), the French Colonial government classification of *French Algeria* as a *settler colony* into, native population and settler colony presupposes the co-existence of two different phenomena, which did not promote uniform development. Not only that, colonialism in Africa led to the emergence of three categories under settler economy: the *Native workers*, the *Colonized Intellectuals*, who think like the European colonizers and third, the *lumpenproletariat*, who are expected to overthrow the settler system through revolutionary means for dehumanizing Africans. *Plantation economy* was not better than the settler economy; as the other form of colonial agricultural economy, sometimes referred to as *absentee capitalists* because the plantations were owned by Europeans living in Europe who left their plantations under the close supervision of their representatives in Africa. Under this model of development, who would doubt that colonial rule was not meant to develop Africa but to simply rip it off.

Under the *peasant colonial economy*, export and food crop production were also geared toward the exploitation of the colonies rather than their development. For instance, the drive toward cash crop production was meant for the supply of raw materials to feed the European industrial system, which depended on peasant subsistence production, using family labor and crude traditional technology of hoe and cutlass in small farm units. Most of the peasant agricultural farms were infertile, *unmechanized*, and depended on weather conditions. Apart from that, Africans were forced to buy imported manufactured goods at very exorbitant prices, while export produce were bought at very cheap prices, far below their real value. A typical example was the accumulated peasant producer prices, which the colonial government in Nigeria refused to utilize to develop the area that led to the establishment of *Produce Marketing Boards* between 1947–1954. As Helleiner (1966, p.162) has shown:

About 42 percent of potential producer income earned from cotton, 40 percent of that from groundnuts, over 39 percent of that from cocoa, over 29 percent of that from palm kernels, and 17 percent of that from palm oil was withheld by the colonial government through taxes and Marketing Board trading surpluses.

What this means is that the enormous reserves or surpluses derived from the Nigerian export producers' income, which could have been used for the development of the colony and as stabilization fund between the two World War periods were siphoned overseas instead of using them to develop the colony.

The deconstruction of the colonial model of development in Africa is not limited to the agricultural economic sector. In the commercial sector, indigenous African participation was alienated from the coastal trade because it involved huge sums of money: This led to constant trade wars between agents of the colonial rule and African middlemen. Similarly, in the industrial sector, the colonial model of development was equally exploitative and far from the idea of development. The colonial industries were small in scale and performance, few and limited to secondary processing. This was called *Import Substitution Industrialization*, which led to the neglect and destruction of local crafts and industries. Thus, all the models of development employed by the different colonial powers were more exploitative than developmental; and more destructive than creative, all of which are diametrically opposed to the idea of development.

Long after independence, the problem of underdevelopment in postcolonial Africa has continued to attract the attention of Marxist scholars including Emmanuel (1972), Nunn (2007), Rodney (1972), and several others; each of who trace the problem to contradictions of colonial past and European imperialism. Emmanuel (1972) referred to this as "unequal exchange on a global scale" and "surplus drain of raw materials from the colonies, leading to the uneven development of factors of production and the current abnormalities in the global system." This scenario is made worse by the international capitalist investments in the ex-colonial territories since the 1990s through the multinational corporations (Ferdausy & Rahaman, 2009). And these account for why African countries remain appendages of their former colonial powers and dominantly poor and one of the least developed regions in the world despite her enormous human and natural resources: "Africa is home to 50% of the world's gold; most of the world's diamond and chromium; 90% of the cobalt; 40% of the world's potential hydroelectric power; 65% of the manganese; millions of acres of fertile and uncultivated farmland and abundance of gas and crude oil" (Ojo, 2016, p.4).

RETHINKING AFRICAN MORAL ECONOMY AND SOCIAL ENTREPRENEURSHIP FOR ENDOGENOUS ALTERNATIVE MODEL OF DEVELOPMENT IN POSTCOLONIAL AFRICA

Rethinking the concepts of African moral economy and social entrepreneurship, which constitute the basis for an alternative indigenous development model, requires a radical shift beyond the colonial models of development in Africa, already discussed above. The need for change is in tandem with suggestions by several scholars as shown in the review of extant literature because of the failure of colonial models of development to develop the African continent. The overall object here is how to achieve sustainable development in postcolonial Africa ultimately as demonstrated in the selected examples in this chapter.

The first two are exogenous in nature and sound like the colonial models of development, as expressed in Macamo (2005, p.18). The first component is that, "African countries must commit themselves to human rights and to free market economy, uphold the rule of law, be fair in their political processes, train their workforce, give education to the young, give succor to the suffering poor, observe gender equality and protect the rights of the minority as, preconditions for African development" (Macamo, 2005, p.18). The second sounds like the first as follows: "Africans should stop blaming others for their economic problems and first put their own house in order," or "pumping more money into Africa is useless and will only prolong its addiction to foreign aid" (Macamo, 2005, p.18) "Let Africa become like us, fully capitalist, otherwise they will never be able to compete with us in world politics and world economics" (Macamo, 2005, p.18).

The third and most critical suggestion is endogenous model of development, led by Amin (1974), which stressed the imperative of thinking differently beyond the European models of development toward plausible alternatives for the emerging African nations. The reason for this is derived from the failure of colonial models of development in Africa. In his, *Accumulation on world scale*, Amin (1974) used different historical experiences to explain why endogenous development strategy is imperative for postcolonial African development. To Amin (1974), development is a product of the existence of two world systems, and a consequence of the development of capitalism, which is responsible for the current underdevelopment in Africa. As I have consistently argued in this chapter, the only way to dislodge African backwardness is to come to grips with Africa's endogenous model through a deliberate policy of rethinking the relevance of *African moral economy* and *social entrepreneurship*. The relevance of the two lies in Africa's production system and social structure, in which productive and reproductive activities *overlap* to mutually support and strengthen social relations of production to guarantee people's safety net. Again, because Africa's moral economy is built on the fabric of African traditions, agricultural production, exchange system, and different types of specialization in craftsmanship, it has an incredible capacity to generate market surplus for the local/urban population and the international trade.

Furthermore, African moral economy and social entrepreneurship both of which are rooted in rural agricultural production and are capable of boosting rural investment opportunities and establishment of Small and Medium Enterprises (SMEs) to facilitate non-farming cash earning nexus if properly managed. Besides that, Africa can also learn from other parts of the world, where institutional support for SMEs in rural communities "have outperformed their urban counterparts in terms of employment growth." Apart from that, African governments should show more serious commitment to sustainable development by devoting large sum of money for the transformation of the rural communities as a matter of priority toward "social entrepreneurship as a recognized economic force in rural development," as re-echoed by Ibrahim (2014, p.14) thus, "SMEs are also the seedbeds for a broad development of the private sector throughout the country, forming the foundation for the national economy and social development at the grassroots." Furthermore, SMEs stimulate rural entrepreneurial skills, provide scarce resources, create non-farm jobs, and add economic value to social engagements in furtherance of economic growth at the grassroots.

The essence of rethinking African moral economy and social entrepreneurship toward sustainable rural development in postcolonial Africa also lies in their capacity to generate diversities of safety nets through social interaction to meet socioeconomic needs in times of distress. This is why Kumiko (2005, p.18) argued that a "deeper understanding of African moral economy will support the paths for subsistence, democracy, and endogenous development in Africa, and provide lessons for the world in creating a new paradigm based on a global moral economy." It is also expected that this will further open the path to a substantial network of researchers working on the economic logic of mobilization in rural areas in the developing countries, including Africa.

This means that endogenous alternative model of development in postcolonial Africa will be geared toward boosting rural productivity through the mobilization of household members working together in groups to meet labor shortfall, especially at peak periods of farming, irrespective of age and gender on the basis of mutual trust and rotational basis. Tosh (1980) has amply demonstrated the efficiency of labor arrangements under colonial rule in Africa tagged cash crop revolution in the international trade system involving diverse cultural, religious, and ethnic groups including Diaspora communities. Austen (2010, p. 9) referred to this as moral community of rural Africa who "believe in one another and overcome problems of mistrust, uncertainties of weather conditions, the seasonal nature of productive activities and other hindrances to cooperation over long distance trade across boundaries."

In the new thinking for Africa's postcolonial development, this is where governments should mobilize/empower social entrepreneurs to leverage on such existing mutual and social interactions in rural communities to work together with the aim of overturning charity-based economy to boost economic returns, growth, and the development of Africa's rural economy. Although peasant "community labor" was not recognized by the colonial administration, but such organizations were successfully used to boost cash crop production for export during the colonial period. The new thinking here again, is that they will work even better in the postcolonial period given the required motivation, increasing consciousness, and re-organization by government.

Finally, apart from the forgoing, because, each mode of production reproduces its own kind of economy, to wit, if the preponderance of the capitalist mode of production is the market economy, in the African context, by implication, the household mode of production constitutes the basis of African moral economy and the much desired sustainable rural development in postcolonial Africa. This means that Africa's economic development should be re-organized on the basis of what the traditional/indigenous economic arrangement consists, just as the East Asian countries did to experience exponential growth as the *Asian miracle* because, they developed their economies along indigenous lines, as Myrdal (1968) demonstrated. What is paramount here is government support, motivation, and follow-up to ensure that indigenous alternative model of development works in different communities throughout Africa, using the right policy framework.

CONCLUSION

By way of conclusion, it is important to cite a number of African economic historians who have demonstrated the resilience of African peasant production and entrepreneurial spirit in the past to illustrate the viability of African moral economy and social entrepreneurship and how the two concepts can be applied to the current drive toward sustainable rural development in postcolonial Africa's growth process: Berry (1975), Hogendorn (1978), Tosh (1980), Dorward (1975), and Hill (1963), to mention just a few. Spring and Barbara (1998) also presented the idea in form of small-scale enterprises and household start-up businesses all over Africa, as "good examples of progressive economic behavior and growth" (p.7). The significance of informal institutions, social inclusion, and wider participation in the formulation of development strategies has been demonstrated all over the world. Furthermore, the synergy between African moral economy and social entrepreneurship debunks social exclusion of the less privileged and vulnerable groups in society and constitutes a dependable linchpin for SMS enterprises in community development. Therefore, the correct development policy of the state economy must first be a dynamic commitment to rural community development, which on the long run will bring about progressive structural transformation, economic reconstruction, and scientific innovation of the development process.

Ayittey's (2005) analysis of Ghana's indigenous peasant farmers, called *Atinga*, is another relevant example, representing a broad spectrum of African rural farmers coming together to solve their problems by embarking on small-scale projects with the support of government and community social interaction. Besides that, Botswana's success story of 8% average growth rate between 1966 and 1986 is another example of how economic growth can be achieved in rural villages through participatory bottom-up development initiatives characterized by social entrepreneurship and moral economy (Ayittey, 2005). Botswana's growth is usually traced to traditional institutions, driven by local chiefs in different rural communities called, *Kgotla* System working together with other local chiefs to deliberate on every development project introduced by government before implementation (Ayittey, 2005). These examples represent the basis of Africa's moral economy and show how social entrepreneurs deal with immediate social problems as a matter of priority to launch into broader issues of growth and development.

The chapter began with literature review on colonial historiography as background for explaining the nature of colonial rule and different models of development in Africa. Three main concepts were conceptualized from different perspectives, namely development, African moral economy, and social entrepreneurship, which is derived from the concept of traditional entrepreneurship. The chapter was an intellectualization of Africa's social and economic indigenous systems on which the matrix of African rural life depends as a basis for sustainable and alternative development.

To bring the argument of the chapter to a conclusion, three principal ideas must be borne in mind: First, it was an attempt to deconstruct the colonial models of development in Africa and second, the arguments were driven by the imperative of rethinking, critically beyond the conventional definitions of development and to engage the philosophy of African *moral economy* and *social entrepreneurship* in the formulation of an indigenous model of development for postcolonial Africa. And third, in doing these, the statement of the problem was resolved accordingly, using the four-set objectives to close the existing gap in African studies.

One of the emerging conclusions from the foregoing is that the most viable models of development in postcolonial Africa must be familiar to the people and be indigenous to Africa; and begin from the rural communities where the vast majority of the rural poor reside. This is because extraneous macroeconomic development models have too many bottlenecks and they are not inclusive or participatory, rather strange to the indigenous population. Indeed, it is difficult to refute the preceding argument for the imperative of rethinking African moral economy and social entrepreneurship for an alternative model of development for postcolonial Africa for the following reasons: First, the deconstruction of the colonial models of development clearly shows that, they were for the interests of the colonial powers and not for the interest of African development. Second, for the postcolonial African development agenda, alternative endogenous model is required, not exogenous ones like the colonial models. Third, the engagement of Africa's moral economy and social entrepreneurship cannot be neglected in the current search for an alternative Africa's rural development initiative because, the two concepts represent a broad spectrum of African traditional life and bring together rural communities with similar historical backgrounds to solve their problems by embarking on small-scale projects, built around subsistence farming with the support of government. and social inclusion.

REFERENCES

Adeyeri, O. & Adejuwon, K. D. (2018). "The Implications of British Colonial Economic Policies on the Nigerian Development". *Journal of Advanced Research in Management and Social Sciences*, 1, (2):1–16.

Ahooja-Patel, K., Drabek, G.A., & Marfin, M. (eds.) (1986). *World Economy in Transition*. Oxford: Pergamon Press, pp. 159–173.

Amin, S. (1974). *Accumulation on a World Scale: A Critique of the Theory of Underdevelopment* (2 volumes). Monthly Review Press.

Austin, G. (2015). The Economics of Colonialism in Africa, In Célestin Monga and Justin Yifu Lin. (eds.), *The Oxford Handbook of Africa and Economics: Volume 1: Context and Concepts.*

Austin, G. (2010). African Economic Development and Colonial Legacies, The Graduate Institute, Geneva pp. 11–32. doi:10.4000/poldev.78 (Accessed, 3rd May 2020).

Ayittey, G. (2005). *Africa Unchained: The Blueprint for Africa's Future*. USA: Palgrave Macmillan.

Berry, S. S. (1975). *Cocoa, Custom and Socio-Economic Change in Rural Western Nigeria*. Oxford: Clarendon Press.

Brundtland Report. (1987). htt ://www.un.documents.nets/our-common-future

Calderisi, R. (2007). *The Trouble with Africa: Why Foreign Aid isn't Working*. New Haven: Yale University Press.

Canale, J. S. (1988). *Essays in African History*. London: Hurst & Co.

Carrier, J. G. (2018). Moral Economy: What is in a Name? *Anthropological Theory,* 18(1):18–35.
Collier, P. (2007). *Bottom Billion: Why the Poorest Countries are Failing and What Can be Done About it.* UK: Oxford University Press.
Croitoru, A. (2012). Schumpeter, J. A., 1934 (2008), The Theory of Economic Development: An Inquiry into Profits, Capital, Credit, Interest and the Business Cycle. A Review to a book that is 100 years old. *Journal of Comparative Research in Anthropology and Sociology.* 3, 2.
Crowder, M. (1976). *West Africa Under Colonial Rule* (4th edition). London: Hutchinson.
Curran, J. & Storey, D. J. (eds.) (1993). *Small Firms in Urban and Rural Locations.* London: Routledge.
Davidson, B. (2005). *The Black Man's Burden.* Ibadan: Spectrum Books
Dees, G. J. (2001). *The Meaning of 'Social Entrepreneurship.* Retrieved from: http://www.fuqua.duke.edu/centers/case/documents/Dees_SEdef.pdf. 28/April/2020
Dorward, D. C. (1975). An Unknown Nigeria Export: Tiv Benniseed Production; 1900-1960. *Journal of African History,* xvi(3): 431–459.
Easterly, W. (2007). *The White Man's Burden.* London: Penguin Books.
El Ebrashi, R. (2013). Social Entrepreneurship Theory and Sustainable Social Impact. *Social Responsibility Journal,* 9(2):188–209. doi:10.1108/SRJ-07-2011-0013
Elkington, J. & Hartigan, P. (2008). *The Power of Unreasonable People: How Entrepreneurs Create Markets to Change the World.* Harvard Business Press.
Emmanuel, A. (1972). *The Theory of Unequal Exchange: A Study of the Imperialism of Trade.* NY: The Monthly Review Press.
Falola, T. (ed.). (2002). *Africa, Volume 3. Colonial Africa, 1885-1939.* Durham: Carolina Academic Press.
Fanon, F. (1967). *The Wretched of the Earth.* Harmondsworth: Penguin.
Ferdausy, S. & Rahman, M. S. (2009). Impact of Multinational Corporations on Developing Countries. *The Chittagong Journal of business Administration,* 24, 111–137.
Filion, L. J. (2011). Defining the entrepreneur. *Journal of World Encyclopedia of Entrepreneurship,* 4152.
Gann, L. & Duignan, P. (1967). *Burden of Empire: An Appraisal of Western Colonialism in Africa, South of the Sahara.* New York.
Götze, N. (2015). Moral economy: New Perspectives, its Conceptual History and Analytical Prospects. *Journal of Global Ethics,* 11(2):147–162. doi:10.1080/17449626.2015.1054556
Helleiner, G. K. (1966). *Peasant Agriculture Government, and Economic Growth in Nigeria.* Richard D. Homewood, IL: Irwin.
Hettne, B. Payne, A. & Soderbuam, F. (1999). (eds). Rethinking Development Theory. *Special Issue of Journal of International Relations and Development,* 2(4):354–478.
Hill, P. (1963). *The Migrant Cocoa-Farmers of Southern Ghana.* Cambridge.
Hisrich, R. D., Peters, Michael & Shepherd, Dean. (2009). *Entrepreneurship,* African edition. Great Britain: McGraw-Hill.

Hogendorn, J. S. (1978). *Origin and Development of Groundnuts Trade in Northern Nigeria*. Zaria: ABU Press.

Hopkins, A. G. (1973). *An Economic History of West Africa*. London: Longman.

Hyden, G. (2007). Affection Economy and Moral Economy Compared: What Lessons"? Revue du MAUSS, 2007/2 (No 30). doi: 10.3917/rdm.030.0161: La Découverte

Hyden, G. (1980). *Beyond Ujamaa in Tanzania: Underdevelopment and an Uncaptured Peasantry*. Berkeley: University of California Press.

Ibrahim, R. O. (2014). Rural Entrepreneurship Development and Poverty Alleviation: A Review of Conceptual Issues, 3rd International Conference of Urban& Regional planning, University of Lagos, Nigeria, 13th to 15th October.

Jan, Z. (2019). *Inequalities and Conflicts in Modern and Contemporary African History: A Comparative Perspective*. Lanham, MD: Lexington Books.

Kamalu, N. C. (2019). British, French, Belgian and Portuguese Models of Colonial Rule and Economic Development in Africa. *Annals of Global History*, 1(1):37–47.

Kumiko, S. (2005). The Role of the African Moral Economy in Endogenous Development: Towards a new perspective", paper presented to the *Moral Economy Workshop*, University of Dar es Salaam, 18 August.

Klugman, J. (ed.). (2002). *A Sourcebook for Poverty Reduction Strategies, Vol. 2 Macroeconomic and Sectoral Approaches*. Washington, DC: The World Bank.

Lugard, F.D. (1965). *The Dual Mandate in British Tropical Africa. Fifth Edition*. London: Frank Cass & Co. Ltd.

Macamo, E. (2005). Against Development, Rethinking African Development: Beyond Impasse, Towards Alternatives, 11th CODESRIA Bulletin Nos. 3 & 4, Maputo, 6–10 December.

Manning, P. (1974). Analysing the costs and benefits of colonialism. *African Economic History Review*, 1(2): 15–22.

Margarian, A. (2011). 4th International Summer Conference in Regional Science, Dresden, June 30 – July 1.

Martin, R. L., & Osberg, S. (2007). Social entrepreneurship: The case for definition. *Stanford Social Innovation Review*, 5(2): 28–39.

Myrdal, G. (1968). *Asian Drama: An Inquiry into the Poverty of Nations. 3 vols*. New York: Pantheon.

Naudes, W. (2008). *Entrepreneurship in Economic Development*. Retrieved from: http://www.wider.Unu.edu/publications/working ers/research papers/2008GB/rp2008-2010.18/05/2020

Nunn, N. (2007). Historical legacies: Linking Africa's past to its current underdevelopment. *Journal of Development Economics*, 83(1): 157–175.

Nwachukwu, J.O. & Abuoma, C. A. (2016). British colonial economic policies and Infrastructure in Nigeria: The rail transport example, 1898-1960. *African Journal of Arts and Humanities*, 2(3): 1–26.

Ojo, E.O. (2016). Underdevelopment in Africa: Theories and Facts. *The Journal of Social, Political and Economic Studies*, 41(1): 89–103.

Polanyi, K. (2001). *Great Transformation: The Political and Economic Origins of Our Time*. Boston, MA: Beacon Press.

Rodney, W. (1972). *How Europe Underdeveloped Africa*. London: Bogle-L'Ouverture.
Rostow, W.W. (1960).*The Stages of Economic Growth*. Cambridge: Cambridge University Press.
Sachs, J, D. (2005). *The End of Poverty: Economic Possibilities for Our Time*. New York: Penguin Books.
Say, Jean-Baptiste. (1803). *A Treatise on Political Economy,* 4th edition. Translated by C.R. Prinsep from 4th Edition in French, Batoche Books. Quoted in J. Gregory Dees (2001). "The Meaning of 'Social Entrepreneurship,'" reformatted and revised, May 30 http://www.fuqua.duke.edu/centers/case/documents/Dees_SEdef.pdf. Retrieved April 28, 2020.
Scholte, J.A. & Soderbuam, F. (2017). A changing global development agenda? *Forum for Development Studies,* 44(1): 1–12. doi: 10.108008039410.2017.1275843 .
Schumpeter, J.A. [1934] (2008). *The Theory of Economic Development*. Cambridge: Harvard University Press.
Scott, J.C. (1976). *The Moral Economy of the Peasant: Rebellion and Subsistence in Southeast Asia*. New Haven, CT: Yale University Press.
Sen, A. (1999). *Commodities and Capabilities and Development as Freedom*. New York: Alfred Knopf.
Sherief, S. R. (2005).*Entrepreneurship as an Economic Force in Rural Development*. http://www.africaeconomicanalysis.org/articles/gen/rural_entrepreneurship.htlm (Retrieved on Oct. 13, 2017).
Slee, B. (1993). Endogenous development: A concept in search of a theory. Proceedings {slee 1993 ENDOGENOUSDA. www.semanticscholar.org. Retrieved May 23, 2020.
Smallbone, D., North, D. & Leigh R. (1993). The growth and survival of mature manufacturing SMEs in the 1980s: An urban-rural comparison. In Curran, J. & Storey, D. J. (Eds), *Small Firms in Urban and Rural Locations*. London: Routledge.
Spring, A., Barbara, E. & McDade, B.E. (Eds). (1998). *African Entrepreneurship: Theory and Practice*. Gainesville: University Press Florida.
Sugimura, K. (2004). African Forms of 'Moral Economy' in Rural Communities: From comparative perspectives". *Tanzania Journal of Population Studies and Development*, 11(2): 21–37.
Thompson, E.P. (1971) .The moral economy of the English crowd in the eighteenth century. *Past and Present,* 50: 76–136. doi: 10.1093/past/50.1.76.23/May/2019
Thompson, J. (2002). The world of the social entrepreneurship. *International Journal of Public Sector Management,* 15: 412–431. doi:10-110810955135502104357 46.
Todaro, M.P. & Smith, S.C. (2002). *Economic Development*, 8th ed. Boston, MA: Addison Wesley.
Tosh, J. (1980). The cash crop revolution in tropical Africa: An agricultural appraisal. *African Affairs: The Journal of the Royal African Society,* 79(314): 79–94.
UN Report. (2020). The Sustainable Development Goals Report, NY, USA, Website https://unstats.un.org/sdgs.
Watts, M.J. (1983). *Silent Violence*. Berkeley, CA: University of California Press.

Chapter 7

Decolonization and Deconstruction of Colonial Development in Postcolonial Africa

Alternative Development Initiatives and the Contentions

Victor I. Ogharanduku

Decolonization and deconstruction of colonial notions and frameworks of development commenced immediately after the attainment of independence in postcolonial Africa and continue to this day. In the process, five notable alternative development initiatives (ADIs) were proposed and adopted between 1980 and 1991 in addition to several development agendas proposed and adopted between 1963 and 1979. However, the decolonization and deconstruction project did not produce successful outcomes because none of the ADIs were ever implemented by postcolonial Africa. This chapter discusses the non-implementation of the ADIs as the result of contentions involving conflicts between African leadership and its people over the meaning of development, its trajectory, outcome(s), and empowerment of the African people. These have been responsible for the non-implementation of the ADIs because the ADIs meant significant transformations of the power relationship between African leaders and the people, particularly the erosion of power which was the goal of development for African leadership. Thus, the unsuccessful decolonization and deconstruction of colonial notions and frameworks of development is an "Afrocentric" issue that can only be addressed by Africans rather than the West which they blame for the underdevelopment of the continent but run to for development aid and assistance.

INTRODUCTION

Decolonizing and deconstructing colonial notions and frameworks of development in postcolonial Africa started since the first decade of independence with the adoption of resolutions and plans by postcolonial Africa—the first in 1963—aimed at charting alternative development trajectories for the realization of development on the continent. This trend continues into the twenty-first century with the New Partnership for Africa's Development (NEPAD) as the latest plan. As a result, various ADIs emerged and each proposal condemned to its early grave due to inaction. So the debate of what ADI best suits postcolonial decolonization and deconstruction continues to this day. Observations of the debate indicate that ADIs have not been in short supply; rather there has been abundance (Onimode, 2004; Tomori & Tomori, 2004; Kankwenda, 2004; Ajakaiye, 2004; Summonu, 2004; Agubuzu, 2004).

Then why has the decolonization and deconstruction not achieved any appreciable result and that real development continues to elude postcolonial Africa? What is postcolonial Africa contending within its decolonization and deconstruction of colonial notions and frameworks of development? And what alternative(s) can it hope to pursue in the process for the actualization of real development? To provide answers to these questions are some of the salient problems the chapter seeks to resolve.

The impressive economic growth of postcolonial Africa in the first decade of the twenty-first century (Elhiraika, 2005; Roxburgh et al., 2010) looked like a new chapter of decolonization and deconstruction was on the way. After two decades of slow and stagnated economic growth, including deepening underdevelopment, much of postcolonial Africa retrogressed into a state of being a global burden and a patient of diverse development policy and plan therapeutics and experiments (Mihevc, 1995; Chossudovsky, 1998; Kankwenda, 2004; Onimode, 2004). This economic growth occurred as a number of countries in the global south emerged as economic forces and poles of growth (China, South Korea, Taiwan, Singapore, India, Brazil, Malaysia, and Hong Kong) (Adam & Dercon, 2009; Todaro & Smith, 2011; Abdelrahman, 2019) in the global economy, giving some renewed impetus to the expectation that postcolonial Africa could achieve decolonization and deconstruction.

Fueling this expectation and aspiration were arguments that the emergence of these economies followed ADIs and trajectories involving complex processes of "inward experimentation" hinged on "intrinsic values and practices" unique to each society and driven by political leadership. This does not however include the "Lee thesis" attributed to the former prime minister of Singapore, Lee Kuan Yew, since more comprehensive inter-country comparison has not provided any confirmation of this thesis, and there is little evidence that authoritarian politics actually improves economic growth (Sen, 1999). However, it is increasingly recognized that political leadership has been the most decisive factor in the development of any nation, and Mills (2010) has argued that Africa's poor political leadership resulted in bad off-policy choices that has been responsible for its underdevelopment. Huntington (1996) observes that the source of the East Asian development success was in its socioculture. The import is that postcolonial Africa looked to exogenous factors at the detriment of endogenous factors which were the most important impediment to its decolonization and deconstruction process.

The development success of these countries revealed that low levels of growth and development were symptoms of deeper concerns about the politics and institutional foundations (Todaro & Smith, 2011) on which any society is built and hence the economic policy choices that emerged (Adam & Dercon, 2009). This suggests that postcolonial African decolonization and deconstruction of colonial notions and frameworks has not been on solid footing. This chapter discusses postcolonial African ADIs and the contentions surrounding the non-implementation of these ADIs—not necessarily that the plans were bad—but that postcolonial Africa was and is contending with endogenous factor(s) that challenge ADIs as tools of decolonization and deconstruction, rather than the exogenous factors that have been the major focus of many observers. Immediately after this introductory section, the chapter is divided into three main sections: the first is a brief conceptualization of development in the context of postcolonial African decolonization and deconstruction of colonial notions and frameworks of development; the second is a review of the various ADIs; the third discusses ADIs and the contentions surrounding the inability of postcolonial Africa to follow through with these ADIs; and the last section concludes the chapter.

A BRIEF CONCEPTUALIZATION OF DEVELOPMENT IN THE CONTEXT OF POSTCOLONIAL AFRICA

This chapter will not achieve its aim if the concept of development is not defined and situated in the postcolonial Africa's decolonization and deconstruction of colonial notions and frameworks of development. This is because development has held various meanings at different times (Ziai, 2019) for different disciplines and purposes such that every modern human activity can be undertaken in the name of development (Rist, 1997). What this implies is that the meaning of development has continued to evolve with changing human and societal circumstances and challenges. Development has evolved considerable such that Ince (2019) observes that it belongs to a family of concepts "whose ideological sway and institutional efficacy bear a paradoxically inverse relation to the clarity of its definition" (p. 179), and that in its relatively short history and circulation among policymakers, academics, and lay publics, development has been variously associated with national industrialization, poverty reduction, satisfaction of basic human needs, integration into global markets, and increasing the choices and capabilities of citizens.

According to Rist (1997) the quest for definition oscillates between two equally irrepressible extremes: (a) the expression of a (doubtless general) wish to live a better life, which seems to deliberately ignore the fact that the concrete way of achieving it would run up against conflicting political choices; and (b) the great mass of actions (also conflicting with one another) which are supposed to eventually bring greater happiness to the greatest possible number. Nevertheless, *development* in its classic social scientific sense refers to long-run social, political, economic, and technological structural transformations that are distinctly modern, although not necessarily conforming to modernization theory (Fischer, 2019). This distinction is important because development as modernization in postcolonial Africa has failed (Scott, 1998) because it became tightly associated with Westernization, an entirely different process. As such the cultures and knowledge systems of African societies have come under serious attack over their perceived antagonistic posture in relation to development prompting the argument by some that Africa's development hinges on its holistic adoption of the cultures and knowledge systems of the developed nations.

"Development must be conceived of as a multidimensional process involving major changes in social structures, popular attitudes and national institutions, as well as the acceleration of economic growth, the reduction of inequality and eradication of poverty" (Todaro & Smith, 2011, p. 16). They explain that development in its essence must represent the whole gamut of change by which an entire social system, tuned to the diverse basic needs and evolving aspirations of individuals and social groups within the system, moves away from a condition of life widely perceived as unsatisfactory toward a situation or condition of life regarded as materially and spiritually better.

As such development anywhere and at any time must have at least three basic components or core values that serve as conceptual basis and practical guideline for understanding the inner meaning of development (Todaro & Smith, 2011). These include sustenance (the ability to meet basic needs)—all people have certain basic needs without which life would be impossible (e.g., food, shelter, health, and protection); self-esteem (to be a person)—a sense of self-worth and self-respect of not being used as a tool by others for their own ends; and freedom from servitude (to be able to choose)—the sense of emancipation from alienating material conditions of life and from social servitude to nature, other people, misery, oppressive institutions, and dogmatic beliefs.

It is a process of institutional, political, cultural, environmental, social, and structural transformation of a society to actualize sustenance, self-esteem, and freedom from servitude for individual and the society. Thus development in postcolonial Africa meant decolonization and deconstruction of colonial notions and frameworks of development as they contradicted development and its core values.

A REVIEW OF POSTCOLONIAL AFRICA'S ADIS

This section reviews the various ADIs proposed by postcolonial Africa in its decolonization and deconstruction aspirations. However, it is pertinent that the review is combined with narrative of a few important events and factors that triggered postcolonial Africa's drive to initiate and develop ADIs. This offers a nuanced understanding of the purpose of these ADIs and the contentions embedded in the decolonization and deconstruction expedition. The statist development model adopted by African states in the first decade of independence paid off with average per capita GDP growing at 1.88%; the second decade however witnessed a decline to 0.31% triggering an economic growth shock that dovetailed subsequently into a development crisis from the beginning of the third decade (Rodrik, 1999 cited in Ajakaiye, 2004). It is important to note that in these first two decades, development in the global south was viewed as homogenous, with economic growth in many postcolonial African countries equaling or surpassing those of many other areas of the world (Olamosu & Wynne, 2015; Abdelrahman, 2019). Despite this assumed homogenous outlook, there were remarkable differences in the global south such that development in this region never reflected a homogenous circumstance and trajectory (Sach, 2008; Sowell, 2017). This homogenous standpoint indeed was an inclusive term that masked the unique underdevelopment condition and challenges of postcolonial Africa. Ince (2019) concludes that the postwar development regime failed to deliver on its promises and nowhere is this so visible than postcolonial Africa.

With the statist or developmental state model failing to enable successful development outcomes (Rapley, 2007), the continents development crisis emerged toward the end of the 1970s. Following the same trajectory as the Marshall plan which involved huge borrowing for development finance in post-WWII Europe and the huge liquidity in the global economy in the 1970s, African governments were encouraged to borrow to finance economic development. The aim was to revive economic growth that would enable them pay back loans. This however did not happen; the situation degenerated precipitating severe economic growth and development shocks which disrupted Africa's development trajectory by 1980. The twin shocks of declining economic growth and a failed statist development model became the rallying point and impetus for the initiation of alternative development policies, plans, and choices to help postcolonial Africa quell the development crisis and put African development on a recovery track. African leaders, civil society organizations (CSOs), trade unions, and academia rose up to this challenge and proffered ADIs for the continent. Five landmark ADIs according to (Onimode et al. 2004) emerged from a decade of intense interactions and debates over what alternative development paradigm postcolonial Africa should follow. They included:

1. Lagos Plan of Action (LPA) for Economic Development of Africa and the Final Act of Lagos (1980);
2. Africa's Priority Programme for Economic Recovery 1986–1990 (APPER) later converted into the United Nations Programme of Action for Africa's Recovery and Development (UN-PAAERD) (1986);
3. African Alternative Framework to Structural Adjustment Programmes for Socioeconomic Recovery and Transformation (AAF-SAP) (1989);
4. African Charter for Popular Participation in Development and Transformation (ACPPDT) (1990) known as "Africa's Magna Carta" (Onimode, 2004); and
5. United Nations New Agenda for the Development of Africa in the 1990s (UN-NADAF) (1991).

Before these five landmark plans, Ake (1996) observes that African governments have been involved in setting development agendas and initiatives aimed at decolonizing and deconstructing colonial notions and frameworks of development. However, this chapter concentrates only on the five major ADIs mentioned earlier but these agendas are worthy of mention for a fuller appreciation of the decolonization and deconstruction voyage. They include:

1. Areas of Cooperation in Economic Problems adopted by heads of state of independent Africa in May 22–25, 1963;
2. Africa's Strategy for Development in the 1970s which was adopted by the United Nations Economic Commission for Africa (UNECA) Conference of Ministers in Tunisia, February 1971;
3. Africa Declaration on Cooperation, Development and Economic Independence, also called the Addis Ababa Declaration adopted by the Organisation of African Unity (OAU) Assembly of Heads of States and Governments in 1973;
4. Revised Framework of Principles for the Implementation of the New International Economic Order in Africa, adopted at Kinshasa in December,

1976 by the OAU Council of Ministers and July, 1977 by the OAU heads of states in Libreville; and
5. Monrovia Declaration of Commitment of the Heads of States and Governments of the Organisation of African Unity on Guidelines and Measures for National and Collective Self-Reliance in Social and Economic Development for the Establishment of a New International Economic Order, adopted in July 1979 by heads of states and governments in Monrovia.

Lagos Plan of Action (LPA) for Economic Development of Africa: This was premised on the cardinal principles of self-reliance (national and collective), self-sustainment, democracy, and sustainable human development (Kankwenda, 2004). Within this plan, a postcolonial development ideological lining was envisaged and attainable through food self-sufficiency, satisfaction of the basic needs of the African peoples, creation of employment opportunities, internal mass production of essential consumer goods, and establishment of the Economic Community for Africa (ECA) by the year 2000 (Sunmonu, 2004). This plan emerged from broad participation of Africa's intelligentsia, civil society, and leaders, and is adjourned to be the best ADI that postcolonial Africa has ever developed (Sunmonu, 2004). Above all it was an inward-looking strategy for collective regional and sub-regional self-reliance (Kankwenda, 2004).

Africa's Priority Programme for Economic Recovery 1986-1990 (APPER): APPER was subsequently converted to the UN-PAAERD because of the conflict between Africa's political leadership and major actors of the International Political Economy (IPE). APPER was assumed to be rooted in the LPA and aimed at translating the broad objectives of radical change in the pattern of production and consumption, social and economic structural transformation, accelerated economic growth and development including integration of the economies of the region into sharply focused, practical, operational set of activities and policies to be implemented between 1986 and1990 as the basis for durable structural change, and improved general level of productivity (Ake, 1996). APPER while not completely discarding the LPA, underplayed it, because African leaders had learned of the futility of trying to determine their development agenda and attempting to follow through without the cooperation of the West (Ake, 1996). More fundamental was its reflection of Sub-Saharan Africa's stumpy power status in the global economic system and the resilience of colonial notions and frameworks of development.

Alternative Framework to Structural Adjustment Programmes for Socio-Economic Recovery and Transformation (AAF-SAP) (1989): AAF-SAP was championed by the renowned economist Professor Adebayo Adedeji, then the head of UNECA. It is also said that he masterminded the LPA and the Final

Act of Lagos (Odunuga, 2004). AAF-SAP was a holistic approach to the issue of adjustment as an integral process of socioeconomic transformation based on the principles of self-reliance and self-sustainment advocated by the LPA (Odunuga, 2004). It aimed for the transformation of African economies from economies "based primarily on exchange to one based on production, with simultaneous democratisation of the development process and pervasive accountability on the part of policy makers and public officials" (Odunuga, 2004, p. xvi). But Onimode (2004) reveals that the World Bank refused to accept this indigenous engineered alternative development plan. Instead it launched its Long-Term Perspective Study (LTPS) in 1989 and hence, African countries failed to implement this plan.

African Charter for Popular Participation in Development and Transformation (ACPPDT) (1990): The charter was an approach to development that represented the continents "rejection of the commodity fetishism and putrid economism of the Western developmentalist or monetisation ideology that was foisted on Africa" (Ake, 1984). This ADI pointed out that the people were the most crucial catalyst of the development process and its most important beneficiaries (Onimode, 2004). It was aimed at giving a new concept to democracy in Africa, it canvassed for popular participation, employment of the people, accountability, social and economic justice, and respect for human and trade union rights and the rule of law (Sunmonu, 2004). The five pillars encapsulated in the charter were the answer to democracy and good governance in Africa as they would ensure "that governance is of the people, for the people, and by the people, without the usurpation of the people's empowerment" by any group especially the continents' political, economic, and military elites (Sunmonu, 2004, p. 64), who are seen as willing tools of the West in the subjugation of postcolonial Africa.

United Nations New Agenda for the Development of Africa in the 1990s: UN-NADAF recognized that African countries were faced with social and economic crisis throughout the 1980s and were entering the 1990s with multiple environmental crises. It also affirmed that SAP had fell short of expectations of African countries and the international community and that the conditions that led to the implementation of SAP still prevailed. In section 3 of the introduction of the UN-NADAF report A/48/334, it stated that this new agenda was a renewed commitment to African development based on "shared responsibility" and "partnership" between Africa and the international community as well as pointed out that African governments and people reiterated their "primary responsibility" for their development and the international community expressed its commitment to give "full and tangible support to the African effort." The responsibilities of African countries in the agenda included: to undertake individual and collective reforms necessary for sustainable growth and development, promote sub-regional and regional cooperation and integration, intensify the democratization process and giving due consideration to key elements such as the human dimension, population, environment, agriculture, and food security, revitalize South/South cooperation and the role of non-governmental organizations (NGOs). A trend in this particular development agenda as with all the other ADIs is that they enunciated what Africans had already articulated in the LPA, in sum it was more of a repetition.

The new millennium saw postcolonial African economies witness significant improvements in economic growth rates 5.1% (2002); 5.2% (2003); 6.1% (2004); 5.9% (2005); 6.3% (2006); 6.8% (2007); 5.4% (2008); 3.1% (2009); 4.1% (2010) (ILO,2010, p. 45). These improvements were associated with expansions in global trade of primary commodities that led to higher demands and prices for these commodities—significant increases in official development aid driven mainly by debt relief and emergency assistance and macroeconomic stability (Elhiraika, 2005; Olamosu & Wynne, 2015); and in part to the emergence of a number of economies in the global south, previously peers of Africa in the early decades of United Nations (UN) development declarations. As this growth began, Africa's political leaders again proposed and adopted a new development plan, NEPAD in 2001, to realize development and in part decolonization and deconstruction. In some quarters it is perceived as an African version of the Marshall Plan with priority areas that include infrastructure, energy, education, health, and agriculture, and very little attention given to industrial development and manufacturing (Onimode et al., 2004).

NEPAD targeted a growth rate of 7% per annum and investment rate of 30% of GDP, an addition of 12% to the previous 18% rate of investment from domestic sources. Mobilization of external resources in the light of resource gap is a key strategy of this plan. In essence, the plan focuses on attracting foreign direct investments (FDIs), instead of paying more attention to domestic mobilization of resources which should be the long-term strategic approach to filling the resource gap observed in the plan. This for Onimode et al. (2004) overshadows wealth creation on a sustainable basis, which, if it was the primary concern of the development plan would lead to the desired postcolonial development transformation. Wealth creation on a sustainable basis has been highlighted as one very crucial factor in the development trajectory of developed economies and the few economies of the global south that have emerged as economic forces and a major reason why postcolonial Africa has failed to catch up with these countries. Successful development outcomes are not due to fast growth as was witnessed in the first decade of independence and the beginning of the new millennium by postcolonial African countries, but having steady growth for a long period of time (Pritchett et al., 2018); and Africa's economic growth has been extremely varied and episodic. Further political governance and economic governance were separated in the plan, a serious fundamental flaw because in the real world both are not just interrelated but also intertwined (Onimode et al., 2004).

Despite achieving improved economic growth rates, Africa is still far from achieving real developments or enhancing appreciably its decolonization and deconstruction of colonial notions and frameworks of development. Onimode et al. (2004) note that Africans applauded and welcomed the five major ADIs because they were based on four fundamental principles of self-reliance (national and collective), self-sustainment, democracy, and sustainable human development. So why did it become difficult for postcolonial Africa to follow through with these plans? The next section discusses the contentions underlying the inability of postcolonial Africa to follow through with its ADIs.

THE ADIS AND POSTCOLONIAL AFRICA'S CONTENTIONS

ADIs were meant to enable postcolonial Africa decolonize and deconstruct colonial notions and frameworks of development and ensure Africans own their development, its trajectory, and make certain successful outcome(s). Onimode et al. (2004) assert that unfortunately all the ADIs were opposed, undermined, and jettisoned by the Bretton Woods institution, and Africans were thus impeded from exercising their basic and fundamental right to make decisions about their future. The World Bank backed by neoclassical economic theories swiftly blamed Africa's development crisis on internal structural problems and domestic policy inadequacies, and quickly launched the structural adjustment program (SAP) as an economic recovery plan. A program which the bank assumed was the solution to development challenges not just in Africa but across the global south. However, many have argued that SAP was not borne out of a desire to really assist African economies wither the crises, rather it was to perpetuate further what Kwankwenda (2004) referred to as the "Development Merchant System" (DMS).

Onimode (2004) and Kankwenda (2004) argued that over-reliance on foreign-dictated development policy and programs has been the crux of the failed development trajectory of postcolonial Africa. "The very narrow sense of massive investment and hopes that the new money will come from Africa's 'partners' particularly in the form of FDIs" (Onimode et al., 2004, p. 246) has left Africa without any control over what development agenda it sets or what trajectory it follows to realize its development. Adedeji (1993), Anyang' Nyong'o (1990), and Onimode (1989) all posit that the postcolonial African development course has been plagued by internal problems such as failure of an African economic integration, foreign debts, poor governance, poor management of resources and the economy, corruption, political instability, and conflicts.

Mohamoud (2007) while not blaming Africa for its unsuccessful attempts to decolonize and deconstruct colonial notion and framework of development, identifies a culturally and idiosyncratic oriented discourse which states that African values and practices inhibit the development of the continent. He explains further that this assumption posits Africa's development quandary as squarely internal and is the result of the continent's bad choices. It blames Africa for the failure of development and leaves African societies with a sense of defeat, including deliberately choosing to focus on problems and things that are going wrong on the continent.

For Ake (1996) the problem is hinged on a number of factors such as: the colonial development albatross imposed on Africa and its legacy, social pluralism and its centrifugal tendencies, the corruption of leaders, poor labor discipline, lack of entrepreneurial skills, poor planning and incompetent management, inappropriate policies, the stifling of market mechanisms, low levels of technical assistance, limited inflow of foreign capital, falling commodity prices, unfavorable terms of trade, and low levels of savings and investments. But of more significance is his twin argument that the political conditions in Africa are the greatest impediment to postcolonial African development, "African politics has been constituted to prevent the pursuit of development and the emergence of relevant and effective development paradigms and programs" (p. 1); and two, that the problem was not so much that development has failed as that it was never really on the agenda in the first place.

Ake's first argument has in the last two decades been supported by a number of authors and development institutions (Heymans & Pycroft, 2003; Burnell and Randall, 2008; Beattie, 2009; Mills, 2010; Pritchett et al., 2018). The consensus is that the politics engaged in by African leadership has been responsible for the kind of development policy choices and institutions that have characterized the region's development trajectory. Politics in African countries remains highly influential in relation to development and that is why in their critique of NEPAD Onimode et al. (2004) noted that it was absurd that African leaders separated political and economic governance and this amounts to "the horse and the carriage—you cannot have one without the other" (p. 244). This has meant that within the context of decolonization and deconstruction ADIs have had to and will have to contend with the politics in African states.

Ake's second argument has some implications; one is that African leaders from the start were not interested in development but "political power" which Ake dwelt extensively on in his book *Democracy and Development in Africa*. The other is that to some extent postcolonial African leadership did not have a full grasp of what development meant outside their euphoria and sentiment and this was responsible for the "confusion of development agendas" narrated in the book. Colonial rule left most of Africa a legacy of intense and lawless political competition amid an ideological void and so development was an attractive idea for forging a sense of common cause and for bringing some coherence to the fragmented political system (Ake, 1996). The "ideology of development" he argued was exploited as a means for reproducing political hegemony, and so development was not an incentive for much of Africa's ruling class that emerged upon the exits of the colonials, but power. Thus, development as defined in the context of postcolonial African decolonization and deconstruction did not commence. As Africa's ruling class craved for and aspired to replace the colonials, it was not fully interested in decolonization and deconstruction beyond rhetorics. Examples of this abound (see Meredith, 2006) in Meredith's (2006) *The State of Africa, A History of Fifty Years of Independence.*

A critical look at the unsuccessful outcomes of postcolonial Africa's decolonization and deconstruction of colonial notions and frameworks of development through ADIs reveals underlying contentions categorized as external and internal. Concentration on the external does not really help explain the region's inability to follow through with its ADIs, especially when compared to economies of the global south that have emerged as examples of development successes driven from within, especially, as the second scramble for Africa by the West and emerging economies of the global south has not changed significantly the underdevelopment state of Africa, indicating that a better understanding of Africa's internal contentions remains very much pertinent to understanding it decolonization and deconstruction failures. This does not mean that some progress have not been recorded as a result of the scramble, at least it provided Africa with some space and opportunity to leverage the interests of these actors. Nonetheless, the unequal power relationship between postcolonial Africa and the West has contributed in some measure to the inability to decolonize and deconstruct but its role is not as important as many have assumed it to be.

Dercon (2018) observes that policy advice and plans are useless or bound to fail when the "political incentives" to act are not well understood. Sowell (2017) observes that although the scope of what political institutions can accomplish has inherent limitations, what they actually do depends also on what those who direct these institutions want to do. What suffixes from this are fundamental contentions involving a conflict with two dimensions; the first is overtly between postcolonial African and Western development ideologues which a significant number of literature have dwelt on. In this dimension, ADIs and their implementation devoid of Western sanctions was sacrilegious and intolerable. This conflict is underpinned by the dogmatic insistence of the IFIs and Africa's creditors (Onimode, 2004) to follow particular development prescriptions which undoubtedly could and do not address the continent's unique development challenges. Todaro and Smith (2011) assert that this conflict of interest is genuine and cannot be ignored and continues even in the twenty-first century; for example, the Copenhagen climate summit (2009), World Trade Organization (WTO) (Doha talks in 2001), and G20 meetings.

The second is a covert conflict between African leaders and its people(s) which has been going on for long and managed to escape attention only becoming very obvious with the Arab Spring in 2010, Zimbabwe in 2018, and Algeria and Sudan in 2019. The reason for the covert character of this conflict is that along with Africa's political problem, it was frozen by the Cold War and never satisfactorily resolved (Scott, 1998). This conflict is over what really constitutes the real end(s) of development and what path should be followed in achieving these end(s). It emanates from the differing views, expectations, and aspirations about development held by African leadership and citizens. African leadership sees development in terms of political and economic power willed over the people and the capacity to control their lives and choice options. African citizens view development in terms of what Amartya Sen (1999) defines as *development*, the freedom to lead the kind of life that one has reason to value. This is further shaped by experiences imbibed from the political economy of everyday life (see Adebanwi, 2017) ("The Political Economy of Everyday Life in Africa, Beyond the Margins" edited by Wale Adebanwi, 2017). This conflict also entails struggles and contestations among the states, social organizations, and actors within states (Migdal, 2001).

The implication is that African leadership and African citizens hold different views of what decolonization and deconstruction of colonial notion and framework of development is, it trajectory, and its outcomes. Examining the development trajectory of Asian economic powers shows that first addressing the conflict between leadership and the citizens is central to creating the enabling conditions for following through with ADIs and realizing successful outcomes. This conflict was quickly recognized and resolved by Chairman Mao of China, General Park of South Korea, and Lee Kuan Yew of Singapore, thereby allowing these nations pursue their ADIs without distraction. However, the manner in which this conflict was resolved is subject to debate, but the examples of these countries indicate that this conflict must be resolved for inwardly developed ADIs to take hold of the development project. Thus Africa's decolonization and deconstruction project was and is ensnared with the burden of African leadership and people(s) resolving this internal conflict. However, there has not been very significant effort, especially from African leadership to resolve this conflict despite the fact that the African people are at a critical juncture involving a realization that this conflict continues to militate against options and choices aimed at the decolonization and deconstruction and opposes the actualization of successful development outcomes.

A critical review of postcolonial Africa's decolonization and deconstruction and its ADIs demonstrates that if ADIs were implemented, certain political and economic incentives of African leadership would have been eroded leaving them open to critical engagements by the people. African leadership sensing the loss of power which it craved for more than development (Ake, 1996) engaged in activities and viewpoints often to inhibit any genuine reform efforts that might benefit the wider population and in some cases this actually led to even lower levels of living and to the perpetuation of underdevelopment (Todaro & Smith, 2011). Sowell (2017) observes that "when the benefits are concentrated in a narrow segment while the costs are diffused over the population at large, the average member of the narrow constituency have far more incentives to promote and maintain the status quo than an average member of the general public has to invest in time and cost to uncover the reality behind the politically generated appearance" (p. 261). Underdevelopment as a coordination failure puts some focus on the potentials of government policies and analyzes government as one component of the development process that may contribute to the problem as well as the solution (Todaro & Smith, 2011).

Thus, the failed attempt of utilizing ADIs as tools of decolonization and deconstruction was and is not so much about the power imbalances with the West or its development ideologues but what the outcomes of implementing these ADIs for African leadership would have been. ADIs meant fundamental restructuring of the political and economic incentives of those in leadership which would have led to a critical altering of relations between them and the people —power—which had become the end of development for African leadership (Ake, 1996). ADIs would not have necessarily fundamentally altered the unequal power relationship with the West but rather transform the powerlessness of the African people and widen the base and structure of power beyond African leadership that is, empowerment of the people. Indeed within the inability to follow through with ADIs was and is the "contention of empowerment" of the African people. These contentions—conflict between African leadership, and people, and empowerment of the people—challenge decolonization and deconstruction. As such the failure of decolonizing and deconstructing colonial notions and frameworks of development has and is mostly an "Afrocentric" issue. This can only be addressed by African leaders and people, not by those they consistently blame for the continents poor development outcomes; but still, run to for development aid and assistance as can be seen in the NEPAD. This Afrocentric challenge has been the unique basis for why postcolonial development has failed in its development efforts and what differentiates it from emerging economies of other regions.

The failure at decolonizing and deconstructing postcolonial Africa through ADIs has left the continent in great despair prompting further: What alternative(s) can postcolonial Africa hope to pursue in the decolonization and deconstruction process? Especially when recent debates on the factors (geography, culture, social, political, and environmental) thought to be impeding development in the region have been scrutinized by scholars (Sowell, 2017; Chang, 2018) and found not to be unique to the continent. What has been unique to postcolonial African development is the failure of African leadership to weave out of the diverse heterogeneous nationalities that inhabit their borders, nation-states (Scott, 1998; Chang, 2018). Thus decolonization and deconstruction of colonial notion and framework of development is challenged by the failure of nation-building by postcolonial Africa.

This awakens debates on the exact impacts of the continents, indigenous knowledge systems and cultural norms, and values and practices on postcolonial African development. Especially since the stock of knowledge held by a society is very important to its development. For example, the rapid reconstruction and development of post-WW II Europe, Japan, and recently China and India shows the importance of knowledge stock and systems. Scholars (Horton, 1982, 1997; Gyeke, 1997) cited in Mapadimeng (2009) posit that Africa has abandoned its own heritage for those of the West and this has not been judicious and has created tensions for postcolonial development. Africa's knowledge stock and systems no doubt experienced some drawbacks by the intrusion of Western cultures through colonialism but this is not necessarily a bane to development. Hungtington (1996) describes three different trajectories in the process of development which include (1) modernization and Westernization; (2) modernization without Westernization; and (3) Westernization without modernization. The second was followed by emerging economies of Asia while Africa adopted the third and this again is one of the distinct differences between of decolonization and deconstruction of development in Asia and postcolonial Africa.

So for postcolonial Africa decolonization and deconstruction efforts, the emulation of Western development systems without refinement to accommodate aspects of African knowledge systems and cultural norms and values contributed to the inability to follow through with its ADIs. African leadership has failed to understand that Western notions and institutions of development emanated from evolutionary processes embedded in Western cultures and knowledge systems at different times and under different circumstances and these are not replicable in postcolonial Africa because contemporary conditions and socioeconomic development realities in Africa have not mirrored that of the West at any given point in time. Consequently decolonization and deconstruction of colonial notion and framework of development as presumed by Africa is an elusive project.

The alternative for postcolonial African development therefore is not necessarily new ADIs but a pragmatic approach to development (Ha-Joon Chang in Abdelrahman, 2019) based on recognition of its unique development constraints and greatly infused with African knowledge systems and positive cultural values and practices. Postcolonial Africa is rife with obvious attempts by Africans to resort to undermining indigenous knowledge systems and cultural values and practices in the hope that development would be fast-tracked. This twisted faulty system has prevailed inducing development failures. Onimode (2004) concludes that developing a political program for the realization of an African agenda starts with the development of a broad consensus around the elements of alternative development to be disseminated widely for awareness about issues involved, implementation, the creation of networking among the social forces or branches of civil society, and coordination of consultative meetings in order to share information, plan common strategies, and pool their typically fragile resources together.

Decolonization and deconstruction is premised on evaluation of development in terms of "the expansion of the 'capabilities' of people to lead the kind of lives they value—and have reason to value" (Evans, 2002, p. 54). It is in African knowledge systems and cultural values and practices that much of the people's capabilities lay; consequently decolonization and deconstruction should embody total inclusion facilitated by distributive justices. Unlocking and encouraging capabilities through debunking the general assumption that development can only be achieved by the elimination of traditional and cultural heritage (Marglin & Marglin, 1993 cited in Sen, 1999) should ultimately be the ADI ideology and pragmatic approach for Africa. The decolonization and deconstruction of colonial notions and frameworks of development problematique as conceived in postcolonial Africa is inscribed at the very core of the Western imaginary, and since there are numerous ways of living a good life, it is up to each society to invent its own (Rist, 1997).

CONCLUSION

The process of decolonization and deconstruction of colonial notion and framework of development has been on since the first decade of independence. Various development agendas and ADIs were proposed and adopted by postcolonial Africa as tools of the decolonization and deconstruction process. Postcolonial Africa adopted five development agendas between 1963 and 1979 and five notable ADIs between 1980 and 1991, but the ADIs especially were never implemented and the unequal power relationship between postcolonial Africa and the West was blamed for this. This unequal power relationship does not completely explain this non-implementation; rather endogenous factors such as the conflict of what development is, its trajectory and outcome(s), and the conflict to empower African people are to blame. These conflicts reveal that African leadership has been unable to implement ADIs because of outcomes that threatened their power base and structure which they craved for, upon the exit of the colonials. After all the economies that emerged from the global south as economic forces in the world economy utilized the same Western economic theories as those that failed Africa. So what is Africa decolonizing and deconstructing?

REFERENCES

Abdelrahman, M. (2019). A Conversation with Ha-Joon Chang. *Development and Change*, 50, 573–591. doi: 10.1111/dech.12482

Abdullah, A. M. (2007). Brief theoretical background and charting alternative perspective. In A. M. Abdullah (Ed.), *Shaping of a New Africa* (pp. 17–26). Amsterdam: KIT Publishers.

Adam, C., & Dercon, S. (2009). The political economy of development: An assessment. *Oxford Review of Economic Policy*, 25, 173–189. doi: 10.1093/oxrep/grp020

Adedeji, A. (1993). *Africa and the World: Beyond Dispossession and Dependence*. London: Zed Books.

Agubuzu, O. C. L. (2004). Regional economic integration: A development paradigm for Africa. In B. Onimode et al. (Eds.), *African Development and Governance Strategies in the 21st Century, Looking Back to Move Forward: Essays in honour of Adebayo Adedeji at Seventy* (pp. 191–205). London: Zed books Ltd.

Ajakiaye, O. (2004). The centrality of planning to alternative development paradigms in Africa. In B. Onimode et al. (Eds.), *African Development and Governance Strategies in the 21st Century, Looking Back to Move Forward: Essays in honour of Adebayo Adedeji at Seventy* (pp. 54–62). London: Zed books Ltd.

Ake, C. (1984). *Revolutionary Pressures from Africa*. London: Zed Books.

Ake, C. (1996). *Democracy and Development in Africa*. Ibadan: Spectrum Books Limited; Jersey: Safari Books (Export) Limited.

Anyang' N. P. (1990). *Popular Struggles for Democracy in Africa*. London: Zed Books.

Beattie, A. (2009). *False Economy: A Surprising Economic History*. New York: Penguin Group.

Chang, H.-J. (2018). *Are Some Countries Destined for Under-Development?* [Video & Powerpoint slides]. Retrieved from www.hajoonchang.net

Chossudovsky, M. (1998). *The Globalization of Poverty – Impacts of IMF and World Bank Reforms*. London: Zed Books.

Dercon, S. (2018). Foreword. In L. Prichett, K. Sen, & E. Werker (Eds.), *Deals and Development: The Political Dynamics of Growth Episodes* (1st ed., pp. v–vii). New York: Oxford University Press.

Heymans, C., & Pycroft, C. (2003). *Drivers of Change in Nigeria: A Preliminary Overview*. London: DfID.

Elhiraika, A. (2005). An integrated approach to Africa's development constraints. In J. J. Teunissen & A. Akkerman (Eds), *Africa in the World Economy-The National Regional and International Challenges* (pp. 192–199). Hague: Fondad.

Evans, P. (2002). Collective capabilities, culture, and Amartya Sen's development as freedom. Studies. *Comparative International Development*, 37, 54-60.

Fischer, M. A. (2019). Bringing development back into development studies. *Development and Change*, 50, 426–444. doi: 10.1111/dech.12484

Hungtinton, S. P. (1997). *The Clash of Civilisations and the Remarking of World Order*. London: Simon & Schuter UK Ltd.

Ince, O. U. (2019). Development. In J. d'Aspremont & S. Singh (Eds.), *Fundamental Concepts in International Law: The Construction of a Discipline* (pp. 179–200). Cheltenham: Edward Elgar Publishing.

Interntional Labour Oganization (ILO). (2010). Employment Sector Employment Working Paper No. 63. Geneva: ILO.

Kankwenda, M. (2004). Forty years of development illusions: revisiting development policies and practices in Africa. In B. Onimode et al. (Eds.), *African Development and Governance Strategies in the 21st Century, Looking Back to Move Forward: Essays in honour of Adebayo Adedeji at Seventy* (pp. 3–19). London: Zed books Ltd.

Mapadimeng, M. S. (2009). Indigenous African cultures and relevance to socio-economic development in the contemporary era. Paper presented at the 2nd International Conference on African Culture and Development, Accra, Ghana.

Meredith, M. (2005). *The State of Africa: A History of Fifty Years of Independence*. London: The Free Press.

Migdal, S. J. (2001). *State in Society. Studying How States and Societies Transform and Constitute One Another*. Cambridge: Cambridge University Press.

Mihevc, J. (1995). *The Market Tells Us So – World Bank and Economic Fundamentalism in Africa, Penang and Accra: Third World Network*. London and New York: Zed Books.

Mills, G. (2010). Why Is Africa Poor? Development Policy Briefing Paper. Washington, DC: Cato Institute.

Odunuga, S. (2004). Preface. In B. Onimode et al. (Eds.), *African Development and Governance Strategies in the 21st Century, Looking Back to Move Forward: Essays in honour of Adebayo Adedeji at Seventy* (pp. xv–xviii). London: Zed books Ltd.

Olamosu, B., & Wynne, A. (2015). Africa rising? The economic history of sub-Saharan Africa. (2015, April 12). Retrieved from http://isj.org.uk/africa-rising/#fo otnote-263-11

Onimode, B. (1989). *A Political Economy of the African Crisis*. London: Zed Books.

Onimode, B. (2004). Mobilisation for the implementation of alternative development paradigms in the 21st Century Africa. In B. Onimode et al. (Eds.), *African Development and Governance Strategies in the 21st Century, Looking Back to Move Forward: Essays in honour of Adebayo Adedeji at Seventy* (pp. 20–29). London: Zed books Ltd.

Prichett, L., Sen, K., & Werker, E. (2018). 'Searching for a "Recipe" for Episodic Development.' In L. Prichett, K. Sen, & E. Werker (Eds), *Deals and Development: The Political Dynamics of Growth Episodes* (1st ed., pp. 1–38). New York: Oxford University Press. https://doi.org/10.1093/oso/9780198801641.003.0011.

Randall, V. (2008). Analytical approaches to the study of politics in the developing world. In P. Burnell & V. Randall (Eds.), *Politics in the Developing World* (2nd ed., pp. 15–34). New York: Oxford University Press.

Rapley, J. (2007). *Understanding Development: Theory and Practice in the Third World* (3rd ed.). Boulder, CO: Lynne Rienner Publishers.

Rist, G. (1997). *The History of Development: From Western Origin to Global Faith.* London: Zed Books.

Roxburgh, C., Dorr, N., Leke, A., Tazi-Riffi, A., van Wamelem, A., Lund, S., Chironga, M., Alatovik, T., Atkins, C., Terfous, N., & Zeino-Mahmalat, T. (2010). *Lions on the Move: The Progress and Potential of African Economies.* Washington, DC: The McKinsey Global Institute.

Sach, D. J. (2008). *Common Wealth, Economic for Crowded Planet.* New York: The Penguin Press.

Scott, T. (1998). Africa and the end of the cold war: an overview of impacts. In: Akinrinade, S. & Amadu, S. (Eds.), *Africa in the Post Cold War International System*, pp. 3–27. London: Bookcraft (Bath) Ltd.

Sen, A. (1999). *Development as Freedom.* Oxford: Oxford University Press.

Sowell, T. (2017). *Wealth, Poverty and Politics* (Revised and Enlarged ed.). Benin-city Beulahland Publication with the permission of Perseus Publishing Group USA.

Sunmonu, H. A. (2004). Implementation of Africa's development paradigms: solution to Africa's socio-economic problems. In B. Onimode et al (Eds.), *African Development and Governance Strategies in the 21st Century, Looking Back to Move Forward: Essays in honour of Adebayo Adedeji at Seventy* (pp. 63–71). London: Zed books Ltd.

Todaro, P. M., & Smith, C. S. (2011). *Economic Development* (11th ed.). Edinburgh Gate: Pearson Education Limited.

Tomori, O. S., & Tomori, O. W. (2004). Revisiting the African alternative framework to structural adjustment programmes for socio-economic recovery and transformation (AAF-SAP) in contemporary Nigeria. In B. Onimode et al (Eds.), *African Development and Governance Strategies in the 21st Century, Looking Back to Move Forward: Essays in honour of Adebayo Adedeji at Seventy* (pp. 30–48), London: Zed books Ltd.

Ziai, A. (2019). Towards a more critical theory of 'development' in the 21st century. *Development and Change*, 50, 458–467. doi: 10.1111/dech.12484.

Chapter 8

Challenging the "Colonial Development Model"

The Quest for an Indigenous African Model in Ngugi wa Thiong'o's Petals of Blood

Solomon Awuzie

African literature has been able to establish the fact that capitalism and all its methods, which are deployed to undermine the values of the African society, are the core of the "colonial development model." The literature has also depicted that the imposition of the capitalist system on the African society institutionalized not just exploitation and discrimination; it is used as a tool to promote and instigate crime in the society. Using Ngugi wa Thiong'o's *Petals of Blood* the "colonial development model" is engaged and in its place, the development model that is indigenous to Africa is stressed. The literature maintains that as long as Africa continues to patronize capitalism, African countries would continue to be imitative of the colonial societies. Consequently, African societies would continue to lag and would continue to be underdeveloped.

INTRODUCTION

African literature has been used to interrogate the suitability of the "colonial development model" to the African system and to advance the claim that Africa has a development model that is home to it before the coming of the Europeans to Africa. Being a part of the postcolonial hegemonic force, the literature has not only been used to engage the postcolonial narratives of African subhumanism but has been used to advance the claim that the "colonial development model" encourages and promotes the discrimination of the postcolonial "others" for the benefit of the center. This historical literary engagement that has continuously projected the African development model above the colonial model has come to be described as part of "Africa Writes Back." "Africa Writes Back" pertains to all forms of postcolonial writings, which include essays, books, interviews, biographies, autobiographies, and literature, which are used to challenge the postcolonial subjugation of Africa to prove Africa was a developing economy before the advent of the European colonialists to Africa. As a postcolonial disposition, "Africa Writes Back" continuously reminds us of the Berlin Conference of 1884, which led to the European occupation of Africa, as well as the aftermath of European colonialization of Africa (Franz Fanon [1967], Walter Rodney [1973] and Edward Said [1978]). The conference which was meant to regulate European colonialization and trade in Africa led to what was described as "the scramble for Africa" or what is now being described in postcolonial studies as "the Rape of Africa." "The scramble for Africa" has to do with the partitioning of African territory by European powers and represents a period when "European powers staked claims to virtually the entire [African] continent" even when their "knowledge of the vast African hinterland was slight" (Meredith, 2005, p.1). With this partitioning, the European powers transited from exercising military influence and economic dominance to the direct rule which brings about colonial imperialism. At this point, the 10% of Africa that was under formal European control in 1870, a period before the Berlin Conference, increased at 90% by 1914 when the partitioning was completed.

The contemporary postcolonial situation began in 1947 through 1960 when many African countries started experiencing self-rule. The period reflects the formal adoption of the European development model together with all its disadvantages and the formal abandoning of the African development model. Through the supports of African literary texts such as Chinua Achebe's *Things Fall Apart*, Mongo Beti's *Mission to Kala*, and Ngugi wa Thiong'o's *Petals of Blood*, the capitalist system, adopted after independence in most African societies, is represented as one of the core systems of the "colonial development model" while African societies are reminded that socialism and communalism are the cores of the African development model. In comparison between the two systems, the literature texts show that capitalism promotes exploitations, prejudices, and all forms of unequal treatment of African people (Ashcroft, 1995, p.2). Capitalism as one of the core systems of the colonial model has continuously subjected Africa to neocolonial domination: a problem which even political independence has not been able to solve. In the view of Ashcroft (1995), rather than revert to and develop their own indigenous model as other postcolonies such as China, India, and Brazil have done, African societies have failed to put theories to practice and have continued to adopt the colonial model of development; hence they have remained perpetually positioned for underdevelopment.

Since the continuous adoption of the colonial development model by most African societies goes to testify, as Ashcroft (1995, p.2) has noted, "to the fact that post-colonialism is a continuing process of resistance and reconstruction," this chapter aims to stress the evil of the continuous patronage of "colonial development model" by the African societies. It questions African societies' continued adoption of the model at a time when the model has practically failed the continent and when many other postcolonies have reverted to the models that are indigenous to their societies. The chapter describes the structure of the African society and the model that is indigenous to it before the advent of the Europeans, using Ngugi wa Thiong'o's *Petals of Blood* (1977). It analyses Ngugi wa Thiong'o's *Petals of Blood* by exposing how he has engaged the postcolonial African problem by linking it to Africa's patronage of the European development model. One of the reasons for the adoption of the novel is, as Nicholls (2014, p.72) explains, it represents the anti-imperial African history in two models. While the first model pertains to Africa as well as the entire Black world's historical struggle, the second model concerns Kenyan national struggle. Our focus in the chapter is on how Ngugi captures the anti-imperial African history. This is reflected through the use of the story that shows how the African society was betrayed not only by former colonial masters but by the African political class (Banik, 2016, p.72). The chapter maintains that Ngugi achieves this by using characters who have been "torn apart between tumultuous past and uncertain future" to reflect on the general Africans disillusionment about the turbulent postindependent African society (Chakraborty, 2016, p.275). Okereke (2017) maintains that this has always been seen in Ngugi's novels so much so that it is also reflected in his latest novel *Wizard of the Crow*. Ngugi uses his fiction as a tool to teach Africans the meaning of colonialism and what it did to the image of the African person. The essence of this engagement is to let Africans know that African colonial experience "is a nihilism so total, so pervasive and so defeatist" (Okonkwo, 2003, p.78). It argues that as long as Africa continues to patronize the colonial model, African countries would continue to be imitative of colonial societies. Consequently, African societies would continue to lag and would continue to be underdeveloped.

THE "COLONIAL DEVELOPMENT MODEL" DISCOURSE AND THE GLORY OF THE AFRICAN PAST

Scholars of African literature have investigated the reason Europeans suddenly became interested in the African continent so much so that they decided to colonize it, and this has led to the identification of several motives which include economic, religious, social, philanthropic, and political reasons.

These motives, however, had both Afrocentric and Eurocentric perspectives. African writers, such as Chinua Achebe, Ngugi wa Thiong'o, Camara Laye, Mongo Beti, Kofi Awoonor, and Hopkins among others, who were proponents of the Afrocentric view, have shown that a study of African history reveals that the precolonial African society was going through substantive, progressive, peaceful, and steady change and development before the advent of Europeans on African soil. In his book entitled *The Breast of the Earth*, Kofi Awoonor (2005, p.7) reiterates that a look at Africa's colonial history shows some evidence of the continuous progress of the societies. In the book, Awoonor describes Africa's cultural progress in terms of its ability to absorb iron, gold, and cotton into African material culture and its ability to erect the centralist organizations around African religious ideas. He also explains the establishment of religion, worship, ritual, and art that were uniquely African in pure cultural sense. Hence it can be said that European colonialists actually arrived into an African society that was rich in every aspect and that their coming marked a very important turning point in the history and culture of Africa. Hopkins (1973, p.10), another Afrocentric scholar, summarizes precolonial Africa before the advent of the Europeans by describing it as the golden age:

> Generation of Africans enjoyed congenial lives in well-integrated, smoothly functioning societies. The means of livelihood came easily to hand for foodstuffs grew wild and in abundance and this good fortune enabled the inhabitants to concentrate on leisure pursuits. [. . .] Europeans [on their advent] disrupted a state of harmony: cohesion based on shared values was replaced by artificial unity backed by force and ruthless exploitation reduced the indigenous peoples to a degree of poverty which they had not known in the past.

Unlike these Afrocentric views, the Eurocentric views of Africa present the picture of African primitivism and savage living and European advent as a mission to savage Africa and to save it from drifting into "uncivility" and "undevelopment" (Osuafore, 2003, p.2). Diala (2002, p. 297) reiterates this view as he posits that in many of their literatures, which picture African subhumanism, Eurocentric scholars justified the European colonial mission in Africa. This is evident in Alfred Marshall's claim that Africans lived under the control of their impulse and the domination of their custom. And that Africans scarcely ever stroke out new lives for themselves and never forecasted the distant future. They were disturbed despite their attachment to their custom and were "governed by the fancy of the moment" and were unable and incapable to keep a long steady work. He argues further that Africans avoided laborious and tedious tasks as far as possible (Osuafore, 2003, p.2). Diala (2002, p. 297) notes that by encroaching into African lands because of their economic necessity as well as their intellectual curiosity, European imperialist defined their relationship with Africa in evolutionary terms. He posits further that the racist stereotypes embodied in European explanation for their encroachment into African space are to justify their dispossession of the African people of anything that they feel is good enough for Europeans, and for colonial subjugation and enslavement. The reason for the ideological advancement of these negative images was to push African "beyond the pale of humanism's grace" and "to render him inaccessible to the ethical prescriptions of humanism" (Diala, 2002, p.301). It was also a systematic and concerted attempt at dehumanizing the African people (Awuzie, 2018). And the ultimate aim of these images in their pieces of literature is to transform into reality the myth which they knew was exclusively their own.

Osuafore (2003, p. 2) regrets that it would have been possible to envisage that African- European contact would have resulted in Africa's growth, change, and development but "on the contrary, the three stages of contact—the slave trade, colonialism and neo-colonialism or neo-independence—has left an abysmal legacy for Africa." The legacy left for Africa questions the views of the Eurocentric argument since it positioned Europe to become richer and Africa to become poorer. This was the case because the labor of African slaves in European colonies, as well as African raw materials, helped in the industrialization of European societies to the detriment of African societies. As if that was not enough, in the postindependent period, Europe devised another mechanism that not only helped them to further plunder the continent but also integrated Africa into the periphery of the world economy of which the former colonial powers are the center (Zabadi, 1992, p.7).

MAPPING AFRICAN INDIGENOUS DEVELOPMENT MODEL

In reaction to the need for Africa to look inward into the effect of colonialism on its people, African leaders, scholars, and writers such as Nkrumah, Nyerere, Achebe, and Ngugi tried to promote the development model that is indigenous to Africa through their different writings. The ideological stance that informs this decision is in connection with the harm the "colonial development model" has done and is still doing to African societies. More than as it is evident in the works of Nkrumah, Nyerere, and Achebe, the African development model is advocated for in Ngugi wa Thiong'o's *Petals of Blood*. Collectively, these African leaders and writers have insisted on the total rejection of colonialism as well as its systems and ideologies. Hence since capitalism remains the core of the European development model, they have not only totally condemned it, they have rejected it because as a model it does not support Africa's development.

In its place, they advocate for socialism vis-à-vis communalism. It is the belief that socialism or a communal system has the potential of making Africa develop quickly despite its many years of exploitation by Western capitalists. The clamor for the socialist system is evident in Nkrumah's (1958) argument:

> Ghana inherited a colonial economy [. . .] We cannot rest until we have demolished this miserable structure and raised in its place an edifice of economic stability, thus creating for ourselves a veritable paradise of abundance and satisfaction [. . .] we must go forward with our preparation for planned economic growth to supplant the poverty, ignorance, disease and illiteracy left in the wake by discredited colonialism and decaying imperialism [. . .] socialism is the only pattern that can within the shortest possible time bring the good life to the people.

He believes that the African societies traditionally lean toward communalism as well as the socialist system. The communal system can naturally be found in African communal ownership of land, the egalitarian character of village life, collective decision making, and extensive networks of social obligation (Meredith, 2005, p.145). It is for this reason these African writers became leading proponents of socialism and communalism. There is no more need of being converted to socialism because it is already rooted in the African past. In an essay on African socialism that he wrote in 1962, Nyerere gave a socialist account of the precolonial African society. According to him, in precolonial African society, everybody was a worker.

Not only was the capitalist or the landed exploiter not known, but capitalist exploitation was impossible. Loitering was an unthinkable disgrace. The advent of colonialism had changed all this. [The precolonial Africa never had any Africans[aspired to the possession of personal wealth to dominate any of his fellows. But then came the foreign, wealthy, and powerful capitalists who implanted the evil seed in Africans and taught them the evil of exploitation. [There is the need for Africans to re-educate themselves to] regain their former attitude of mind [and] their sense of community.

He maintains that to do this, Africans must reject the capitalist attitude that colonialism brought to Africa, as well as all capitalist methods. However, this ideological stance did not continue for too long as Africa witnessed a "dark revolutionary period" which not only desecrated the plans to revert Africa to its indigenous development model as well as discontinue Africa's patronage of capitalism and all its methods. This was as a result of the fact that some of Africa's educated elites who were clamoring for this ideological change were either killed or forced to go on exile. The fates of the African societies were once again left in the hands of the colonial stooges and the hands of some African literature writers.

Of course, African colonial stooges were not helpful in the battle to restore the lost values of the African continent and that made African literature the lone voice in the struggle. Hence, African literature is used to continuously engage the ruination of the African societies by the colonial systems. As African literature effectuates this role of being the social gadfly, it also runs the risk of being accused of being mere anthropological documentation of the African societies (Onuekwusi, 2001, p.29). The sociological perspective of the literature is implicated in Chinua Achebe's idea of African literary output as a great festival of Africa's cultural harvest to which African writers are expected to bring their literature to the global arena. He maintains that African literature must speak of a particular African space, evolve out of the necessities of its current and past history, and be the aspiration and destiny of its people. This he describes as the socio function of the African writer. When the writer ceases to function along this line, he has ceased to function as the conscience of his society and his relevance to that society comes seriously into question. In order to function as the conscious of the people, the African writer must call into use all resources available to him, not only to sensitize his community but also to proffer to them ways by which they can make their overall conditions better (Ezejideaku, 2001, p.48). This is what gave the writer the image of not just the communal drum but a town crier with an iron bell, "shouting himself hoarse from the mountain top" (Ezejideaku, 2001, p.51). By implication, the message of the African writer is replicated as being urgent and crucial.

THE AFRICAN DEVELOPMENT MODEL VERSUS THE COLONIAL DEVELOPMENT MODEL IN NGUGI'S *PETALS OF BLOOD* (1977)

Apart from engaging the postcolonial African problems such as the ill-gotten wealth of the African middle class and the worsening plight of the unemployed peasants of the postcolonial African society, Ngugi wa Thiong'o's *Petals of Blood* (1977) points to the need to guard against the development of capitalism which would replace "African indigenous development model." The novel represents a period in the postindependent African society when Africa is seeking to reconcile the force of modernism and also depicts the failure of the "colonial development model" to address present African sociopolitical situation. The novel made a significant comparison between the two development models by beaming its light at the sociopolitical development in Ilmorog, a community which grows from a small traditional village into a modern capitalist complex. While the small traditional village details the African setting where the African communalism is operational—as it allows everyone the opportunity to contribute his or her own quota to the development of the community—the setting of the modern capitalist complex reflects the chaotic African experience under the capitalist system. Writing about similar classification in the novel, Griffiths (2000, p. 160) argues that this did not happen in Ilmorog alone; it can also be seen in Kamiriithu village. Even though the novel is also set in Kamiriithu village, Ilmorog is prominently focused on, in that it is given a broader political context than other villages in the novel. Ilmorog is reflected upon as the microcosm of the entire African society in the novel. Its experiences are represented as the paradigm of what has happened to several African communities. Using one of Ilmorog's citizens, Karega, the trade union leader, Ngugi states one of the overall messages of the novel: "We must not preserve our past as a museum; rather, we must study it critically, without illusions, and see what lessons we can draw from it" (p.39). By this character's assertion, Ngugi reveals that even though the totality of the African past is not without blemish, the African past should be seen as the store house of all the good things that can be tapped for the development and betterment of the present African societies. Palmer (1979, p. 289) refers to this as "regeneration." This concept of "regeneration" is fully demonstrated in the novel through the use of "the symbolic cluster that relates to flowers and other forms of vegetation." It is expected that after plucking a flower leaf from its stem, it would regenerate by replacing the leaf with a more tender and beautiful one. Karega explains it further in another part of the novel, during one of the times we may have represented him as Ngugi's spokesperson for the African historical awareness, thus: "To understand the present, you understand the past. To know who you are, you must know where you come from." This assertion also finds its analogy in present-day Africa. This is the reason the novel is seen to have the characteristics of an epic. Its epic characteristics is evident in the stretch of the action of the novel over a sufficient span of years, evoking Kenya of the 1940s, the liberation struggle of the 1950s–1960s, and the contemporary Kenyan situation.

Before the imposition of the capitalist system on Ilmorog, Ngugi represents it in the novel as a purely traditional society that is untouched by Western values. It is portrayed as a community where the dignified, courageous peasants reckoned their wealth in land, cows, and goats. Not only is Ilmorog's past a glorified one, but the novel also celebrates the life of its men and women as well as the valor of its warriors. The stories of Ilmorog's past reflect the stories of when Africa was in full control of its own destiny. It is a typical example of the story of "heroic resistance." These are the kind of stories Karega got into trouble trying to impart to his students. These stories are legendary passed from generation to generation. Nykinyua, a character occasionally referred to as the "Mother of men" is used most of the time to tell the stories. Ngugi used her as the living embodiment of the values of this society and the character through which the traditional songs of the initiation ritual is performed. As she performs these traditional rites, she invests them with dignity which exposes the rich tradition and undefiled past of Ilmorog. The difference between authentic and literary myth in the novel is made plain by Ngugi. The mythic figures such as legendary and heroic, which have their sources in the past, have their stories told alongside contemporary heroes whose songs are composed following the resistance efforts of actual historical figures in the immediate, colonial past (Killam, 1986, p. 157). Ngugi also depicts the legend and oral lore of the first heroes of the community and progresses into showing the gradual change from a largely nomadic to an agrarian civilization—presenting their prosperity, contentment, and sense of community. In his use of myth and legend, Ngugi conveys impressions of precolonial Ilmorog where barter was seen in terms of equivalent exchange of the wealth of the land and where the folk heroes through their valor might justly be described as epic heroes. He also presents a precolonial society where the peasants are represented as being at one with their hero-leaders in the traditional Ilmorog. All these can also be evident in Nykinyua's assertion:

> It had had its days of glory: thriving villages with a huge population of sturdy peasants who had tamed nature's forest and, breaking the soil between their fingers, had brought forth every type of crop to nourish the sons and daughters of men. (p.120)

Using the characters who tell stories that reflect the past African history, Ngugi is primarily concerned with restoring Africa to its history to enable it to find its identity in this essentially colonial situation as well as to enable it to discover a source of pride in African people's past accomplishments. The efforts of these characters are made to exemplify the courage and determinations of the African nationalists. Cook and Okenimkpe (1983, p.158) explain that the tales and the songs in Ngugi's novel provide the Kenyan characters with vital links with their ancestors. They maintain that Ngugi's aim is to arouse in his Kenyan readers, especially the peasantry, a sense of history that would unify and dignify them as they find both meaning and sustenance from contemplating the past. They used Karega as a typical example of a character on whom the stories have some significant effect. According to them, "Karega discovers pride and hope in Nyakinu Inyua" remembrance of the past, while Abdulla's stories of the Mau Mau make Karega and his comrades "aware of a new relationship to the ground on which they trod."

With the imposition of the capitalist system, or what is referred to as the "colonial development model," on the society together with the inhumane activities that came with it, Ilmorog experiences the first blow to its pride. Consequently, capitalism becomes the disruption that heralded the beginning of Ilmorog's decline. The fate of Ilmorog at this time depicts, to use the words of Nkosi (1981, p.57), that "the once-thriving community of Ilmorog has fallen on evil times" and starts to appear "a desolate, unprogressive place from which the young are only too happy to get away." This is evident in the novel as we discovered that after the imposition of capitalism on Ilmorog, young people who come to Ilmorog to stay were spiritually maimed in one way or the other. This is also represented in the symbol of the petal flower. The flower, which "belongs to a plant that grows wild in the plains," has been infested by worms, which are another agents of corruption in the novel. The flower symbol "petals of blood" is used to represent Ilmorog as a victim of evil. It is portrayed as a community whose innocence is destroyed by the agents of the "colonial development model." "Blood" that is associated with the petals suggests suffering while the flower is a symbol of Ilmorog—a potentially beautiful, healthy, and productive society. But this society has its potential unrealized and consequently got itself destroyed by the agents of corruption. Though through the narration of the flower symbol, Ngugi introduces the symbolism upon which the title of the novel is based, it is in his later narration that he further depicts the motif of the novel as contained in the analysis of the flower:

> He stood looking at the flower he had plucked and then threw the lifeless petals away. Yet another boy cried: "I have found another. Petals of blood—I mean red ... It has no stigma or pistils ... nothing inside." He went to him and the others surrounded him: "No, you are wrong," he said, taking the flower. "This colour is not even red ... it does not have the fullness of colour of the other one. This one is yellowish red. Now you say it has nothing inside. Look at the stem from which you got it. You see anything?" "Yes," cried the boys. "There is a worm—a green worm with several hands or legs. Right. This is a worm-eaten flower ... It cannot bear fruit. That's why we must always kill worms ... A flower can also become this colour if it's prevented from reaching the light." (pp. 21–22)

Ngugi portrays "the colonial development model" as lacking the values which gave the traditional African culture its admirable stance. One of the things we saw in the novel is that the modern peasants have no heroes. Their leaders are their exploiters, the collaborators, and sometimes the dupes of the capitalist exploiters. The peasants are either unconscious or unaware of alternatives to their way of life, but they recognize the need to achieve an alternative to their present circumstances. The idealist peasants, who are capable of courageous action "symbolized by the drought-ridden march to Nairobi" (Killam, 1986, p.158) are brought to disillusion and despair through betrayal. As one of the agents of the "colonial development model," the aim and content of colonial education in modern African society is seriously checked and questioned. In the novel, education is seen by the people as the hope for the future, although those who plunge their fates into it usually end in disillusionment since they would certainly have to come face-to-face with the political reality. In the novel, Ngugi presents colonial education as an oppressive, irrelevant, and racial system geared toward perpetuating White domination and imprinting into the pupils' mind, a respect for British institutions and attitudes. While arguing along similar lines, Palmer (1979, p.303) notes that "Cambridge Fraudsham, the eccentric headmaster who terrorizes his pupils" in the novel and who eventually provoked students to riots, is the embodiment of this educational system.

The novel also details the activities of some Africans clamoring for Africa's adoption of their indigenous model of development having experienced the bad side of the colonial model of development. Among the characters upon which this is advanced in the novel are Karega and his revolutionary contemporaries, who organized strikes first against the White Fraudsham and then against the Black Chui, while demanding the inclusion of African content to the education students are given. They demand that the students be taught African literature and African history and to know themselves and their environment better. Karega and his revolutionary contemporaries object to the colonial education system which teaches about white snow and "spring flowers fluttering by icy lakes," and insist in African headmaster and African teachers who understand the educational needs of the African students:

> We wanted to be taught African literature, African history, for we wanted to know ourselves better. Why should ourselves be reflected in white snows, spring flowers fluttering by on icy lakes? Then somebody shouted: we want an African headmaster and African teachers. We denounced the prefect system, the knightly order of masters and menials. That did it. And imagine. The newspapers took up this aspect of the crisis and denounced us. Since when did students, a mob, tell their teachers what they ought to teach? If the students were so clever and already knew what they ought to be taught and who was fit to teach them, why had they bothered to enroll in the school? And a school with such a record! A headmaster whom even the very best school in England, like Eton, would have been proud to have in their midst? They counted the money spent on a student and compared it with the income of the poor peasants. (p. 170)

When Cambridge Fraudsham is eventually succeeded by Chui, an African who in his student days has been victimized by the oppressive imperialist system and who ought to have effected changes, he turns out to be more British in his attitude and policies than Fraudsham himself. This led to disillusionment on the part of the characters. It was the lawyer who first showed his disillusionment in the novel. Hence he asked Karega: "I do not understand—so different from our time—I mean the demands. Was it because of independence?" (p.173). And surprisingly, Karega says he himself does not know.

In Ngugi's *Petals of Blood*, we find a similar situation where after independence majority of the peasants in Ilmorog became disillusioned. Ngugi used a number of characters to demonstrate this and among these characters are Karega and Wanja. Ngugi also plays out Karega's disillusionment in the novel, where having returned to Ilmorog, when he was expelled from school for getting himself involved in a riot where the students clamor for a change in the administrative system and the things they were taught, he was worried and wondering if the independence of most African societies were only a mere child's play. Wanja's disillusionment in the novel is also stressed, when having turned a prostitute, she made love with Munira, and then suddenly turned and asked him to pay because, according to her, "there is no free thing in new Kenya." To Cook and Okenimkpe (1983), Wanja's portrayal in this part of the novel represents what modern capitalist complex can do to a hard-working female in modern African societies. Having been forced to do the unusual to survive in that jungle of African society and even after her regeneration in Ilmorog, she discovered a new sense of purpose in helping to engineer that society's revival and by so doing she is thrown back into high-class prostitution through the intrigues of the new Black imperialists.

Religion is also seriously challenged in the novel. The novel reveals that bad people hide under the cloak of religion to perpetrate their evils. The Christian religion is presented here as oppressive, unsympathetic, and hypocritical. The portrayal of Munira's father in the novel is central to this exposure to religion. Munira's father, who is a patriarch of the church as well as a pillar of the state, is presented as a capitalist and a Black slaver. In his younger days, he turned his back on his traditional society and joined the White man while in his later years, he supported the White oppressors against the Mau Mau freedom fighters, and now he participates wholeheartedly in the exploitation of the masses. His religion is a life-denying force that has stifled the life of Munira's wife and children. He is an irreligious and ungodly man who cannot see that his Christianity should not include the taking of an oath geared toward the consolidation of tribalism. What astonishes one is not just the man's hypocrisy but his utter insensitivity. The behaviors of the Reverends Kamau and Jerrod also reinforce this impression of religious bankruptcy in modern Africa. The latter would rather read a sermon to starving itinerants about the need to give the colonial industry that succor it wants than help a sick boy receive medical attention.

The church is represented as a great proprietor and its priests presented as individuals who are not different from the other modern Black capitalists and their imperialist counterparts. The novel *Petals of Blood* can be summarized, using Griffith's (2000, p.160) claim that the theme of corruption and betrayal is central in the novel and is linked with the problem of postindependent African society. The novel expresses the belief that the future is determined by the past and is concerned with the betrayal of the ideals of the freedom movement.

CONCLUSION

This chapter has been able to reveal that colonial-imposed development model such as capitalism and its related methods have contributed to Africa's underdevelopment. By the continuous patronage of the capitalist system in most African societies, the vindictive exploitation and discrimination that it exposes the society to would become endemic and would push African societies out of the debacle of human society. In its place, different scholars' claims, as well as examples from Ngugi wa Thiong'o's novel *Petals of Blood*, have been deployed as a mechanism to detail the development model that is indigenous to the African society. It reflects on the precolonial African society as having a peaceful, steady, and progressive development model that would work properly for Africa. This indigenous African development model was only destroyed by the colonial imposition of capitalism on the society as well as Africa's continuous patronage of the system. This continuous patronage of the capitalist system however reveals the postcolonial resistance of the adoption of the African indigenous model by the powers that be and the determination of the center to continuously subjugate the periphery on the African space. The central message in the chapter is that as long as Africa continues to patronize capitalism, African countries would continue to be imitative of the colonial societies. Consequently, African society would continue to lag and would continue to be underdeveloped.

REFERENCES

Ashcroft, B., Griffiths, G. and Tiffin, H. (1995). *The Post-colonial Studies Reader*. London: Routledge.

Awoonor, K. (2005). *The Breast of the Earth*. New York: Nok Publishers International.

Awuzie, S. (2018). Narratives and the African Experience: The Dialectical Consideration of the Writings of First and Second Generation African Writers in Africa. *Africology: The Journal of Pan African Studies* 11(5):1–124.

Banik, S. (2016). Ngugi wa Thiong'o's notion of historical change in petals of blood IOSR. *Journal of Humanities and Social Science* 21(1):72–74.

Chakraborty, A. (2016). The polemics of class, nationalism and ethnicity in Ngugi wa Thiong'o's petals of blood. *Africology: The Journal of Pan African Studies* 9(10):275–293.

Cook, D. and Okenimkpe, M. (1983). *Ngugi wa Thiong'o: An Exploration of His Writings.* London: Heinemann Educational Books.

Diala, I. (2002). Mistah Kutz: He dead' English and the African writer. In P.A. Anyanwu and E. Otagburuagu (Eds.), *Concepts and Issues in Language Studies.* Owerri Spring Field.

Ezejideaku, E. (2001). Protest and propaganda in Igbo written poetry. *Journal of Humanities.* 5(2): 54–57.

Fanon, F. (1967). *The Wretched of the Earth.* Harmond-Sworth: Peginin.

Griffiths, G. (2000). *African Literature in English: East and West.* London: Pearson Education Limited.

Hopkins, A.G. (1973). *An Economic History of West Africa.* London: Longman.

Killam, G. (1986).Themes and treatments in Ngugi wa Thiong'o's Novels. In Samuel Omo Asein and Albert Olu Ashaolu (Eds.), *Modern Essay on African Literature Vol. 1.* Ibadan: Ibadan University Press, pp. 198–206.

Meredith, M. (2005). Introduction. In Meredi, M (Ed.) *The State of Africa: A History of Fifty Years of Independence.* Britain: Simon & Schuster. (1–3)

Ngugi, T. (1977*). Petals of Blood.* Oxford: Heinemann.

Nicholls, B.L. (2014). History, intertextuality and gender in Ngugi wa Thiong'o's petals of blood. *Moving Worlds: A Journal of Transcultural Writings* 14(1): 71–76.

Nkosi, L. (1981). *Tasks and Masks: Themes and Styles of African Literature.* London: Longman.

Nkrumah, K. (1959). *Ghana: The Autobiography of Kwame Nkrumah.* Edinburgh: Thomas Nelson.

Nyerere, J. (1968). *Freedom and Socialism: A Selection from Writings and Speeches, 1965-67.* Oxford University Press.

Okereke, E.C. (2017). The maggot within: The state security apparatus in Ngugi's wizard of the crow. *Tydskrif vir Letterkunde* 54(1): 211–227.

Okonkwo, C. (2002). The African writer as a teacher. *Journal of Educational Studies* I: 75–84.

Onuekwusi, J.A. (2001). New directions in the Nigerian novel: Munonye's a kind of food and Onyekwere's the keepers. *Journal of the Humanities* 1(4): 23–37

Osuaforr, C. (2003). *The Colonial Experience and African literature.* Owerri: Amvaly Press.

Palmer, E. (1979). *The Growth of the African Novel.* London: Heinemann.

Rodney, W. (1973). *How Europe Underdeveloped Africa.* Dar-Es-Salaam: Tanzanian Publishing House.

Said, E. (1979). *Orientalism.* New York: Vintage.

Chapter 9

Nationalism and the Decolonization of the Ideology of Development in Africa

Matthew D. Ogali

The imperative of development in Third World states has become so emotionally consuming and frustrating that concerns about its real meaning, viable models, and appropriate strategies call for urgent intellectual reevaluation. In particular, the complexity of the relationship between the nationalist spirit, the decolonization process, and the development agenda, in different contexts, needs to be properly articulated. In Europe these three elements blended effectively to produce the modern liberal democratic state through the Thirty Years War and various bourgeois revolutions. However, the nationalism-inspired decolonization struggle has failed to generate development in Africa, attributable to the fractured and factionalized approach adopted, the distraction of divisive identities in state policy formulation, and the absence of a determined transformative decolonization policy to create a new society. How the decolonization of the ideology of development could be operationalized to achieve an indigenized socioeconomic transformation in Africa is the crux of this chapter. Undeniable therefore is the urgency of a return to the fundamental basis for an endogenous model of development for Africa, an issue addressed by this chapter with the adoption of Franz Fanon's revolutionary decolonization as theoretical framework with textual and historical analysis of secondary data and qualitative rational inference as methodology.

INTRODUCTION

Locating and interrogating the nexus between nationalism and development within the historical dynamic of the relationship between the advanced countries and the postcolonial states has obviously become very expedient.

Its intricacies are embedded in the lopsidedness of the exchange relations between the two categories of states, relationship that is constantly fed with false hope, deceit, manipulation, arm-twisting tactics, and even military threats for its sustenance. The futility of this linkage is underscored by the objective developmental disaster in many contemporary postcolonial African states after several decades of interaction (Frank, 1967; Chinweizu, 1978; Onimode, 1983; Rodney, 2005). Colonialism could be characterized as the illegitimate child of a rampaging, expansionist, and unfaithful begetter in the mold of capitalism, made to continually suffer ill-treatment, rejection, degradation, and indignity, having been abandoned in a rented, dilapidated, and inhabitable domicile, and ultimately struck down with an incurable paralysis, lunacy, and stunted growth.

Capitalism, having transmuted into imperialism (Brewer, 2001), has created a world sharply divided into extremities in the form of bourgeois and proletarian states (Ake, 1978) operating within the same global milieu with livelihoods affecting and reshaping each other in complex and often times inexplicable dimensions. Sadly, all the medical prescriptions offered by an ill-tempered physician, hired for a mysterious purpose, have only succeeded in sapping the patient's residual energy in measured spasms but ensuring that he remains in that condition, neither dead nor alive. Accordingly, the colonized victim is systematically disempowered from any productive capacity but is rather being provided with toxic food, tattered clothing, and lots of intoxicating wine. Consequently, this decolonized heir, having been led out of captivity with an apron string, still remains in perpetual stupor, staggering under the control of his numerous profit-seeking predators.

Other dichotomies that follow closely relate to the products of that same imperialistic connection that enigmatically and conspicuously define the contemporary world such as development and underdevelopment, internationalism and nationalism, globalization and localization, neocolonialism and decolonization, affluence and poverty, freedom and captivity, security and terrorism/insurgency, domination and peripheralization, all in perpetual conflict several decades after national liberation. Arguably, the greatest enigma that confronts the contemporary world is the well-packaged delusion called development, a concept the definition of which is infested with quarrels and dissonance.

Ironically, the same forces that preach the gospel of development with so much passion also consistently throw spanners into the works and clog down its realization in the Third World. Development is a major component of the Western-modeled modernization panache. The clear message is that the Third World must be made to remain in the wood. Can slaves dine with their masters on the same table? But if not, why shouldn't slaves cast away their burdens and shackles and at least create a befitting table for their own elevated status through an indigenous system like *Ujamaa*? Global politics is full of ironies, one of which is the perpetually enslaving disposition of nations that had earlier taken up arms in a bloody struggle for their freedom, equality, and justice. Now on the saddle the drumbeat of freedom delivers a whole new litany of songs with sweet-sounding but vacuous titles such as comparative advantage, development partnership, stabilization package, globalization, international credit and cooperation, and so on. The north beats the drum and the south keeps dancing and smiling.

Permanent revolutionary decolonization to ensure sustainability of an indigenously evolved development program, its dispersal across Africa, and diffusion into the rural peasant communities, should have been orchestrated as a driving and guiding principle for a new postcolonial Africa. But the colonized simply seized the throne of his master and swiveled around in comfortable self-adulation. His roots of misery are forgotten and his kith and kin only gather under his table expecting dispiritedly to feed from the crumbs. These issues are discussed below, but for now the chapter addresses some methodological issues.

METHODOLOGY

This is essentially a theoretical study with data collection principally from secondary sources such as books, journals, newspapers, documentaries, and internet sources, and data presentation mainly logical reappraisal and analysis of historical and contemporary facts and records. The method of analysis was qualitative, normative, analytical, conceptual, and historical. Generally, the chapter adopted a methodology of textual extraction and analysis, including periodization and content analysis of data that is "thorough examination of documents in order to generate information for inference based on the canons of scientific research" (Biereenu-Nnabugwu, 2010, p. 253).

To provide a framework for properly situating this study Franz Fanon's (1991) theory of revolutionary decolonization is preferred. It is a self-conscious, self-sustaining, liberating, and transformative decolonization theory that insists on violence, not for its sake, but rather to successfully combat the colonizer's disposition to perpetuate a vicious system of underdevelopment. "The violence which has ruled over the ordering of the colonial world, which has ceaselessly drummed the rhythm for the destruction of native social forms and broken up without reserve the systems of reference of the economy . . . that same violence will be claimed and taken over by the native" (Fanon, 1991, p. 31) to repossess his land and reconstruct it into a modern state.

Where decolonization is not perceived as a revolutionary process, possibly involving violence and vigorously pursued with a conscious democratic agenda, transformative change would be difficult to achieve. Nationalism could be conceptualized and utilized as the ideological companion, the driving spirit of separation and identity, as well as a sense of repossession that irrigates the decolonization process. Permanent nationalism is a regenerative mental attitude that sustains the sense of national ownership internalized by the citizens and serves to prevent the seizure of the decolonization process by a new set of buccaneers pretending to be statesmen. Such is the framework that would illuminate the rest of the chapter.

THE POLITICAL THEORY OF NATIONALISM

Historically, nationalism has been the most potent ideological weapon for challenging and knocking down foreign domination. Virtually every nation of the world has had reason to incite nationalist sentiments and emotions against some form of domination.

Nationalism, however, was not a simple force acting in a single direction or with a single motive. It might mean democracy and the rights of man, as in general it did in the age of the Revolution, but it might mean also an alliance between the landowning gentry and the new middle-class aristocracy of wealth. It might sweep away the remnants of feudal institutions only to build in their place new institutions that would rely no less heavily on traditional loyalties and the subordination of classes (Sabine & Thorson, 1973, pp. 545–546).

Revolutions involving the active participation of the peasantry and other lower classes have often turned out to put fetters on them and subordinated them into conditions even worse. For instance, peasants and serfs participated in the Thirty Years War only for the negotiations at Westphalia in 1648 to produce the equally tyrannical absolutist states across Europe constructed on the conceptualizations of nationalism, decolonization, and self-determination, but denied human freedom, equality, human rights, and even constitutionalism. Absolutist state repression evoked resentment and peasant uprisings across Europe, but more devastating in "different parts of France in 1639, 1662, 1664, 1670, 1674, and 1675" (Moore Jr., 1993, p. 70). Hence, nationalism also involved the enthronement of democratic rule and legally codified human rights. The concepts of freedom, equality, property, inalienable rights, and the pursuit of happiness, which the French Revolution idolized, romanticized, and modernized were precisely the same arsenal with which papal absolutism was battered down, including the American War of Independence (1765–1783) from British absolutism under King George III, with French assistance.

In the Thirty Years War (1618–1648) France played the key role of rallying the forces of freedom, equality, and justice from "papal imperialism or plenitudo potestasis or papal absolutism" (Sabine & Thorson, 1973, p. 258). As an instrument of freedom nationalism is the usual battle cry against political or economic domination of one people by another. Kedourie (1979, p. 13) observed quite correctly that "the French Revolution showed, in a resounding manner, that such an enterprise was feasible. In this it greatly strengthened a tendency for political restlessness implicit in the reforms preached by the Enlightenment and ostensibly adopted by Enlightened Absolutism." Reformation thinkers were quite explicit, eloquent, and dogged in their intellectual struggle for political liberty from a higher constitutive authority. If the French Revolution had consolidated and strengthened the modern state it was the Peace of Westphalia that laid the solid foundation, while the Enlightenment flowered it with glorious ideas such as the equality of states, self-determination, and sovereignty.

Ignited by the Bohemian Revolt and the Defenestration of Prague in 1618 the fundamental kernel underlying the Thirty Years War was freedom from Catholicism and equality before God, while the European kings exploited the opportunity to assert sovereign authority over their territorial possessions with nationalism providing the driving spirit. Consequently, one after the other the Protestant kings of Europe, first Denmark, Holland, and England, and later Sweden, France, and Spain eventually got involved in the final and most devastating part of the War. From an internal conflict within the Holy Roman Empire the War was transformed into a competitive struggle between the monarchical powers of Europe for their freedom, territoriality, and sovereignty (Nuhoglu, n.d.) just as the same pattern of struggle resulted in the partitioning of Africa into a modern states structure, which the nationalist struggle consolidated.

Furthermore, the germ of what broke out into the 17th century War started festering from the twelfth century in form of a rudimentary doctrine of monarchical sovereignty which gradually exalted "the one and only Ruler to an absolute plenitude of power" (Gierke, 1988, p. 35). One of the most notable achievements of the War was the launch of Europe into a new political phase dominated by the doctrines of sovereignty, collective security, balance of power, equality of states, and the state system itself (Sotirovic, *Oriental Review*, 2017/12/09). With these objective facts, the idea that "ideology and nationalism are coeval terms since their origins equally lie in the French Revolution" (Conversi, 2012, pp. 13–34) would appear to be a misconception. The Thirty Years War may have been the culmination of a historically deeper, festering struggle for freedom from papal supremacy beginning with the conflict between Pope Boniface and King Philip of France in continuation of the Investiture Controversy.

The nature of the issue between Philip and Boniface had much to do with developing the theories advanced on either side. The most important issues arose from Philip's efforts to raise money by imposing taxes on the French clergy, an attempt met by the Bull Clericis laicos in 1276, in which Boniface declared such taxation to be illegal and forbade the clergy to pay without papal permission. From this position he was forced to recede a few years later because he discovered, to his surprise, that even the French clergy would stand with the French King on a question which, in modern terminology, would be called national (Sabine & Thorson, 1973, p. 253).

Underlying and sustaining these struggles was the inspiring and stimulating Renaissance and Enlightenment intellectualism (Berlin, 2017) that produced such notable theories as the social contract, inalienable human rights, rule of law, separation of powers, federalism, sovereignty, checks and balances, and so on from thinkers such as Hobbes, Locke, Hume, Burke, Bodin, Althusius, Montesquieu, Rousseau to mention a few (Sabine & Thorson, 1973). Earlier, the intellectual ground for the flourishing of Enlightenment political thought had been prepared by medieval thinkers such as Dante Alighieri, Marsilio of Padua, and William of Occam (Curtis, 1981) whose efforts had succeeded in rescuing the state from papal absolutism. Both objective and theoretical imperatives had necessarily and effectively combined in the struggle for freedom from papal imperial domination. "Obviously, a new force of political cohesion was at work" (Sabine & Thorson, 1973, p. 253), that is, nationalism, as opposed to papal loyalty.

Nationalism as a combination of sacred and temporal forces in the struggle for political liberation from overarching ecclesiastical authority had manifested eloquently even as early as the thirteenth century in course of the Investiture Controversy. French and other nationalisms could not have just sprung up in that contest for political power against papal authority if not already ingrained in the consciousness of the people or if these were not sentiments that already served as instruments of national cohesion even in the womb of the medieval Holy Roman Empire and Roman Catholic Church. It is instructive to note certain salient points in this discourse on the emergence of the absolutist states as they relate to the contemporary ideology of decolonization and development in African countries, that is, the utilization of nationalism to achieve decolonization and restructuring of the new states. Next, the chapter demonstrates how this transformation occurred from Europe to Africa.

PAPAL IMPERIALISM AND NATIONAL CONSCIOUSNESS IN THE MEDIEVAL ERA

Nationalist sentiments like those of the French, English, and Germans strongly coalesced within the medieval double-cross of the Holy Roman Empire and the Roman Catholic Church. There can be no stronger evidence of the specificity of the lineages along which the Thirty Years War was fought and the national outcome it produced than the absolutist state (Anderson, 2013). Imperial colonialism and ecclesiastical domination were categorical realities of the medieval era in European history. From this perspective, the War was deeply an anticolonial or liberation struggle for a reorganization of society along nationality lines.

The unique power possessed by the pope alone is, therefore, in a special sense, a "divine right"; it confers a peculiar superiority, a power of revision and supervision over all the other forms of authority, whether ecclesiastical or secular. In this sense all power, both temporal and spiritual, resides in the church and is vested in the pope (Sabine & Thorson, 1973, p. 257).

Such was the enormity of the political and spiritual power wielded by the pope and clearly implied that only an equally violent struggle would guarantee any form of concession toward national liberation (Fanon, 1991). Political power is not ceded but can only be won through a dedicated and compulsive struggle. Domination and colonization were viewed as divine rights under papal supreme political authority and the only avenue for national rescue was warfare also with the same appeal to freedom and equality before God. So far-reaching were the effects of the Treaty of Westphalia that even articles 2.1 and 2.7 of the United Nations Treaty which secured the equality of states and sovereignty are said to be its derivatives (Nuhoglu, n.d.).

COLONIALISM AND ECONOMIC DISARTICULATION IN AFRICA

Wherever it occurs a uniformity of the destructive effects of colonization and domination is unmistakable. Papal imperialism ensured a centralization of resources that almost completely impoverished the lower rungs of the feudo-ecclesiastical hierarchy. The massive and unmitigated corruption that ruined the Catholic Church and the gradual loss of its internal cohesion with the reformation revolt as the inevitable result are attributable to papal wealth accumulation. Imperialism and colonialism, wherever and whenever they have held sway historically, have always had an economic motive in the background. This forms the basis of Ake's (1981, pp. 22–24) critique of Schumpeter, and Robinson and Gallagher, who argued that imperialism was "objectless," not rational, had no economic motive, and even contradicted capitalism, as well as Adam Smith (2012, p. 553) who insisted that "the establishment of the European colonies in America and the West Indies arose from no necessity." Marx's specificity in his definition of the capitalist mode of production was intended to avoid its theoretical conflation with similar forms of precapitalist productive and commercial activities, unlike Weber (2005, p. 17) who would emphatically argue that "capitalism existed in China, India, Babylon, in the classic world, and in the Middle Ages." Sabine and Thorson (1973, p. 253) rightly observed that if "Boniface had made good what seemed to be the literal meaning of Clericis laicos, no monarchy in Europe could have existed except on sufferance of the pope. Even feudal monarchy could not have survived if all the land held by churchmen had been exempt from feudal rents."

With a Papal Bull hanging over their heads like the Sword of Damocles monarchical resistance supported by medieval imperial intellectualism, which could leading to an open conflict was only a matter of time. Postwar negotiations had produced the absolutist state based on nationalist sentiments and consciousness, a trend that was consummated by the series of revolutions that produced the modern state armed with modern capitalism and liberal rights as the last man (Fukuyama, 1992). In turn capitalism evolved into imperialism that has enabled the few capitalist states of the West to hold captive, with sophisticated modern technology, a large number of states in Africa, Asia, and Latin America, using the most potent instruments; the International Monetary Fund (IMF), the International Bank for Reconstruction and Development (World Bank), the Multinational Corporation, and the World Trade Organization (WTO) (Nabudere, 1980; Tandon, 1982; Stiglitz, 2002), and also backed by the global mass media.

It is particularly instructive that France, England, and Germany that utilized the ideological instruments of nationalism, freedom, equality of states and citizens, sovereignty, rule of law, democracy, human rights, and so on have resorted to denying the same fruits of civilization and held captive and voraciously and perpetually colonized and exploited another set of weaker nations collectively called the Third World. Colonialism, between the nineteenth and early twentieth centuries, ensured that the development process that had been naturally set in motion was truncated through deliberate policy and these nations effectively transformed into underdeveloped, poverty-stricken, crisis-ridden, and beggarly dependencies (Frank, 1967; Amin, 1974; Ake, 1981; Roxborough, 1981; Onimode, 1983; Rodney, 2005). A polarized global economy ensured a perpetuation of the condition of sustained transfer of vital resources from the poor countries of the Third World to the advanced nations through various unethical mechanisms. In the Communist Manifesto Marx and Engels had anticipated that capitalism would create a world in its own image but a more critical study of the role of colonialism in India revealed the contrary.

The bourgeoisie, by the rapid improvement of all instruments of production, by the immensely facilitated means of communication, draws all, even the most barbarian nations into civilization . . . It compels all nations, on pain of extinction, to adopt the bourgeois mode of production; it compels them to introduce what it calls civilization into their midst, i.e., to become bourgeois themselves. In one word, it creates a world after its own image (Marx & Engels, 1977, p. 112).

Marx's original perception, anticipation, and interpretation of the relationship between the Western capitalist countries and the Third World was elaborately developmental until he studied India and China more closely. Indeed, capitalism had drawn all nations into its operational orbit. Anderson (2010, p. 10) points out that "Marx and Engels's praise for Western colonialism's conquests in Asia in the Manifesto can be seen as part of their overall sketch of the achievements of capitalism in Western Europe and North America." Western capitalism's glorious achievements in Europe were never intended to be replicated in Asia, Africa, and Latin America because it was only in search of sources of raw materials and markets for its products. He was fully aware that the only possible outcome would be the emergence of a bourgeois class like what obtained in the West, but certainly not one that would simply play a subordinate comprador role and a coterie of nations reduced to perpetual misery.

> It was the British intruder who broke up the Indian handloom and destroyed the spinning wheel. England began with driving the Indian cottons from the European market; it then introduced twist into Hindustan and in the end inundated the very mother country of cotton with cotton . . . This decline of Indian towns celebrated for their fabrics was by no means the worst consequence. British steam and science uprooted, over the whole surface of Hindustan, the union between agriculture and manufacturing industry . . . England has broken down the entire framework of Indian society without any symptoms of reconstitution yet appearing. This loss of his old world, with no gain of a new one imparts a particular kind of melancholy to the present misery of the Hindu and separates Hindustan, ruled by Britain from all its ancient traditions and from the whole of its past history (Marx & Engels, 2008, pp. 34–36).

Capitalism that glorifies and thrives so much on foreign commerce in raw materials and finished goods simultaneously and deceptively not only closes its markets against foreign goods but also takes action to kill such industries in the colonies right at the roots, variously conceptualized as "plunder and exploitation" (Onimode, 1983, p. 8), "economic disarticulation" (Ake, 1981, p. 43), and "disintegration of African economies and their technological impoverishment" (Rodney, 2005, p. 279). That precisely was the mission of colonialism in Asia, Africa, and Latin America. In so doing, the development process was stultified, terminated, and redirected to serve the purposes of capitalism through structural integration (Roxborough, 1979). The years of colonial rule ensured the violent deployment of political power to disarticulate the domestic or indigenous economy, pitch the existing ethnic groups against each other in perpetual hatred, struggle, and conflict (Fanon, 1991). Thus "the entire framework of Indian society," the entire structural foundation, was broken down, disconnected, and alienated from the people and then restructured to serve global capitalism, as Marx and Engels have demonstrated.

IDEOLOGY OF DECOLONIZATION

In order to entrench itself perpetually, on an alien soil, capitalism set out to inflict a comprehensive or "absolute" violence on the subsisting and blooming structures that constituted the foundation of autochthonous development in the colonized territory (Fanon, 1991, p. 29). Societal stagnation is an impossible concept because change is a continuous process. The presumption of a developmental inertia, "static and totally unchanging," in the colonized territory is a puerile and unsustainable argument (Roxborough, 1979, p. 1). Colonialism's claim of initiating a development process in the colony is equally jejune (Rodney, 2005). Ideological indoctrination is the greatest and most potent weapon of colonialism because it introduces a mirror for the colonized to view and accept a new distorted vision of himself. He begins to realize the inferiority of his products, values, education, technology, and himself. Fanon (1991, p. 32) captures it very effectively thus:

The native is declared insensible to ethics; he represents not only the absence of values but also the negation of values. He is, let us dare to admit, the enemy of values, and in this sense he is the absolute evil. He is the corrosive element, destroying all that comes near him; he is the deforming element disfiguring all that has to do with beauty or morality; he is the depository of maleficent powers; the unconscious and irretrievable instrument of blind forces.

Virtually every evil, error, inefficiency, dysfunctionality, or failure has the native or colonized to blame. It is to the credit of the Indian and the Chinese that he rejected the values, nomenclature, fashion, culture, diet, and so on of the colonizer, and successfully defended and maintained his cultural integrity. He was not totally consumed by the fantasies of the colonizer's foreign culture, whereas the African even took over the task of ideological devaluation of his personality by himself. This is the meaning when the more he acquired the strange values of the colonizer the more he despised and disparaged his kith and kin lagging behind in the race of self-devaluation. The colonized was blamed for his inability to develop with explanations to convince him that he is less intelligent, less innovative, less prepared to adopt new production techniques, and so on. The subtle ideological disorientation of the African has turned him against his neighbor, blaming him for everything and reducing anything of value to an object of cut-throat struggle. Consequently, inter-ethnic, inter-communal, and inter-religious struggles now pervade the African continent. The neighbor is made to take the place of the colonizing stranger as the real enemy to be eliminated. Wars, conflicts, terrorism, insurgency, banditry, abductions, ritual killing, sex slavery, human trafficking, and modern slavery have become the defining features of the new African inter-personal and inter-communal relations. Spellman (2011, pp. 159–160) laments that:

> most disturbingly, allegedly homogeneous nation-states now discovered plural voices within their midst emphasizing the primacy of religious, ethnic, linguistic, and even regional identity over common civic bonds ... Ethnic nationalism and a focus on what divides, rather than unites people, reached genocidal proportions in the former Yugoslavia during the mid-1990s and, beyond the West, in the impoverished state of Rwanda in 1995.

The nationalist horizon of the contemporary African is consistently getting narrower, and so also are his agitations. Rather than identify the unifying elements of wider national configurations it is the dividing factors that receive greater emphasis and attention. His loyalty and commitment are usually attached to narrow primordial enclaves. Such tendencies are shared between Eastern Europe and Africa owing, perhaps, to the already achieved levels of development and less aggressive imperialist exploitation. Europe has successfully contained the trend, whereas Africa keeps boiling uncontrollably.

It is also expedient to review the African style of nationalist struggle. Unlike the English and French what afflicted Africa was a three-pronged, fractured, and deformed nationalism that was also envious of the posh statuses and perquisites of the colonizer. Hence, the African nationalist leaders fought simultaneously for wider national liberation, alongside parochial portions as bases for their future political battles and opportunities for self-aggrandizement. These multiple regal attractions and commitments easily distracted the African nationalist from the need for national cohesion and also distorted his sense of development. For instance, the "Great Zik of Africa" became the President of Igbo State Union (Nnoli, 1978a, p. 165). Awolowo converted Yoruba cultural organization *Egbe Omo Oduduwa* into the Action Group that dominated the Yoruba Western Nigeria. Northern Nigeria was arguably the worst with their Northern Peoples Congress, and so on (Sklar, 1963, p. 321).

Ake provides several examples of African leaders that degenerated into ethnic champions, such as Arap Moi of Kenya, Eyadema of Togo, Paul Biya of Cameroun, Milton Margai of Sierra Leone, Idi Amin of Uganda to name a few. The weapon of such "exclusionist regimes is ethnic appeal" (Ake, 2008, p. 40). It was a lost opportunity that is extremely difficult to regain.

In that state of psychological and ideological confusion they abdicated their responsibility for fashioning a developmental route and direction for Africa to "multilateral development agencies" such as the IMF and World Bank (Ake, 2001, p. 43).

Having been so battered and disoriented, the task of searching for and discovering the point at which the African developmental trajectory was halted and "uprooted" was abandoned, like the self-reliant and indigenous *Ujamaa*. The futility of the struggle for development in Africa appears to vindicate the view that nothing meaningful can be achieved in Third World development without tracing and returning to this starting block of national self-rediscovery, like an original sin.

The new and most disturbing trend in Africa, particularly West Africa, is the expansionist ambition of some ethnic groups, also driven by religion, to conquer territories, exterminate communities, and dispossess them of their property, including land, converting vast territories into cattle grazing fields with the active connivance of the state (Chinweizu, 2013). With such deep-seated and implacable divisions among the occupants of the African continent the road to regional peace and development is fast receding. It is a new form of colonialist expansion and ironically also driven by a new form of parochial nationalism. The core message of postmodern African leadership, thought, and action is the rise of new emphasis on parochial identities. This is a deviation from "the Enlightenment formulation which, we recall, stressed a democratic citizenry where a common education and a uniform civil spirit were actively pursued" (Spellman, 2011, p. 159). Such holistic, unified, and people-oriented leadership sustained by Rousseau's "General Will" or Hegel's "National Spirit" has obviously eluded the African states. For an imperialized Africa the battle is overwhelming.

NATIONALISM AND THE IDEOLOGY OF DEVELOPMENT

Development is one of the prevalent catchwords in contemporary discourse and, as a concept, has accordingly been subjected to multiple interpretations. As the scope of its definition expands so also does it increasingly become elusive to an ever-widening percentage of the global population. Developmental disparities have bifurcated the world into two huge camps (Ake, 1978), at one pole the developed or advanced countries while attached to the others is a babel of appellations such as developing, underdeveloped, transitional, less developed, Third World, least developed, and so on, the categorization depends on the level of developmental disaster that has afflicted a particular state.

Though as old as human existence, the concept of development has a contemporary specificity and complexity with an institutionalized sense of urgency that distinguish it from previous usages. More than any other global organization, the United Nations is the most prominent driver of the modern development process using various specific indicators for comparative studies, setting standards of achievement and encouraging nations to work toward the targets. For purposes of easy measurability it has been further broken down into smaller and more specific strands than the broader indices such as human capital development, economic development, political development, technological development, territorial (spatial) development, and so on. The United Nations adopts the Human Development Index (HDI) with three indices which are averaged in order to identify a nation's achievements in health/longevity, education and living standards in terms of life expectancy, adult literacy/enrollment, and real GDP per capita in purchasing power parity (Bellu, 2011). Various agencies of the United Nations such as the United Nations Development Programme (UNDP) and the United Nations Conference on Trade and Development (UNCTAD) have their own indices for measuring development among nations with measuring indices such as poverty levels, life expectancy, adult literacy, access to education, average income, and so on. The publication of annual human development reports for all countries is designed for comparative purposes (Soares Jr. & Quintella, 2008, pp. 104–124).

The concept of sustainable development, introduced by the Brundtland Commission (WCED, 1987) Report, is another strand to the conceptualization of development, particularly to ensure the availability of resources for future generations to meet their own needs. The UN approach is setting standards and targets for nations across the globe. The specific concept of sustainable development has three major objectives with minor specifics. These are Social objectives in education, equity, full employment, health, cultural identity, participation, and so on; Economic objectives in growth, stability, efficiency, and so on; and Environmental objectives such as healthy environment, conservation, and rational use of natural resources. Cross-national development comparative studies in the form of what the World Bank calls development diamonds are also utilized rather than the use of the more broad-based GDP or GNP per capita countries categorized as high-income, upper middle income, lower middle income, and low income of the citizens (Soares Jr. & Quintella, 2008, pp. 104–124). Income levels are also measured against primary/secondary school enrollment, life expectancy at birth, access to safe water, and GNP per capita.

Primarily, the United Nations aims to eradicate poverty or at least reduce the scourge drastically across the globe but that still remains a tall dream in many Third World countries. Bellu (2011) has identified several paradigms of development, most of which are UN-sponsored. They include Free-Market Trickle-Down Growth-Led development, which though accrues to the rich trickles down to the poor through the functioning of the free-market mechanism and Adam Smith's (1976) "invisible hand," the preferred model usually advocated by the West for the Third World, to keep them within the orbit of global capitalism. Pro-poor growth-led development emphasizes economic growth as the basis for development accompanied by equitable distribution of income. Low-wage labor-intensive export-led development based on the export of labor-intensive manufactured commodities factored within low wages. China is said to fall within this paradigm. Agriculture-based development depends on local peasant communities to facilitate socioeconomic development through agriculture. It ensures poverty reduction because of its extensive practice.

Endogenous growth-based development anchors on the development and utilization of endogenous technology sustained by constant innovation through learning-by-doing skill development. It discourages exogenous or imported technology but rather emphasizes "policies favouring local processes, context-specific technologies and the creation and maintenance of human capital" (Bellu, 2011). Rural development paradigm is another form of community-based development emphasizing the socioeconomic relationships among agents of production within the rural milieu while also relating to urban and semi-urban producers. The Washington Consensus-based development thrives on globalization and encourages nations to liberalize their markets, foreign trade and tariffs, privatize public corporations, reduce marginal tax rates, liberalize exchange and interest rates, control labor, encourage the flow of modern technologies, and so on. Essentially, IMF-programmed policies dominate this model.

Strategic openness is a development model which balances openness and protection by strategically applying policies based on types of commodities and trade partners rather than blindly adopting the "Washington Consensus," Protectionist policies are selectively adopted. Exhaustible-resource export-led development model is usually adopted by mineral-oil, timber, and other primary commodity-exporting countries, which invest the enormous resources derived from export to finance the development process. Middle East and some oil-producing African countries fall within this category. Agricultural commodity export-led development is another primary commodity export-oriented model but based on agricultural products such as tea, coffee, cocoa, cotton, groundnuts, bananas, palm produce, and so on (Nigeria, Ghana, Kenya, Uganda). Emigration-based development is associated with countries with a weak industrial sector and therefore have to export their excess labor force to earn foreign exchange and further develop the economy (Philippines, Indonesia).

Conversely, immigration-based development model focuses on the ability to attract foreign labor with a strong resource base but small population. Examples are the Gulf countries like UAE. FDI-based development model depends mainly on attracting foreign direct investment to take advantage of the availability of cheap labor and natural resources such as oil and other minerals. Finally, the foreign aid-based development model depends on foreign aid to finance its development efforts (almost all African states). Funding could be directed at specific projects or to support the public budget. While these development models are not mutually exclusive some may not really qualify to be identified as such because countries adopting them may never develop. It is also instructive that almost all of them are pro-capitalist blue-print models imposed on Third World countries by UN agencies such as the IMF and World Bank, and controlled by the Western capitalist countries. That also explains why despite their adoption development has eluded many of these countries where poverty and other forms of social crises reign supreme.

The objectives of these development paradigms may appear laudable and commendable but are nonetheless laden with an ideological burden. The IMF and the World Bank usually present themselves as the champions of development in Third World countries but these same institutions impose conditionalities that make development almost impossible. Perpetual poverty and underdevelopment are the usual objective results of their prescriptions. As agents of imperialism they only ensure, through their policies and activities, the continued exploitation and transfer of the resources of Third World countries for the development of the advanced capitalist countries. The economic distortions, political crises and instability, insurgency, resource wars, poverty, unemployment, the debt burden, and so on, associated with Third World countries are all the inevitable outcomes of the policies and actions of the Western capitalist countries and the UN development agencies, robbing with one hand and paying with the other, creating problems and providing the solution, which in turn leads to another crisis. Consequently, Third World countries must sustain the search for a viable alternative to the Western-oriented and imperialistically imposed development paradigms as attempted below.

TOWARD AN AFRICAN PARADIGM OF DEVELOPMENT

Development is not a commodity to be purchased or much less a free gift to treasure, hence an authentic and feasible path to the transformation of Africa, through a sustained and persistent engagement in the decolonization of the ideology of development is a sine qua non. Primarily, it is the product of constant intercourse between man and his natural environment. It has been stated unequivocally above that the search for a viable development paradigm for Africa must begin at that same point where it was halted, thwarted, and uprooted. The authentic nationalist spirit is that which decolonizes the African from the mentality of refusing to think for himself and believing that development can only come from the West. It is that spirit which seeks to disengage from soul-ties with both West and East, and return to the basics. China's current competitive parity with, if not edge over, the United States is attributable to the evolution of its own indigenous paradigm of development. Africans need to revisit, revitalize, and modernize the indigenous egalitarian pattern of political leadership and decision making. Modern technology should be adapted to suit the peculiar needs of the African societies. Nnoli (1981, p. 36) captures it thus:

> Development is a dialectical phenomenon in which the individual and the society interact with their physical, biological, and inter-human environments, transforming them for their own betterment and that of humanity at large and being transformed in the process. The lessons learned and experiences acquired in this process are passed on to future generations, enabling them to improve their capacities to make further valuable changes in their inter-human relations and their ability to transform nature. Development is first and foremost a phenomenon associated with changes in man's humanity and creative energies, not in things.

Development is embedded in the indigenous people and their creative and innovative capacities, in their constant intercourse with their environment or nature, in seeking solutions to their own challenges. It is not borrowed, awarded, or purchased from an oppressor pretending to be a development partner. Africa has all it takes to become a developmental giant if the leaders could jettison their petty quarrels, greed, jealousy, superiority and inferiority complex, if they could stop killing their industries and capacities in favor of importation, if they could cherish what they have and improve on it rather than flaunt that sophisticated and expensive but imported gadget or apparel. Discipline is key in all such efforts. The Chinese exercised self- and national discipline and the results speak eloquently.

> The Reports, not surprisingly, noted that the remarkable Chinese success derived from their transformation of the rural class structure and that little could be expected in India without similar charge: To create an atmosphere favorable to the formation of agrarian cooperatives . . . (the) atmosphere should be one of equality and non-exploitation. In creating such an atmosphere, land reforms

will play a vital role . . . Two things must happen: (i) the power of the village oligarch must be broken . . . and (ii) the Government must become an instrument of the ordinary people . . ." The limits of gradualism and incremental changes were manifest; progress could not be achieved without a major assault on the classes that dominated the countryside (Alavi, 1975, p. 163).

The Chinese success inspired Nyerere of Tanzania in Africa whose shining example was the Ujamaa villagization program enunciated under the Arusha Declaration of February 5, 1967. Its ideological backbone was the philosophy of self-reliance, that is, belief in the productive capacity of Tanzanians or the African, deploying his ingenuity, mastering his environment, harnessing his resources, and processing them into higher-quality products to satisfy his needs. It was a declaration of war on poverty, ignorance, and disease, and under such conditions "self-reliance means the maximum possible mobilisation of existing resources, the minimisation of waste in their extraction and allocation, and the activation of most of the country's potential wealth" (Nnoli, 1978b, p. 205). It involved public-sector dominance over the commanding heights of the economy through a nationalization program as priority, through with active private-sector participation.

Ujamaa was motivated by the ideology of African Socialism, the idea that socialism is natural to the egalitarian lifestyle of the African. It was essentially a villagization program for cooperative living, involving communal ownership of land and other resources, formation of village governments with power to plan and execute local projects, and provision of social services such as electricity, health facilities, and water supply. In 1969 there were 180 Ujamaa villages involving about 60,000 people, but by 1972 about 5,500,000 people had been villagized (Hartmann, 1983, p. 5). It eliminated poverty and beggarliness on the streets, children were in school, no luxury goods, great inequalities were eliminated, everyone had access to basic necessities, and the rich were denied luxuries.

It was a combination of revolutionary decolonization, an indigenous brand of socialism, emotionally nationalistic, uniquely ideological, economically emancipatory, socially egalitarian, and politically self-governing, democratic, and participatory; a unique indigenous model for Africa. Ujamaa was however short-lived because it was up against formidable imperialist forces and their internal collaborators, their propaganda, smear campaigns, gluttony, and their capitalist wealth orientation. Though largely abandoned and ignored in Africa Ujamaa is being successfully adopted among Black communities in the United States, termed Ujamaa Kwanzaa cooperative economics; "local people cooperating with each other to provide for the essentials of living, including food, clothes, education, housing and entertainment, particularly the hip-hop music industry" (Redmond, Economist's View, 2005), which underscores the adaptability and viability of Ujamaa as a universal development model.

CONCLUSION

It took a determined struggle to liberate Western Europe from the clutches of despotism and tyranny under papal and the absolutist states, and entrench popular democratic rule. In the same vein, a determined and detached nationalist spirit that is also ideologically decolonized is crucially needed to launch African countries on the path of genuine democracy and development. Africa will change only when the real and genuine spirit of nationalism becomes the driving force in its developmental struggle. It is a patriotic spirit, non-partisan, non-parochial, selfless, people-based, people-focused, people-oriented, and people-driven. The nationalist spirit of development is simultaneously a spirit of decolonization and anti-imperialist. African leaders must begin to believe in their people, make them the centerpiece in all national decisions, programs, and policies, and evolve an endogenous paradigm of development. An *Ujamaa* style of indigenous development model holds the key for Africa.

REFERENCES

Ake, C. (1978). *Revolutionary Pressures in Africa*. London: Zed Publishers.
––––––– (1981). *A Political Economy of Africa*. London: Longman.
––––––– (1982). *Social Science as Imperialism: The political Theory of Development*. Ibadan: Ibadan University Press.
––––––– (2001). *Democracy and Development in Africa*. Ibadan: Spectrum Books Ltd.
––––––– (2008). *The Feasibility of Democracy in Africa*. Dakar: CODESRIA.
Alavi, H. (1975). India and the Colonial Mode of Production, Socialist Register.
Amin, S. (1974). *Accumulation on a World Scale*. New York: Monthly Review Press.
Anderson, K. B. (2010). *Marx at the Margins: On Nationalism, Ethnicity and Non-western Societies*. Chicago: University of Chicago Press.
Anderson, P. (2013). *Lineages of the Absolutist State*. London: Verso.
Bellu, L. G. (2011). Development and Development Paradigms: A review of prevailing Visions, EASYPol Resources for Policy Making, EASYPol Module 102, a publication of the United Nations Food and Agriculture Organisation (FAO), Rome, May.
Berlin, I. (2017). *The Age of Enlightenment*. In Hardy, H. (Ed.), *The Age of Enlightenment: The Eighteenth-century Philosophers*. Oxford: Isaiah Berlin Literary Trust.

Biereenu-Nnabugwu, B. (2010). *Methodology of Political Inquiry: Issues and Techniques of Research Methods in Political Science*. Enugu: Quintagon Publishers.
Brewer, A. (2001). *Marxist Theories of Imperialism: A Critical Survey*. London: Tailor and Francis e-Library.
Chinweizu. (1978). *The West and the Rest of Us*. Lagos: NOK Publishers.
———. (2013). *Caliphate Colonialism: The Taproot of the Trouble with Nigeria*. Shekere. n.a.
Conversi, D. (2012). Modernism and nationalism. *Journal of Political Ideologies*, 17(1): 13–34.
Curtis, M. (1981). *The Great Political Theories Vol. 2*. New York: Avon Books.
Dodd, C. H. (1972). *Political Development*. London: Macmillan Press Ltd.
Fanon, F. (1985). *The Wretched of the Earth*. Middlesex: Penguin Books Ltd.
Frank, A. G. (1967). *Capitalism and Underdevelopment in Latin America*. New York: Monthly Review Press.
Fukuyama, F. (1992). *The End of History and the Last Man*. New York: The Free Press.
Gierke, O. (1988). *Political Theories of the Middle Ages*, translated with an introduction by Frederic William Maitland. Cambridge: Cambridge University Press.
Hartmann, J. (1983). Development Policy Making in Tanzania 1962-1982: A Critique of Sociological Interpretations. Unpublished PhD Thesis. University of Hull.
Hassan, D. (2006). The rise of the territorial state and the treaty of Westphalia. *Yearbook of New Zealand Jurisprudence*, 9: 62–70.
Kedourie, E. (1979). *Nationalism*. London: Hutchinson & Co. (Publishers) Ltd.
Marx, K. & Engels, F. (1977). *Selected Works*, Volume 1. Moscow: Progress Publishers.
Marx, K. & Engels, F. (2008). *On Colonialism, Second Impression*. Moscow: Foreign Languages Publishing House.
Moore Jr., B. (1993). *Social Origins of Dictatorship and Democracy: Lord and Peasant in the Making of the Modern World*. Boston, MA: Beacon Press.
Nabudere, D. (1980). *The Political Economy of Imperialism: Its Theoretical and Polemical Treatment from Mercantilist to Multilateral Imperialism*. London: Zed Publishers.
Nnoli, O. (1978a). *Ethnic Politics in Nigeria*. Enugu: Fourth Dimension Publishers.
———. (1978b). *Self-Reliance and Foreign Policy in Tanzania: The Dynamics of the Diplomacy of a New State 1961-1971*. Lagos: NOK Publishers.
———. (1981). *Path to Nigerian Development*. Dakar: CODESRIA Book Series.
Nuhoglu, M. S. (n.d.). 1648: The Treaty of Westphalia. https://www.academia.edu/29524207/1648 retrieved 24/05/2019.
Onimode, B. (1983). *Imperialism and Underdevelopment in Nigeria: The Dialectics of Mass Poverty*. London: Macmillan Press Ltd.
Redmond, L. (2005). Ujamaa, the Cooperative Economics of Hip-Hop. The Economist's View. Austin Weekly News. December 29.
Rodney, W. (2005). *How Europe Underdeveloped Africa*. Lagos: Panaf Publishing Inc.

Roxborough, I. (1981). *Theories of Underdevelopment*. London: Macmillan Press Ltd.

Sabine, G. H. & Thorson, T. L. (1973). *A History of Political Theory*. New Delhi: Oxford & IBH Publishing Co. Ltd.

Scruton, Roger. (2007). *The Palgrave Macmillan Dictionary of Political Thought*, 3rd edition. New York: Palgrave Macmillan.

Seth, A. (1989). Marxism and the Question of Nationalism in a Colonial Context: The Case of British India, Unpublished PhD thesis Australian National University.

Sklar, R. (1963). *Nigerian Political Parties: Power in an emergent African nation*. Enugu: NOK Publishers.

Smith, A. (1976). *An Inquiry into the Nature and Causes of the Wealth of Nations*. Oxford: Oxford University Press.

Soares Jr., J. and Quintella, R. H. (2008). Development: An analysis of concepts, measurement and indicators. *Brazilian Administration Review*, 5(2): 104–124.

Sotirovic, V. B. (2017). The peace treaty of Westphalia (1648) and its consequences for international relations. *Oriental Review*. https//orientalreview.org›2017/12/09›peace-treaty westpha

Sowell, T. (2017). *Wealth, Poverty and Politics*. Benin City: Baulahland Publications.

Spellman, W. M. (2011). *A Short History of Western Political Thought*. New York: Palgrave Macmillan.

Stiglitz, J. (2002). *Globalization and its Discontents*. London: Penguin Books.

Tandon, Y. (Ed.) (1982). *University of Dar es Salaam Debate on Class, State and Imperialism*. Dar es Salaam: Tanzania Publishing House.

WCED (1987). *Our Common Future, World Commission on Environment and Development (WCED)*. Oxford: Oxford University Press.

Weber, M. (2005). *The Protestant Ethic and the Spirit of Capitalism*. London: Routledge Classics.

Chapter 10

Women, Resistance Movements, and Colonialism in Africa

Evidence from Egypt, Kenya, and Nigeria

Moses J. Yakubu and James Olusegun Adeyeri

In Africa, narratives on resistance movements against colonial administrations have not adequately captured the status and position of the female gender. While most scholars expend time and spaces on the experiences of men, without reference to women, others who attempt a feminist perspective have not significantly presented a holistic role of women. Besides, a comparative analysis with the view of highlighting the continental experiences of women in the fight against colonial rule and implications for decolonization of gender inequality in Africa is yet to be critically addressed. It is the position in this study to re-examine the roles of African women in resistance movements against colonial governments. Anchoring on evidence from Egypt, Kenya, and Nigeria, the chapter discusses the convergences and divergences of women's activities during colonial resistance. The study adopts the relative deprivation theory of war and radical feminist theory. The study reveals that colonial women, like their male counterparts, were fighters who demonstrated a profound level of camaraderie as they agitated and fought against the travesties of European imperialism. It demonstrates that these women bequeathed an enduring legacy of decolonization, political activism, and militancy to postcolonial African women. It argues that to decolonize colonial development, gender equality must be frontal as women in postcolonial Africa remain increasingly marginalized and underrepresented.

INTRODUCTION

The history of resistance movements against imperialism or any form of subjugation toward Africans and elsewhere is rife with male-dominated perspectives. Most available materials on the subject discuss the role of men more than women. Though, in Africa, a few scholars have attempted a reconstruction of women's political activism and militancy in colonial society, the place of women in the struggle for political independence is yet to be adequately documented. The exploits of African women under colonial rule, especially during nationalist agitations and wars of liberations, lack adequate presentation like those of men. Female warriors of African extraction are undermined when discussing the long walk to independence. The reconstruction of African history therefore should entail a balanced coverage of both the male and female genders.

Since the colonial era, the female gender has been actively involved in agitations and struggles for self-determination. Women have played leadership roles in revolutionary situations in Angola, Namibia, Mozambique, Eritrea, and a host of other struggles (Ferris, 1993). In Africa, women were part of wars of liberation against colonial powers as well as in contemporary rebel insurgencies. During these armed conflicts women have served in various capacities, ranging from foot soldiers to high-ranking positions as commanders (Bennett, 1995).

Colonial African women defied the essentialist worldview of the unchanging nature of women (Heyman and Giles, 2006). Two great essentialists were Aristotle and Plato. The essentialist approach to gender difference in any human society is based on the notion that gender is determined by the fundamental characteristics of an individual's biology, and cannot be changed (Heyman and Giles, 2006). However, through dint of hard work, women have showcased the dynamism in gender identity. Women have proved that gender difference is a cultural construct subject to constant changes. Like their male counterparts, colonial women demonstrated that the fight for freedom and political emancipation is also their business.

Against this backdrop, this chapter seeks to re-examine the role of colonial African women in the fight against colonial administration. It re-appraises the different experiences and activities of women from Egypt, Kenya, and Nigeria. Significantly, the study is a pointer to the fact that colonial women passed the baton of political activism to postcolonial African women.

THEORETICAL FRAMEWORK

The study anchors on two theories: feminist theory and the relative deprivation theory of war. These theories are relevant because they both capture the plights women found themselves during colonial rule. Also they provide plausible explanations for the involvement of girls and young women in liberation struggles. The tenets of the theories form the underpinning ideologies and principles of women liberators in colonial Africa. In the first part of this section, the feminist theory is discussed.

There are several feminist theories such as liberal, socialist, cultural, and radical. These theories are intended to sharpen political analyses and inform strategies for social change. Feminist theory makes unique contributions to our understanding of the demeaning and appalling situation of women. Feminist theorists have attempted to answer questions about the roles women could play and/or reasons behind the situations of women during war.

For a better understanding, however, the Radical feminist theory is adopted in this study. In 1960, this theory emerged as a perspective of feminism that calls for a radical reordering of society in which male domination is eradicated in all social and economic contexts, while at the same time recognizing that women's experiences are also affected by other social divisions such as race, class, and sexual orientation (Willis, 1984; Giardina, 2010; and Martins, 2019). Some foremost proponents and/or founders are Ellen Willis, Kathie Sarachild, Ti-Grace Atkinson, Carol Hanisch, and Judith Brown (Love, 2006).

The above proponents and many others around the globe challenge male domination and oppression against women. They view society as a patriarchy in which male gender subjugates women, and on the other hand, seek to put an end to patriarchy. Radical feminists oppose sexual objectification of women and oppressive policies/laws, create public awareness about issues such as rape and violence against women, challenge the concept of gender roles, and challenge racialized and gendered capitalism.

Radical feminists, through the platform of Women's Liberation Movement (WLM), agitate against unjust society (Giardina, 2010). Unjust society, in radical feminist viewpoint, includes the experiences of humans during colonialism in Africa. Although this theory emanated from America and/or the West, African feminism, like the experience elsewhere, challenged injustice, oppression, and male domination over women.

Radical feminism is relevant to this study as it explains and supports women's agitations against oppression, obnoxious policies and laws, unjust society, and unequal opportunities between the sexes. The theory gives credence to women's struggle against colonial powers whose policies subjugated women to the last rung of societal ladder. Though it has been criticized on the ground of extreme radicalism and for being "bourgeois," or "anti-left," it has, in many ways, transformed women's lives, particularly in terms of freedom, justice, and women's rights. It thus explains the involvement of women in resistance movements across Africa.

The second theory, relative deprivation is especially useful in describing the origins of liberation struggles and internal wars. *Relative deprivation theory of war* is defined as the experience of being deprived of something to which one believes oneself to be entitled. This refers to the discontent people feel when they compare their positions to others and realize that they have less of what they believe themselves to be entitled than those around them (Walker and Smith, 2006).

The theory maintains that political rebellion and insurrection become inevitable when people (men and women) believe that they are receiving less than their due. To achieve greater benefits or to relieve the frustration of denial, groups may turn to aggression and political violence (Gurr, 1970).

To Crane Brinton (1965) and James Davies (1962), the objective or absolute conditions of poverty and oppression do not lead directly to rebellion, but rather, the subjective or psychological response to these conditions is a precipitating factor for rebellious activity. Crane's work the *Anatomy of Revolution* and James's "Toward a Theory of Revolution" emphasize the psychological perspective of relative deprivation theory. To these scholars, since 1945, civil wars have been more frequent in the developing world than in already developed states.

This theory is relevant to this study because it sees war as the business of men and women, since both experience the psychological effects of poverty and oppression. The theory played an important role in the development of modern feminism. It appreciates the capability of women to cause war and participate in war.

However, several objections arise. Rich countries have engaged in many hostile confrontations outside their own borders, usually in the territory of dependent Third World client states. Another objection to this theory of political violence concerns the separation of physical bloodshed from other forms of abuse. Singling out violence alone as a social disease ignores the everyday suffering of millions of people.

In spite of these criticisms, relative deprivation theory of war is relevant and appropriate in explaining the participation of women in resistance movement against colonial powers because it captures the frustration experienced by women, and how this informed their canon for resistance and freedom from socioeconomic and political subjugation of the Europeans. It provides background explanations for rebellious activities against unethical standards and/or policies.

UNDERSTANDING WOMEN'S PLIGHT UNDER COLONIAL RULE

In precolonial setting, African women alongside their male counterparts were team players in virtually all spheres of human endeavors such as economic, social, cultural, and political areas. Though male supremacy as the head of the family existed, women were not relegated to the background. Like men, they participated in the aforementioned sectors actively and meaningfully contributed to the development of their various societies. Women through their agricultural activities supported the economy of their families and the communities in general (Nzemeka, 2009).

Also, before the European incursion into Africa, women were relevant in the decision-making processes. For example, in South Africa there were female chiefs in the Tswana and Rhonda Kingdoms. Similarly, high-ranking female chiefs were found among the Thongs of Zambia and the Nzinga of Angola (Balogun, 1999). In Nigeria, women played relevant political roles in precolonial society. Among the Igbos, women were involved in the activities of "Umuada" institution (Falola, 2019). They played definite ritual roles within the village. Their opinion on sociopolitical issues was sought after and highly considered. More so, among the Yoruba, women actively participated in politics. For example, in Ijebu Igbo, gender dualism existed in the valuation of contribution to the administration of the society. While it did appear that the male gender dominated the scene, women's contribution was significant. For instance, Erelu and Iya Abiye were titled members of the Osugbo secret cult which is one of the legislative arms of the town. The roles of these women were so crucial in the administration of the community that it assumed a proverbial dimension:

Da' gi ge, da' gi ge
Aake kan ko lee da gi ge
Da' gi la, da' gi la
Eele kan ko le da gi la
B' o s' erelu
Osugbo o lee da awo se

Cutting alone, cutting alone
The axe cannot cut alone
Splitting alone, splitting alone
The wedge cannot split alone
Without Erelu (the Women's representative)
Osugbo (the secret society) cannot operate alone (Balogun, 2019)

The above narrative was an indication that men and women, though not equal in terms of status, were recognized in the political administration in precolonial Africa. It demonstrated that in Egbaland, if Erelu was absent from Osugbo, no decision would be reached. And that women in other climes within Africa were not just recognized but played meaningful roles which were capable of instilling positive change.

In addition, Efunsetan Aniwura of Ibadan was a notable businesswoman who, through her economic accomplishments, influenced political decisions in Yoruba land. Studies have shown too that Moremi was one precolonial African woman who played significant role in the political and social spheres of life in Yoruba land (Falola, 2017). In Lagos and Abeokuta Madam Tinubu demonstrated the power of the traditional Yoruba woman in the political sector of her society up to 1914 (Nzemeka, 2009). In Hausaland, there were cases of women activists and political leaders with titles and offices. For example, the "Iya," "Magajiya," and "Mardani" were title holders who occupied outstanding positions in the society (Falola, 2017) Also, Queen Amina was a female political and military leader in ancient Zazzau Kingdom, present-day Zaria, Nigeria. She embarked on several military expeditions with successful conquests that contributed to the development of the economy of Zazzau (Falola, 2017).

In Baganda, women, under the auspices of a group known as "Olukiko," played sociopolitical and economic roles. These women were actively involved in deciding over issues that affected them. They had powerful female royal title holders known as the "Namagole" (Queen Mothers) and "Nalinya" (Queen) (Balogun, 1999). In fact, the "Namagole and Nalinya" did not only possess large estates but successfully commanded large followership and maintained a large number of slaves. More importantly, the queen mother and the queen had their own courts with titled officers (Balogun, 1999).

Suffice to say that prior to European imperialism African women were central to the economic, social, and political activities within the various societies in the continent. At virtually all fronts, women supported and complemented men's role in Africa. Women were neither relegated nor pushed aside, rather they were, like men, active participants in community development. Male dominance did not translate to women subjugation and marginalization.

AFRICAN WOMEN UNDER COLONIAL RULE

This part of the chapter will focus on women under colonial administration. It examines the factors responsible for the changing pattern of the role of women in the colonial period. This part also discusses the initial reactions of women to colonial rule, which include the formation of women organizations. This part provides a succinct explanation for the involvement of women in resistance movements against colonial systems of government in Africa. It demonstrates "why" and "how" women fought for political independence alongside men.

Women under colonial power experienced an unprecedented retrogressive change within the various African states. This obnoxious paradigm shift in the role of women was informed by certain uncontrollable factors instigated by the colonial masters. The European policies and strategies in Africa significantly altered the existing status which had been on ground before their arrival. Greek philosophy of not according women equal status with men was replicated in Africa. For example, Aristotle's assertion on women being equal or a little bit above slaves was upheld by Western democracies entrenched by the colonizing nations (Bradford, 1996).

The notion of a woman being portrayed as chattel, slave, or object to be acquired, used, and discarded forcibly pushed women further down the societal ladder. Western philosophy never saw women as integral part necessary for community development; rather they project women as object for men's amusement and/or entertainment. Frederich Nietsche, a German philosopher, opined that when visiting a woman, one (a man) should go with a cane, that the woman is an object to be toyed with (Balogun, 1999 and Bradford, 1996). The introduction of Western philosophy and democracy in Africa had legal implication for women. The entrenchment of Western legal concepts and the codification and redefinition of customary law gradually kept women silent in the political sphere.

That as it is, Christian missionaries, the accompanying agencies of colonialism, further subjugated women to the background (Yakubu, 2009). The doctrine of women keeping quiet in the church was a regress for the female gender. The church forbids women from being heard, and this doctrine became generalized through the teachings of the missionaries and the Mission Schools. It should be noted that during colonial rule Western education was the prerogative of the missionaries and that the teachers were Christians. Western education thus became the vehicle for the perversion of women's status. The nature and pattern of Western education helped promote the doctrine of women not being heard. By implication, women's sociopolitical status dwindled compared to that of men. This trend subsequently strengthened and promoted patriarchy in Africa. Masculinity and the control of women by men became phenomenal. Men tended to assert more power over women while women found themselves in a pitiable situation.

Worse still, the cash crop system introduced by the imperialists did harm to the female gender. The cash economy was predominantly under the control of men. Unlike the precolonial society where women and men were actively involved in agricultural activities, the policy of the colonial era ostracized women from the scheme of economic intercourse. The European traders interacted more with men while the female gender was sidelined. The economic interaction between African men and the colonialists financially empowered the former to the detriment of the latter. The male gender earned more income during colonial rule through production for export. Higher income strengthened men's power vis-à-vis the women in the family (Nzemeka, 2009).

Restricted access to Western education also affected women's access to the modernizing sectors of the government and the economy (Erumuo, 1999). As a result, women's incomes continued to reduce. Women became more dependent on men who possess financial capability and featured more in the cash economy (Yakubu, 2009).

In addition, European incursion into Africa informed negative land reforms across Africa (Erumuo, 1999). Women who had previously in the precolonial society possessed adequate land for cultivation and other agricultural purposes were displaced. The once cared and cultivated lands were taken away from them. They were alienated from land that once defined their roles for centuries (Ogundipe-Leslie, 2009). This reform impaired their access to food and reduced their economic prowess in the society. It gradually instilled a sense of male supremacy in the women, and also brought about the loss of female identity. The inadequate land left for the women limited their agricultural yield significantly.

European wage labor system deployed by imperialists was another mechanism that trampled on women's right in colonial society. Hardworking colonial women were forced to forego their once cherished duties for European service (Ogundipe-Leslie, 2009). These women worked for the European farmers, especially at the peak of the seasons. A gory side of the wage or forced labor was that women became vulnerable to physical and sexual abuses from their European masters, and also their husbands who saw their new roles as worthless, and resented them for neglecting their homely duties (Ogundipe-Leslie, 2009). Wage labor and its disheartening characteristics had negative impact on women. Their absence from home affected the raising of children and attention to their husbands.

African women under colonial rule witnessed significant decline and disparity in gender role separation. The separation of spheres of activities along gender lines which previously enabled women ample space for freedom and achievements within their own spheres whittled away. In addition, colonialism led to the loss of traditional economic and political rights. Women found themselves confined within the domestic spheres without empowerment for efficiency (Bradford, 1996). The tenets of colonialism deprived the female gender the opportunity to contribute, through subsistence production, to the growth and development of their communities Nzemeka, 2009).

More perturbing was the introduction of tax by European powers in some African states. The policy of tax system not only angered the men but also women who felt the colonial governments were chewing more than necessary, especially in the wake of economic downturn. Besides, extending the payment of tax to women who had already been frustrated and pushed to the rear worsened the tensed socioeconomic and political atmosphere. Women's agitations against the payment of tax significantly increased.

In their dealings in continental Africa, the imperialists failed to acknowledge African women and their age-long substantial status and positions in the society. The projected gender roles instigated by the Europeans were setback for women, and this however became an impetus for women agitation, protest, and active participation in the resistance movements. It is crystal clear to discerning observers that the colonial government presented African women varieties of challenges and negative effects. However, as a display of their resilience, the women reacted, in most cases, by learning to protest and stand up for their rights. African women adapted as they needed to and were ferociously determined to preserve their identities.

Disgruntled and disenchanted colonial African women started evolving with diverse female-based associations and organizations, with the purpose of addressing the plights of women and the society in general. It should be stated here that before female participation in resistance movements against colonialism and its scourging underpinnings, colonial women found solace in the establishment of certain organizations which addressed women's issues. These organizations, which cut across the different African societies, became the initial rallying points for ill-treated and frustrated women, and the platform for political awareness and activism. For example, in 1929, Nigerian women established the British West Africa Ladies Club. The women club was designed to encourage women to express themselves, and also provided the platform upon which to do so (Falola, 2017).

The Lagos Market Women's Association (LMWA) was another notable organization established for the promotion of women's interest in the colonial period. The association started in the mid-1920s as an interest group for the promotion and protection of women's rights in colonial Nigeria. Madam Alimotu Pelewura, the leader of the association, proved that women had the capability to organize and control affairs relating to them. The LMWA challenged British regulation and policies. In 1932, rumors surrounding a tax on Lagos women arose, and in response the association set up a committee that met with the administrator of the colony, C. T. Lawrence. The committee was however assured that there is nothing of such. Eight years later in 1939, the LMWA rose up against the war-time regulations that called for an income tax ordinance to generate revenue to help take care of British forces. During this protest, 200 illiterate market women came together to challenge the colonial authority. They closed the market and marched to the commissioner (Ogundipe-Leslie, 2009). The commissioner assured the women that the tax was only for wealthy women. Although all women were still taxed in subsequent years, the efforts of the LMWA demonstrated that women in Nigeria and elsewhere in Africa were not passive and pushovers as they protested against colonial policies (Ogundipe-Leslie, 2009).

In Ghana, women organizations played a major role in the sensitization of the female gender on their plights and the unfolding outrageous colonial policies. Women traders in urban cities mobilized themselves and supported the United Gold Coast Convention (UGCC) and later Convention Peoples Party (CPP). It was in 1951 during the struggle for independence that the CPP led by Dr. Kwame Nkrumah established the Women's Wing of the party called the CPP Women's League (Prah, 2019).

Similarly, in the 1900s, Black women in South Africa resisted outrageous government policies, legislations, and laws which threatened their existence. For example, in early twentieth century, Black women successfully prevented proposed legislation that require them to carry passbooks, while in 1956, they actively opposed the "Pass Laws" restricting the movement of Africans (Van Heyningen, 1999).

The case of women protesters and activists in Tanzania is another worthy example. In the 1950s, women formed part of the Tanganyika African National Union, the principal political party in the struggle for independence of Tanganyika, now Tanzania (Geiger, 1987).

All over colonial African societies the above trend was phenomenal. Women from all walks of life, especially market unionists, instilled political consciousness in their members. The various associations across Africa prepared women for the struggle against colonialism. No wonder before and during the nationalist struggles women were well informed of the appalling sociopolitical and economic situations that precipitated the clamor for independence. The next section focuses on three case studies—Egypt, Kenya, and Nigeria. These countries were former colonies of the British Empire, and they are also from three different regions that is, North, East, and West Africa. They provide different backgrounds and perspectives needed in this chapter.

WOMEN AND RESISTANCE MOVEMENT IN EGYPT

Before attempting an analysis of the role of women in the revolt against British rule in Egypt, it is imperative to examine the situation and status of Egyptian women. Women under British rule were relegated to the background. They lacked equal opportunities and privileges as their fellow men. For example, the British colonial government narrowed education opportunities, with the few to isolate and demean the female gender. While they claim to be doing everything they could to improve the status of Egyptian women, they indirectly sought to undermine the existing feminist movement in Egypt by dividing women by class, occupation, and residence. Schooling for a male child was a right, while for the girl child it was a privilege. The British harped on the constraints of the Islamic religion on women as an explanation for their lack of attention to female reforms during their occupation (Ramdani, 2019). The situation on ground however gave credence to women's political activism. Egyptian women became aware and more abreast of happenings around the society.

The uniqueness of the Egyptian state was that prior to British occupation, an Egyptian feminist awareness and ideology had existed alongside the nationalist movement in the late nineteenth century. Feminist consciousness dated back to the reign of Mohammed Ali (1805–1848) (Ramdani, 2019). Ali's efforts at modernizing Egypt through industrial, educational, social, and technological reforms did not only bring enlightenment but also provided necessary opportunities for both the upper- and middle-class Egyptian women (Ramdani, 2019). The reforms transformed the lives of women. In 1832, Ali established a school for midwives, while in 1837 he opened the first girl's state school. In fact, women were allowed to have home tutors, especially for those who could not attend the structured school. As a sign of progress, in the late nineteenth and early twentieth centuries Egyptian women began to teach in schools and also published books and journal articles (Daly, 1988; Ramdani, 2019).

Apart from the educational reform, the Egyptian women's press played a significant role in the construction of feminist national identity alongside the Egyptian nationalist movement. Historians and other scholars marked 1907 as a turning point for women periodicals because of the effect their publications had on the British occupation (Linhares, 2018). Women's writings and publications were exceedingly vocal against the British government. For example, Fatima Rashid formed Jami'iyyat Tarqiyat al-Mar'a (The Society for Women Progress) and held series of meetings in her home that addressed the status of Muslim women in Egypt. Jami'iyyat Tarqiyat al-Mar'a published articles that promoted women's rights and supported the nationalist party's activities (Chirol, 1922; Linhares, 2018).

It is seen here that the formation of a feminist consciousness in Egypt was in tandem with the country's rapid development as a modern state at the beginning of the nineteenth century (Chirol, 1922). Mohammed Ali's technological advancements and lofty reforms in Egypt positively affected all sectors of the country including women. Therefore, women alongside men had all reasons to criticize the system of governance of the British government, who had exploited the country's resources for their selfish gains, while neglecting the interests of the indigenous population.

Having discussed a background scenario of the situation of women, and the pre-nineteenth-century feminist consciousness, next space would be on the role of women in the 1919 revolution. Egyptian women agitated for their civil rights through the nationalist platform. In 1910, Egyptian feminist,

Inshira Shawqi declared an unflinching support for the nationalist movement in a document read by the congress chairman at the Nationalist Congress in Brussels (Linhares, 2018). At the turn of the twentieth century, feminists' activities and women activists confidently entered the public sphere to join cause with the nationalist movement.

Within the nationalist movement, feminist elements and women activists were both vocal and powerful, as women rallied under the "Egypt for the Egyptians" slogan. The two dynamic and overlapping groups—nationalists and feminists—combined to create an impressive and formidable force, capable of dismantling the strongholds of imperialism in Egypt. It should be stressed that radical demands being made by a pioneering women's movement strengthened the nationalist cause (Quaraishi, 1967).

Unlike the Urabi Revolt of 1881–1882, which was exclusively men's business, the 1919 Egyptian revolution against British government was led by female participants (Quaraishi, 1967 and Chirol, 1922). Upon the popular support that the Wadf Party and its leaders enjoyed, and fearing social unrest, the British government moved to arrest Zaghlul on March 8, 1919, and exiled him with two other movement leaders to Malta (Quaraishi, 1967; Ellis, 1992). Following the exile of male nationalist leaders in March 1919 by the European power, women took over the reins of affairs, protested and rallied for the release of male nationalist leaders and for Egypt's independence (Ellis, 1992). Elite women, including Safiya Zaghloul and Huda Sharawi, led the masses, while lower-class women were actively involved in street protests alongside men. Rural-class women provided the economic labor that sustained the protesters. In the countryside, the rural class provided food and assistance to male activists. Besides, masses of poor women rushed and supported the activists.

The revolt was remarkable in that members from all religions and classes of Egyptian society were moved to action. The demonstration became a national general strike that dragged the economic and political affairs of Egypt to a halt (Ellis, 1992 and Ramdani, 2019). Courtrooms were deserted by lawyers, while railroad tracks and telegraph lines used by British officials were sabotaged at strategic locations. Peace demonstrations erupted all over the country, sometimes accompanied by small-scale violence in the form of rioting especially in Cairo, the city of Tanta, and in Asyut Province (Linhares, 2018 and Chirol, 1922). Between March and April, demonstrations and strikes throughout Egypt by students, elite, civil servants, merchants, peasants, workers, and religious leaders became a regular occurrence. In the Egyptian countryside the uprising was more violent in that attacks were carried out on British installations, civilian facilities, and personnel. By July 25, 1919, 800 Egyptians were feared dead, while 1,600 others were severely injured (Ramdani, 2019).

In March 16, 1919, several hundred traditionally veiled women gathered to demonstrate openly against the British government. At the forefront were wives of the exiled nationalist leaders Safia Zaghlul, Huda Sharawi, and Mana Fahmi Wissa (Linhares, 2018). In the ensued mass movement, women adopted the tactics of civil disobedience. These women and others from the upper classes of Egyptian society played crucial roles in the protest by organizing strikes and boycotts of British goods, and petitioning foreign embassies on behalf of the independence movement (Linhares, 2018).

In February 28, 1922, the British pronounced limited independence for Egypt. The British however retained for themselves the control of Sudan and the right to intervene to defend foreign interests in Egypt. By April 19, 1922, a constitution was approved, and an electoral law establishing parliamentary elections was established few weeks later (Ramdani, 2019). Also, the British government was in charge of certain sectors such as control over the security of the communications of the British Empire in Egypt; and defending Egypt against foreign aggression.

Having achieved limited independence in 1919, women played notable role in the build up to the 1952 independence. Elite women had established a political culture in Egypt by the late nineteenth and twentieth centuries. This political base was built upon by women in the next national protest. During the second phase of the Egyptian revolution, between 1940 and 1952, the likes of Doria Shafik and the Bint El Nil (Daughters of the Nile) group were active participants. Their involvement revolved around political rights, equal pay, education and literacy campaigns, and health and social service programs (Ramdani, 2019).

Althoug the 1952 free officers' revolution had been tagged male business because it was planned and carried out by the free officers in Egypt's army, women still provided a complementary and valuable role. Like the 1919 revolution, women adopted letter writing campaigns, petitions, strikes, marches, and demonstrations against the British (Quaraishi, 1967; Ramdani, 2019).

THE WOMEN'S REVOLT IN SOUTH EAST NIGERIA

The women's revolt, sometimes referred to as "Aba Women Riot" or "Women's War," took place during the colonial period (Dike, 1995). It is christened the women's war because although the menfolk of Eastern Nigeria also criticized the tax policy and complained about being taxed, it was the women who exclusively organized and led the anti-tax demonstrations. Though there were related outstanding offensive and provocative impositions such as indirect rule, native courts, and provincial courts on Easterners, the direct taxation was a major catalyst for the uprising (Dike, 1995).

Before the introduction of taxation, the generality of the people of South East had grudgingly existed under the colonial administration. The people experienced worse forms of oppression. In fact, the whole of Southern Nigeria criticized the indirect rule system, and the roles of the native and the provincial courts. The use of Warrant chiefs within these offices met with stiff oppositions within the Eastern communities. The introduction of direct taxation lightened up the South Eastern communities.

In 1926, the British colonial government declared that direct tax would be paid by all male adults in South Eastern Nigeria. As a follow up to the policy, in 1927, the Native Revenue Ordinance was introduced, while in 1928, male adults were made to pay taxes according to the Ordinance (Onaolapo, 2009). The large collections of taxes from male adults made Captain John Cook, the acting District Officer for the Old Bende Division, to embark on an extensive nominal role to capture compounds and families with details of wives and livestock unlike the previous year when only the adult males were counted (Obaro Ikime, 1995). Captain Cook directed the Warrant Chiefs to count the men and from them get data on the number of their wives, goats, sheep, and chickens. Since past head counts ended up with men being taxed and the current exercise was to include women, it was naturally regarded by the people to mean taxation for the women folk.

It is instructive to note that the timing of the introduction of tax system was problematic. The year 1928/1929 witnessed a worldwide economic depression in that the price of palm produce was declining while imported goods for daily use were attracting increased custom duties. During this period the people's income suffered a noticeable downturn. At this time, life was becoming unbearable for most families. Also, there was the belief that taxation implied "head money", which created the impression that the people were slaves and must pay for their freedom (Akpan,1995). More disheartening was the lack of due consultation and conceptual clarifications. One, the people, especially women, were not consulted before attempting to collect tax. And second, there was no form education or information to enlighten the people on what the policy entails.

By November 1929, Chief Okugo of Oloko, one of the Warrant chiefs who had received Captain Cook's instructions to carry out the tax collection order, subsequently sent his messenger Mark Emeruwa, a teacher in one of the local Mission Schools, to count some of his people (Onaolapo, 2009 and Osuji, 1995). This enumeration officer entered a compound and directed one woman, Nwanyeruwa, who was pressing palm oil, to count her goats and sheep. In the process there was a misunderstanding which led to physical confrontation between the two (Obaro Ikime, 1995). This incident resulted in a protest which attracted all the women in the community. As the news spread to other parts of South Eastern Nigeria, more women got involved and received mass sympathy because the fate of the entire peasant populace under colonial administration was at stake.

Suffice it to say that Nwanyeruwa started the women's revolt from Oloko. The riot escalated from her village to a protest that spanned across two provinces and over 6,000 square miles (Okonjo, 1974). The movement covered women of Ngwaland, Mbano, Mbaise, and the neighboring Annang community around Ikot Ekpene, in the Old Calabar Province (Nicolas, 1969). In early November over 10,000 women gathered outside the district administration office demanding the Warrant chief of Oloko provide a written guaranty that they would not be taxed. The women were scantily dressed, girded with green leaves and carrying sticks. Some women wore chalk markings and carried palm fronds on the one hand and sticks on the other, symbolizing peace and war. They chanted solidarity songs against the Warrant Chiefs, Courts Clerks, and Court Messengers.

The rebellion was directed against all forms of constituted authority and control. Women's struggle was also against the Warrant chief system, the brazen corruption, and high-handedness of some of those chiefs who were seen as puppets and agents of the imperial government, especially in the operations of the Native Courts over which they presided. The Aba women's war was essentially anti-government, a rejection of the colonial order. It was a movement of women to protect the economic and political interests which were endangered by taxation.

Women's daring and sacrifice in the 1929 rebellion affected the political landscape in South East and other regions. In 1931, the Royal Commission's Report on the Women's Uprising was published. In the same year, Sir Donald Cameron was appointed Governor of Nigeria with the clear mission of introducing and implementing comprehensive political, administrative, and judicial reforms based on the findings of the Royal Commission's Report (Afigbo, 1972). More so, there was judicial reform. By the protectorate Courts Ordinance, the oppressive provincial courts were abolished. Protectorate Courts were managed by trained officers not associated with political functions as had been the case with the provincial courts. Though the direct taxation continued, it was henceforth operated by persons in whom the public reposed confidence (Afigbo, 1972 and Akpan, 1995).

WOMEN FIGHTERS IN THE MAU MAU MOVEMENT

The Mau Mau movement in Kenya was yet another revolutionary group in which women demonstrated their militancy against a European power. The movement broke out in 1952 following the policies of the colonial master, which frustrated the Kenyans, especially the Kikuyu, and the imperial government declaration of a State of Emergency that led to a colony-wide hunt for members of Mau Mau Association (Lewis, 2007). Also, the changing pattern in the socioeconomic and political milieu of the Kenyan society made the Kenyan revolution inevitable.

Before colonial rule, Kenyan women were actively involved in the agricultural economy by performing various tasks. While men were responsible for harder agricultural tasks such as breaking of land and felling of trees, women were preoccupied with certain basic subsistence crops such as beans, millet, sweet potatoes, maize, and so on. Women also participated in joint ventures such as brewing of beer, trading, harvesting, house building, and other tasks performed by both sexes. The efficiency with which women performed their responsibilities determined their social status with the family and community. In addition, women had influence in the political and institution. Since political and religious matters were closely related, and women featured prominently in religious rites, the latter therefore, through religion, indirectly participated in political issues (Gachihi, 1986).

However, under colonial administration, women in Kikuyu and other societies experienced oppressive measures which made them readily available to any movement that would deliver them from their precarious situation, even if it includes violence. The British government established a system of labor for the European Settler Community using Africans as cheap labor. Land holdings drastically reduced as significant number of lands were appropriated by the settlers (Ogot, 1974). The accession to power of the Conservative government in 1927 and its negative disposition toward Africans, which later led to the restoration of White supremacy, subjugated women further (Tamarkin, 1976). It should also be stated that women were disadvantaged in the education system throughout the colonial period. The traditional belief that the place of women was the home became strengthened under colonial administration (Gachihi, 1986). Women were living in a society that was rapidly losing the concept of "tribal cohesion." The colonial policies relegated the womenfolk further to the background in that the gap between men and women became widened.

Against this backdrop, women decided to join the Mau Mau movement to fight for national freedom. To start with, in order for loyalty, cohesion, and unity of purpose, the leaders of the movement adopted the use of oath or pledge. Taking of oath became the strongest binding factor that created a common bond of secrecy (Gachihi, 1986). Women were involved in the acquisition of weapons in preparation for war. Alongside the men, women stole, smuggled, and bought guns and ammunition. In the ensued battle women, like their male counterparts, fought the colonial force. In 1953, Nyaguthii Theuri, popularly known as Mwago, joined the fighters in the forest. She was a member of one of the several platoons under the command of

Kimathi (Gachihi, 1986). She was one of the staunchest fighters in the Mau Mau.

Some women were responsible for the organization of food and its supply to the fighters, while other women leaders had the task of recruiting girls and young women. For example, Mama Habiba Ali from Majengo area of Nyeri town had several girls who transported food. These girls reported their activities directly to her (Lewis, 2007). It is important to state that for those with specific duties, disobedient or the failure to perform the given task had severe penalty including death. Once an individual decided to stay in the movement, the expectation was that instructions must be obeyed unreservedly and without questions.

Women provided a life-link to the combatants for the first two years of the rebellion. Village women established an organizational pattern responsible for the delivery of resources from the reserves to the forest. All women who had been initiated into the secrets of the movement through the Mau Mau oath performed several varied functions. Women played both meaningful and destructive roles. Some were in the forest as fighters alongside men, some were in the economic sphere, intelligence and information, and espionage.

ANALYSIS OF THE REBELLIOUS MOVEMENTS AND IMPLICATIONS FOR DECOLONIZATION OF GENDER

Deduced from the above, it is a fact that Egyptian women were involved in and instrumental to the 1919 and 1952 national revolutions that saw the country through to political independence. Their level of indocility against obnoxious British policies needs to be appreciated. It is apt to assert that the feminist movement of the late nineteenth and twentieth centuries, and the participation of women from different walks of life in the revolutions, has been the precedent and foundation upon which the twenty-first-century Egyptian women premised their involvement during the 2011 revolution that upturned the regime of Hosni Mubarak. However, it is worrisome to note that in narrating the Egyptian revolutions against colonial rule, the experiences of women protesters and fighters have not attracted much attention. Also, the situation of women in postcolonial Africa has not significantly improved compared to male gender. Gender balance and equity in Africa is far from being achieved. Men and their exploits dominate most discourses, while women's positions are underrepresented. Since men and women are central to the dismantling of the colonial shackles, a balanced analysis is imperative.

In Nigeria, the women's revolt was predominantly the business of the female gender. When in the first instance the colonial government introduced taxation, men did not in practical term protest against the policy, they only criticized passively but at the instance of the introduction of direct taxation on men and women, the latter did not only condemn the policy verbally, but violently protested and fought the colonial government. Unlike the Egyptian revolution that had feminist elements, the Aba revolt was orchestrated by illiterate market women. Their agitation, though organized, was not under watchful eyes of any prominent organization. It was gathered that some men disguised and dressed like women to participate alongside women. The revolt took place in South East and had nothing to do with guerrilla approach like what was happened in Egypt and Kenya.

For the Mau Mau revolt, it is apt to say that the female gender though was actively involved in virtually all departments of the movement had a different experience. Unlike the Egyptian revolutions and the Nigerian women's war, the Mau Mau movement adopted oath taking for its members, including women. Oath taking in the Mau Mau was shrouded in ritual and secrecy, and was inherently violent. Members of Mau Mau were not to divulge the secret of the group to non-members. In fact, the movement was more of a cult. More so, in the Mau Mau, the rank and file and other women with specific duties were faced with severe punishment and in some cases death sentence when found disloyal, disobedient, or unsuccessful in their functions.

The rebellious activities of the above-mentioned African women and their likes in other contexts had profound implication on the status of women. Women resistance movements promoted the decolonization of gender. It invariably repositions the female gender for subsequent involvement in community development. Women participation in resistance movements brought recognition to the female gender in postcolonial Africa. It demonstrates that women, like their male counterparts, possess inherent skills and potentials which can translate to meaningful change in any society.

To decolonize development in gender contexts is imperative not only to strike gender balance but for an inclusive development. This chapter has substantially demonstrated the pivotal role of women in colonial resistance. Ironically, postcolonial African women have been increasingly marginalized. For decolonization of development to be effective, it must be inclusive and take account of the plights of women who are the most vulnerable.

CONCLUSION

The chapter examined the role of Colonial African women in anticolonial resistance across the continent, with particular focus on Egypt, Nigeria, and Kenya. Women, as it is seen, played both destructive and meaningful roles. They were central to the emergence of the various revolts examined. Their complementary roles maintained and sustained the rebellion. More importantly, their legacies had been bequeathed to postcolonial African women. However, their situations have not fared better in the postcolonial African society.

Women's rebellion suggests a genuine clamor for gender transformation against colonial and postcolonial vestiges. However, to decolonize gender is to resist the patriarchal colonial notion, which placed women in a subordinate and unequal position with men and subjugated women's freedom, rights, social existence, and equality. Decolonization of gender is a research agenda which advocates for gender equality by confronting the colonial policies that undermine African women's transformation.

There is therefore the need for African governments to operate an inclusive system where the female gender that had played significant roles in the traditional society would be given the opportunity to contribute to national development.

REFERENCES

Afigbo A. E. (1972). *The Warrant Chiefs: Indirect Rule in South-eastern Nigeria, 1919-1929.* London: Longman.

Akpan, E. E. (1988). The women's war of 1929: Its cultural, social and political aspects. A paper presented at a Mamser symposium on women activities in Uyo, Akwa Ibom State in March.

Akpan, N. U. (1995). The political and social heritages of the 1929 women's uprising in Nigeria. In Chike Dike (Ed.), *The Women's Revolt of 1929.* Lagos: Nelag & Co. Ltd., pp. 20–32.

Balogun, A. O. (1999). Gender crisis in Yoruba thoughts: An aftermath of western experience. *Journal of Cultural Studies* 1(1): 99.

Bennett, O., Bexley, Jo and Warnock, K. (Eds.) (1995). *Arms to Fight – Arm to Protect: Women Speak Out About Conflict.* London: Panos.

Bradford, H. (1996). Women, gender and colonialism. *Journal of African History* 37(3): 351–360.

Brinton, C. (1965). *The Anatomy of Revolution.* New York: Vintage.

Chirol, V. (1922). The Egyptian question. *Journal of the British Institute of International Affairs* 1(2): 34.

Daly, M. W. (1988). *The British Occupation, 1882-1922.* Cambridge Histories. Online: Cambridge University Press, 89.

Davies, J. (1962). Toward a theory of revolution. *American Sociological Review* 27(1): 35.

Falola, T. (2019). The role of Nigerian women. Available at http://www.Britannica.com, accessed September 25.

Ferris, E. (1993). *Women, War and Peace.* Uppsala: Life and Peace Institution.

Erumuo, F. C. (1999). Gender and empowerment. In Remi Anifowose and Francis Erumuo (Eds.), *Elements of Politics*. Lagos: Sam Irognusi Publications, p. 226.

Gachihi, M. W. (1986). The role of kikuyu women in the Mau Mau. Unpublished Master's Thesis submitted to the Department of History, University of Nairobi, Kenya, pp. 40–89.

Geiger, S. (1987). Women in nationalist struggle: Tanu activists in Dar es Salam. *International Journal of African Historical Studies* 20(1): 2–3.

Giardina, C. (2010). *Freedom for Women: Forging the Women's Liberation Movement, 1953-1970*. Gainesville, FL: Florida University Press.

Goldberg, E. (1992). Peasants in Revolt-Egypt 1919. *International Journal of Middle East Studies* 24(2): 44–50.

Gurr, R. T. (1970). *Why Men Rebel*. Princeton, NJ: Princeton University Press.

Heyman, G. D. and Giles, J. W. (2006). Gender and psychological essentialism. *Enfance; Psychologie, Pedagogie, Neuropsychiatrie, Sociologie* 58(3): 293–310. doi: 10.3917/enf.583.0293.

Heyningen, E. (1999). The voices of women in the South African war. *South African Historical Journal* 41: 22–43.

Ikime, O. (1995). Of governors and the governed. In Chike Dike (Ed.), *The Women's Revolt of 1929*. Lagos: Nelag & Co. Ltd., pp. 10–16.

Lewis, A. E. (2007). A Kenyan revolution: Mau Mau, land, women, and nation, Electronic Theses and Dissertations, Paper 2134, pp. 45–66.

Linhares, J. (2018). Egyptian pieces of the empire's puzzle: Peasants, women, and students in British official issued after the 1919 revolution in Egypt *Senior Theses*, Trinity College, Hartford, pp. 3–6.

Love, B. (2006). *Feminists Who Changed America, 1963-1975*. Champaign, IL: University of Illinois Press.

Martins, A. (2019). Feminist consciousness: Race and class, *Meeting Ground*, Retrieved 15 September, 2020. http://:meetinggroundonline.org/feminist-consciousness-race-and-class/

Nabila, R.(2019). Egyptian women in the 1919 revolution: Political awakening to nationalist feminism. Available at http://www.nabilaramdani.com accessed on September 25.

New York Times (1919). 800 natives dead in Egypt's uprising; 1,600 wounded, 25 July.

Nicolson, I. F. (1969). *The administration of Nigeria (1900-1960), Men Methods and Myths*, Oxford: The Clarendon Press.

Nzemeka, J. (2009). The position of women in pre-colonial Africa. In Eno B. Ikpe (Ed.), *Women and Power in the Twentieth and Twenty First Centuries*. Lagos: Fragrance Publications, p. 28.

Ogot, B. (1974). Kenya under the British, 1895-1963. In B. A. Ogot (Ed.), *Zamani: A Survey of East African History*, Nairobi: East African Publishing House, p. 267.

Ogundipe-Leslie, M. (2009). African woman, culture and another development, In Eno B. Ikpe, (Ed.), *Women and Power in the Twentieth and Twenty First Centuries*. Lagos: Fragrance Publications, p. 27.

Okonjo, I. N. (1974). *The British Administration in Nigeria 1900-1950: A Nigerian View*. New York: Nok Publishers, p. 33.

Onaolapo, A. F. (2009). Patriarchy and the acquisition of state powers by African women in the twentieth century. In Eno B. Ikpe (Ed.), *Women and Power in the Twentieth and Twenty First Centuries*. Lagos: Fragrance Publications.

Osuji, C. (1995). The Aba women's revolt of 1929: A study in the mass mobilisation process in Nigeria. In Chike Dike (Ed.), *The Women's Revolt of 1929*. Lagos: Nelag & Co. Ltd., pp. 40–48.

Prah, M. (2019). Chasing illusion and realising visions: Reflections on Ghana feminist experience. Available at http://www.quartafrica.com, accessed on September 24.

Quraishi, Z. M. (1967). *Liberal Nationalist in Egypt: Rise and Fall of the Wafd Party*. Kitab Mahal Private Ltd., pp. 99–102.

Tamarkin, M. (1976). Mau Mau in Nakuru. *Journal of African History* 17(1): 7.

Walker, L. and Smith, H. J. (2006). *Relative Deprivation: Specification, Development and Integration*. London: Cambridge University.

West, H. G. (2000). Girls with guns: Narrating the experience of war of FRELIMO'S female detachment. *Anthropological Quarterly* 73(4): 180–194.

Willis, E. (1984). Radical feminism and feminist radicalism. *Social Text* 9(10): 91. doi: 10.2307/466537.

Yakubu, M. (2009). Power relations between the genders in African families during the twentieth century. In Eno B. Ikpe (Ed.), *Women and Power in the Twentieth and Twenty First Centuries*. Lagos: Fragrance Publications, pp. 151–160.

Chapter 11

African Migrations to Europe
A Historical Appraisal of Transcultural Exchanges and Decolonization in the Age of Globalization

John Ebute Agaba and Emmanuel S. Okla

Globalization has created an avenue for people to interact and relate across borders. Africans have offered their host countries their cultural heritage and have also imbibed such from their hosts in terms of culture and belief system. Even so, there has been an accentuation of cultural imperialism where African migrants are often short-changed in their bid to gain the acceptance of their hosts. Based on historical methodological approach and data from secondary sources, the chapter argues that whereas some African migrants in Europe have suffered from pseudo cultural mentality by losing their sense of dressing, belief, and accent, others insist on sustaining their cultural heritage and transmitting the same to their host who tend to be vulnerable to discriminatory policies. Thus, the chapter points to the need for decolonization in the age of globalization and recommends that the walls of cultural inhibition often erected through state policies and laws be de-emphasized for the free flow of cultural exchanges among nations of the world.

INTRODUCTION

At the turn of the twentieth century, Oripeloye (2011) reechoed McLuhan assertion that the old world had become a global village as the old world order was being dismantled in response to the massive technological inventions of the period. The resonance of this assertion has been felt in virtually all human endeavors. In the world today, the phenomenon of globalization has completely altered the human perception of culture, and the nature of cultural identities as a form of interaction in the global village. The traditional view of culture as state- or nation-centered as manifested in individual attachment to the state for an identity is thus being de-emphasized, and there is a shift from the state to the examination of events beyond its borders. It is in this wise that geographical boundaries are becoming less significant in the context of globalization (Oripeloy, 2011)

Since the end of the Cold War and the emergence of the New World Order (NWO) characterized by unipolarity in 1992, communications and transportation have become more rapid, markets for goods and services have transformed immensely, and money can be moved freely and instantaneously from one country to another with little or no hitches at all (Okpeh, 2000). All of these, coupled with the spate of violent conflicts that erupted across Africa at the end of the Cold War, created avenue for mass migration from Africa to Europe and Asia, among others. The two variants of migrants from Africa were the legitimate migrants who emigrated in pursuit of career, business, scholarship, safe haven (refugees), medication, and on religious grounds; the other variant were the illegal migrants, usually made up of people of low skill in search of menial jobs, and illicit transactions such as commercial sex work and drug peddling.

Migration has major effects on the economy and the people of Africa at large. Most of Africa's best brains are lost as a result of brain drain through migration to Europe, America, and Asia where they are offered better remunerations and work environment. However, it has been argued that migration has often been used as a solution to the problems of poverty at home, since many migrants send remittances to their families. These remittances reach major proportions in some countries. For instance, as a proportion of exports, migrants' remittances in 1988 were over 50% in Jordan, Burkina Faso, Egypt, Sudan, Bangladesh, and South Yemen (Hadjor, 1993). While it is true that migrants often suffer discrimination and low wages in the countries to which they migrate, they nonetheless often succeed in ameliorating their own, their families, and even their countries' economic situations (Hadjor, 1993). This is evident in the case of Nigerian diaspora, particularly in the last two decades, some of which had been documented by the Central Bank of Nigeria with the following figures, $1.34 billon in 2002, $2.26 billion in 2004, $6.47 billion in 2005 and $15 billion in 2007 (Englama, 2007, P.34).

It is imperative to state without mincing words that the crisis of development in Africa is fundamentally responsible for the perennial spate of human movement from Africa to other continents. It is against this backdrop that the chapter problematizes the key issues to be addressed, thus: When did the African migration to Europe begin? What were the remote and immediate causes (factors) that led to these migrations? What were (are) the impact of these migrations on the host countries (Europe) and source countries (Africa), especially on the economy and culture of the two continents over time? How has globalization accentuated these migrations and transcultural exchanges and what strategies can be adopted to mitigate the tides of these migrations that have caused several frictions, the very foundations of diplomatic relations between the source and destination countries. For the purpose of clarity of analysis, the work is structured into five segments, including the introduction. The other segments include conceptual clarifications and theoretical framework, factors responsible for the migration of Africans to Europe, transcultural exchanges between Africa and Europe, and the last being conclusion with some few suggestions.

CONCEPTUAL CLARIFICATIONS AND THEORETICAL FRAMEWORK

In this chapter, there are some key concepts and theoretical framework that need to be clarified for the purpose of deepening our understanding of the subject matter. These include migration, culture and cultural imperialism, cultural mutation and decolonization, and globalization and transcultural. The above concepts are conceptualized thus:

Human migration is a phenomenon that has attracted attention of so many disciplines and scholars over time. Due to the complexity of human life and the fast changing socioeconomic and even political conditions, human migration is gaining importance day by day. Different scholars have tried to define the concept of *migration* distinctly because of their different approaches.

Migration is defined as shifting of people or an individual or group of individuals from one cultural area to another, which may be either permanent or temporary. Eisenstadt (1953, p. 167) looked at *migration* as "the physical transition of an individual or a group from one society to another. This transition usually involves abandoning one social setting and entering another and permanent one." It is also defined as "act of moving from one area to another in search of work." The principal directions of migrations are illustrated by more or less continuous movements from rural areas toward the city, from areas of stable population toward centers of industrial or commercial opportunities, from densely settled countries to less densely settled countries, and from the centers of the cities to their suburbs (Eisenstadt, 1953). *Migration* can also be defined as permanent or semi-permanent movement from one place to another which leads to culture diffusion and social integration (Eisenstadt, 1953, p. 3).

Many migrant scholars have equally looked at the facts of migration and have established that these factors can be classified into two, namely "push" and "pull" factors. Pull factors include better employment, education, recreational facilities, housing and medical facilities, and so, whereas push factors include poverty, indebtedness, social outcaste, unemployment, natural calamities, and host of others. It has been assumed that the confluence of some migratory factors differ from time to time. In other words, there can be many factors combined together that determine the migrants' decision to move from one place to another. It has been found in many migration studies that the economic factors play an important role as most migrations appear to be economically motivated (Gullive, 2000, p. 12).

Also important to state here are the different types of migration. These include rural–rural, rural–urban, urban–urban, and international migrations. The last type of migration is of interest to us to conceptualize it because the subject matter of this chapter is contextualized in it and therefore needs to be briefly defined. International migration happens when the movement of people cross the international borders. This phenomenon of migration has become very common in recent times, due to industrialization and technological revolutions and indeed information and communication technology accentuated by the influence of globalization, which is one of the issues being addressed in this chapter. Following this conceptualization of migration are the concepts of culture and transcultural exchange which are explained below.

Culture is a phenomenon known to all human society. In every human group, there is a desirable pattern of life dominantly observed by the people (Ehindero, 2008). This is why broadly speaking, Ehindero (2008) argues that culture has often been referred to as a way of life of a people; the way they speak, dress, cook their food, serve it, build houses, bury their dead, farm, dance etc. According to Okpaga (2005), "culture connotes the whole range of human activities which are created and learned and are transmitted from generation to generation through various learning processes." The import of Okpaga's submission is that culture is both flexible and dynamic. In the views of Weihrich and Koontz in Ameh (2007, p. 154) culture is "the general pattern of behaviour, shared beliefs and values that members have in common." Haralambo and Heald in agreement with Mark Kirby et al. have postulated that "culture is learnt through socialization rather than that which is gotten by instinct" (Cited in Ehindero, 2008, p. 172). Having explored the variegated standpoints of scholars on culture, it is imperative to submit in tandem with Edward Taylor that culture is "that complex whole which includes knowledge, belief, art, morals, law, customs and any other capabilities and habits acquired by man as a member of society" (Yemisi, 2008, p. 172).

Another concept that deserves attention is cultural imperialism. The term *cultural imperialism* refers most broadly to the exercise of domination in cultural relationships in which the values, practices, and meanings of a powerful foreign culture are imposed upon one or more native cultures. In this broad sense, cultural imperialism could be used to describe examples of the enforced adoption of the cultural habits and customs of actual imperial occupying powers from antiquity down to nineteenth- and twentieth-century European colonialism. In practice, however, the term is nearly applied to relations between sovereign nation-states and their colonies from the mid-twentieth century onward (Tomlinson, 2012, p. 1). Ekeanyanwu (2005) states that cultural imperialism is the subjugation of a local culture and the imposition of an alien culture on the local culture.

Writing on cultural imperialism, a media scholar, Uche (1996), has drawn a clear and distinct line between cultural imperialism, cultural synchronization, and culture juxtaposition. He states that what most persons call cultural imperialism may actually be regarded as cultural synchronization. According to him, cultural imperialism means an external culture that is imposed upon another against its will, cultural synchronization means an external culture that is welcomed and imitated by another culture which the external eventually supersedes in an evolutionary fashion, and cultural juxtaposition means the placing together of locally produced cultural elements with the externally produced (or as the opposition and co-existence) of distinct types of cultural productivity within late capitalism. The next conceptualization is cultural mutation.

Understanding the meaning of cultural mutation in our context here is very crucial, possibly to expand our knowledge about cultural imperialism already conceptualized. Cultural change has similarities to generic evolution, but the study of culture using evolutionary models remains contentious. Analogously to genetic evolution, cultural traits are transmitted by replication (i.e., learning), and cultural change involves mutation of cultural traits, drift, and selective processes favoring the persistence of certain cultural traits and the loss of others. Genes and cultural traits also differ in many ways, but many of those differences do not affect evolutionary dynamics in a fundamental way. For example, some cultural traits have a particular nature similar to genes (terms memes in such cases) and others do not, but this has superficial effects on the outcome of evolutionary modeling (Henrich & Boyd, 2004; Mesoudi, 2004). Evolutionary models similar to population genetics could, therefore, provide useful tools to study cultural change. An unresolved source of contention, however, concerns the role of cultural mutations in cultural change (Pinker, 1997; Henrich & Boyd, 2008). On the basis of the above explanations, among others, we define *cultural mutation* as any modification of existing cultural traits or the creation of new cultural trait altogether. Cultural mutations may also result from adaptive cognitive biases and thus be common and non-random relative to the selective landscape (Henrich & Boyd, 2008). The concept of decolonization is the next and last to be discussed before we lay the basis of the theoretical framework that underpins this chapter.

Decolonization can be conceptualized as the process of revealing and dismantling colonialist power in all its forms. This includes dismantling the hidden aspects of those institutional and cultural forces that had maintained the colonialist power and that remain even after political independence is achieved (*Stanford Encyclopedia of Philosophy*, 2006).

Initially, in many places in the colonized world, the process of resistance was conducted in terms or institution, appropriated from the colonizing culture itself. This was only to be expected since early nationalists had been educated to perceive themselves as potential heirs to European political systems and models of culture. This occurred not only in settler colonies where the White colonial elite was a direct product of the system, but even in other colonies of occupation (*Stanford Encyclopedia of Philosophy*, 2006). It is pertinent to state here too that the contradiction inherent in the decolonization process whether in India, Africa, or the West Indies in the nineteenth and early twentieth centuries, the first nationalists were also modernizers, whose program was less to effect a rejection of colonialists' culture than to adopt its practices. This process of political and cultural "brokerage," as some historians have called it, involved these early decolonizers in a profound complicity with the imperial powers from which they sought to emerge as free agents. Their general attitudes and practices were necessarily imbued with the cultural and social values they had been taught to regard as those of a modern, civilized states (de Morases & Barber, 1990). Consequently, political independence did not necessarily mean a wholesale freeing of the colonized from the colonialist values, for these, along with political, economic, and cultural models, persisted in many cases even after independence.

Furthermore, this becomes more glaring, as has been analyzed in the main text that the globalization of the modern world economy especially in Africa has meant that political independence has not really affected the kinds of changes in economic and cultural control that the early African nationalists might have expected. It has even been argued by some recent commentors that the colonial powers deliberately avoided granting independence until they had, through internal discriminations and hegemonic educational practices, created an elite (comprador) class to maintain aspects of control on their behalf but without the cost or the opprobrium associated with the classic colonial models.

Thus, as well as direct and indirect economic control, the continuing influence of Eurocentric cultural models privileged the imported over the indigenous, colonial languages over the local languages, writing over orality, and linguistic culture over inscriptive cultures of other kinds (e.g., dance, graphic, arts, which had often been designated as "folk culture"). Against all these, occlusions and over writings of precolonial cultural practices, a number of programs of decolonization have been attempted. Notable among these have been those that seek to revive and revalue local languages. Thus, decolonizing processes that have advocated, for instance, a return to indigenous languages have involved both a social program to democratize culture and a program of cultural recuperation and reevaluation. In Africa, the work of Ngugi WaThiong'o has been at the forefront of this decolonizing model, (Ngugi 1981a, 1986, 1993). By and large, however, decolonization, whatever else it may be, is a complex and continuing process rather than something achieved automatically at the moment of independence.

Globalization no doubt remains one of the most talked about issues in recent times around the world by both specialists and non-specialists alike. The intensity of this continuing debate has generated a frenzy-like situation, encapsulating all aspects of the phenomenon's ongoing processes—historical, political, economic, cultural, environmental, technological, and ideological, that rage on without any sign of abating.

Although the phenomenon of globalization is not "new," its renewed vigor and interest, especially within the humanities however stem from the accelerated pace of global economic integration, occasioned by the widening and intensifying of international linkages in trade, finance, and communications; underpinned by the liberalization of economic policies and by technological discoveries that have facilitated transport and communication networks. It has engendered "a process whereby national borders cease to be an impediment to the movement of products and capitals" (Grant, 1996, pp. 23–26), where the "interlinking of national economies into an independent global economy and the development of a shared set of global images" (Nazombe, 1995, p. 2) have resulted in an "integrated global economy in which not only exchange but also production and finance are organized and articulated on a planetary scale" (United Bank for Africa, 1994, pp. 32–33). This interlinking of hitherto wholly independent economies; the increasing irrelevance of physical national boundaries; and the emergence of shared set of images characterizes the contemporary global society, which Renato Ruggiero has described as borderless economy or to borrow the popular expression of McLuhan (1996) a "global village."

In the submission of Dicken (1992, p. 1), globalization represents a more complex and advanced form of internationalization, implying a degree of functional integration between internationally dispersed economic activities. To Khor (1995, p. 1) "it is what we in the third world have for several centuries called colonization." McLuhan (1996, p. 206) puts it simply as another "phase of exploitative capitalism, a pretext for socially regressive governmental economic policies and the means by which both domestic and international inequalities are further entrenched." To Jinadu (2000, p. 68), the concept involves "the diffusion or trans-nationalization of capital and of the dominant ideas of social and cultural organization which underlie it and propel it to other societies from the most advancing societies." It is "the transformation of the relations between states, institutions, groups and individuals, the universalization of certain practices, identities and structures, and perhaps more significantly, the expression of the global restructuring that has occurred in recent decades in the structure of modern capitalist relations" (Aina, 1997, p. 2).

As Nnoli (2000, pp. 173–174) succinctly puts it, "globalization is imperialism. Like imperialism, globalization is a dynamic phenomenon, which changes in accordance with the laws of capitalist expansion; consequently, it has assumed different focus in the past, such as slave trade, legitimate trade, colonialism, neocolonialism. Today it is simply called globalization." Similarly, Olorode (2000, pp. 15–20) argues that "globalization is the current stage of centuries old capitalist expansion process leading to the commodification of people's creativity and resources faster than ever before"; thereby resulting in the "thingification" of people: reducing human beings to "things" to be exchanged at the market place with profit as the main consideration. The net result of which they argue would be increased poverty, unemployment, instability, corruption, distortion, and negation of local or indigenous sociocultural institutions and values (Ihonvbere, 1993).

Nevertheless, the reality of our time amply suggests that the phenomenon of globalization represents an irreversible and inescapable trend that nations must wake up to, and accept along with its prospects and challenges. As Oscar Arias, former president of Costa Rica and a winner of the Noble Peace Prize cited in Abe (2004, p. 234) rightly avers:

> [S]ome have engaged in debate about whether globalization is good or bad for humanity. This is as ridiculous as trying to decide if Tuesday is a better day than Thursday. The truth is that globalization is not an ideology, or a religion, or a philosophical vision of the world. What it is, like the climate of our planet, is an inescapable part of reality neither good nor bad in itself. It is simply here, in our day and age, and societies and individual must adapt their presents and plan their futures within globalization [*sic*].

Having conceptualized the main concept in this chapter, what follows is the discussion on theoretical framework. Cultural imperialism/theory was developed in the 1970s to explain the media situation as it existed at that time. After a critical analysis of the arguments put forward by most of the theorists and other scholars who have written on the subject of cultural imperialism, the major propositions could be summarized in the work of Schiller (1976) as follows:

> Firstly, theory proposes that "a society is brought into the modern world system when its dominating stratum is attracted, pressured, forced and so met.

Secondly, it is bribed into shaping its social instructions to correspond to, or even promote, the values and structures of the dominating centre of the system." (Schiller 1975, cited in White, 2001)

The summary of this view is that the essence of cultural imperialism is the domination by one nation by another and the environment for this is created by transnational media organizations.

Third, another assumption of this theory, according to White (2001, p. 4) citing Tomlison (1991) is that Media play a central role in creating culture. This axiom is linked to the interchangeable use of various terms to refer to cultural imperialism Writers, who talk about "cultural imperialism" as "Media Imperialism," treating the two terms as synonyms bring into question the centrality of the media in claims of cultural imperialism. This practice implies that the media have such an overwhelming role in the process deferred.

What follows after the discussion of the theoretical framework is the analysis of the key factors that led Africans to migrate to Europe.

FACTORS RESPONSIBLE FOR MIGRATION OF AFRICANS TO EUROPE

The factors behind the mass movement of Africans to other continents during the Cold War era up to the heightened phase of globalization were essentially the same. The plethora of conditions at the root of African migration in our contemporary time can be divided into internal and external factors. The internal factors which migration experts refer to as push factors are those conditions and circumstances that are generic to the African setting and compel individuals and groups to migrate. The external factors commonly referred to as the pull factors on the other hand denote conditions and circumstances in the industrially developed countries that serve as attractions and thereby compel groups to desire and seek to emigrate (Ogaba, 1999)

What then are these internal factors? They include conflicts, wars, famines, drought, poverty, and bad governance. It is important to look at how all of these issues contributed to the phenomenon of migration within and from Africa all through the period of the Cold War to the era of globalization. The African continent just like other Third World countries served as a major theater of proxy wars orchestrated by the United States of America and the now-defunct Soviet Union between 1945 and 1991. The violent conflicts witnessed in Africa during this period ravaged four regions in the continent, namely Southern and Eastern Africa, Central Africa, and West Africa. The major consequences of the violent contestation across Africa were massive stockpiling of weapons at the detriment of agriculture and industry, widespread destruction of lives and properties, and ultimately large-scale displacement of people within and outside the continent.

At the end of the Cold War, the general expectation was that of a global peace and cessation of conflicts and indeed wars. The paradox is that new theater of violent conflicts erupted in Africa as hitherto totalitarian regimes could no longer sustain the support of their patrons who were more concerned about how to handle the crisis precipitated in Eastern Europe as a result of the disintegration of the Soviet Union. Pent up grievances then snowballed in the forms of ethnic-based conflicts in places such as Liberia and Sierra Leone in West Africa and Rwanda and Burundi in Central Africa. The conflict in Sudan also heightened at the end of the Cold War following the assumption of power by President Omar Bashi, a diehard Islamist, in 1989 (Ingham, 2017). Bashi did not only overthrow a democratically elected government but also blocked a process put in place for the secularization of Sudan. His support for militia group such as the jarija weed led to the outbreak of the Dafur conflict in 2003. More than 2.3 million Darfurians were displaced in one of the world worst humanitarian crises (Dosomething.org, nd). By the end of the twentieth century, almost all the regions in Africa had witnessed violent conflicts that had forced people to flee from their homes. It is estimated that close to the end of the twentieth century, 14 million or 40% of the 35 million refugees around the world were Africans (Ogaba, 1999).

In the first quarter of the twenty-first century some of the violent conflicts in Africa were caused by contestation for power by ethnic groups in countries such as Kenya, Central African Republic, and Burundi. In the same period, the penchant for monopolization of leadership had generated tensions and caused violence in nations such as Cote d'Ivoire, Bourkina Faso, Guinea Bissau, and Gambia. The activities of religious extremists or terrorists had also contributed enormously to the incidences of violence across Africa in the twenty-first century—from the activities of Alshabab in Somalia and Kenya to that of Alqueda in Mali, Mauritania, Senegal, and Burkina Faso and Boko Haram in Nigeria, Chad, Niger, and Cameroun, and ISIS and ISIL in Algeria and Libya—such that the atmosphere that pervaded the entire continent was that of fear and trepidation, thereby creating fundamental reason for migration. Although the bulk of the refugees generated by all these violent conflicts confronting Africa remained within the continent, a substantial number still find their way to other continents in search of security and survival.

Another internal factor responsible for the influx of migrants from Africa can be situated in the economic predicaments of most African states at the advent of globalization. Prior to the end of the Cold War, most African economies were unable to generate or sustain development in the critical sectors of health, housing, roads, water, food, and labor. Most of the development attained by African countries in the decades of the 1960s and 1970s were dramatically curtailed in the 1980s and 1990s due to a combination of bad governance, improper government policies, draught, economic recession, conflicts, and wars (Ogaba, 1999, p. 128). When most of the countries approached the World Bank and the International Monetary Fund (IMF) for succor, they were made to embrace the Structural Adjustment Program (SAP) as the only alternative panacea. It turned out, most unfortunately, that the SAP became an albatross for all those countries that implemented the policy.

The concomitant effects of SAP on Africa were the abysmal decline in living standard due to devaluation of currencies, job cut, or rationalization and privatization of public enterprises. As cost of goods and services skyrocketed beyond the reach of the masses, many Africans also lost their jobs. Most governments in the continent were constrained to impose embargo on employment at a time when universities and polytechnics were turning out graduates in large numbers. Lack of employment or underemployment for an energetic and restless mass of African youth thus became a major ground and motivation for emigration to other countries in search of the proverbial green pasture.

The fall out of the above was the endemic spread of poverty across the African landscape. With little or no government intervention in national economies, coupled with a prostrate private sector, Africa stepped into the envisioned "global village" at the end of the Cold War on an unequal footing and has since remained at the mercy of Western capitalist interests. Africa is reputed as the poorest region in the world (Bairo & Le, 1993) with 33% of an estimated African population of about 640 million people living in poverty at the verge of globalization (Todaro, 1989). The desire to break out of the cycle of poverty by most Africans who possessed the skills to thrive in the global labor market domiciled in Europe, America, and Asia was also at the root of the quest by most African professionals to migrate out of the continent for either temporary or permanent residency.

The pull factors on the other hand are external in nature and located outside Africa. The quest and increasing demand for cheap labor in Europe served as motivating factor for those willing to take advantage of such opportunities to better their economic fortunes outside Africa. With the intensity of globalization, European countries imposed strict immigration laws through the introduction of visa policies in the bid to regulate the inflow of immigrants from outside Europe. Instances of these immigration policies could be seen in some European countries as analyzed below.

The Danish authorities introduced a series of measures during the period to enforce "Danish values," designating certain areas as "ghettos" based on a high proportion of residents with ethnic minority or immigrant backgrounds, and low social status. Children in those areas would be subject to mandatory daycare in the name of integration. In the same period a ban on wearing face veils in public came into effect (European Union, 2018). There were also instances of racist intolerance or violent hate crimes in many EU states, including Bulgaria, France, Germany, Greece, Hungary, Italy, Slovakia, Spain, and the United Kingdom. Issues of xenophobia became rampant in most EU member states (European Union, 2018, p. 3).

However with these stringent immigration policies desperate African migrants who are termed as illegal migrants still find their ways to Europe through unauthorized channels. Two categories of African illegal immigrants are found in Europe, the majority are those who had traveled through illegal routes across the North African deserts and the Mediterranean Sea without proper clearance and documents from their countries of origin (Wikipedia, 2017). The second category of illegal immigrants are those who initially traveled to Europe as legal immigrants under the guise of business trip or academic pursuits but could not revalidate their visa after expiration.

There also exists an established pattern of international connection based on historical link between Africa and especially Europe that has over time fueled the incidences of immigration and emigration between the two continents. Ogaba (1999, p. 132) aptly observes that:

> Migrations are not random occurrences, rather they follow pre-established routes and directions which are usually established as far back as the days of colonialism. For example, most African migrants to France come from former colonies of France and most African migrants to the United States and Canada come from Anglo-phone African States.

The influence of Western media, especially the information super highway in the age of globalization, has had a tremendous impact on Africans through the spread of Western value and culture. It is the over "glamouralization" of Western life that most often stimulates the interests of young Africans to emigrate even at the slightest opportunity.

The phenomenon of "chain migration" as argued by migration experts such as Meissner, Hermits, Walker, and Ogaba (1993, p. 9) is also contributory to the spate of migration from Africa to the industrialized world. They state thus:

> Once migration footholds are established, family members join successful migrants, remittances link communities across great distances, and established immigrant groups help the newly arrived find work and negotiate seemingly alien ways and practices.

Thus, it is evident that individual migrants most often formed the bridge heads that act as catalysts for their relatives at home (i.e., Africa) to emigrate and integrate with them abroad. The Igbo, Yoruba, Hausa, and Edo ethnic groups in Nigeria have greatly utilized this approach, placing them ahead of several ethnic groups from Africa in the industrialized world. In the elections of June 2016 in the United Kingdom where seven Nigerians won seats in the parliament is a classic example to reinforce this viewpoint.

Having discussed the factors responsible for migration of Africans to Europe, what follows is an appraisal of transcultural exchanges between Africa migrants and their hosts in Europe.

TRANSCULTURAL EXCHANGES BETWEEN AFRICAN MIGRANTS AND THEIR HOSTS IN EUROPE

Europe for reasons of historical link with Africa since the Atlantic Slave Trade era and the emergence of colonialism has served as a destination point for most African migrants. While the initial phase of African migration to Europe was by compulsion, especially during the Trans-Atlantic Slave Trade, as from the twentieth century, the migration trend was dictated by motivation or inducement from Europe and desire on the part of Africans to explore the opportunities that abound in Europe, particularly the attainment of independence by some African states (European Union, 2018).

A precise population estimate of African migrants in Europe is yet to be ascertained due largely to the fact that the population of irregular migrants from Africa far outstripped that of regular migrants. Between 2000 and 2005, an estimated 440,000 people per year emigrated from Africa, most of them to Europe (Townsend, 2015). The position often advanced by migration experts while explaining in the causative factors of irregular migration is the simplistic narrative that acute poverty was at the root of the quest for emigration by Africans and that most irregular emigrants are people of low skills and of low literary level. It has been proven that not all irregular immigrants were victims of acute poverty as some of them had to sell out their valuable assets such as houses and cars to be able to pay their fares through the various routes and channels of transportation. It is also verifiable that most of the immigrant population are well educated but were only attracted to Europe because of the opportunities of cheap labor provided by the informal labor sectors there (Wikipedia, 2017). According to a BBC report (2007) the International Organization for Migration (IOM), estimated that around 4.6 million African migrants live in Europe. The Migration Policy Institute on the other hand put the population of irregular migrants from Africa in Europe at between 7 and 8 million (BBC, 2017).

At the end of the Cold War and with the intensification of globalization in the last decade of the twentieth century some scholars have advocated for cultural hybridization and harmonization (Oripeloye, 2011). In explaining this concept, Rushdie makes an illustration in *Imaginary Homelands* when he states thus:

> (We) are Hindus who have crossed the black water; we are Muslims who eat pork . . . our identity is at once plural and partial. Sometimes we feel that we straddle two cultures; at other times, that we fall between two stools. (cited in Oripeloye, 2011. p. 92)

The fate of African migrants in Europe in the post–Cold War era is not in any way different from the picture of Asian migrants in Europe painted above by Rushdie. However, from the angles of the host continent of Europe, the citizens appear to have issues assimilating the culture of African migrants.

The influence of Western media on the psyche of most African migrants cannot be overemphasized. For most African migrants, the drift toward European culture starts right from their places of origins in Africa. This development has serious implication for African migrants as it often places on them the burden of truly defining their "cultural make up and identity."

The current generation of African migrants in the post–Cold War era in Europe is confronted with myriads of challenges to their survival and cultural expression. The events that followed the collapse of Soviet Union in 1991, especially the conflicts that erupted in some of the new states that emerged out of Union of Soviet Socialist Republic (USSR), had negative implications for African migrants in Europe. With the upsurge in the influx of Eastern European refugees into Western Europe, most of the European Union member states, such as United Kingdom and France, embarked on strict immigration policies. The contest between Afro-Asian and Eastern European migrants for available job also became fiercer.

One of the reactions of Africans to the harsh immigration policies in Europe was the high incidence of marriages between Africans and Europeans. Through marriage to Europeans most African migrants became naturalized citizens in their host countries. Though many Africans adopted this approach as survival strategy, the union between Africans and Europeans nevertheless has far reaching social and cultural implications. It is a common thing to see a product of Afro-European union in European cities bearing African names and relating with African cultural norms and practices. Schools abound in major cities of Europe where young children of African parents and Europeans married to Africans attend language classes taught by African migrants. The African homeland culture of inclusiveness and extended families has continued to thrive among some migrants in Europe to the admiration of Europeans. Different African migrant communities, through their sociocultural organizations from time to time, organize cultural-related events such as naming ceremonies, marriage, and other special days to celebrate and create awareness about their ethnic identities. In most of these events, African foods and delicacies, including fashion, are showcased. While it is difficult to gauge the level of assimilation and acceptance of African culture through this approach, it has however stimulated the interest of some Europeans in the study of African culture and heritage. Even though this is evident as a research gap, it may not receive emphasis in this discourse.

As the tempo to deny African migrants immigrant rights and status heightened in most European countries, acquisition of language skills and proficiency in national history and culture were made state policies and enshrined as prerequisite for granting and retention of immigrant status in some countries. For instance in the pre-Nicolas Sarkozy era in France, the learning of French culture and history was a compulsory requirement for all those seeking immigrant status in that country (Globalisaion101, 1997). In the Netherlands, the government embarked on a program called "inburgering" which is translated as "citizens making" in which potential immigrants cannot become citizens until they have passed courses in Dutch culture and social norms. Immigrants are compelled to speak Dutch in order to receive welfare and must be in the country for seven years before they can apply for nationality (Globalisaion101, 1997, p. 3)

Many Africans in Europe, especially labor migrants and students, speak multiple languages in order to cope well in workplaces and in schools. They did not have to struggle much to adjust to European fashion style, especially the Christian populations from predominantly Sub-Saharan Africa. However, the population of Muslim immigrants from predominantly North Africa have to adjust to Western fashion and dress code because of the climatic condition of Europe and also the need to comply with recommended dress code and ethics in the work place. Most Western governments in recent years had banned hijab used by Muslim women to cover their heads, a state policy due to the rising waves of terrorist activities across Europe (Aljazeera, 2017). The Muslim immigrant community in Europe found it very difficult to accept the reason advanced by their host countries that terrorists often disguised with hijabs and also hid bombs and other dangerous weapon in them. They viewed the entire development as an assault on the religion of Islam which prescribes the use of hijab for women, especially in public places. This issue has been a subject of litigation in many European courts (Aljazeera, 2017).

There has been a rising wave of resentment against African immigrants and what they stand for, especially their culture in Europe. In France, with a population of 5 million Muslims, mostly from Africa (Lohma, 2017), the immigrants population are not fully integrated into the society as they are always considered as security risks, especially since the aftermath of the annulment of Algerian elections in 1993 and the September 11, 2001, terrorist attacks in the United States of America. In Paris, for instance, there are suburbs where Muslims immigrants mostly from Africa reside in clusters. These areas, apart from the occasional raids carried out in them by government security agencies to fish out perceived terrorists and criminals, appeared largely to lack government presence in terms of provision of infrastructure and social amenities (Walt & Bajekal, 2015). In the Netherlands, Pin Fortuyin, a popular politician who was assassinated in 2002, was so vociferous against immigrants, particularly from Africa whom he accused of eroding traditional liberal Dutch tolerance for homosexuality and commitment to equality for women (Globalisation101, 1997).

In a so-called age of globalization, the major advocate of the concept may pretend, but we cannot gloss over the fact that cultural issues are a significant factor in the response of Europeans to global migration (Globalisation101, 1997, p. 4). This is why in recent years the European public has questioned the effects of immigration on culture and national identity. Fear and distrust of immigrants have led to the creation and flourishing of anti-immigrant political parties in several European countries such as Britain, Switzerland, Denmark, Italy, Sweden, France, and the Netherlands (Globalisation101, 1997, p. 4). Most often, many of the anti-immigrant political parties have linked social ills, such as unemployment and crime, to immigration. The activities of these parties have given rise to xenophobia and hatred for immigrant communities in Europe, thereby laying formidable obstacles to cultural crystallization envisioned at the dawn of globalization (Globalisation101, 1997, p. 6).

CONCLUSION

The presence of large pool of African immigrants in Europe and Asia was in response to the internationalization of labor. That African migrant labor force has contributed enormously to the economies of European member states is no longer in doubt. However, with all the contributions and sacrifices made by African migrants to enhance the socioeconomic well-being of their host countries, they are always and still perceived as cultural irritants. While it is expected that host governments would create conducive environment for African migrants to unleash their full potentials by encouraging cultural cohabitation between Africans and their citizens, they have at most time played into the hands of right-wing elements and irredentists in the guise of populist politics. The resultant outcome is the imposition of strict immigration policies, mostly aimed at denying the African migrants the capacity for cultural expression. For an effective transcultural exchange between African migrants and their hosts in Europe to thrive, the EU member states should endeavor to dismantle all the walls of cultural inhibitions erected through state immigration policies, particularly in this age of globalization.

REFERENCES

Abe, T. (2004). Global Village Phenomenon: Nigeria and Globalization. In Kolawole, D. (ed.), *Nigeria's Foreign Policy Since Independence: Trends, Phases and Changes*. Lagos: Julius and Julius Associates.

Aina, T. A. (1996). Globalization and Social Policy in Africa CODESRIA Bulletin, No. 4.

Aina, T. A. (1997). *Globalization and Social Policy in Africa: Issues and Research Directions*. Dakar: CODESRIA.

Aljazeera. (2017). Employers Allowed to Ban the Hijab: EU court. Retrieved from https://www.aljazeera.com/news/2017/03/employers-allowed-ban-headscarves-eu-court 170314092627483.html (Accessed on June 22, 2017).

Ameh, A. A. (2007). Culture and its Implications for Effective Management in Africa. In A. Menegbe & G. Omachonu (eds.), *Cultural Renaissance and National Development in the 21ˢᵗ Century* (p. 154). Abuja, Nigeria: Roots Books.

Bairo, R. V. & Le, J. (1993). Losers and Winners in Economic Growth. In *Proceedings of the World Bank Annual Conference on Development Economic 1993*, Washington 1994.

BBC. (2017). Key Facts: Africa to Europe Migration. Retrieved from http://news.bbc.co.uk/2/hi/europe/6228236.stm on 15/6/2017.

de Moraes-Farias, P. F. & Barber, K. (1990). Self-Assertion and Brokerage: Early Cultural Nationalism in West Africa. Retrieved from https://www.cambridge.org/core/journals/africa/article/p-f-de-moraes-farias-and-karin barber-eds-selfassertion-and-brokerage-early-cultural-nationalism-in-west africa-birmingham unive rsity-african-studies-2-birmingham-university-of birmingham-centre-of-west-african studies-1990-242-pp-950-isbn-0-7044-1096-6 paperback/F7C27721AE210F1 DF7FDD510E016048D.

Dicken, P. (1992). *Global Shift* (2nd edition). New York: Guilford Press.

DoSomething.org (n.d.). 11 Facts About Darfur. Retrieved from https://www.dosomething.org/us/facts/11-facts-about-darfur (Accessed on October 26, 2021).

Ehindero, J. T. (2008). The Nexus Between Culture and Integration as an implication for National Development. In A. D. Menegbe & G. S Omachonu (eds.), *Cultural Renaissance and National Development in the 21st century* (p. 31). Abuja: Roots Books.

Eisenstadt, S. N. (1953). Analysis of Patterns of Migration and Absorption of Immigrants. In *Population Studies*. London: London School of Economic.

Ekeanyanwu, N. T. (2005). *International Communication: Issues, Concepts and Research in the 21st Century*. Lagos: Standard Mass Concept.

Enejo, E. K. (2000). Globalization and the Culture of Third World Economy: Implications for National Development In A. Menegbe & G. Omachonu (eds.),

Cultural Renaissance and National Development in the 21st Century. (p. 47). Abuja, Nigeria: Roots Books.

Englama, A. (2007). "The Impact of Remmittance on Economic Development", Central Bank of Nigeria (CBN) Bullion 31(4): October-November 2007.

European Union. (2018). Migration and Asylum. Retrieved from https://ec.europa .eu/homeaffairs/sites/homeaffairs/files/docs/pages/00_arm2018_synth sis_report _final_en.pdf.

Globalisation101. (1997). Culture and Globalization. Retrieved from https://www .globalization101.org/uploads/File/Culture/cultall.pdf.

Grant, W. (1996). Making Economic Policy in a Global Economy. *Political Review*, 6: 11–38.

Gullive, B. (2000). Concept and Theories of Migration: An In-Depth Understanding. Retrieved from https://shodhganga.inflibnet.ac.in/bitstream/10603/37372/9/09_ chapter%203.pdf

Hadjor, K. B. (1993). *Dictionary of Third World Terms*. London: Penguin Books.

Henrich, J. & Boyd, R. (2004). *Foundations of Human Sociality: Economic Experiments and Ethnographic Evidence from Fifteen Small-Scale Societies*. Oxford: Oxford University Press.

Ihonvbere, J. O. (1993). Economic Crisis, Structural Adjustment and Social Crises in Nigeria. *World Development*, 21: 141–153.

Ingham, K. (2017). Omar al-Bashir President of Sudan. Retrieved from https://www .britannica.com/biography/Omar-Hassan-Ahmad-al-Bashir.

Jinadu, L. A. (2000). Globalization and the New Partnership: An African Perspective. In G. Lachapelle & J. Trent (eds.), *Globalization, Governance and Identity: The Emergence of New Partnerships* (pp. 67–81). Montreal: Les Presses de l'Universitaire de Montreal.

Khor, M. (1995). Address to the International Forum on Globalization, New York City, November, 1995. Retrieved from https://core.ac.uk/download/pdf/7028178 .pdf on 22nd May, 2020.

Lohma, M. (2017). *Teaching Immigration with the Immigrant Stories Project: Lesson Plans*. Minnesota: University of Minnesota.

Marshall, D. D. (1996). Understanding Late-Twentieth Century Capitalism: Reassessing the Globalization Theme. *Government and Opposition*, 31(2): 200–232.

Meissner, D. M. et al. (1993). *International Migration Challenges in a New Era*. New York: Trilateral Commission.

Mesoudi, A. (2004). Is Human Cultural Evolution Darwinian? Evidence Reviewed from the Perspective of the Origin of Species. *Pub Med*, 58: 1–11.

Nabende, J. S. (2010). Theories and Concepts in the Study of Governance in Africa. In S.A. Nyanchoga, et al. (eds.), *Governance in Africa: Historical and Contemporary Perspectives* (p. 14). Nairobi: CUEA Press.

Nazombe, E. (1995). Democracy in Africa: NGOs, Education, Action. *Hunger Teachnet*, 6(3): 1–15.

Nnoli, O. (2000). Globalization and Democracy in Africa. In D. Nabudere (ed.), *Globalization and the Post Colonial African State Harare-Zimbabwe* (pp. 173–189). AAPS Books.

Ogaba, O. (1999). The Security Implications of Contemporary African Migration. In W. O. Alli (ed.), *Africa and the African Diaspora* (p. 127). Jos: Mazlink Nig Ltd.

Okpaga, A. (1999). The Globalization of Western Cultural Values: Some Implications and Consequences for National Development in Nigeria. *Journal of Globalization and International Studies,* 11(1): 60–72.

Okpeh, O. O. (2000). Globalisation and the African question in the Twenty-First Century. *African Journal of Economy and Society,* 2(2): 43–60.

Olorode, O. (2000). *Globalisation in Perspective.* Ile-Ife: LST Publisher.

Oripeloye, H. (2011). Globalisation and Cultural Identity Discourse in the Exilic Poetry of Tanure Ojaide and Odia Ofeimun. In J. T. Tsaajor (ed.), *Politics of the Post Colonial Text: African and its Diasporas* (pp. 90–99). Lagos: Concept Pub. Ltd.

Schiller, H. I. (1976). *Communication and Cultural Domination.* New York: International Arts and Sciences Press.

Stanford Encyclopedia of Philosophy. (2006). Globalization. Retrieved from http://plato.stanford.edu/entries/globalization

Todaro, M. P. (1989). *Economic Development in the Third World.* New York: Longman.

Tomlinson, J. (2012). Cultural Imperialism. Retrieved from doi:10.1002/9780470670590.wbeog129 (Accessed on May 22, 2020).

Townsend, R. M. (2015). The European Migrant Crisis. Retrieved from https://books.google.com.ng/books/about/The_European_Migrant_Crisis.html?id=612SCgAAQBAJ&redir_esc=y

Uche, L. U. (1996). Cultural Imperialism Hypothesis Revisited. In L. U. Uche (ed.), *North-South Information Culture: Trends in Global Communications and Research Paradigms.* Lagos: Longman.

United Bank for Africa. (1994). Monthly Business and Economic Digest, 17 (1) January.

UNRISD. (1995). *States of Disarray: The Effect of Globalization.* Geneva: UNR1SD.

Walt, V. & Bajekal, N. (2015). Muslims in Neglected Paris Suburbs Worry Conditions Could Produce More Terrorists. Retrieved from time.com/.../muslims-france-alienated/ (Accessed on June 22, 2017).

White, L. (2001). Reconsidering Cultural Imperialism Theory. Retrieved from https://www.arabmediasociety.com/reconsidering-cultural-imperialism-theory/

Wikipedia. (2017). Migrants. Retrieved from https://en.wiki.pedia.org/.../migrants%2... (Accessed on June 21, 2017).

Wikipedia. (2017). Illegal Number. retrieved from https://en.wikipedia.org/wiki/Illegal_number (Accessed on June 15, 2017).

Yassine, F. (1999). Globalization, Its Institutions and African Women's Resistance. In F. Yassine (ed.), *Africa: Gender, Globalization and Resistance* (pp. 75–76). New York: Anword Book Series.

Yemisi, J. (2008). Culture: Implications for Managers of Organizations in Nigeria. In A. D. Menegbe & G. S Omachonu (eds.), *Cultural Renaissance and National Development in the 21st century* (p. 172). Abuja: Roots Books.

Chapter 12

Beyond Colonial Development Model and the Quest for Alternatives in Africa

Olayinka Akanle and Chukwuka Blessing Chidiogo

This chapter examines the ramifications of the colonial development model and the possibilities of achieving development through alternative non-Western approaches in Africa. Furthermore, the chapter explains how Africa's current colonial epistemic traditions can be decolonized. The role of indigenous knowledge systems and social thoughts is explored. The chapter concludes that until colonial perspectives and processes of development are de-emphasized, Africa's development aspirations will remain evasive. This is a decolonial approach that needs to be adopted to drive development in Africa.

INTRODUCTION

The issue of development is a practical one. This is particularly so when Africa comes into focus. Africa is better known globally today as a continent of underdevelopment than for any other reason (Akanle and Adejare, 2019; Akanle and Okewumi, 2019). This has led many to wonder if Africa is actually synonymous with anything other than underdevelopment. This is because all the measures of underdevelopment are very visible on the continent while elements of development appear very distant from the continent. For instance, Africa today is very popular for war, terrorism, political instability, godfatherism, poverty, brain drain, corruption, human trafficking, illegal international migration, unemployment, child abuse, child marriage, violence, election rigging, illiteracy, uncontrolled urbanization, subsistence farming, poor industrialization, dilapidated infrastructures, desperate international migration, destitution, and gender inequality just to mention a few (Adelakun, 2008;

Abdi, 2010; Akanle, 2012; Akanle and Abayomi, 2013; Akanle and Adesina, 2018; Akanle and Okewumi, 2019; Akanle and Shittu, 2019; Adewusi and Akanle, 2020; Akanle and Omotayo, 2020). The continent depends more on aids, loans, grants, and numerous assistances from the West and more recently from China. Africa lacks the capacity to engage in giving assistance to other continents because it is always seeking assistance from even unusual quarters and corners (Adelakun, 2008; Abdi, 2010; Akanle, 2012; Akanle and Abayomi, 2013; Akanle and Adesina, 2018; Akanle and Okewumi, 2019; Akanle and Shittu, 2019; Adewusi and Akanle, 2020; Akanle and Omotayo, 2020). In terms of development, Africa is best described as an incapacitated continent constantly seeking help.

An increasing concern is the fact that the continent as a whole appears to be fixated in underdevelopment. The route to development in Africa depicts an unclear pathway and as somewhat confusing as no country in the continent has achieved progressive sustainable development (Akanle and Adesina, 2019). Even the North African nations that previously showed great prospects of development are dropping into underdevelopment at an increasing rate and are bedeviled with conflicts and unrests, while South Africa with huge development potentials is gradually slipping into underdevelopment. South Africa is submerged in corruption, state capture, political infighting, xenophobic and homophobic attacks, and outright racism. Unfortunately, these are very dangerous counter-development variables. A very important question raised and engaged in this chapter is this: Why is Africa rooted so intrinsically in underdevelopment? Our theoretical, pragmatic, and epistemological interventionist perspective is that as long as colonial development perspectives and orientations continue to serve as the development frameworks for African nations, original development can never be achieved in the continent. Furthermore, colonial development models such as modernization theory and globalization theory which have been the basis of measuring development in Africa have proven to be ineffective in the attainment of sustainable development across all indicators, and this is because these models lack the ability to incorporate indigenous and cultural development factors. The "Eurocentric" nature of the colonial development models is a contributing factor to the development issues bedeviling Africa. On this basis, the importance of alternative development approaches cannot be overemphasized. Decolonial frameworks are therefore very important as alternative approaches across levels and systems on the continent and this is the focus of this chapter.

Sustainable routes to development must begin with an appreciable understanding of development as a concept and a practice. According to Akanle and Adebayo (2013), development usually means different things to different people depending on the scholars' aims, interest, context, and perspective. Development, according to Akanle (2012), was coined from the old French word *des envolupper* which means unfolding. This refers to development as being a process of evolving, expanding, and opening discoveries of new things and a new way of life. This indicates that development is never a mistake; it does not happen unconsciously but it is often premeditated and objectively postulated by people for reaching a desired state of living. Rodney (1973) looked mainly into the concept of development and underdevelopment. Development can be considered and interpreted from individual perspective, national perspective, and/or continental perspective. The most important point is that development must be objective by indicators and subjective by value with primary effects on totality of quality of lives of people and groups in society. It must also be sustainable by meeting the needs of current generation and at the same time must not destroy the chances of the future generation (Akanle and Adesina, 2018; Akanle and Shittu, 2019). From the individual perspective, one can say that development means a good job, a good family, a steady source of income, an intelligent person with skills and capacity, a morally upright person, and so on (Akanle and Adebayo, 2013). Development could also be seen from the level of social groups. In other words, have people been able to improve in their general lifestyle and in their relationship with fellow people? At the level of social groups, therefore, development means an increasing ability to control relationships at both internal and external level (Akanle and Adejare, 2019; Akanle and Okewumi, 2019).

Even though development shares huge relationships with growth, growth is not synonymous with development. Growth is only a necessary but not sufficient factor for development. Development is unlikely to happen without growth but growth does not translate to development. Growth is commonly related to the economy but development transcends the economy and the figures. Development includes the social, cultural, economic, political, family, educational, health, technological, environmental, climate, geographical, religious, and the other inexhaustible forces that determine the quality of life of people, nation, continent, and the world (Rodney, 1973; Akanle and Adesina, 2018; Akanle and Okewumi, 2019; Akanle and Shittu, 2019; Akanle and Omotayo, 2020).

Development is a process and not an event. Development is also not a destination but a constantly shifting process. This is why it is necessary to argue that describing a nation as developed and others as developing is a mirage. All nations are by and large developing because development is a process that all nations are essentially passing through and will forever pass through. This has become very clear with the destructions occasioned by the Coronavirus (Covid-19) pandemic. Covid-19 actually led to thousands of deaths and infections in the United States of America, United Kingdom, Italy, Germany, Russia, China, and France among other affected *developed countries*. These supposedly *developed countries* experienced far more deaths and infections than the so-called underdeveloped countries of Africa to the extent that the supposedly *developed* healthcare system of the *developed world* was overwhelmed and clueless in the face of ravaging Coronavirus pandemic. This case study of Covid-19 pandemic empirically showed that all nations are developing in the final analysis ultimately because development is a process and not a destination. Development is a means through which humans increase or maximize control and use of resources in the environment. Hence, development is the ability to attain self-sufficiency within the context of the available resources (Olutayo, 2018). This presupposes that as human beings exist within a social environment they continue to widen their horizon as to the knowledge and needs of their environment and state of living. From inception, development has always been a totalistic movement. However, as much as development is germane to human survival, it has remained one of the most controversial yet very important phenomena globally especially as some nations claim and appear developed while others are rooted and gripped by underdevelopment.

Development is a multi-dimensional process by which the productivity, income, and welfare in terms of health, nutrition, education, and other features of satisfactory life of people can be improved upon or transformed (Akanle and Adesina, 2018). For Walter Rodney (1972), development is a many-sided process implying for the individual, skills and capacity, greater freedom, creativity, self-discipline, responsibility, and material well-being. The process involves the development of tools, skills, and the mobilization of required resources for development purpose. Swanepoel and De Beer (2006) emphasized that development involves a series of stages by which individuals having recognized their capabilities, ensure that knowledge is acquired and also work collectively to meet their needs. In the same vein, Korten (1990) defined *development* as a process which involves the ability of members of a particular society to improve individual capabilities as well as their institutional capacities to manage successfully the available resources, ensuring sustainable improvements in their state of living (see also Singh, 2009), who documented how development should be perceived using an index. To him, development must include aspects such as increase in real income per capita which is basically viewed as an economic growth; improvement in distribution of income, thereby ensuring equity, ability to ensure political and economic freedom; and lastly, equitable distribution and access to resources, education, health care, employment opportunities, and justice.

According to Nnoli (1979), development refers to checklist of technical artifacts. To him, the availability of schools, hospitals, road networks, electricity, boreholes, and other infrastructural faculties are indications of development. To Lenin (1964) development is a progressive movement, ascension from lower to higher stages and from simple to complex situations—the simple/lower stage(s) refers to the state of nature in which society finds itself in the process of social evolution. However, development can also be drastic and radical as seen from historical developments and revolutions. By implication therefore, this presupposes that this expansion is a continuous process, it never ends because human desires never end. As human beings exist, they continue to widen their horizon as to the knowledge and needs of their environment and state of living. One can therefore say that an essential aspect of development is the quest to improve lives.

The World Bank in the World Development Report (1991) believed that the concept of development has economic, social, and political attributes such as sustainable increase in living standards including consumption, education, health and environmental protection, equality of opportunity, and liberties and political freedom. It should, however, be noted that development goes beyond quantity in terms of economic growth, gross domestic product, and so on; it also encompasses the quality of life of the people in a particular society. Development gives measurements of the number of goods and services produced in various economies. Besides, for development to be understood, certain qualitative assessments have to be made concerning the way that a given economy is put together. Development must of necessity translate to the improvement of people's lives through improved education, incomes, skills development, and employment (Umekachikelu, 2011). Similarly, development thus represents the comprehensive process of change through which an entire national/continental system moves away from a condition of life widely perceived as unsatisfactory toward a situation of life or condition regarded as subjectively and objectively more desirable. And since humans are at the center of development, for development to have true meaning it must have to do with a progressive improvement of the quality of human life in society (Echikwonye and Beetseh, 2011). The various issues central to the concept of development underscores the need for more development experts. Akanle (2012) buttresses the importance of development studies in understanding and explaining how societies can achieve optimal health, the best of useful knowledge, and optimal resources utilization for a common goal, appropriation of their participatory rights, and achievement of an optimum standard of living without external imposition.

DECOLONIAL THEORETICAL FRAMEWORK

The proponents of decolonial framework cannot be traced to a single person as several scholars in sociology and across other disciplines have contributed to the theoretical framework. The focus of most decolonial scholars is not only on global economic relations but also on the effects of colonialism on the colonized. One major proponent of decolonial framework is W. E. B. Du Bois, the founder of U.S. Sociology whose works suggested the views of decolonial methodology. Smith (2012) described decolonial framework as a methodology that focuses on recovering the lost identities of colonized people. It is pertinent for a decolonialist to realize that "indigenous ways of knowing were excluded and marginalized" (Smith, 2012, p. 71) and then initiate a move to reclaim, reconnect, and reorder "those ways of knowing which were submerged, hidden or driven underground" (p. 72). To Smith (2012), *decolonization* can be defined as the manner with which "indigenous populations share experiences as peoples who have been subjected to the colonization of their lands and cultures, and the denial of their sovereignty, by a colonizing society that has come to dominate and determine the shape and quality of their lives even after it has formally pulled out" (Smith, 2012, p. 7). Decolonial theory served as the framework guiding this book chapter and this is suitable as it makes provision for Africa to propose alternative approaches to development from the experiences of the indigenous people.

Rodney, in his book *How Europe Underdeveloped Africa*, emphasized that when using comparative standards, it is evident that Africa today is underdeveloped in relation to Western Europe and a few other parts of the world; and that this present position has been arrived at, not by the separate evolution of Africa on the one hand and Europe on the other, but by exploitation. As it is well known, Africa has had prolonged and extensive contact with Europe, and one has to bear in mind that contact between different societies changes their respective rates of development. It is generally believed that Africa today is seen to be underdeveloped while certain parts of the world are considered developed. To think that Africans were cultureless before the coming of the Europeans is a fallacy and an aberration. Prior to the coming of the colonialists, African countries had their own lifestyle and culture. They had their agricultural/ economic system, political system, religious system, educational system, and so on. Prior to colonialism, Africans had their distinct culture. A *culture* is the total way of life of a group of people. It encompasses what such people ate and what they wore; the way they walked and the way they talked; the manner in which they treated death and greeted the new-born, the way they learned, the way they met their needs and the likes. Obviously, unique features came into existence in virtually every locality with regard to social details. This distinct African culture helped to bind people together. Their art was rich and symbolic in its own way. The people reached the pinnacle of achievement in various spheres of life. There were traces of development in various African countries such as the Ancient Egypt, Ethiopia, Nubia, Zimbabwe, the Maghreb, Western Sudan, and so on; these countries were altered by culture contact with the Europeans.

Rodney (1973), however, emphasized that to set the record straight, four operations were required. First, the reconstruction of one's understanding of the kind of development in Africa prior to the arrival of the Europeans. Second, the reconstruction of the nature of development that existed in Europe before expansion abroad. Third, the analysis of how Africa had contributed to Europe's development. Last, the analysis of how Europeans contributed to Africa's underdevelopment. Rodney (1973) revealed that extensive research has been carried out in the second operation; however, all other operations deserve extensive and further attention. Having realized the importance of reconstructing the nature of African development, this chapter seeks to deconstruct the colonial development models while prescribing alternative development approaches. This chapter emphasizes the need for Africa to come up with alternative development approaches to their nation and go beyond the colonial development model that was bequeathed to Africa.

COLONIAL DEVELOPMENT MODELS: THEORETICAL PERSPECTIVES

Colonialism is a form of temporarily extended domination by people over other people and as such part of the historical universe of forms of intergroup domination, subjugation, oppression, and exploitation (Horvath, 1972). According to Reyes (2001), modernization theory and globalization theory are the core theoretical paradigms that have been used to make sense of the development concept especially as it relates to developing countries. African economies obviously lack comparative technical expertise partly as a result of the historical strangulation of their rudimentary technological base in the age of colonialism.

MODERNIZATION THEORY

According to Olutayo (2002), this theory is the oldest of all attempts at assisting the Third World nations to develop. The concept of modernization incorporates the full spectrum of the transition and drastic transformation that a traditional society has to undergo in order to become modern (Hussain, et al., 1981; Lenin, 1964). *Modernization* refers to the experience of social change in the new nations, that is, the countries that are emerging from the centuries of colonial exploitation and domination. Modernization theory is also a description and explanation of the processes of transformation from traditional or underdeveloped societies to modern societies. Eisenstaedt (1966) holds that historically *modernization* is the process of change toward those types of social, economic, and political systems that have developed in Western Europe and North America from the seventeenth century to the nineteenth century and have then spread to other European countries to South American, Asian, and African continents. (Eisenstaedt, 1966). Modernization theory attempts to identify the social variables which contribute to social changes and development of societies, and seeks to explain the process of social evolution. Modernization theory does not only stress the process of change but also the responses to that change. It looks at the internal dynamics while referring to social and cultural structures and the adaptation of new technologies.

Modernity is a term used to characterize the stage in the history of social relations dating roughly from the end of the eighteenth century that is characterized by political and industrial revolutions of the time. It is established to this effect that sociology as a discipline developed as a response to the advent and challenges of modernity. Modernity is typically contrasted with traditional forms of society along lines parallel to Durkheim's contrast between mechanical and organic solidarity. To state simply, *modernization* is referred to as the process of becoming modern. It doesn't carry much weight to make declarative statements that suggest that the antithesis of modernity or modernization in its entirety is tradition or traditionalism. Western writers and scholars that propound theories for Africa's development usually make this assumption neglecting the fact that our ideological orientation of communalism is different from theirs that is capitalist in nature.

Modernization theory emerged in the 1950s as an explanation of how the industrial societies of North America and Western Europe developed. Internal factors in the countries of the "Third World" such as illiteracy, the traditional attitude of the population, ideological orientation of communalism, agrarian structure, the low division of labor, and the lack of communication and infrastructure among other factors are the causes of underdevelopment. The theory argues that societies must develop in fairly predictable stages through which they become increasingly complex.

According to Agugua (2018), modernization in itself is believed to be an irreversible process that once kick-started cannot be stopped. It is believed that once "Third World" comes in contact with the West, it will not be able to resist the impetus toward modernization. For one, this implies that the covert function and basis of modernization as a theory of development and a state of being is without mincing words to be Westernized. Since the "Third World" is prescribed upon contact with the West to drop its own indigenous way of life and emulate the features of the Western societies, it is not becoming modernized in itself, but Westernized outside of itself. Again, this suggests a race in futility because, in as much as the '"Third

World" may venture into the process of "modernization," it is not locally driven by them, it is rather out of their context and they go out of their way to copy and emulate what holds for other people. So we can exercise that while modernization may not be reversible as suggested, it may equally not be attainable since it is not the "Third World" setting their pace or target themselves.

Again, Levy (1967), in Agugua (2003), maintains that "as time goes on, the west and the 'third world' will increasingly resemble one another because the patterns of 'modernization' are such that the more highly modernized societies become, the more they resemble one another"; in essence, it stated that modernization is a homogenizing process (Agugua, 2018). So far so good; from observations, we cannot submit that "Third World" nations in any way look like or replicate successfully the "First World." All they have is a situation of trying to adopt and buy the ways of living and technology produced and created for the "First World." Ironically, we "Third World" are chronic consumers of whatever junk is produced by the West, hence serving as a ready and stable market for the economic advancement of a "First world." In essence, "Third World" does not readily create or innovate any genuine products as such like the "First World" does; it only wants to acquire and use what the First World is using. We end up being consumers for their excesses, which are oftentimes from raw materials gotten cheaply from us. This is a case of the Third World not knowing what they have nor how to use them, so they come to take from them and dictate to them how and what to use their resources for. Our needs are now based on their own discoveries and innovations. It is in line with these features that the modernization theory is grounded.

Hence, for Armer and Katsillis (2001), modernization theory has been one of the major perspectives in sociology of national development and underdevelopment since the 1950s. Primary attention focused on ways in which the past and present premodern societies become modern (for instance, Westernized) through the thought process of economic growth and change in social, political, and cultural structure (Armer and Katsillis 2001). In general modernization theorists are concerned with economic growth within societies as indicated, for example, by measures of gross national product. They are also of the opinion that for a society to develop they have to follow the way of living of the Western world. Societies should copy the West that is, the way they eat, dress, modes of production, culture, and so on, and they would develop. This is a strong claim among these theorists and they also believe that the reason why some societies are not developed yet is because they still practice their own archaic way of living, once these societies drop that lifestyle they would develop.

GLOBALIZATION THEORY

Globalization theory emerged from the assumptions that there is a global interaction and integration of nations on the basis of socioeconomic transactions with much emphasis placed on cultural and communication ties (Akanle, 2011; Reyes, 2001). Globalization scholars are of the opinion that cultural links are pivotal in explaining the elements of modern development (Reyes, (2001)). Globalization itself entails the increasing international integration of markets for goods, services, and capital bringing about noticeable changes to the face of the world economy which has frequently been described as gravitating toward a global village (Akanle, 2011; Obadan, 1999).Globalization has brought about considerable improvement in nation's development; this includes the commercialization of agriculture and expansion of agro-industries, the liberalization of international trade and marketing for food and other agricultural products, the intensification and internal labor migration, the increasing privatization of resources and services, and the wider use of information and communication and technologies (Akanle, 2011).

Giddens (1991) views globalization as the intensification of worldwide social relations which link distant localities in such a way that local happenings are shaped by events occurring many miles away and vice versa. Akanle (2011) simply referred to globalization as the world becoming a global village with the ease of interaction, even though the world is so big, gigantic, and massive with different kinds of people numbering over seven billion with many non-identical languages, different cultures, and weather, it has become very possible and easy for the people of the world to relate seamlessly. Ritzer (2008) viewed globalization as the spread of worldwide practices, relations, consciousness, and organization of social life.

DECONSTRUCTING THE COLONIAL DEVELOPMENT MODELS: ALTERNATIVE APPROACHES

According to Gordon and Sylvester (2004), development is construed from the sociocultural and political ideologies of the Westerners. The development models are made up of theoretical assumptions that demand to be interrogated. These assumptions are based on Eurocentrism whereby the belief systems and practices of the West are considered superior to that of other nations. This Eurocentric relation documents the many reasons for the failure of development of the Third World as it portrays the non-Westerners in a degrading light. Having established that colonial development models such as modernization theory and globalization theory have been idolized as Western constructs which have continued to serve as the basis for measuring development in other parts of the world particularly that of Asia and Africa, there is massive need for Africans to deconstruct the imposed and adopted models.

In other words, there is need for Africans to develop indigenous and African development trajectories in measuring the continent's development status. According to Olutayo (2018), gaining independence from colonialist was expected to genuinely create an independent nation that could handle things in their own way. However, the level of dependence has seemed to continue, especially, or perhaps, despite the socialist regime in the world economy. Years after colonial freedom, African nations inherently model their development pathways to that of the West, thereby creating unnecessary developmental challenges for the nation. Western life, beliefs, and culture are being emulated and looked upon as the ultimate, neglecting indigenous cultural beliefs prior to our contact with the West. While this dependency act continues, it continuously poses a threat to the development of African nations which increases our underdeveloped state and greater dependence on core countries.

Development in Third World countries should be meticulously defined in line with the natural resources at disposal. Rather than being a primary producer of commodities and pave the way for the exploitative nature of global supply chain, is it not normal to kick start development in the Third World nations through indigenous industrialization? Hence Olutayo (2010) suggested that to ensure development at the country level, indigenous industrialization should be strongly encouraged based on our level of technical expertise, because as long as investible capitals continued to be expropriated from the African economies under whatever guise, growth and development would continue to be a mirage. The Third World countries need to review their economic relation with the capitalist countries and consider the economic interest that would engender development. It would be better to focus on raw materials and other economic resources in the local and indigenous areas to achieve developmental goal. In order to adequately decolonize our development ideologies, it involves a process of prioritizing and valuing indigenous knowledge and practices so much so that our thought processes are shifted away from the Western ideas to that of indigenous ideas.

Olutayo (2018) in his inaugural lecture expressed that having researched how nations develop, he has come to the foremost knowledge that a nation cannot develop by copying the ways of other nations; hence, to develop, such nations must indigenize what it has learned from other nations. He further buttressed that indigenizing development can be made possible when the means of survival is owned and controlled by the inhabitants of such nation. Development should entail a well-planned process directed toward a specific ideological postulation which reflects the beliefs, values, and thought processes of a particular community.

INDIGENOUS KNOWLEDGE SYSTEMS

Indigenous knowledge and Western science have been established as two sides of the same coin. This dichotomy in knowledge systems is a result of the various epistemological orientations attached to them (Briggs, 2005). *Indigenous knowledge* according to Sillitoe (2006) is any understanding that is linked and deeply rooted in a particular culture. He further buttressed that indigenous knowledge includes all understanding and cultural ways of "doing things" held together by a defined set of people that inform the interpretation of their social environment. The concept of indigenous knowledge has been referred also to mean endogenous knowledge, traditional knowledge, and local knowledge (Sillitoe, 2006; Rist, et al., 2011; Akanle, et al., 2017). Indigenous knowledge system has been conceptualized differently and has been a controversial topic at the national and international discourses. Scholars have defined indigenous knowledge system from the aspect of culture, people's values, and their way of life. Homann and Rischkowsky (2001) emphasized that indigenous knowledge is a social product. Ellen and Harris (1966) characterized indigenous knowledge to be local in practice and deeply rooted in geographical location as well as people's contextual experiences. The scholars also characterized indigenous knowledge to be practiced and transmitted orally; embedded in everyday lived experiences, it involves empiricism, and also must be situated within the tradition of a cultural heritage.

Indigenous knowledge has been increasingly identified as a solution to most of the challenges brought about by the many development strategies which have failed over time (Agrawal, 1995, p. 420). Briggs (2005, p. 3) emphasized indigenous knowledge as the "possible alternative for development" therefore the concept *buen vivir* comes to mind. This simply refers to an alternative concept of development that tends to bring to limelight the attainment of good life in a broad sense, only attainable within a community, this presupposes that Western development pathways should be neglected such that members of a particular community focus solely on indigenous methods of achieving development (UNPFIL, 2010; Gudynas, 2011; Olutayo, 2012). Indigenous knowledge system therefore, emphasizes that development is situated within a particular sociocultural environment, thereby ensuring that the necessary intervention needed by people to meet their needs is considered within their cultural exposure. This way, sustainable development can be easily achieved.

From the foregoing, one can categorically emphasize that in order to properly deconstruct colonial development models, indigenous knowledge system is seen to be pivotal to ensure Africa's development framework as it involves grassroots practices and also offers development models that are ecologically friendly and sound socially (Senanayake, 2006). A self-initiated development should be encouraged at all levels involving the sociocultural indigenous development paradigms. According to Olutayo (2018), it is saddening to know that our state of development is being dictated for use rather than considering development as the process of exploiting our environmental resources. There are many natural resources that are left untapped or made redundant in the country due to the colonial conquest and the advent of Westernization. To redefine paths to sustainable development, it therefore becomes imperative to revive and promote the indigenous knowledge systems to ensure that our indigenous culture does not get eroded in the waves of globalization. According to Oladimeji (2013), reviving the local crafts, agriculture, and indigenous technology offers an unexploited succor capable of salvaging the people from chronic and transient poverty. Indigenous knowledge ensures that people's needs are enriched through the cultural practices. However, indigenous knowledge systems have been criticized for a number of reasons. It is often referred to as being backward (Briggs (2005)), causing low levels of development and leading to development stagnation since its focus has been shifted from modern to local. Other scholars allude to the fact that indigenous knowledge cannot sufficiently contribute to economic development without the help of Western technologies (Bebbington, 1993; Sinclair and Walker, 1999; Briggs, 2005).

AFRICANIZING DEVELOPMENT MODELS

To Africanize development is to frame development within African's existential realities. The colonial invasion altered Africa's indigenous knowledge systems and replaced it with Western development concepts and models that lacked the foresight for a sustainable development in the contextual ways. There is no gainsaying the fact that the deepest root of development failure of Africa is not a lack of resource for development, rather, it is lack of sustainable indigenous development practices. For many years, development of Africa has been modeled after the foreign, incompatible, capitalistic, and individualistic frameworks of the West/colonial *masters*. It is truism that indigenous development strategy is a systematic, comprehensive, and reliable measure with capacity to bring about desirable transformation to African nations. It is essential for the African continent to develop in all spheres of life, including but not limited to the economic, social, and political dimensions.

Africans should ensure this by involving the populations and ensuring that the policies and strategies aimed at ensuring development are indigenously driven from below. The real bottom-top approach to development of Africa is strongly and forcefully recommended here. Not the imported models and frameworks that never work when infused into African contexts. Decolonized development approaches that accommodate nature of Africans and encapsulate the "Africanness" are needed as sustainable alternative approach to development on the continent. In essence, domestic markets should be strengthened, intra-Africa exports should be encouraged, and massive energy development should be promoted to avoid reliance on external models. Indigenous theories and social thoughts should be encouraged. Gender inclusion and general inclusive social policy frameworks that are inward looking are needed as alternative. All that is foreign is not always good. Indigenous knowledge systems and decolonial perspectives are more functional and must be prioritized for Africa's development.

Africa is blessed with abundant human and natural resources and Africans must begin a new process of social orientation as well as entrench social relations in the context of localized social needs. Africans should engage democratic nationalists who exhibit proven attributes of credibility and integrity with the expertise of harnessing the potentials deposited in contextual and external natural and human resources for sustainable development. In order to attain sustainable development, it must begin and end with the people as they develop their individual and collective potentials in the interest of the nations and the continent. The African social thought should be appraised and appreciated through rigorous research and analysis to promote and encourage African development capacities. Indigenous sustainable development can only be achieved when the deconstruction of colonial development models is total and when Africans base their development practices and policies on local, contextual, and indigenous knowledge systems, cultural heritage, beliefs systems, and values.

Social thoughts have the ability to aid decolonization of African development processes. Social thoughts are capable of assisting in understanding the prevailing experiences of people in their local environments. These experiences are coded in norms and values accepted by societies. Social thoughts explain the societal arrangements within a community such that patterns and forms of behaviors are understood. According to Olutayo (2018), it is impossible to develop a society without ensuring that all the constituent units of the social institutions (family, religious, political, economic, educational, media), and indeed, the attendant deviances that may arise from these institutions, are put into consideration. As a result, the structural analysis of the society comes to the fore. As Africans there is need to rethink alternative and new approaches to development relegating to the background the colonial development approaches bequeathed on Africans.

By so doing Africans will move closer to ensuring an indigenous sustainable development alternative. In order to ensure development, and to improve standards of living and quality of life, Africans need to create a path for Africans and reduce reliance of the foreign colonial approaches. This presupposes that Africans would engage their thought processes so much so that they consider their indigenous characteristics in ensuring that Africans are properly taken care of and that Africa can be developed by focusing on strengthening domestic markets at its pace, though this process might be slow, it will definitely ensure a steady progress. African countries should focus on domestic and regional markets, orientations, thought processes, and modeling rather than focusing on Western approaches and recommendations. It is imperative to prioritize African social thoughts if Africa will achieve sustainable economic, political, social, and inclusive development. Africans have a part to play in ensuring that indigenous knowledge systems and decolonial alternative approaches are embraced, instituted, sustained, and preserved to the extent that these decolonial alternative approaches can even be exported.

CONCLUSION

The indices of development in Africa are Eurocentric bequeathed upon by colonialists; however, these have not translated to better and sustainable development over the years, hence scholars are of the opinion that alternative development models be adopted. This chapter has provided insights on how the colonial development models have failed to comprehensively ensure that Africa attain sustainable development. In this chapter, these models were deconstructed and alternative development approaches were provided. Decolonial framework laid emphasis on how indigenous knowledge systems and Africanizing development models were better alternatives to the colonial development models of modernization and globalization theory. Going forward, the ideas proposed by these authors in this chapter would be beneficial to policymakers in Africa to adopt a more indigenous approach to development.

REFERENCES

Abdi, A. A. (2010). Globalization, Culture and Development: Perspectives on Africa. *Journal of Alternative Perspectives in Social Science,* 2(1): 1–26.

Adelakun, A. O. (2008). *Theoretical Approaches to Development and Underdevelopment, Nigeria.* University of Jos Press.

Akanle, O. & Omotayo, A. (2020). Youth, Unemployment and Incubation Hubs in Southwest Nigeria. *African Journal of Science, Technology, Innovation and Development,* 12(2): 165–172.

Adewusi, A. O. & Akanle, O. (2020). *Ose Dúdú*: Exploring the Benefits of Yoruba Indigenous Black Soap in Southwest, Nigeria. *The International Indigenous Policy Journal,* 11(1), 1–20.

Agrawal, A. (1995). Dismantling the Divide Between Indigenous and Western Knowledge. *Development and Change,* 26(3): 413–439.

Agugua, A. (2013). Social Change in Nigeria since Independence. In A. Osuntokun, D. Aworawo, & F. Masajuwa (eds.), *History and Cultures of Nigeria up to AD 2000.* Somolu: Frankad.

Agugua, A. (2018). Africa and the development Narratives: Occurrences, Histories and Theories. In O. Akanle, & J. Adesina (eds.), *The Development of Africa: Issues, Diagnoses and Prognoses.* Springer International Publishing.

Akanle, O. (2011). Nigeria Culture and Identity in a Globalized World. In B. Owasanoye, O. Akanle, & J. Olusanya (eds.), *Youths and Nigeria's Intangible Cultural Heritage.* Lagos: Human Development Initiatives (HDI).

Akanle, O. (2012). Introduction to Development Studies. In I. S. Ogundiya & J. Amzat (eds.), *The Basics of Social Sciences* (pp. 45–68). Sokoto: Usman Dan Fodio University.

Akanle, O. & Adebayo A. A. (2013). Sociology of Development. In R. Aborisade, A. O. Omobowale, O. Akanle (eds.), *Essentials of Sociology.* Ibadan: Ibadan University Press.

Akanle, O. & Adejare, G. S. (2019). Foundation of Development Sociology. In A. A. Abdullahi & E. M. Ajala (eds.), *Contemporary Issues in Sociology and Social Work* (pp. 98–115). Ibadan: College Press, Lead City University.

Akanle, O. & Jimi, O. A. (2018). Introduction: The Development of Africa: Issues, Diagnoses and Prognoses. In O. Akanle & J. O. Adesina (eds.), *The Development of Africa: Issues, Diagnoses and Prognoses* (pp. 1–8). Berlin: Springer.

Akanle, O. & Okewumi, O. E. (2019). Contemporary Sociological Theories: An Africanist View. In A. A. Abdullahi & E. M. Ajala (eds.), *Contemporary Issues in Sociology and Social Work* (pp. 27–44). Ibadan: College Press, Lead City University.

Akanle, O. & Shittu, Olamide. (2019). When Development Appears Impossible: The Unending Development Question of Nigeria. 42nd AFSAAP Annual Conference. November 26–27, 2019. Africa's Diversity and Development. University of Otago, Dunedin, New Zealand.

Akanle, O., Adesina, J., & Fakolujo, O. (2017). Jedijedi: Indigenous Versus Western Knowledge of Rectal Haemorrhoids in Ibadan, Southwestern Nigeria. *African Studies,* 76(4): 530–545. doi: 10.1080/00020184.2017.1372121.

Amin, S. (1976). *Unequal Development: An Essay of the Social Formation of Periphery Capitalism.* New York Monthly Review Press.
Briggs, J. (2005). The Use of Indigenous Knowledge in Development: Problems and Challenges. *Progress in Development Studies*, 5(2): 99–114.
Dos Santos, T. (1971). The Structure of Dependence. In K. T. Fann & Donald C. Hodges (eds.), *Readings in U.S. Imperialism* (p. 226). Boston: Porter Sargent.
Echikwonye, R. A. & Beetseh, Kwaghga. (2011). The Role of Public Policy Making and Development. *Nigeria. Journal of Social Science and Public Policy*, 3: 44–64.
Eisenstadt, S. N. (1966). *Modernization: Protest and Change.* Englewoods Cliffs, NJ: Prentice- Hall.
Ellen, R. & H. Harris. (1996). Concepts of Indigenous Environmental Knowledge in Scientific and Development Studies Literature – A critical Assessment. Draft Paper Presented at East-West Environmental Linkages Network Workshop 3, Canterbury.
Frank, A. Gunder. (1967). *Sociology of Development and Underdevelopment of Sociology. Catalyst* (University of Buffalo), No. 3.
Giddens, A. (1991). *The Consequence of Modernity.* Cambridge: Polity Press.
Gordon, R. E. & Sylvester, J. H. (2004). "Deconstructing Development" Villanova University Charles Widger School of Law. Working Chapter Chapter Series.
Gudynas, E. (2011). Buen Vivir: Today's Tomorrow. *Development*, 54(4): 441–447.
Harrison, D. (2005). *The Sociology of Modernisation and Development.* London/New York: Routledge.
Homann, S. & Rischkowsky, B. (2001). Integration of Indigenous Knowledge into Land-Use Planning for the Communal Rangelands of Namibia. *Indigenous Knowledge and Development Monitor*, 9.
Hussain, A. & Tribe, K. (1981). *Marxism and the Agrarian Question: German Social Democracy and The Peasantry 1890-1907.* Hong Kong: Macmillan Press Ltd.
Korten, D. C. (1990). *Getting to the 21st Century: Voluntary Action and the Global Agenda.* United States of America: Kumarian Press.
Lenin, V. I. (1964). *The Development of Capitalism in Russia.* Moscow: Progress Publishers
Levy, M. (1967). *Social Patterns and Problems of Modernization.* Englewood Cliffs, NJ: Prentice-Hall.
Nnoli, O. (1979). *Path to Nigerian Development.* Senegal: CODESRIA.
Obadan, M. (1999). Features and Implication of Globalization. Being Text of the Welcome Address Delivered at the Globalization Seminar in NES Newsletter, 40(1), June.
Oladimeji, Y. (2013). Potentials of and The Socio/-Economic Benefits Of Blacksmithing Production in Promoting Agricultural Development and Poverty Alleviation in Kwara State, Nigeria. *International Journal of Modern Engineering Research*, 3(6): 3809–3817.
Olutayo A. O. (2002). The Concept of Development in Historical Perspective: The Third World Experience. In U. C. Isuigo- Abanihe, A. N. Isamah, & J. O.

Adesina (eds.), *Currents and Perspectives in Sociology*. Lagos: Malthouse Press Ltd.

Olutayo, A. O. (2010). Engendering Rural Development through Indigenous Production Relations in Africa: Society in Focus. In Lindy Heineken & Heich Prozesky (eds.), *Change, Challenges and Resistance: Reflections from South Africa and Beyond*. Cambridge, UK: Cambridge Scholars Publishing.

Olutayo, A. (2012). "Verstehen", Everyday Sociology and Development: Incorporating African Indigenous Knowledge. *Critical Sociology*, 40(2): 229–238.

Olutayo, A. O. (2018). Sabiticate is equal to what; an inaugural lecture 2017/2018 of the Social Sciences, University of Ibadan.

Reyes, G. E. (2001). Four Main Theories of Development: Modernization, Dependency. World Systems and Globalization. *Nómadas. Revista Crítica de Ciencias Sociales y Jurídicas*, 4(2): 109–124.

Rist, S., Boilla, S., Gerritsen, P., Schneider, F., Mathez-Stiefel, S., & Tapia, N. (2011). Endogenous Knowledge: Implications for Sustainable Development. Research for Sustainable Development: Foundations, Experiences and Perspectives. *North-South Perspectives*, 119–146.

Ritzer, G. (2008). *Sociological Theory*. Boston: McGraw-Hill.

Rodney, W. (1973). *How Europe Underdeveloped Africa*. Tanzania: L'overture.

Sanderson, Stephen K. (2005). World-Systems Analysis after Thirty Years. *International Journal of Comparative Sociology*, 46: 179–213.

Scott, J. & Marshall, G. (2005). *Oxford Dictionary of Sociology*. New York: Oxford University Press.

Senanayake, S. G. J. N. (2006). Indigenous Knowledge as a Key to Sustainable Development. *The Journal of Agricultural Sciences*, 2(1).

Sillitoe, P. (2006). Introduction: Indigenous Knowledge in Development. *Anthropology in Action*, 13(3): 1–12.

Singh, K. (2009). *Rural Development: Principles, Policies and Management* (3rd edition). New Delhi: Sage Publications.

Skocpol, T. (1997). Wallerstein's World Capitalist System: A Theoretical and Historical Critique. *American Journal of Sociology*, 82(5): 1075–1090.

Smith, L. T. (2012). *Decolonizing Methodologies. Research & Indigenous Peoples* (2nd edition). London: Zed.

Swanepoel, H. & De Beer, F. (2006). *Community Development: Breaking the Cycle of Poverty*. Kenwyn: Juta.

Umekachikelu, F. C. (2011). 'African Development and the Problem Leadership'. Nigeriavillagesquare.com.

UNPFIL. (2010). Ninth session E/C.19/2010/CRP.425. The Human Development Framework and Indigenous people self-determined development or development with culture and identity. 19-30 April 2010. New York: United States.

Wallerstein, I. (1974). *The Modern World System: Capitalist Agriculture and the Origins of the European World in the Sixteenth Century*. New York Academic Press.

World Development Report. (1991). *The Challenge of Development*. New York: Oxford University Press. World Bank.

Chapter 13

Colonialism and Misconception of Development in Benin Province
The Case of the Oil Palm Industry
Fred Ekpe Ayokhai

This chapter posits that, like elsewhere in Africa where colonialism once prevailed, Nigeria's Benin Province had its share of the colonial development experience, which the colonialists brutally enforced. In the process, all socioeconomic and political structures were ruthlessly transformed to fit its construct of development. One of the sectors which experienced this brutal enforcement of colonial development construct was the oil palm industry. Despite the sector's contribution to the colonial economy, it has largely remained comatose and neglected in the postcolonial development endeavors of Nigeria, thus necessitating a reconsideration of the colonial development construct and its implications for the postcolonial development. Using systematic content analysis, this chapter examines, in historical context, the colonial development construct with a view to understanding and explaining its logic in the oil palm industry in Benin Province. In the historical context of Benin Province, the chapter argues that colonial development was not only exogenous but also a case of development misconception. It also argues that the colonial development construct was transposed on the postcolonial state with all its exploitative structures. It finds that these structures resulted in the postcolonial development crisis just as they did in the colonial epoch. The chapter concludes that as long as the misconceptions of the colonial development construct continue to predominate, the postcolonial oil palm industry will continue to replicate the contradictory logic (or illogicality) of the colonial era. As a way out of the postcolonial development conundrum, it recommends a radical break with this heritage of colonial development construct and an aggressive engagement with an endogenous development construct.

INTRODUCTION

Nigeria, the most populous Black nation in the global system, remains a sad reminder of the Africa's most failed hope of development. At independence in 1960, Nigeria was one of the very few countries, south of the Sahara, which the African race and the rest of the world looked up to for the fulfilment of the dream and aspiration of development. Nigeria, like some of the erstwhile colonies in Asia, was perceived as an emerging African giant and legend because of her development potentials. Most of her counterpart, erstwhile colonies such as Malaysia, Indonesia, India, and even China, among others, have made the bookmakers proud by living out their potentials of greatness and development and cut a niche for themselves as the Asian Tigers.

Nigeria, on the other hand, has disappointed all expectations and made herself the development *hobble de cup* of the world. According to a Brookings Institute report of 2018, Nigeria has overtaken India to become the country with the largest number of extremely poor people in the world (Kharas, Hamel and Hofer, 2018). Yet, Nigeria is not only Africa's greatest reservoir of human capital but also one of the world's "Treasure Islands." Nigeria's estimated population is currently over 190 million. This population is complemented with abundant natural resources, a clement weather, and a vast and safe land resources. In addition, the nation has neither experienced any major natural disaster nor been under any major attack (real or perceived) from a hostile neighbor since her coming into being as a postcolonial entity. Rather, Nigeria is a land blessed with abundant agricultural and mineral resources. By every standard of measure, she is a potentially great country.

Despite the favorable conditions predisposing Nigeria to greatness and development, she has not been able to rise beyond her potentials, rather has frittered them away. While some of her counterpart erstwhile colonies in Asia and Latin America have resolved their postcolonial development quagmire and made steady progress on the development ladder, she has been locked down by the development conundrum. Even sectors such as cocoa, groundnut, rubber, timber, cotton, and oil palm that were viable in the global market under the colonial dispensation are now prostrate. Similarly, the hydrocarbon sector that has given her the most needed oxygen in the postcolonial period is currently in critical crisis. To add a chronicle of her sociopolitical maladies and experiences to the list of the economic woes of the country is to paint a picture of a doomed postcolonial state. That Nigeria is still surviving as a corporate entity would, probably, pass for the eighth wonder of the world as the reality of her continued existence and survival as a corporate entity defies simple logic. Having gone through a bitter civil war earlier and plagued by political instability, insurgencies, terrorism, and fraudulent democratic experiments throughout her postindependence existence, the world became apprehensive of her possible disintegration during the build-up to the 2015 general elections after the U.S. National Intelligence Council and informed observers predicted its possibility (Campbell, 2013a, 2013b; U.S. Intelligence Expert Report, 2005).

This gloomy image of a once perceived potentially great country has persisted and bleakly stares her future in the face. Nigeria's several out of school children, particularly in the northern part of the country who beg for alms for their subsistence, have now grown into gun-wielding men who are reinforcing the criminal gangs perpetuating various acts of violent crimes ranging from terrorism to all forms of banditry. Their unemployed youthful counterparts in the southern divide of the country are not any less vicious and desperate for survival. In many respects, Nigeria now shares many of the attributes of a failed state and an ungoverned space. The rest of the world, particularly the West, blames, principally, the profligacy and ineptitude of the Nigerian ruling class for the inability to transform the country's huge human and material resources into greatness and development. While it could be argued that the Nigerian ruling class shares a fraction of the blame for Nigeria's development crisis and backwardness, there is no doubt that these malaises are mostly symptomatic of the structures of the postcolonial development crisis. The real culprit is the postcolonial development construct which was transposed from the colonial experience and structures, which are themselves outcomes of the colonial construct of development.

To illustrate this view, the specific case of the oil palm industry of Benin Province is examined in this chapter. The oil palm sector expanded and provided a significant part of the revenue of government during the colonial dispensation. The oil palm revenue to the postcolonial Nigerian government began to decline toward the second half of the 1960s when the fortunes of the industry began to nose-dive. From the 1970s, the petro-dollar had established itself as the undisputed and indispensable revenue base of the monolithic Nigerian economy, thereby nailing the coffin of the oil palm sector. Since then, despite the half-hearted efforts of some governments to breathe some lease of life into the oil palm sector as a result of the crisis in the petroleum sector, it has remained comatose. Why has the postcolonial Nigerian oil palm sector failed to respond to the stimuli of growth and development? This chapter answers this question by arguing and establishing the fact that colonial development constructs in the oil palm sector of Nigeria's Benin Province were misconceived and that the misconceptions have been transposed on the postcolonial oil palm economy of Nigeria, including the erstwhile Benin Province. This transposition of colonial development crisis has led to Nigeria's postcolonial development crisis. Before we pontificate further over this question, let us quickly interrogate the theoretical roots of the misconceptions of the colonial development construct with a view to understanding its practice in the oil palm industry in Nigeria's Benin Province.

THEORIZING COLONIAL DEVELOPMENT CONSTRUCT

Development constructs, like all other social theories, are anchored on empirical assumptions. Colonial development constructs, particularly in Africa, are anchored on the empirical assumptions of two theories prominently advanced by colonial apologists. These are the vent for surplus theory propounded by Adam Smith and later revised by Hla Myint (1958) who stressed the importance of export orientation as the most useful "engine of growth" based on his thesis of South East Asia and the modernization theory whose pristine ideas are traced back to Marquis de Condorcet (Gilman, 2003).

The vent for the surplus theory came about as a result of the need to explain the nature and causes of the wealth of nations. It asserts that when a country produces more than it consumes, it produces a surplus. It thus asserts that the under-utilization of such surplus causes an inward movement on the production possibilities frontier and that trade with another country is used to vent off this surplus. This, in turn, brings the production possibilities frontier back to full capacity (Smith, 1776, 1982; Myint, 1958). In other words, it argues that international trade makes for the fuller use of economic resources than domestic trade. When this theory is applied to the economies of precolonial Africa, including the Benin area, it assumes that surplus was being created, but because of its presumed subsistence level of development, the surplus produced was under-utilized. It, therefore, suggests that the under-utilized surplus was inhibitive of its productive potentials. It also assumes that surplus was created because of the existence of surplus land, the major means of production, and voluntary or involuntary surplus labor before colonial incursion (Smith, 1979). It is therefore assumed that trade between a colonial state (or a section of it) and the colonizing state necessarily improves the production possibilities frontier of the latter. In this process of international trade, it is presumed that the developed colonizing state helps to bring about development in the underdeveloped colonized state. Therefore, the international trade in palm kernel and palm oil between Britain and Nigeria, of which Benin Province was a part, based on this theoretical premise, stimulated development in the latter, including its constituent part of Benin Province.

Modernization theory, on the other hand, presents development as a straitjacket path which all societies desirous of a transition to modernity must take if they must transit from agricultural, rural, and traditional societies to post-industrial, urban, and modern forms (Bradshaw, 1987; Shrum, 2000). Put differently, all traditional economies embarking on a journey of transition to modernization must follow a predetermined and sequential order of development stages which include transition to take-off, the take-off stage, drive to maturity, age of high consumption, and post-industrial society (Chirot and Hall, 1982: 82) as outlined by Rostow (1990).

Unlike the vent for surplus theory, the modernization theory emphasizes internal forces and other sources of socioeconomic development such as formal education, market-based economy, and democratic and secular political structures. Nonetheless, according to Jenkins and Scanlan (2001), modernization theory does not rule out external forces as sources of social change and economic development, but focuses less on foreign influences. However, science is considered exceptional among the external influences because it is beneficial to developing societies through "knowledge and technology transfer" from developed countries (Shrum, 2000). In this vein, it is assumed that science and technology is alien to the societies to which they are exported by the foreigners. Essentially, modernization theorists see science and technology as catalyst for development. In other words, societies can be fast-tracked into modernization by borrowing Western technical capital, forms of organization, and science and technology (Shrum, 2000; Herkenrath and Bornschier, 2003). In this way, it is a one-way top-down development schema that holds true for all societies irrespective of time, place, and historical context.

Thus, the theory assumes that Nigeria's Benin Province was a traditional, agrarian, and rural society in dire need of the influence of European technology, forms of organization, technical capital, and science and technology. In the case of Benin Province, the colonizers assumed the place and role of the foreign agency that brought in the predisposing elements of modernization and development.

Undoubtedly, both the vent for surplus and the modernization theories provided the underlining assumptions of the colonial development construct in Nigeria's Benin Province. This is because the colonial policies enunciated and implemented in the province exuded an overdose of these assumptions as will be seen in the next section of this chapter.

The province was expected to go through the modernization stages of development in a process facilitated by colonialism. If the theoretical assumptions encapsulated in the colonial development construct were to be true for all societies, times, and historical contexts, why then did it fail to deliver the envisioned transition to modernity in Nigeria's Benin Province and her oil palm sector under colonial tutelage? The answer to this question belies the colonial development construct, as shall be demonstrated in this chapter.

"COLONIAL DEVELOPMENT" FROM THE LENS OF COLONIAL POLICIES

Benin Province was brought into the global network of capitalism through the instrumentality of colonization by Britain after her brutal subjugation in 1897. It was integrated into the Oil Rivers Protectorate, which later came to be known as the Niger Coast Protectorate. By 1906, the Protectorate and others established in the southern part of the River Niger, including the Colony of Lagos established earlier in 1861, were unitized and the entire British Estate, south of the Niger, became known as the Colony and Protectorates of Southern Nigeria. This was the precursor to the unitization of the Colony and Protectorates of Southern Nigeria and the Protectorates of Northern Nigeria, which gave birth to the Colony and Protectorates of Nigeria in 1914. Further political developments in the colonial state resulted in its division into three provinces viz: Northern Province, Eastern Province, and Western Province. Benin Province became part of the Western Province and remained so until Nigeria attained independence in 1960. As part of the efforts to transform societies in the Benin Province into Western forms of organization, it was divided into four divisions which included Benin Division, Ishan Division, Asaba Division, and Kukuruku (later Afemai) Division.

In an attempt to rationalize the colonization of Africa, the Europeans had explained their imperial ventures as a philanthropic mission in the service of God and humanity. Consequently, they argued that the incursion and invasion's primary objective was to rescue the uncivilized peoples of the "Dark Continent" from their barbaric trade in humans, which was still flourishing on the continent despite its abolition in Europe and to integrate the region into the more humane global trade in primary commodities ("legitimate trade"). The veil on this humanitarian pretense has since been removed by irrevocable pieces of evidence from studies that identified the objective social, political, and economic conditions prevalent in Europe at the time as the main reasons for the abolition of slave trade and the launch of the trade-in primary produce (Smith, 1979; McPhee, 1926; Hopkins, 1973; Iweriebor, n.d.; Dike, 1956; Ajayi and Crowder, 1971; Falola and Heaton, 2008). Reinforcing this view, Iweriebor (n.d.) states that:

> [T]he European imperialist push into Africa was motivated by three main factors, economic, political and social. It developed in the nineteenth century following the collapse of the profitability of the slave trade, its abolition and suppression, as well as the expansion of the European capitalist Industrial Revolution. The imperatives of capitalist industrialization – including the demand for assured sources of raw materials, the search for guaranteed markets and profitable investment outlets—spurred the European scramble and

the partition and eventual conquest of Africa. Thus, the primary motivation for European intrusion was economic.

These same reasons explain the invasion of Benin Kingdom and its incorporation as Benin Province into the Colony and Protectorates of Nigeria. It is important to note that under the logic of colonialism, African colonies, including Nigeria and its constituent provinces such as Benin, were not only mere spheres of political influence but also mostly strategic enclaves of trade monopolies. It is in the context of the latter that the study of Benin Province and its oil palm industry is strategic for our understanding and explanation of the misconceptions inherent in the colonial development construct.

Benin Province was an area rich in the primary agricultural commodities that were of vital interest to Britain's industries. While recapping this view, Ayokhai (2017: 62) observes that:

> Located in the Southern Protectorate of Nigeria, Benin Province was a rich source of cheap rubber, oil palm products, cocoa and timber. Most of these resources had become important in the economic calculations of Europe since the Industrial Revolution but they assumed new and critical importance during the Second World War with Britain's loss of her Far East territories.

The international trade potentials and activities of the area had drawn it into a complex economic relationship with Europe since the fifteenth century. It is therefore not surprising that the Benin area became a major region of interest and consequent hostilities for the British colonizers early in their imperial enterprise in Nigeria.

Having subjugated the area, the British immediately set out on the principal business of exploiting the province's human and natural resources. In addition to being a market for finished European consumer goods, it became a source of cheap cocoa, rubber, timber, palm oil, and palm kernel. To ensure a favorable balance of trade in the resultant international trade, the subjugated societies' political and socioeconomic structures were immediately transformed to align them with the new role of sources of supply for the cheap primary produce desperately needed to service the bourgeoning industrial sectors of Europe and a market for their finished consumer goods to keep the global capitalist economy afloat. Central to this agenda was the need to maintain a monopolistic control over trade in the province.

To achieve its dual objectives, the British colonial administration immediately set out to establish the political structures of capitalist exploitation such as the needed state bureaucracy, the police, and the native authority courts and the prisons to ensure the unfettered attainment of the type of law and order conducive for the maximum exploitation of the people and their primary agricultural resources. Having established these structures of colonial power, the colonial administration formulated and implemented a number of policies to drive its objective of exploitation. They included the introduction of British currencies, the provision of social amenities and infrastructures, facilitation of the establishment of banks to ease access to, and repatriation of capital and profit. Other policy measures included the provision of agricultural extension services, the supply of requisite European manufactured technology, and the introduction and enforcement of market reforms and price mechanisms aimed at stimulating the expansion of the production of export produce. In addition, colonial policy ensured that the peasant mode of production was sustained. Through the implementation of these policies, the colonial administration was to ensure that the human, land, and the oil palm resources with specific reference to its derivatives such as palm kernel and palm oil were maximally exploited for the benefit of British industries. However, these policies were couched and presented as efforts aimed at the overall development of the colonial state, including Benin Province.

COLONIAL OIL PALM APPROPRIATION POLICIES IN BENIN PROVINCE

This section of the chapter embarks on a critical examination of each of the colonial administration's policies, which together constituted the colonial development construct and practice. However, our analysis is limited to those policies which had specific implications for the oil palm industry in Benin Province. When we appraise the impact of these policies holistically, it will lead us to the inevitable conclusion that the colonial development constructs and practice which they exemplify constitute a misconception. For instance, the colonial agricultural policy on which the oil palm industry was anchored stated expressly the British colonial administration's position on the traditional mode of agricultural production. It demonstrates a firm lack of desire to mediate its transformation as long as the British supply of agricultural commodities was sustained and kept expanding to meet its export needs. This can be gleaned from Clifford's assertion that:

> [A]gricultural industries in tropical countries which are mainly, or exclusively in the hands of the native peasantry (a) Have a firmer root than similar enterprises when owned and maintained by Europeans, because they are natural growths, not artificial creation, and are self-supporting, as regards labour, while European plantations can only be maintained by some system of organized immigration or by some form of compulsory labour, (b) Are incomparably the cheapest instrument for the production of agricultural produce on a large scale

that has yet been devised; (c) Are capable of rapidity of expansion and progressive increase of output that beggar every record of the past. (Clifford, 1920; Ayokhai, 2011: 47; Ayokhai, 2017: 69)

The above text clearly states that the priority of the colonial administration in the agricultural sector of the colonized societies was the "rapidity of expansion and progressive increase of output." It was on the premise of this stated objective that Clifford anchored Britain's colonial agricultural policy not to mediate the transformation of the mode of production in the oil palm sector of Nigeria, including Benin Province (Clifford, 1920; Ayokhai, 2011: 47; Ayokhai, 2017: 69).

Since Britain's overriding interest was in promoting export trade, the colonial administration maintained that it was "the business of government not to itself engage in commercial enterprises of any kind, but to prepare and maintain the conditions—political, moral and material—upon which the success or failure of such enterprises in a very large measure depends" (Clifford, 1920; Ayokhai, 2011: 47).

This policy did not change till the end of the colonial regime. Rather, there was a slight modification as the appetite for more oil seeds expanded according to the imperatives of the changing times. For instance, the first modification to colonial policy in the oil palm sector occurred in 1928 with the introduction of privately owned small oil palm plantations. The plantations were owned by peasant farmers. Farmers were encouraged to own private oil palm plantations as against the communal ownership of the wild oil palms. Though Benin Province had the most successful experience of this policy, its overall impact on the production of export oil palm products was quite negligible. The idea of privately owned plantations did not appeal to the people who had an abundance of wild oil palm which met their needs (Bauer, 1957). Similarly, Ayokhai (2017: 70), observes that "Since there were sufficient stands of uncultivated palm trees to meet the needs of the people, the idea of cultivating them . . . did not appeal to most farmers." Similar to this policy was the idea of regenerating wild oil palms by substituting them with the improved varieties from the Department of Agriculture. Even then, the disposition of the colonial administration was that "investigation can show that it is likely to prove economically sound" (Nigeria: First Annual Bulletin, 1922: 5, Ayokhai, 2011: 49).

Some other policy innovations have introduced the course of World War II. In the course of the war, Britain did not only lose its Far East territories in 1942 which were its alternative sources of oil seeds supply (Ayokhai and Rufai, 2017: 73) but also was desperate to meet its deteriorating domestic need for fats. It also had a dire need to supplement its European allies demand for fats.

The exigencies of the war arising from Britain's loss of the Far East, its effect on the domestic supply of nutritional fat, and its assumption of responsibility for supplying the needs of its European allies during World War II aggravated her demand for Nigerian oil palm products. Another policy initiative in the colonial development construct closely related to the pressures arising from World War II was the conscription of more provinces into the official oil palm belt. This became imperative since increases in the production of palm oil and palm kernel depended solely on the scope and intensity of labor and oil palm exploitation. This is because production tools, techniques, and methods remained largely the same (Ayokhai and Rufai, 2017: 90 – 91; Ayokhai, 2017: 67). To achieve the export production target of Nigeria, the scope of the oil palm exploitation had to be extended. This led to the conscription of more provinces into the official oil palm belt. Consequently, Benin Province and the entire Western Provinces were formally declared oil palm belts. Benin Province was formally declared a "production zone" by Public Notice 301 in 1943 (NAI No. B.P. 2140/566, 1943). Closely related to this initiative was the reactivation of the forced labor policy as through Regulation 89 of 1943.

The forced labor regulation was used to conscript and compel peasants in Benin Province to not only maximally exploit labor but also ensure the optimum production of palm oil and palm kernel for export to Britain. This assertion is supported by evidence from the instructions of the Acting Chief Commissioner (1943) to the Resident Officer, Benin Province that "When the need is so pressing we must consider again making use of the powers conferred by Regulation 89 of 1943" and the Chief Commissioner's statement that:

> I am not suggesting that compulsion, as authorised by regulation 5 of Regulations 89/1943, should be employed wholesale but in areas where the resident believes that the people could do more than they are doing, then I think that neither he nor the Native Authority concerned can hardly fail to make use of regulation 5. (Secretary W.P. 21050 vol. 1)

According to Ayokhai and Rufai (2017: 80) and Ayokhai (2017: 76) compulsion was of general application in Benin Province concerning the export production of palm oil and palm kernel. This is substantiated by the evidence from the District Officer (D.O), Kukuruku Division's instruction to the Clan Councils that:

> I hereby direct you to arrange for the reaping of this palm fruit, and for cracking the nuts and marketing the kernels. You may order anybody to do the work. I suggest the occupants of farms (where the palms are in farmlands) and the

working companies where they are in the unoccupied bush. (N.A.I. No. K.D. 546/B/43)

The fact that the entire force of the state was mobilized for the implementation of the forced labor ordinance can be gleaned from the D.O's declaration that "You may prosecute in the native court anybody who does not obey your orders. If you do not work properly every member of the council will be prosecuted in my court" (N.A.I. No. K.D. 546/B/43). This is further supported by additional evidence from Benin Division where the Resident Officer, Benin Province stated that:

> I have also authorised the Oba of Benin to act for me under Regulation 5 (1) for Benin Division and the District Officers for the other Divisions. Each will direct suitable persons to harvest and process the fruits where this is not being done. (N.A.I. B.P. 2140/678; Secretary W.P. 21050 vol.1)

There is no doubt that the full weight of compulsory labor was brought to bear in Benin Province and that the powers of the colonial state as exemplified by the native authority courts, the police, and prisons were all culpable in the process.

To ensure that no stone was left unturned, the colonial government introduced the monitoring and inspection of production to ensure that the orders to harvest and process the oil palm fruits were "carried out and report areas in which the fruit is not being reaped" (N.A.I. B.P. 2140/678). For effective monitoring and inspection of production, the colonial administration appointed inspectors who were paid either salaries or allowances to assist the D.Os who had earlier been appointed Deputy Controllers who oversaw production activities at the districts level to underscore the importance it attached to the export production of palm oil and palm kernel. For instance, three inspectors were appointed to monitor production activities in Ishan Division, five for Kukuruku Division, and one for Asaba Division, while Forest Officers and Rangers monitored and reported to the Oba in Benin Division (Secretary W.P. 21050 vol. 1).

In addition, some reforms in market and price mechanisms were introduced by the colonial administration to stimulate increase in production. It is believed that there was a relative stability and general improvement in the prices offered for palm oil and palm kernel in Benin Province relative to the pre–World War II period. Closely related to this was the market reform which eliminated the middlemen and replaced them with licensed buying agents. This had the added advantage of eliminating incidences of underpayments by the middlemen because under the new dispensation the prices offered by both the foreign merchants and the marketing boards were announced in advance and the producers were aware of them.

Similarly, buying stations were opened either in the villages or close to them. Notwithstanding the reforms that attended the establishment of the marketing boards, the peasant producers did not consider such improvements significant enough and as adequate compensation for their labor and as such they failed to stimulate production as producers merely produced and sold barely enough to enable them to make enough money to meet their immediate needs. The Resident Officer, Benin Province, had lamented in 1944 that the peasant producers "'did not consider that they get sufficient remuneration for the work involved when they have a much easier way to earn the required cash by selling food in very flourishing black markets" (N.A.I. Ministry of Agriculture/1/433; N.A.I. B.P.2134/409; Ayokhai, 2017: 78). Despite the improvements in the price and market mechanism, there were no significant increases in production.

Despite the realization of the colonial administration that the drudgery of labor was a significant consideration for the producers, its policies did not show that it was genuinely interested in significantly ameliorating it. Its intervention in the area of technology was quite insignificant. The establishment of mills, though came much later, were too few to make any significant change. Similarly, the introduction of hand-pressers and nut-crackers which came earlier did not make a significant impact as only three farmers owned pressers, while one owned both presser and a nut cracker as at July 1935 (Superintendent of Agric, 1935; Ayokhai, 2017: 67). This was because they were too few where they were available at all and generally too expensive to acquire by the peasant producers in Benin Province (Ayokhai, 2017: 68). Consequently, the majority of the producers were simply doomed to the hazardous and labor intensive traditional methods, techniques, and tools. As noted in respect of Eastern Provinces by Usoro (1974), only a few people could afford hand-pressers because of their cost and those few used them to process fruits for other producers for a few pence. To worsen matters, the market reforms were accompanied by the introduction of price/grade differentials in export palm oil and palm kernel. The classification of palm oil and palm kernel into different grades was to improve the quality and check adulteration of export products (Nigeria: Annual Reports of the Department of Marketing and Export, 1954). This grading system led to either outright rejection or low pricing of products considered less than grade 1.

CONCLUSION: TOWARD DECONSTRUCTING COLONIAL DEVELOPMENT

A critical appraisal of all the colonial policies in the oil palm industry of Benin Province points to the fact that they were merely interested in the expansion of export production. Therefore, they were focused on increases in the production of palm oil and palm kernel and the improvement of products' qualities. These were completely at variance with the interest of the peasant producers of Benin Province. The conclusion arising from this is that the colonial development construct and practice were as externally oriented as the policies' roots. Consequently, it is argued that the development of export oil palm products was misconceived as development for the peoples and societies in Benin Province. Unfortunately, the situation of Benin Province merely approximates the situation of all other oil palm products producers in the British colony of Nigeria. This conclusion is supported by the decline of Nigeria's export palm oil and palm kernel trade once Britain repudiated its contract with Nigeria to procure all the palm kernel and palm oil from Nigeria in 1965. Since then, the sector, which once proved a viable sector of governmental revenue for both the colonial and the First Republic Nigerian governments, began to nose-dive until it finally petered into insignificance.

Subsequent efforts encapsulated in the agricultural policies of postindependence Nigerian governments have failed woefully to nudge back to life her oil palm sector. This is understandable because both the postindependence Nigerian state and governments have their existential structures rooted in the structures of the colonial state and development construct and practice. For instance, the postindependence Nigerian state still remains a peripheral state in international economics, which continues to perceive its role as that of a supplier of primary agricultural commodities and minerals to the industries of the metropolitan Western states. The Nigerian government continues to perceive its role in this process as that of providing the enabling environment for its facilitation. Hence, all the agricultural policies of the Nigerian government have been conceived through the prism and practice of capitalist and neocolonial development. For instance, from the 1960s, policies have been driven by the expansion and diversification of agricultural export commodities, import substitution, export promotion, and Integrated Rural Development. From the 1980s, policy regimes have been characterized by privatization and commercialization and the Structural Adjustment Program (SAP). When we contextualize these postcolonial development constructs, we can only come to a conclusion that they have not dared to deviate from the theoretical prisms and praxes of both the vent for surplus and the modernization theories, in which the colonial development constructs were anchored. On this note, it can only be concluded that as long as Nigeria continues to exist as a hangover of the colonial state and her government continue to conceive their roles as the extension of the colonial public bureaucracy, so long shall all her economic sectors, including the oil palm industry, continue to wallow in crisis.

To break the jinx of perpetual development crisis, Nigeria and her postcolonial government must rethink their place and role in international economic relations by looking inward in terms of overall sectoral policy constructs in a manner that not only radically depart from the exogenous orientations of the colonial policy heritage and the misconceptions of the postcolonial development construct but also substantially take into account the endogenous dynamics of her economy.

REFERENCES

Ajayi, J.F.A. & Crowder, M. (Eds.) (1971). *History of West Africa, vol. 1*. London: Longman.

Ayokhai, F.E.F. (2011). African women in changing economic system: An examination of the oil palm industry among Uzairhue women of Benin Province, 1900 – 1960. *Jalingo Journal of African Studies*, 1(1): 41–54.

Ayokhai, F.E.F. (2017). Between exploitation and profitmaking: Ttravails of women in oil palm products expansion in Benin Province during WW II. *Umewaen Journal of Benin and Edo Studies*, 2: 61–85.

Ayokhai, F.E.F. & Rufai, B. (2017). West African women and the development question in the post World War II economy: The experience of Nigeria's Benin Province in the oil palm industry. *Journal of Global South Studies*, 34(1): 72–95. https://www.jstor.org/stable/48517875.

Bauer, P.T. (1957). *Economic Analysis and Policy in Underdeveloped Countries*. London: University Press.

Bradshaw, Y W. (1987). Urbanization and underdevelopment: A global study of modernization, urban bias, and economic dependency. *American Sociological Review*, 52(2): 224.

Campbell, J. (2013a). Cited in Oluwarotimi, Abiodun, '2015: Revisiting Campbell's Prediction on Nigeria's Disintegration'. *Leadership*, 11/1/2015.

Campbell, J. (2013b). *Nigeria: Dancing on the Brink*. Rowman & Littlefield. https://www.cfr.org/book/nigeria-dancing-on-the-brink. Retrieved May 23, 2019.

Chirot, D. & Hall. T.D. (1982). World system theory. *Annual Review of Sociology*, 8: 81–106.

Clifford, H (1920). National Council, Address by the Governor, Sir Huge Clifford (20 December, 1920).

Condorcet, de Marquis. Cited in Gilman, N. (2003). *Modernization Theory: Its Origin and Rise in Cold War America*. Baltimore: Johns Hopkins pbk. ed. Johns Hopkins University Press.

Dike, K.O. (1956). *Trade and Politics in the Niger Delta, 1830 – 1855: An Introduction to the Economic and Political History of Nigeria*. Great Britain: Clarendon Press.

Falola, T. & Heaton, M.M. (2008). *A History of Nigeria*. Cambridge: University Press.

Hopkins, A.G. (1973). *An Economic History of West Africa*. London: University Press.

Iweriebor, E.E.G. (n.d.). The Colonization of Africa. http://exhibitions.nypl.org/af ricanaage/essay.colonization-of-africa.html. Retrieved May 23, 2019.

Jenkins & Scanlan. (2001). Food security in less developed countries, 1970 – 1990. *American Sociological Review*, 66(5): 718–744.

Kharas, H., Hamel, K. & Hofer, M. (2018). The start of a new poverty narrative. https://www.brookings.edu/blog/future-development/2018/06/19/the-state-of-a -new poverty-narrative/. Retrieved May 23, 2019.

McPhee, A. (1926). *The Economic Revolution in British West Africa*. London: University Press.

Myint, Hla. (1958). Cited in Fuglie, K.O. (1991). Vent for Surplus as a source of agricultural growth in northeast Thailand, 1958 – 1980. *The Journal of Developing Areas*, 25(3): 331–346.

Oluwarotimi, A. (2015). 2015: revisiting Campbell's prediction on Nigeria's disintegration. *Leadership* 1/11.

Rostow, W.W. (1990). *The Stages of Economic Growth: A Non-communist Manifesto*. Cambridge: Cambridge University Press.

Shrum. (2000). Cited in Ynalvez, M.A. & Shrum, W.M. (2015). Science and development, *Elsevier International Encyclopedia of the Social & Behavioral Sciences*, 2nd edition. Oxford: Elsevier, pp. 150–155.

Smith, A. (1776). *An Inquiry into the Nature and Causes of the Wealth of Nations*. London: W. Strahan and T. Cadell.

Smith, S. (1979). Colonialism in economic theory: The experience of Nigeria. *The Journal of Development Studies*, 15(3): 38–59.

US Intelligence Expert Report. (2005). Conference Report on 'Mapping Sub-Saharan Africa's Future by Experts assembled by United States National Intelligence Council, Presented to the US Senate http//www.cia.gov/nic/confreports_africa_ future.html. Retrieved 23/5/2019.

Usoro, E.J. (1974). *The Nigerian oil Palm Industry, 1906 – 1965 (Government Policy and Export Production, 1906 – 1965)*. Ibadan: Ibadan University Press.

Ynalvez, M.A. & Shrum, W.M. (2015). *Science and Development*, Elsevier International Encyclopedia of the Social & Behavioral Sciences, 2nd edition. Oxford: Elsevier, pp. 150–155.

ARCHIVAL SOURCES

National Archive Ibadan. B.P. 2134/409. Palm Oil Production, Review.
N.A.I. B.P. 2140/678. Palm Production; Compulsory Measures.
N.A.I. No. B.P. 2140/566/1943. Palm Production; Compulsory Measures.
N.A.I. K.D. 546/B/43. Compulsory Reaping of Palm Fruits.
N.A.I. Ministry of Agric/1/433. Palm-Oil and Kernels – General.
N.A.I. Secretary W.P. 21050 Vol. 1. Palm Production: Compulsory Measures.
N.A.I. Superintendent of Agriculture, 1935.
Nigeria First Annual Bulletin, 1922, 5
Nigeria Annual Report of the Department of Marketing and Export, 1954.

Chapter 14

Decolonizing State Fragility and Forced Migration in Postcolonial Nigeria

Olanrewaju Faith Osasumwen

State fragility and forced migration have become recurrent themes in the international political system, particularly in failing states like Nigeria. While these themes are quite evident in the postcolonial Nigerian state, they are undoubtedly manifestations of the ills of antecedent colonial legacies. Extant literature indicates that these twin factors are directly linked to broader conflict and insecurity challenges such as ethno-religious conflicts, electoral violence, terrorist insurgencies, banditry, abductions, and escalation of general insecurity in the country. Utilizing a robust combination of secondary data and analytic arguments, this chapter advances the causal roles of fragility in displacement episodes in postcolonial Nigeria. It adopts the social contract and frustration aggression theories and argues that state fragility and its resultant forced migration perils are caused by deep-seated colonial and foundational socio-cum-ethno-political problems that Nigeria's ruling elite and weak state institutions have failed to address. It demonstrates that the culture of political and economic exploitation, social injustice, and breached social contract, inherited from the colonialists by the Nigerian political elites, trigger violent agitations, conflicts, or acts of terror, which account for continued fragility, and lead to forced migration. It concludes by emphasizing that, to effectively decolonize state fragility and forced migration in Nigeria, there is need for the political elite to be committed to the social contract between the state and its citizens. It recommends that the government and political elites must embrace the reality of the need for political restructuring of the heavily centralized federal system by adopting regional federalism that allows for adequate self-determination, political, and economic control of each region to fizzle out most interests, conflicts, and colonial vestiges that trigger state fragility and forced migration.

INTRODUCTION

Decolonizing state fragility and forced migration in postcolonial Nigeria has been an issue of recent scholarly interest following persistent insecurity in postcolonial Nigeria. State fragility has emerged as one of the important themes in the social sciences in decolonization studies, international relations, and global politics of the twenty-first century (Gravingholt, Ziaja and Kreibaum, 2012). The concept of fragility is an elusive one and often criticized for its lack of clarity (Betts, 2013). The word *fragility* according to OECD (2016, p. 16) is defined as the "combination of exposure to risk and insufficient coping capacity of the state, system and/or communities to manage, absorb or mitigate those risks." On the other hand, states are fragile when state structures lack the political will and/or capacity to provide the basic functions needed for poverty reduction, development, and to safeguard the security and human rights of their population (OECD DAC, 2007). The United Kingdom Department for International Development defines *fragile states* as those where the government cannot or will not deliver core functions to its people. (Duruji and Oviasogie, 2013).

Forced migration is an umbrella term used to describe the situation of involuntary movement from a person's place of abode to other locations within a state or outside the state. There are two categories of forcefully displaced persons: internally displaced persons (IDPs) and refugees. Refugees are persons who due to reasons of threat to their lives and/or violation of their human rights flee out of their former country of residence to another country. On the other hand, IDPs flee their native homes or residence to safer abodes within a state/country due to security threats to their lives and/or violation of their human rights but do not cross an internationally recognized state border. The forced migration dynamic this chapter focuses on is the dimension associated with IDPs. This is because of scant scholarship on state fragility and IDPs in postcolonial Nigeria.

State fragility and forced migration are contemporary fallouts of colonialism and colonial heritage. The concept of colonialism has different meanings for different scholars. Colonialism is a form of imperialism. It represents a signature of European encounter, penetration, and exploitation of Africa. To Cohen (1973), colonialism entails "economic exploitation combined with political domination and the superimposing of European control over indigenous political authorities of Africa." Colonialism is a forceful weapon which was used to subjugate and alter the African continent and by extension, Nigeria's political, economic, and social structures. As quoted in Nkrumah (1973:19), the Colonial Secretary of State for France said in 1923, "What is the use of painting the truth? Colonialism is not an act of civilization. The origin of colonialism is nothing else than an enterprise of individual interests, a one-sided egotistical imposition of the strong upon the weak."

Colonialism is a practice of domination, which involves the subjugation of one people to another. According to Akorede (2010:158), it could simply mean one country dominating another country and its people. Bala (2019) argued that this could be effectively achieved by substituting ancient norms, values, and practices with the ways of the colonial powers. To Fadeiye (2005:161), it could mean the establishment and maintenance of foreign rule by a colonizing power over some people with the aim of getting full economic benefit. Colonialism could also imply the extension of control often politically motivated by a powerful nation over another that is presumed weaker (Aderibigbe, 2006:164).

Nigeria is one of the African countries that experienced colonialism under Britain. The enterprise of British colonialism in Nigeria was economically exploitative, politically domineering, and socially oppressive. Historically, Nigeria has witnessed series of native versus colonialist conflicts prior to independence in 1960. These conflicts happened as a result of the introduction of various policies of the British administration such as coercive and coarse modes of production, forceful resource expropriation, unequal terms of trade and exchange, imposition of taxes, indirect rule, slavery and slave trade, and so on. Notable examples of such conflicts or uprisings were the 1916 Iseyin-Okeho uprising in a town in the Oke-Ogun area of Oyo State, the 1929 Aba women riot, the Kano crisis of 1953, various labor protests, strike actions, and nationalist agitations against the oppressive and exploitative colonial administration.

This conflict trends, crisis, political turmoil, and disconnect between the colonial government and the Nigerian polity, which is symptomatic of fragile state systems transited into political independence and was inherited by the immediate political ruling class that took over from the colonialists. The state handed over to the Nigerian ruling elites could not have been more fragile. The tension, deadlock, and crisis that trailed the 1959 pre-independence elections, the 1963 census, and the attendant controversies, ethnic rivalry, unhealthy competition for political power, violence, and political instabilities that bedeviled the first republic are still resounding in memory and effect to date.

Furthermore, the gory violence and arson that characterized the Western region crisis of 1962–1963-styled *Operation Weti E*, the January 15 coup and July 28 counter-coup of 1966, the reprisal killing of Igbos in the North, and secession attempt and civil war that climaxed state fragility in the First Republic engendered a wave of IDPs and forced migration across the country.

Not unconnected with these are the frequent wave of religious fundamentalism and ethno-religious violent conflicts, which are often politicized to instigate ethno-religious intolerance and killings which usually result in massive internal displacements and forced migration. Examples of these are the Maitatsine uprising of 1980–1985 and the ongoing Boko Haram insurrection. Indeed, displaced Nigerian families affected by these gruesome holocausts are traumatized by the memories and effects of their experiences including loss of lives, property, livelihood, and the rigorous task of having to rebuild the ruins of their homes or start life afresh in new destinations.

The advent of military rule between 1967 and 1996 are also manifestations of colonial antecedents of state fragility as the country witnessed a sequence of military coups and counter-coups evident in the ethno-political fragmentation, value/interest-based differences, and power struggle within the military. Examples are the Dimka 1976, Vatsa 1985, Orkar 1990, that were aborted coups while those of Murtala 1975, Buhari 1983, Babangida 1985, and Abacha 1993 were successful coups.

The same unresolved colonial antecedents of state fragility have haunted the current fourth republic since the return to democracy in 1999. Among these manifestations are political turmoil and violence during transitional elections, militancy in the Niger Delta by Movement for the Emancipation of the Niger Delta (MEND) and other militant groups, Movement for the Actualisation of a Sovereign State of Biafra (MASSOB), and the ongoing Indigenous People of Biafra (IPOB)/Eastern Security Network (ESN) agitations in Eastern Nigeria, the Sunday Igboho-led campaign for the creation of Oduduwa republic in Western Nigeria, Boko Haram terrorism in the North East, herdsmen crisis, and the general state of insecurity in the country. Appalling is the evidence of weak capacity of the current Buhari-led government/state institutions to manage the political, economic, and security affairs of the country as all aspects of the Nigerian state seem to be helplessly dwindling in an irrecoverable spiral.

These chronicled issues and periods in Nigeria have all had untold hardship and negative impacts on displaced persons, the image and unity of the country at large. These colonial and postcolonial crises attest to the failure of the British colonial administration as well as the fragility of the state system handed down by which the architecture of Nigeria's fragility was established for the future. Thus, the linkage between state fragility, forced migration, and the colonial state is glaring.

This chapter utilizes secondary data obtained from existing academic journals, books, and online resources on state fragility and forced migration to offer theoretical and analytical arguments for the causal roles of state fragility in instigating forced migration in postcolonial Nigeria. It also interrogates the colonial root causes and contemporary manifestations of state fragility and forced migration in Nigeria. It argues that Nigeria's current fragility and forced migration crisis are vestiges of colonial legacies despite sixty-one years (1960–2021) of independence.

THEORETICAL FRAMEWORK

The social contract and frustration aggression theories were adopted for this chapter. A social contract is the implicit or explicit agreement between the relevant actors or social groups that constitute a society and the government, about mutual obligations and rights; in specific terms, the exchange of public goods and services. It is the collection of informal and formal rules as well as behavioral norms that standardize society-state relations in a given country, with benefits or relevance to both individuals and social groups that form a given society (Kaplan, 2017). The social contract theory argues that persons' political and moral obligations are dependent upon agreements among them to create the society they live in. This posits that the state is formed or exists on the mutual agreement among individuals to achieve certain social needs. It is therefore an instrument conceived by humans for their collective benefits.

On the other hand, Gurr's Frustration-Aggression theory principally provides an efficient explanation of why people rebel. The main thrust of the theory is that the manifestation of aggressive behavior always presupposes the occurrence of frustration and, inversely, that the presence of frustration would always lead to aggression. Gurr (1970) thus elucidates that when the worth of material conditions decreases or increases and their expectations of material conditions do not match, there will be the perception of deprivation that leads individuals to an attitude of violence and discontent.

This argument is in line with the unmet needs thesis, which has similarities with the frustration-aggression theory defined as the difference between achievements and expectations. According to Kelman (1999,p.174), conflict is caused and escalated to a considerable degree to unfulfilled needs—not only material needs, but also such psychological needs as security, identity, self-esteem, recognition, autonomy, and a sense of justice. Parties in conflict, in pursuit of their security and identity and related needs and interests, undermine and threaten the security and identity of the other.

According to OCED (2018), broken social contracts exacerbate the root causes of displacement and forced migration especially those associated with state repression, injustice, and inter-communal conflicts. This posits that underperforming and weak social contracts are defining factors in state fragility. The theories are very germane to the discourse of this study in that they argue that the failure of state institutions to meet citizens' needs causes frustration that generates agitations such as protests, uprisings, and crises accounting for state fragility and forced migration. Odesuge (2020) draws attention to the debilitating circle of state fragility and its attendant connection to forced migration and vulnerability. The Nigerian situation explicates the failure of the social contracts between the government and the people which has led to state fragility and the large number of forced migrants the country has recorded in the past decade. This chapter focuses on the governance attributes and administrative abilities of the states as the fundamental indicators for interrogating the fragility of Nigeria. In other words, it can be deduced that the indices of fragile states are weak institutions that produce poor policies and weak governance structures that affect the welfare of citizens as well as the stability of the state.

STATE FRAGILITY AND FORCED MIGRATION IN COLONIAL NIGERIA

Protests, agitations, and confrontations have been part of the Nigerian system prior to her political independence in 1960. From the colonial era, decades before political independence, there have been various forms of agitations. In the early 1900s, the protests in Nigeria, took new dimensions. At this period, disgruntled masses over government policies took to the streets to vent their grievances. Some of the evidences of state fragility during the colonial era in Nigeria were the 1916 Iseyin-Okeho uprising in South Western Nigeria and the Aba Women's Riot of 1929 in South Eastern Nigeria.

Britain at that time was recovering from the infrastructural, financial, and human losses of World War I. In order to meet up with the financial demands, Britain resorted to internally generate revenues within its colonies. With this strategy, there was the introduction of new tax policy in Nigeria which included the imposition of direct taxation on women and enumerating children, personal properties, livestock, and other taxable possessions. This did not augur well with the women because they were already fraught with the heavy financial burdens levied on them by the warrant Chiefs. Their peaceful consultation with the colonial government to preserve their tax-exempt status was not granted. The Aba Women's riot lasted for two months and was waged by local market women against the excessive powers as well as the economic and sociopolitical oppressions of the warrant Chiefs and British government. They saw the riot as necessary to preserve their tax-exempt status that the Igbo traditional system bestowed on them (Anoba, 2018). Over 25,000 Igbo women of South Eastern Nigeria came out to protest (Onyeakagbu, 2020). About fifty-one women and one man were killed and others severely beaten and displaced (Anoba, 2018). It was the first of its kind. The protesters massively destroyed government factories and infrastructure across Igboland, which colonial police and troops met with brutal repression. It was the first major revolt by women in West Africa. Among other impacts, the Aba women's riot led to the cancellation of taxation of women and even men which was the foremost essence of the conflict. This created the impetus for the struggle for liberation from colonialism. It also confirmed the frustration aggression narrative that at the height of frustration, there will be reactions that will challenge existing status quo and breed state fragility (Onyeakagbu, 2020).

Another event buttressing the fragility of the colonial Nigeria was the 1953 riot in Kano. In May 1953, there was an eruption of conflict in Kano, Nigeria's largest city. It was a four-day reaction to the divergent opinions between the Northerners and Southerners on deliberations bothering on Nigeria's independence. On the one hand, the Southerners supported the immediate independence of Nigeria, while on the other hand, the Northerners opposed it. Most likely, they feared the dominance of the more educated Southerners and preferred to support the continuation of the colonial regime that protected them.

On March 31, 1953, the motion to grant Nigeria self-government in 1956 was moved by Chief Anthony Enahoro who was a prominent member of the Action Group (AG) political party. While other members of AG supported this motion, including majority of the members of the National Council of Nigeria and the Cameroons (NCNC), the Northern People's Congress (NPC) did not agree with their compatriots. Rather the NPC argued that the Northern region was not yet ready for self-governance. Alhaji Ahmadu Bello, leader of the NPC, then proposed an amendment to Enahoro's motion suggesting instead that self-governance should be granted "as soon as practicable," replacing "in the year 1956" from the earlier bill. This suggestion escalated tensions and disagreements and resulted in strained relationship between the Southern and Northern leaders. While leaving the House, the Northern delegates were attacked by the aggressive crowds from Lagos, who jeered and insulted them. Embittered by this, members of the Northern delegation, in an "Eight Point Program" in the Lugard Hall in Kaduna State, sought for secession which was opposed. A delegation of the NCNC and AG led by Samuel Akintola took a decision to tour the North to campaign for self-government because of their refusal to agree with the concerns of the Northern elites. This tour is believed to be the immediate cause of the Kano riots. The riot deteriorated into an ethnic conflict in which the Northerners were first to clamp down on the Yoruba. However, the casualties of the conflicts were mostly people of Igbo origin because of their refusal to accept Islam and their economic aggressiveness/business acumen (Fasan, 2021). Hundreds of people were killed and lots of them displaced.

Forced migration was also caused by the trans-Atlantic slave trade. By the fifteenth century, the patterns of migration between Africa, including Nigeria and other parts of the world, were altered by the advent of European colonialism which was characterized by force. Natural resources, commodities and labor from the African colonies were extracted to meet the economic needs of the colonial state. During the trans-Atlantic slave trade between the sixteenth and nineteenth centuries, there was the forceful movement of millions of Africans to the "new world." In other words, the colonial design managed human mobility, regulation, and control to meet the colonial labor needs at the plantation and mining-based economies. The slave trade made the Nigerian state fragile as able-bodied men that should have constituted the manpower and developed the societies were carted away.

STATE FRAGILITY AND FORCED MIGRATION IN POSTCOLONIAL NIGERIA

The immediate post-independent Nigeria was not free from the crisis of state fragility and forced migration. Conflict-induced causes such as inter-ethnic, ethno-religious, as well as inter and intra-communal and political crises were major causes of state fragility and forced migration. These conflicts have occasioned large upsurge of internal displacement of people.

In 1962, the foremost and major ethnic violence in the postcolonial period ensued in the Western region between Chief Ladoke Akintola and Chief Obafemi Awolowo. The discord led to crises which eventually resulted in the declaration of a State of Emergency.

Another region that experienced ethnic violence was the North, specifically in Kaduna State, which was capital of the region and seat of government. The conflict was caused by the assassination of Sarduna of Sokoto, Sir Ahmadu Bello, in a bloody coup d'état of January 15, 1966, that was led by Kaduna Nzeogwu, an Easterner. While the coup failed, Gen Thomas Aguiyi-Ironsi who was also an Igbo took over power. The coup was described by the plotters as a temporary and brief revolution to put an end to the corruption and ethnic rivalry in Nigeria—including those feuds against Hausa-Fulani dominance. As no Igbo leader was assassinated in that coup, there was resentment mostly by the Northerners, which triggered a reprisal attack against the Igbo. The Northerners construed the coup as a conspiracy led by the Igbos to impose Igbo domination and suppress the North.

After six months, there was a counter-coup mainly by Northern officers seeking revenge. It was bloodier than the initial coup. Aguiyi-Ironsi was killed and Colonel (later) Gen. Yakubu Gowon took over power. Colonel Emeka Odumegwu-Ojukwu, appointed by Ironsi as the Governor of the Eastern region, rebuffed Gowon's authority. After months of political bottleneck, in May 1967 the independent Republic of Biafra was declared. The Nigerian civil war (1967–1970) was the outcome of this mounting resentment. About 30,000 Igbos were killed by Northern mobs and thousands of Igbos that lived in the North at that time fled to the South. It was a major displacement crisis in Nigeria's history as millions of persons were internally displaced.

Post-1999, Nigeria continues to experience fragility and forced migration caused by poor governance. Going by the Fragile State Index of 2006 and 2020, Nigeria ranked poor in indices such as security issues, group grievances, weak and ineffective central government, economic decline, brain drain, widespread corruption and criminality, non-provision of public services, human rights/ state legitimacy, demographic pressures, rule of law, and forced migration.

The Niger Delta crisis cannot be overlooked. Since oil was discovered in the region, the region has known no peace. The region is at the heart of Nigeria's oil exploration from which Nigeria earns about 95% of her foreign exchange and 80% of the government's budgetary revenue since oil was discovered in Oloibiri in present-day Bayelsa state (Rotimi and Abdul-Azeez, 2013). While this was a gain for Nigeria, it has been a curse for the people of the region whose sources of livelihood are predominantly dependent on primary economies such as hunting, farming, and fishing. The region has been devastated by enormous oil-induced environmental degradation from gas flaring and oil spillages which destroyed the land and water resources and have led to agricultural decline, soil fertility loss, fisheries decline, forest loss, and biodiversity depletion. Oil exploration created the realities of a paradox of poverty and underdevelopment in the midst of plenty. Rather than development, the region is confronted with exploitation, inter-ethnic feuds, and inter-communal conflicts. The challenges of resource exploitation and contradictions of environmental degradation and poverty led to the rise of militant groups such as the Movement for the Emancipation of the Niger Delta (MEND) that rose in demand for justice (Ajodo-Adebanjoko, 2017) and post-amnesty militia groups such as the Niger Delta Avengers (NDAs). The effects of the Niger Delta crisis in terms of the forced migration impacts has been different during the military and civilian eras. While in the military era, the approaches for the demand for social justice took more peaceful approaches such as peaceful protest, persuasive dialogue, and petitioning, during the post-1999 era, Niger Delta militancy and the use of force went full scale causing unprecedented displacements.

Between 2007 and May 2011, Yar'Adua's/Jonathan's administration, there were various forms of violence that perpetually led to the displacement of thousands of people mostly in Northern Nigeria and fewer numbers in the southern part of the country. Between 4,500 and 5,000 persons were displaced following sectarian violence in Bauchi in February 2009 (IRIN, February 25, 2009). The fight between the militant groups such as MEND and government forces in May 2009 caused the displacement of thousands of people. The Joint Task Force (JTF) was charged with the assignment of restoring order in the Niger Delta. To achieve this and uproot the militants, JTF launched Operation Restore Hope. The JTF launched air and land strikes around the city of Warri in Delta State, and later the offensive attacks spread to the neighboring areas in Rivers State (Reuters, November 19, 2009). Although the number of casualties among the civilian population due to the conflict was not known, the IDPs' figures varied between 1,000 people displaced in various locations in Ogbe Ijoh and the 10,000 residents that fled to the forest (IRIN, May 22, 2009).

The resource curse arguments and "rentierism" also provide another line of argument to the fragile state analysis and forced migration challenge. The underdevelopment of the Niger Delta has been widely used to explain Nigeria's resource curse crisis (Amadi and Alapiki,2014). The post-amnesty resurgence of militant groups such as the NDAs resonant their quest for resource justice against the marginalization and neglect that have resulted in underdevelopment of the region. The agitations became more pronounced and violent in the post-1999 civilian administration. Following the repressive responses of successive civilian administrations such as the Olusegun Obasanjo's era, the agitations took a militant approach that ignited massive displacement. The strategies adopted included bombings of oil facilities, kidnapping, and oil bunkering. One of the reasons that accounts for Nigeria's resource curse crisis is the expensive nature of the federal system that Nigeria practices. This made Nigeria's federal arrangement non-responsive to the needs of the people. For instance, the difference between the minimum wage and the money earned by politicians are worlds apart; in May 2010, most of the Legislators in the lower chamber of the National Assembly requested for a new quarterly allocation of $277,000 each, that is, N42 million. This does not include their monthly salary of about $8,600 each, that is, N1.3 million. To date, the state Governors and the President have access to security votes, which is an unspecified amount of money they often spend without giving account. In the same country, the vast majority of the citizens earn less than $2 or N300 daily (Yagboyaju, 2011).

One major cause of the forced displacement is the human needs/socioeconomic analysis premised on the assumption that unmet human needs are the fundamental cause of violence. In line with the unmet needs argument, banditry and crime such as abduction and kidnapping have been embraced as lucrative businesses across Nigeria as the government fails to provide employment for the youths to meet their basic needs. Poverty and unfavorable socioeconomic conditions made it easy for insurgent groups such as Boko Haram to recruit youths for suicide missions. Also, Niger Delta youths have taken up arms against the federal government. The import of unmet needs on the state fragility and forced migration discourse is that fear is widespread in communities that have had persistent criminal attacks, making it imperative for people to flee their communities for safer places. For instance, after the kidnapping of about 276 Chibok girls from their school in Chibok, residents of the localities and suburbs fled to other areas so that they could be safe and protect their other children that had not been abducted by bandits (Ajakaye, 2019).

Across several adjoining communities, beyond abduction for ransom, victims were raped, killed, and others forcefully conscripted into militia/criminal groups. Unaffected individuals had to flee.

Crises between Fulani pastoralists and farmers have caused tension in the North Central geopolitical zone, especially in the Middle Belt resulting in violence and displacement. Long-existing ethnic conflict between the pastoralists and Hausa farmers in North Western Katsina, Sokoto, and Zamfara states also trigger the displacement of thousands of people every year (IDMC, 2020).

Nigeria's North Central and North West Zones are plagued with multidimensional ethnic and religious crisis and attacks by criminal groups such as grand larceny and kidnapping along major highways. The crisis intensified during the past years and resulted in extensive displacement throughout the region. For instance, between the May 3 and 9, 2021, armed clashes between herdsmen and farmers and those between bandits and local communities led to new wave of population displacement. The attacks affected 1,258 people in Keana Local Government Area (LGA) of Nassarawa State and Safana LGA of Katsina State. The series of attacks caused people to flee to neighboring vicinities. The crisis affected 1,351 individuals in Qua'an Pan LGA of Plateau State and Wamba LGA of Nassarawa State. The armed clashes that occurred between the farmers and herders, and the local communities and bandits on the April 26 and May 2, 2021, affected 2,121 individuals in Sabuwa and Dandume LGAs of Katsina State and Guma LGA of Benue State. These also resulted in forced migration to neighboring localities for safety (DMT, 2021).

Ethnicization and religious coloration of Nigerian institutions have also weakened Nigeria's security apparatus. It is imperative to mention that in Nigeria, the professionalism of the military has been traded for political ambition, which has not been helpful for the preservation of the country's security and that of its citizens. Terrorist groups such as Boko Haram, the Islamic State in the Greater Sahara (ISGS), al-Qaeda in the Islamic Maghreb, Fulani herdsmen of West Africa, and the Islamic State in West Africa Province (ISWAP) took advantage of the weakness of the Nigerian military security complexes to dominate ungoverned spaces so as to entrench their existence, carve out territories, and take over villages. Additionally, despite the huge budgets allotted to the security institutions, corruption among public office holders at the federal and state levels made investments in the security sector a secondary affair. The result of this has been the weakness of the police and military to withstand the sophistication of armed groups operating within the Nigerian geographical space (Bumah and Adelakun, 2009). For instance, Danjibo (2009) pathetically mentioned that the military officers and police deployed to confront Boko Haram ran for their lives when they found it difficult to withstand the prowess of the sect.

Religion and religious fundamentalism play a predominant role in Nigeria's displacement and state fragility discourse. Religious fundamentalism is a faith-based or religious-superiority complex that creates the consciousness that a religion is better than others. Religion plays a crucial role in the fragility discourse because "religious belief, practice and the high capacity to impose and assert its perspective on the country's political agenda" can induce conflicts (Rasheed, 2013:23). Nigeria is not a conventional nation-state because it is not united by religion, language, culture, or even a common national history. The Islamic fundamentalist ideologies of the sect have led to the deliberate attacks on churches, the bombing of Christian communities, and the abduction of clergymen who are Christians or moderate Muslims. According to the U.S. Commission on International Religious Freedom (2013), between January 1, 2012 and August 2013, Boko Haram's religiously motivated attacks have included: 50 churches that either were bombed, burned, or attacked, killing at least 366 persons; 31 separate attacks on Christians or Southerners perceived to be Christian, killing at least 166 persons; 23 targeted attacks on clerics or senior Islamic figures critical of Boko Haram, killing at least sixty persons; and twenty-one attacks on "un-Islamic" institutions or persons engaged in "un-Islamic" behavior, killing at least seventy-four.

The religious inclination of the group is evident in the abduction of the 276 Chibok school girls. The abducted girls were predominantly Christians. The terrorists killed seven people, burned down ten homes, and looted food supplies that were meant to be distributed to residents to celebrate Christmas. A clergy was also abducted. Also, on April 20, 2021, at least twenty-three students and staff of Greenfield University, a private university acclaimed to be owned by a Christian, were kidnapped by armed gunmen. This was Nigeria's fourth kidnapping from a tertiary institution between January and April 2021 alone.

Ethno-religious violence has mostly occurred in the North due to religious and inter-ethnic intolerance. It has led to the displacement of several persons. Between 1999 and 2003, there were forty incidents of violence such as inter-ethnic conflict, ethno-religious, and communal nationwide in which 10,000 lives were lost while a large number were displaced. The Federal Commissioner for Refugees estimated that around 500,000 people were displaced between 1999 and 2005 (Bronwen, 2002). For example, the clash between and Muslims in the city of Kaduna due to the imposition of sharia in 2000 saw the death of Igbos and Christians. This also led to displacement and forced migration as Muslims and Christians relocated to zones dominated by people of their own faith as thousands of people fled from the far north while religious tension amplified in other areas.

In 2001, religious conflicts broke out in Jos Plateau state, which sits on the divide between the largely Christian South and Muslim North. Thousands of people were displaced and over 1,000 were killed. Many of them settled permanently and temporarily in neighboring Bauchi state (Madueke, 2015). The major inter-ethnic violence that took place in Plateau, Taraba, Benue States, and Nassarawa between 2000 and 2002 centered on the matters of boundary and land and indigenes/settlers. In Obasanjo's second term as President of Nigeria between 2003 and 2007, there were a number of ethno-religious, inter-ethnic, communal, and political conflicts that featured across the country. For instance, there were series of clashes over farmland in Gombe and Adamawa States, which led to the displacement of over 3,700 and 20,000 people, respectively (IRIN, February 25, 2009).

Border porosity is another facilitator of state fragility in Nigeria. One of the characteristics of the Nigerian state is the porosity of its border and it constitutes a major facilitator and protraction of conflict-induced displacement. Nigeria has porous borders with Niger (1,497 kilometers) in the north, Cameroon (1,690 kilometers) in the east, Chad (87 kilometers) in the northeast, and Benin (773 kilometers) in the west (Bearzotti, et al. 2015). The fact that most of the Nigerian border regions are either mountainous or located in the jungle makes it permeable. Musa (2013) and Onuoha (2013) assert that Nigeria shares with Niger, Chad, and Cameroon between 1,000 and 1,500 illegal or unmonitored trans-boundary routes leading in and out of Nigeria.

In the 2009 conflict between Boko Haram sect and security agents, security forces killed some of the persons that committed atrocities in Nigeria under the umbrella of Boko Haram who were identified as aliens that took advantage of the porous borders to perpetuate evil and thereafter return to neighboring countries for refuge. In addition to this, Musa (2013) opines that the sect has been able to use the porous condition of the borders in Yobe and Borno States to smuggle arms for its activities and increase in military hardware of the terrorists. Over time, the illegal movement of arms has been done with the aid of nomadic herdsmen that pack the hardware attached to cows, donkeys, and camels to conceal their identity. However, sometimes the arms are stocked into cartons of goods and bags of grains and are transported via trucks and lorries. Citing specific examples, Onuoha (2013) argued that the porosity of the border led to the trafficking of weapons by al-Qaeda in the Islamic Maghreb (AQIM), mercenaries, and other terrorist groups into Nigeria during the Libyan civil war.

Porous border allows for the fluidity and movement of members of the armed groups from one neighboring country to another. It has helped in the conscription of fighters (Omale, 2013). Akinyemi (2013) advances that the porous nature of the Nigerian borders has empowered Boko Haram to establish connections with other terrorist groups and violent extremists in East, North, and West Africa for trainings, logistics, funding, and weaponry. The sect joined some other Islamic Jihadist groups to fight against the French troops in Mali (ICG, 2014). For instance, Boko Haram provided support for the coup in Mali in 2012, about 100 of its members joined other sects to lay siege to the Algerian consulate in Gao (Copeland, 2013). There are also claims that the facilitators of the Herders/Farmers crisis in Nigeria's Middle Belt and other regions are not Nigerians but infiltrators from Niger, Cameroun, and other neighboring countries that share similar cultural, physical, religious, and historical linkages with tribes from Northern Nigeria. These similarities and the porosity of the borders have made it very difficult for the security institutions to effectively nip terrorism and other conflicts inducing forced migration in the bud.

A 2016 report by Oxfam estimated that Nigeria had 2 million small and light arms weaponry in 2012, the number has tripled in just four years. A recent speech given by General Abdulsalami Abubakar, former Head of State of Nigeria stated that Nigeria has over 6 million small arms in circulation. The existence of over 10 million of these weapons in West Africa, means that Nigeria accounts for roughly 60% of the region's total. Their proliferation easily makes them get into the hands of gangs, insurgents, armed robbers, and individuals who often use them to terrorize the masses. Easy access to small arms enables crime and terrorism to spread faster than they would otherwise, thus increasing the fragility of the Nigerian state.

Nigeria's security force still follows the sequence of the pattern bestowed to them by the departed colonial officials as regards oppression and the use of force. Nigeria's postcolonial history has been that in which security forces wield power and force to suppress agitations and unrest. State response to the October 2020 #EndSARS protest suggests the use of repression in Nigeria's fourth republic. Members of the military were authorized to open fire on peaceful #EndSARS protesters, which was a movement that responded to the litany of abuse by the Special Anti-Robbery Squad (SARS), which is a special unit of the police.

There are other cases such as Gbaramatu Niger Delta (May 2009), Odi Bayelsa State (July 2003), Zaki Biam Benue State (October 2001), and the Shi'a Muslims in Zaria Kaduna State (December 2015) where the security forces habitually use disproportionate force on civilians, killed many, and forced thousands of them to flee.

Asides conflict-induced displacement, Nigeria has been exposed to natural disasters that have triggered forced migration and state fragility over the years. The commonest are floods that occurred in the lowlands and the basins where the people lived in densely inhabited informal settlements (Amadi, 2013). The floods were caused by rainfall, overflowing watercourses, and water released from dam reservoirs both in Nigeria and upstream countries as well. Adamawa and Borno states which have experienced displacement and protracted conflict also bore some of the brunt of floods in 2019 during an unusually lengthened rainy season. Also, the floods in the Niger River basin between August and September destroyed 2,667 homes in Niger State, thus, displacing the inhabitants from their places of habitual residence (IDMC, 2020). Between January 1 and December 31, 2020, Nigeria had 279,000 new displacements caused by disasters. This was higher than the figure of the previous year. In 2019, there were 143,000 people displaced by disasters. Within the same period, there were 248,000 new displacements by conflict and violence across nineteen states. At the end of 2020, the total of persons still displaced by conflicts and violence in Nigeria totaled over 3.2 million. Of this figure, Nigerian refugees in Chad, Cameroun and Niger totaled 304,562, while others were displaced within Nigeria (UNHCR, 2021).

Self-determination and secessionist struggles are the most recent cause of state fragility and forced migration. Right from the colonial days there have been agitations of minority groups in Nigeria by reason of their population and the "smallness" of the territory that they occupy as well as the level of the political and socioeconomic influence/relevance they hold. In this wise, certain geopolitical/ethnic groups in the country have been agitating for self-determination or increased relevance in the political affairs of the country or in the control of their own economic resources or determination of their own affairs as a people. The foremost, in the early postcolonial days, were the people of Ogoja in Cross River, and the Bakassi minorities in Cameroun.

Recently, groups such as Amotekun in Yorubaland in the South West and the Indigenous People of Biafra (IPOB) in the South East have risen for this purpose of secessionist agitations. The most prominent one in the present administration has been the IPOB's and Biafra's self-determination and secessionist agitations. They can be traced back to 1967 after the first military coup. The Eastern Security Network (ESN) is the paramilitary organization of IPOB. The pro-Biafra separatist movement is particularly informed by the fact that since the federal government is weak in providing security for the eastern region particularly against the Fulani herdsmen whom they accuse of grazing on farmlands and committing crimes against local residents as bandits and kidnappers, there is the necessity for the creation/emergence of militant or vigilante security outfit to protect them. According to Ojewale (2021), the conflict between herders and farmers in North Central zone of Nigeria has made the herders to be ranked six times deadlier than Boko Haram insurgents. Yet the government has looked away and preferred to label ESN an illegal group challenging the government's authority.

The import of this is the fact that the Fulani herdsmen and bandits' attacks on the citizens of the South East have led to forced migration because many people have abandoned their homes, businesses, farmlands, and source of livelihood to seek safer haven for their lives. More so, the government's consideration of the IPOB and ESN as a threat to its authority and an attempt to further achieve the goal of secession by the disgruntled and divergent entities/groups of the South East has led to government clampdown with its military might on the South East in a manner that has unleashed a high scale of forced migration due to military attacks and killings that has forced citizens to flee for safety in other places (Peckham, 2021). The Orlu massacre in January 2021 is a very good example.

DECOLONIZING STATE FRAGILITY AND FORCED MIGRATION IN POSTCOLONIAL NIGERIA

The previous sections have established that the challenges in postcolonial Nigeria have their roots in its historical linkages to the predatory colonial experiences such as the inherited federal system of government. The post-1999 fragility throve on the inherited colonial legacy such as federal system of government rooted in the pre-independence Sir Arthur Richard's 1946 constitution of Nigeria. With the approval of the 1954 Lyttleton Constitution, federalism as a system of government was fully launched in Nigeria with its strong divisive ethnic tendencies (Epelle, 2019).

Bringing the subject back to how the decolonization of state fragility and forced migration in postcolonial Nigeria can be achieved, first, there is need to decolonize Nigeria's federalism by restructuring it for regionalism. *Federalism* is a system of government or a political arrangement in which power is shared between the central government and other subsequent components of governments such that each of the tiers exists as a separate government operating independently from each other (Ita and Inimo-Etele, 2019). This stipulates that none of the tiers of government is an appendage of each other. Power ought to be shared so as to prevent the preponderance of power in the hands of any of the tiers. However, this has not been the case in Nigeria. The President who is at the central government and at the apex of the national leadership wields much of power concentrated in the office with the other tiers of government as mere appendages. Due to this, the federal government accumulates and misappropriates the revenue that is accrued to the nation. The challenge with this is that the massiveness of the wealth and resources at the center makes the tussle for political power a "do-or-die-affair," deepens ethnic and religious politics, breeds corruption, and limits electoral credibility and transparency (Orunbon, 2020).

Thus, decolonizing Nigeria's federalism for regionalism will mean dissolving the federation's unitary character for a system that diffuses power; each union will have political autonomy; and will be largely independent of the federal authority. According to Campbell (2021), between 70 and 80% of political power would be exercised by the regions rather than the federal government. Political restructuring will in no small measure address the challenges of state fragility and forced migration because the elements of state fragility such as resource control tension, ethno-religious tension (jihad and sharia), economic instability, self-determination, regional discrimination, and so on will naturally fizzle out. This is because a new political arrangement such as regionalism will allow for more equity in the distribution of wealth and resources as well as allow for better representation of citizens' opinions.

It is essential to mention that the quest for restructuring is built on the fact that it has had some level of success in the past in terms of enhancing competition for rapid development among the regions; this was even when oil was not yet discovered. On this note, this chapter disagrees with the argument by Babalola and Onapajo (2019) that the call for restructuring has increasingly become a strategy in elite politics for power and its associated material opportunities and because of ethno-regional politics surrounding the restructuring debate, there are contradictions in the demands of regional elites and their groupings. Given that the issue of political restructuring, as advocated, is elite-driven and has the tendency to lead to endless agitations for change, Bbalola and Onapajo (2019) conclude that restructuring is not the solution to the problems of the country.

This chapter argues that this is not a viable reason to rebuff the clamor for restructuring because there are more gains such as rich regions becoming productive and moving away from poverty and the mobilization of internal resources than just the politicization of power at the region.

Second, the chapter demonstrates that if the clamor for political restructuring is not going to be allowed by the main powerful bloc, mostly the Northern bourgeoisies, then Nigeria can tow the path of separation into different political units/systems like the separation of Sudan into South and North Sudan, with each being independent from each other. It is very likely that the separation of Nigeria into either two (North and South) or three independent nations (North, South, and East) can quell the engulfing menace of state fragility and forced migration. The evidence from Sudan supports this claim. North and South Sudan no longer have such intense warfare like they did before their disengagement. They can focus their attention and resources to economic growth and stability and citizens' welfare and infrastructural development, and not crisis management. This can also be achieved in Nigeria.

CONCLUSION

Nigeria's forced displacement or migration crisis due to state fragility has exhibited cogent and indisputable connections between colonial heritages, government's breach of its social contract with its people, and the resultant violent conflicts and instability that have bedeviled the Nigerian state. As already explicated, the inept institutions of government and colonially initiated ruling elite have over time bred a system of economic deprivation and repression, social inequality, injustice, ethno-political marginalization, and unequal distribution of state resources, which are all in tandem with the underlying characteristics of state fragility. Furthermore, the situations of forced migration across the country are also capable of further weakening the already fragile institutions of government by fomenting demographic challenges. The increased population density in the refuge destinations creates new problems associated with economic and security management, particularly with the risk of bandits and terrorists using the opportunity to penetrate target areas under the guise of seeking refuge after forced displacement.

To effectively decolonize Nigeria's forced migration crisis, state institutions and the political ruling class must do away with their corrupt interests and adopt a new political will for good governance. In doing this, there must be commitment to social contract between the state and its citizens in order to earn the trust and loyalty of the already fragmented citizenry.

Similarly to decolonize state fragility, the Nigerian government and political elites must disconnect from the hitherto failed colonial experiment and immediately adopt the solution of political restructuring of the heavily centralized federal system. The adoption of a decentralized or deconcentrated federal system will allow for federating states' political and economic control of their resources, tax, security apparatus, and so on, in addition to constitutional review and immediate amendment of other draconian sections of the Nigerian constitution that are stifling true federalism. This will naturally result in the fizzling out of most interests and value-based conflicts as causes of the colonial vestiges of state fragility and forced migration.

The impact of forced migration arising from the problems of state fragility as discussed in this chapter portends a clarion call to action by concerned state and non-state actors, policymakers, local and international humanitarian actors and organizations, among other stakeholders concerned with conflict resolution, humanitarian action, and responsibility to protect IDPs.

REFERENCES

Aderibigbe, S. (2006). *Basic Approach to Government*. Lagos: Joja Educational Research and Publishers Ltd.

Adesote, S. and Peters, A. (2015). A historical analysis of violence and internal population displacement in Nigeria's fourth republic, 1999-2011. *International Journal of Peace and Conflict Studies* 2(3):13–22.

Adeyeri, O. and Adejuwon, K. D. (2012). The implications of British colonial economic policies on Nigeria's development. *International Journal of Advanced Research in Management and Social Sciences* 1(2):1–16.

Ajakaye, R. (2019). Poor economy, governance weaken Nigeria's security: Experts. Retrieved on May 18, 2021 from https://www.aa.com.tr/en/africa/poor-economy-governance-weaken-nigeria-s-security-experts-/1472178

Ajodo-Adebanjoko, A. (2017). Towards ending conflict and insecurity in the Niger Delta region. Retrieved on May 25, 2021 from https://reliefweb.int/report/nigeria/towards-ending-conflict-and-insecurity-niger-delta-region

Akinyemi, O. (2013). Globalisation and Nigeria border security: Issues and challenges. *International Affairs and Global Strategy* 11:1–7.

Akorede, E.I. (2010). Colonial experience in Africa: How it affects the formation of a United States of Africa. *International Journal of Issues on African Development* 2(4): 23.–45.

Amadi, L .(2013). Climate change, peasantry and rural food production decline in the Niger delta region: A case of the 2012 flood disaster. *Journal of Agricultural and Crop Research* 1(6):94–103.

Amadi, L. & Alapiki, H. (2014). Perspectives and dynamics of the natural resource curse in post 1990 Niger delta, Nigeria. *Journal of Advances in Political Science* 1(2):45–62.

Anoba, I. (2018). The aba women's riots of 1029: Africa's great tax revolt. Retrieved on May 25, 2021 from https://www.africanliberty.org/2018/10/01/the-aba-womens-riots-of-1929-how-women-led-africas-great-tax-revolt/

Babalola, D. and Onapajo, H. (2019).At issue- new clamour for 'restructuring' in Nigeria: Elite politics, contradictions, and good governance. *African Studies Quarterly* 18(4):41–56.

Bala, A. (2019). *Colonialism and the Development in Nigeria: Effects and Challenges.* International Affairs and Global Strategy, p. 70.

Bearzotti, E., Geranio, A., Keresztes, V. K. and Müllerova, M. (2015). *Containing Boko Haram's Transnational Reach: Toward a Developmental Approach to Border Management.* Regional Academy on the UN.

Betts, A. (2013). State fragility, refugee status and survival migration. *Forced Migration Review* 43:5–6.

Bumah, J. and Adelakun, A. (2009). *The Boko Haram Tragedy and Other Issues.* The Punch (Lagos), p. 40.

Campbell, J. (2021). Yoruba Debate "Restructuring" of Nigeria or "Autonomy". https://www.cfr.org/blog/yoruba-debate-restructuring-nigeria-or-autonomy

Cohen, B. J (1973). *The Question of Imperialism: The Political Economy and Dependence.* New York: Basic Books.

Copeland, F. (2013). The Boko Haram insurgency in Nigeria. Civil-Military Fusion Centre. Retrieved on March 3, 2016 from http://reliefweb.int/sites/reliefweb.int/files/resources/20130220%20Boko%20Haram%20in%20Nigeria.pdf

Danjibo, N. D. (2009). *Islamic Fundamentalism and Sectarian Violence: The 'Maitatsine' and 'Boko Haram Crises in Northern Nigeria.* Peace and Conflict Studies Paper Series, pp. 1–21. Nigeria: Institute of African Studies.

DTM (May 11, 2021). Nigeria — North Central & North West Flash Report #51 (03 – 09 May 2021). Retrieved on May 18, 2021 from https://displacement.iom.int/reports/nigeria-%E2%80%94-north-central-north-west-flash-report-51-03-%E2%80%93-09-may-2021?close=true

Duruji, M. and Oviasogie, F.O. (2013). State failure, terrorism and global security: An appraisal of the Boko haram insurgency in Northern Nigeria. *Journal of Sustainable Society* 2(1): 20–30.

Epelle, A. (2019). Challenges of political restructuring in Nigeria's fourth republic: A prognostic analysis. *European Journal of Scientific Research* 152(4): 370–383.

Fadeiye, J. O. (2005). *A Social Studies Textbook for Colleges and Universities.* Vol. 2. Ibadan: Akin- Johnson Press and Publishers.

Fasan, O. (January 21, 2021). Restructuring Nigeria: The North is on the wrong side of history again. https://www.vanguardngr.com/2021/01/restructuring-nigeria-the-north-is-on-the-wrong-side-of-history-again/

Gravingholt, J., Ziaja, S. and Kreibaum, M. (2012) *State Fragility: Towards A Multi-Dimensional Empirical Typology.* Deutsches Institut für Entwicklungspolitik. ISBN: 978-3-88985-546-6.

Gurr, T.R. (1970). *Why Men Rebel.* Princeton, NJ: Princeton University Press. ISBN: 9781594519147.

Integrated Regional Information Networks (IRIN). (May 22 2009). Nigeria: Thousands Flee Violence, Hundreds Suspected Dead.

Integrated Regional Information Networks (IRIN). (February 25 2009). Uneasy calm in Bauchi after deadly clashes.

Internal Displacement Monitoring Centre (IDMC). (2020). Nigeria: country information. https://www.internal-displacement.org/countries/nigeria

International Crisis Group (2014). *Curbing Violence in Nigeria (II): The Boko Haram Insurgency.* Belgium: ICG.

Ita and Inimo-Etele, 2019). Restructuring Nigerian federalism: A prognosis for nation-building and socio-political stability. *Journal of Political Science and Leadership Research* 5(1): 1–18.

Kaplan, S. (2017) *Inclusive Social Contracts in Fragile States in Transition: Strengthening the Building Blocks of Success.* Barcelona: Institute for Integrated Transitions.

Kelman,H C. (1999).Experiences from 30 years of action conflict. In K. Spillman and A. Wenger (Eds.), *Zeitg Kinflite VII: Zucher Beitrage zur Sicherheitspoliti,* pp. 173–179. Zurich: Forschungsstelle fur Sicherheitsp Zurich

Imhonopi, D., Urim, U. M. and Iruonagbe, T. C. (2013). Colonialism, social structure and class formation: Implication for development in Nigeria. *A Panoply of Readings in Social Sciences. Lessons for and from Nigeria.* Department of Sociology- Covenant University. Nigeria. Ibadan: Cardinal Prints Ibadan.

Madueke, K. (2015). From neighbours to deadly enemies: excavating landscapes of territoriality and ethnic violence in Jos, Nigeria. *Journal of Contemporary African Studies* 36(1): 87–102.

Mukoyama, N. (2019). Colonial origins of the resource curse: endogenous sovereignty and authoritarianism in Brunei. *Democratization* 27(2): 224–242.

Musa, S. (2013). Border security, arms proliferation and terrorism in Nigeria. Sahara Reporters. Retrieved April 1, 2016 from http://saharareporters.com/article/border-security-armsproliferation-and-terrorism-nigeria-lt-col-sagirmusa?goback=.gde_4451300_member_234179302

Nkrumah, K. (1973). *Revolutionary Path*. London: Panaf Books Ltd.

Odesuge, A. (2020). *State Fragility as Drivers of Forced Migration and Displacement in South and Central Somalia*. University of Nairobi Library.

OECD. (2016). *States of Fragility 2016: Understanding Violence*. Paris: OECD Publishing.

OECD. (2018). MENA-OECD Resilience Task Force Annual Meeting, Jeddah 4 – 5 December 2018 Background Paper for Session 1: Rebuilding a Social Contract Based on aSocial Dialogue. Retrieved on May 18, 2021 https://www.oecd.org/mena/competitiveness/ERTF-Jeddah-2018-Background-note-Social-Contract.pdf

OECD DAC. (2007). OECD DAC Handbook on security sector reform: Supporting security and justice. Paris: OECD Publishing. OECD. (2016). *States of Fragility 2016: Understanding Violence*. Paris: Authors.

Ojewale, O.(2021). Rising insecurity in northwest Nigeria: Terrorism thinly disguised as banditry. https://www.brookings.edu/blog/africa-in-focus/2021/02/18/rising-insecurity-in-northwest-nigeria-terrorism-thinly-disguised-as-banditry/

Omale, D.J.O. (2013). Terrorism and counter-terrorism in Nigeria: Theoretical paradigms and lessons for public policy. *Canadian Social Science* 9(3): 96–103.

Onuoha, F.C. (2013). *Porous Borders and Boko Haram's Arms Smuggling Operations in Nigeria*. n.p: Al Jazeera Center for Studies.

Onyeakagbu, A. (2020). The real story behind the Aba women's riot and the list of people that died. Retrieved on May 25, 2021 from https://www.pulse.ng/lifestyle/food-travel/the-real-story-behind-the-aba-womens-riot-and-the-list-of-people-that-died/605kbl1

Orunbon, A. (2020). Why regionalism/restructuring of Nigeria is vital. Retrieved on May 25, 2021 from https://businessday.ng/opinion/article/why-regionalism-restructuring-nigeria-is-vital/

Page, M. (2019). Nigeria struggles with security sector reforms. *Chatham House*. Retrieved on May 25, 2021 from https://www.chathamhouse.org/2019/04/nigeria-struggles-security-sector-reform

Peckham, N. (2021). Deepening security crisis in south east Nigeria. https://www.spear-fish.com/blog/8fyf6a4gdcg5jygh8xswn9344zg4z6

Rotimi, O. and Abdul-Azeez, A. (2013). Revenue generation and transparecy in Nigeria oil and gas industry: Position of Nigeria extractive industries transparency initiative (Neiti). *Research Journal of Finance and Accounting* 4(6): 99–114.

The U.S. Commission On International Religious Freedom. (2013). Nigeria: August 2013 Boko Haram's Religiously-Motivated Attacks. Retrieved on May 18, 2021 from https://www.uscirf.gov/sites/default/files/resources/Final%20Nigeria%20Factsheet%20%20August%2019,2013.pdf

UNHCR. (2021). Nigeria Emergency. Retrieved on May 18, 2021 from https://www.unhcr.org/nigeria-emergency.html

Yagboyaju, D. A. (2011). Nigeria's fourth republic and the challenge of a faltering democratization. *African Studies Quarterly* 12(3): 93–106.

Author Index

Abayomi, 236
Abdelrahman, M., 1, 143, 154
Abdi, A. A., 236
Abe, T., 222
Abrahams, P., xxv
Abuoma, C. A., 127
Acemoglu, D., xv
Achebe, C., xxv, 165
Adam, C., 1, 141
Adam, S., 186
Adama, O., 10, 13
Adebanwi, W., 151
Adebayo, A. A., 145, 236, 237
Adegoju, A., 6
Adejare, G. S., 235, 237
Adejuwon, K. D., 125
Adelakun, A. O., 235, 236, 280
Aderibigbe, D., 12
Aderibigbe, S., 271
Adesina, J., 236–38
Adewusi, A. O., 236
Adingupu, C., 14
Afigbo, A. E., 207, 211
Agbetiloye, A. B., 6
Agboola, T., 9
Agena, xxiv
Agozino, B., vii, 43–46, 48–50, 52, 54, 56, 58, 59
Agrawal, A., 246

Agubuzu, O. C. L., 1, 155
Agugua, A., 242, 243
Ahooja, P., 114
Aina, T. A., 222
Ajakaiye, 1, 143
Akanle, O., 235–39, 244, 246, 248
Ake, C., xvi, 4, 38, 144–46, 149, 150, 152, 174, 179–81, 183, 184
Akinsanmi, G., 15
Akinsete, E., 6, 10
Akpan, N. U., 206, 207
Alabi, B. O., 14
Alavi, H., 1
Althusser, L., xxvii
Amadi, L., xxii, xxiii, xxiv, 278, 283
Amadiume, I., 56
Ameh, A. A., 218
Amin, S., xv, xvi, 24, 25, 34, 39, 56, 114, 116, 130, 180, 183
Amnesty International, 11, 15, 16
Anderson, A., 24
Anoba, I., 274, 275
Appiah, K. A., 23, 24
Armah, A. K., xxv
Armer, 243
Arowasegbe, J. O., 38
Arruzza, C., 38
Ashcroft, B., xvi
Atkinson, Ti.-G., 195

Austen, 131
Austin, G., 86, 116
Awoonor, K., 162
Awuzie, S., 159, 164, 166, 168, 170
Ayittey, G., 133
Azikiwe, N., 48, 56

Babu, A. M., 56
Bajekal, N., 230
Bala, A., 271
Balogun, A. O., 7, 197–99, 211
Banik, S., 1
Banks, J., 124
Barbara, E., 132
Barber, K., 220
Basinski, S., 13
Bebbington, 247
Beetseh, K., 239
Bellu, L. G., 185, 186
Bennett, O., 194, 211
Berry, S. S., 1, 132
Bhabha, H. K., 34, 35
Bhattachrya, T., 38
Biereenu-Nnabugwu, B., 175
Bigon, B., 7
Biko, S., 56
Bongie, xxiii
Bornschier, H., 257
Boukhobza, M., 66, 70
Boyd, R., 219
Bradford, H., 199, 200, 211
Bradlow, B., 14
Bradshaw, Y. W., 257
Brennan, T., 25, 28, 32, 36
Brennen, 32, 33
Briggs, J., 246, 247
Brinton, C., 196
Bronwen, 280
Brookes, M., 38
Brown, J., 195
Brundtland Report, 114

Cabral, A., 52, 56, 94, 104–6
Cain, A., 5
Calderisi, R., 1
Campbell, J., 255, 285

Caring, 216
Carrier, J. G., 1, 124
Castels, xxiv
Cerny, xxiv
Chakrabarty, D., xxiii, 96
Chang, H.-J., 153–155
Cheah, P., 25, 29, 35
Chen, K-H., 34
Chilisa, B., xxiv
Chinweizu, J. O., 104, 174, 184
Chirol, V., 203, 204, 211
Chirot, D., 257
Chittick, C. W., 69, 78
Chossudovsky, M., 1
Chow, R., 37
Chui, B., 169
Clark, G., 49
Clarke, C. G., 3
Clifford, J., 35, 36
Coleman, J., xx
Cooper, F., 4
Croese, S., 6, 13, 14
Croitoru, A., 123
Crowder, M., 115, 116, 125, 126, 258

Daly, M. V., 203, 211
Daniel, 15
Daoud, K., 66, 69
Davidson, B., 116
Davies, J., 196
Davis, A., 45
Dees, G. J., 123
De Gramont, D., 12, 14
Delanty, G., 38
de Morases, P. F., 220
Dercon, S., 1, 141, 150
Diala, I., 162–63
Dicken, P., 221
Dike, K. O., 205, 258
Dirlik, A., 36
Dos Santos, T., xv
Drayton, 124
Driessen, P., xxv
Du Bois, W. E. B., 46, 50, 56, 240
Duignan, P., 126
Dunwoodie, P., 66

Easterly, W., xv, xxv, 116
Echikwonye, R. A., 239
Ehindero, J. T., 218
Eisenstadt, S. N., 217
Eisler, R., xvi
Ekeanyanwu, N. T., 219
El Brashi, R., 124
Elhiraika, A., 1, 147
Ellen, R., 246
Ellis, 204
Emmanuel, S., 125, 129, 215, 216, 224, 226, 228, 230
Engels, F., 181
Engerman, S., xvi
Epelle, A., 284
Escobar, A., xv, xxiii
Esteva, G., xv
Evans, P., 154
Ezeonu, I., 57

Falola, T., 4, 96, 115, 197, 198, 201, 258
Fanon, F., x, 25, 28–31, 33, 37, 44, 45, 49, 54–56, 70, 73, 96, 126, 128, 173, 175, 179, 182
Ferdausy, S., 129
Ferguson, J., xxiii
Ferris, E., 194, 211
Fieldhouse, D. K., 49
Filion, L. J., 123, 124
Fischer, M. A., 1
Folarin, S., 9, 10
Forward, C. N., 3
Foucault, M., xxiii
Frank, A. G., 174, 180
Fraser, N., 38
Frederick, 3

Gachihi, M. W., 208, 209
Gandy, M., 7
Gant, K., 6
Gardner, S., 67, 80
Geiger, S., 202
Gellner, E., 24, 25
Giardina, C., 195
Gibson, J., 67, 70

Giddens, A., xxiii, 244
Giles, J. W., 194
Gilley, B., xx
Gilman, N., 256
Gleave, M. B., 4
Gordon, R. E., 244
Götze, N., 1
Gramsci, A., 55, 57
Griffiths, G., xvi
Gurr, T. R., 196, 273
Gyeke, 153

Haack, M., 38
Hadjor, K. B., 216
Hall, S., 45, 49, 275
Hall, T. D., 257
Hallward, P., xxiv, xxv
Hamel, K., 254
Hani, C., 56
Hanisch, C., 195
Hansard, 48
Hardt, M., xx, xxiii, xxv
Harris, H., 246
Harvey, D., xiv, 5, 6
Helleiner, G. K., 128
Henderson, D., xvi
Henrich, J., 219
Heyman, G. D., 194
Heymans, C., 149
Hirji, K. F., 45
Hisrich, R. D., 123
Hofer, M., 254
Hogendorn, J. S., 132
Hopkins, A. G., 123, 258
Horton, 153
Horvath, 241
Huntington, S. P., 141
Hurley, A., 3
Hyden, G., 1
Hyden, L., 121

Ibiwoye, D., 14
Ibrahim, R. O., 131
Ikime, O., 206
Ince, O. U., 1, 143
Index Mundi, 66

Ingraham, C., xxii
Inimo-Etele, 284

James, C. L. R., 37, 56
Jan, Z., 126
Jinadu, A. M., 9
Johnson, S., xv
Jones, C., 56

Kamalu, N. C., 126, 127
Kankwenda, M., 1, 145, 148
Kant, L., 26–29, 31, 32, 85
Katsillis, 243
Kharas, H., 254
Khor, M., 2
Killam, G., 167, 168
Klugman, J., 1
Koolhaas, R., 16
Koontz, 218
Korten, D. C., 238
Kumiko, S., 1, 123, 131
Kwankwenda, 148

LaCapra, xxiv
Laye, C., 162
Lefebvre, H., 4, 35
Lenin, V. I., 50, 54, 57, 238
Levy, M., 243
Lewis, A. E., 101, 208, 209
Lin, K., 38
Linhares, J., 203–5
Love, B., 195
Lugard, F. D., 116, 127, 275

Macamo, E., 128, 130
Machel, J., 56
Madunagu, B., 56
Madunagu, E., 56, 57
Magdoff, H., xvi
Makoko, A., 2, 3, 9–14
Mamdani, M., 4
Manning, P., 1, 125, 126
Mapadimeng, M. S., 153
Marcinkoski, C., 5, 6
Margarian, A., 1

Marglin & Marglin, 154
Martins, A., 195
Marx, K., 26–29, 32, 52, 67, 71, 86, 101, 179–82
Matsinhe, D., 55
Mbembe, A., 4, 6
McLuhan, 215, 221
Mendelsohn, B., 4
Mercer, K., xix
Meredith, M., 150, 164
Merleau-Ponty, M., 67
Mernissi, F., 69
Mesoudi, A., 219
Meynen, N., 2
Mignolo, W., 34, 73, 96
Mihevc, J., 1
Minca, C., 3
Ministry of Physical Planning and Urban Development, 15
Mohamoud, 149
Mulele, P., 56
Murray, M. J., 4, 5
Myers, G. A., 3, 4
Myint, Hla., 256
Myrdal, G., 1, 132

Nandes, G., 120
Nazombe, E., 221
Ndi, A., 4
Ndlovu-Gatsheni, S. J., 24, 29, 93, 94, 96
Negri, A., xxii, xxv
Nehusi, K., 45
Nicholls, B. L., 1
Nicolas, I. F., 207, 229
Njoh, A. J., 4
Nkrumah, K., 44, 50, 56, 164, 202, 271
Nnoli, O., 183, 238
Nnolim, C., xxv
Nossiter, A., 14
Nowell, C., xvi
Nunn, N., 129
Nwachukwu, J. O., 127
Nwanna, C., 2, 5, 9
Nyman, J., xviii

Nzegwu, N., 60
Nzemeka, J., 197–200

Obadan, M., 244
Obono, O., 2
Odunuga, S., 146
Ogaba, O., 223–26
Oglu, M., 69
Ogot, B., 208
Ogundipe-Leslie, M., 200–202
Ogunlesi, T., 11
Ojewale, O., 283
Ojo, E. O., 2, 129
Okereke, E. C., 1
Okewumi, O. E., 235–37
Okonjo, I. N., 207
Okpaga, A., 218
Okpeh, O. O., 216
Oladimeji, Y., 247
Olamosu, B., 143, 147
Olorode, O., 222
Olukoju, A., 3, 4, 7
Olusina, O., 14
Olutayo, A. O., 238, 241, 245–47, 249
Omoegun, A. O., 10
Omotayo, A., 236, 237
Onaolapo, A. F., 206
Onimode, B., 144, 146–49, 151, 154, 174, 180, 181
Onuekwusi, J. A., 165
Onwudiwe, I. D., 57
Onyeakagbu, A., 274, 275
Opeibi, T. O., 6
Oriola, T., 57
Oripeloye, H., 215, 228
Orunbon, A., 285
Osuafore, 1, 163
Osuji, C., 206
Oyelowo, A., 3
Oyewunmi, O., 60

Palmer, E., 166, 169
Parnell, S., 6
Pile, S., 4
Pinker, 219

Polanyi, K., 1
Prah, M., 202
Prichard, xxiv
Pritchett, 147, 149
Prodger, M., 66
Pycroft, C., 149

Quaraishi, 204, 205
Quijano, A., xxiii, 30

Rahaman, M. S., 129
Rahnema, M., xix
Rakodi, C., 4
Ramdani, 203–5
Rapley, J., 143
Rasheed, 280
Reyes, G. E., 2, 244
Rist, G., xv, xxv, 154, 246
Rist, R., xvii
Rist, S., 246
Ritzer, G., 244
Robinson, J., xv, 6
Rodney, W., ix, xvi, 30, 43–48, 51, 52, 56, 59, 92, 93, 95, 97, 126, 129, 174, 180–82, 237, 238, 240
Rodrik, 143
Rostow, W. W., 93, 101, 257
Roxburgh, C., 140
Russel, D., 67, 80

Sabine, G. H., 176–79
Sachs, J. D., xv
Sachs, W., xv
Sada, P. O., 7
Sahlin, M., 68
Said, E., vii, xxiii, xxvii, 28, 37, 96, 97, 160
Said, E. W, 7
Saleh-Hanna, V., 56
Salm, S. J., 4
Samora, M., 56
Sarachild, K., 195
Say, J-B., 123
Schiller, H. I., 222, 223
Scholte, J. A., 114

Schuurman, F., xv, 30
Scott, J. C., 123
Scott, T., 151, 153
Seers, D., xiv, xv
Sen, A., xxv, 151, 154
Senanayake, S. G. J. N., 247
Sessou, E., 14
Sharp, J., xviii
Shittu, O., 236, 237
Shrum, W. M., 257
Sillitoe, P., 246
Simek, N., xxiii–xxv
Sinclair, 247
Sklar, R., 183
Slee, B., 114, 115
Slovo, J., 56, 57
Smallbone, D., 119
Smith, C. S., 152
Smith, H. J., 196
Smith, J., 38
Smith, L. T., 95, 151, 152, 179, 256, 258
Soares Jr. J. & Quintella, R. H., 185
Soderbuam, F., 114
Sokoloff, K., xxvi
Sowell, T., 143, 150, 152, 153
Spellman, W. M., 183, 184
Spivak, G., xxiii, xxv, 27, 28, 96, 98
Spring, A., 132
Stiglitz, J., xxv, 180
Storm, 38
Sugimura, K., 122
Summonu, 140
Swedberg, 123
Sylvester, J. H., 244

Thompson, J., 124
Thornton, B., 49
Thorson, T. L., 176–79
Tiffin, H., xvi
Todaro, M., xiv, xv, 31, 151, 152, 225
Todaro, P. M., 118, 119

Tomlinson, J., xxiv
Tomori, O. S., 140
Tomori, O. W., 140
Tosh, J., 131, 132
Townsend, R. M., 227
Toyo, E., 57
Ture, K., 56

Uche, L. U., 219
Ujamaa, 94, 106, 175, 184
Umekachikelu, F. C., 239
Uva, A., 13

Walestein, xxii
Walker, L., 196, 247
Walt, V., 230
Warren, M. E., 17
wa Thiong'o, N, 10, 159, 165
Watson, V., 5, 6
Watts, M. J., 127
Webster, R., xvi
Weihrich, 218
Weinstein, B., xv
White, L., 223
White, xii, 32, 45, 46, 52, 100, 102, 105, 116, 117, 169, 170, 208
Whiteman, K., 10, 14
Wikipedia, 226, 227
Williams, E., 49
Willis, E., 195
World Bank, 2, 12–14, 106, 146, 148, 180, 184, 185, 225, 239
Wynne, A., 143, 147

Yagboyaju, D. A., 278
Yemisi, J., 218
Young, R., 31, 35

Zeleza, P. T., 9
Ziai, A., 102

Subject Index

absentee capitalists, 128
Accra, 5
administrative power, 4
Africa, 1, 3, 5–12, 14, 17, 24, 51–60, 253–54, 256, 258, 259, 270, 276
Africana Mass Party, 55, 56, 58–60
African cities, 4–7, 17
African condition, 92
African continent, 23, 91–93, 97, 101, 124, 130, 161, 165, 183, 184, 223, 242, 248, 270
African Critical Race Theory, ix, 91, 93, 100
African decolonization, 4, 141
African development, 92, 96, 105, 113, 114, 116–18, 125, 130, 134, 144, 146, 153, 160, 163, 171, 184, 241, 245, 248
African Diaspora, 60
African economic integration, 149
African History and Dance, 105, 108
African independent states, 4
African indigenous histories and dances, 91
Africanize development, 247
African leaders, x, 94, 102, 106, 107, 139, 144, 145, 149, 151, 152, 163, 183

African leadership, x, 139, 149, 151, 152
African literature, 159, 161, 164, 165, 169
African material culture, 162
African migrants, 215, 226–30
African migration, 216, 223, 227
African moral economy, 113, 115, 118, 122, 130–34
African nations, 102, 106, 108, 109, 130, 236, 245, 248
Africanness, 30, 248
African peoples, 23, 24, 30, 31, 104, 105, 145
African politicians, 5, 6
African production systems, 120
African religious, 162
African society, 159, 161, 162, 164–66, 168, 170, 171
African space, 163, 165, 171
African states, 3, 17, 54, 55, 57, 93, 143, 149, 184, 187, 198, 200, 224, 227
African theorists, 92
African traditional training, 103
African troops, 52
African Union, 54
African unity, 30, 31

African women, x, 49, 54, 59, 193, 194, 196, 198, 200, 201, 210, 211
African workers, 45, 46, 128
Afrocentric, viii, xii, xv, 109, 139, 152, 162
Algeria, ix, 53, 65–69, 71–73, 75, 77, 79, 81, 83, 128, 151, 224
Algerian territory, 83
Algerian women, 71, 74, 83
alternative development initiatives (ADIs), 139
America, xvii, xxiii, xxiv, 92, 102, 117, 179–81, 195, 216, 223, 225, 230, 237, 242, 254
Amnesty International, 11, 15, 16
Angola, 13, 52, 99, 102, 194, 197
Angolan national government, 13
Arab Bureau, 72
archaic, 28, 54, 59, 71, 243
Asian, x, 24, 32, 45, 46, 119, 120, 132, 151, 228, 242, 254
Asian Drama, 119
Atlantic Slave Trade, 227

backward traditions, 92
Bangladesh, 119, 216
Bar Beach, 3
Belly Dancing, 72, 74, 77, 78
Benin, 11, 93, 253, 255–65, 281
Benin Kingdom, 259
Benin Province, xi, 253, 255–65
Black, 45, 46, 50, 51, 53, 117, 161, 169, 170, 189, 202, 254
Black Africans, 45
Boko Haram, 224, 272, 278–83
Boko Haram terrorism, 272
bourgeois propagandists, 49
The Breast of the Earth, 162
Britain, 25, 51–53, 181, 230, 256, 258, 259, 261, 262, 265, 271, 274
British colonial government, 202, 206
British West Africa Ladies Club, 201
Burkina Faso, 102, 216, 224
Burundi, 224
Bus Rapid Transit (BRT), 13

Cameroon, 281
Camp de Thiaroye, 49
capitalism, 40, 160, 174, 181
Cartesian dualism, 66
Casablanca, 5
Catholic Church, 179
Catholic South, 53
Central African Republic, 224
Central and Northern Zimbabwe, 99
centralist organizations, 162
Chad, 224, 281, 283
Chibok school girls, 280
China, 34, 37, 71, 94, 101, 102, 106, 140, 151, 153, 160, 180, 181, 186, 188, 236, 237, 254
Chinese nationalist language policy, 37
Christianity, 104, 170
Christian missionaries, 199
Christians, 199, 280, 281
Christian South, 281
city planners, 4–6, 8
Cold War, vii, xii, xxiv, xxv, 106, 151, 216, 223–25, 227, 228
Colonial African women, 194, 210
colonial apologists, 125, 256
Colonial education, 104
colonialism, xviii, 44, 50, 53, 91, 93, 95, 97, 99, 101, 103, 105, 107, 109, 197, 199, 201, 203, 205, 207, 209, 211, 241, 253, 255, 257, 259, 261, 263, 265, 270, 271
colonial revolution, 116
colonial school curriculum, 98
colonial setting, 75
Colonized Intellectuals, 128
Conference on Trade and Development (UNCTAD), 185
contemporary African cultures, 23
Contemporary Algerians, 65
Convention Peoples Party (CPP), 202
Coronavirus, 237, 238
Court Messengers, 207
Courts Clerks, 207
Covid-19, 237, 238
culture, 28, 35, 40, 218

Culture and Imperialism, 28

Daily Service, 8, 9
dance, ix, 65, 67, 69, 71, 73, 75, 77, 79, 81, 83, 85, 95, 99, 100, 108
decolonization, vii, xxvii, 66, 139, 141, 143, 145, 147, 149, 151, 153–54, 173, 175, 177, 179, 181, 183, 185, 187, 189, 211, 215, 220
decolonizing state fragility, 270
Denmark, 177, 230
developed countries, 117, 119, 223, 237, 238, 257
developed world, 70, 117, 119, 238
development, vii, xiv, xv, xvii, xix, xx, xxvii, 1, 3, 5, 7, 9, 11, 13, 15, 17, 43, 65, 67, 69, 71, 73, 75, 77, 253, 255–57, 259, 261, 263, 265, 270
development constructs, 256
Development Merchant System, 148
Dubai Marina, 15

East Asian, 132, 141
Eastern Europe, 183, 224, 228
Eastern European, 228
Eastern Nigeria, 48, 205, 272
Eastern Province, 258, 264
Eastern Security Network (ESN), 283
Economic Anthropology, 120
Economic Community for Africa (ECA), 145
economic development, 134, 144, 145
economies of affection, 123
Edo, 227
Egypt, x, 93, 94, 193, 194, 202–5, 210, 216, 240
Egyptians, 95, 204
Eko Atlantic City, 3
Eko o ni baje, viii, 1–3, 6, 7, 10–16
electricity, 13
endogenous development, 114
EndSARS, 282
England, 45, 51, 97, 169, 177, 180, 181
Enlightened Absolutism, 177
Enlightenment formulation, 184

entrepreneur, 123
entrepreneurial spirit, 123, 132
entrepreneurship, 120, 123, 124, 134
epistemicide, 98
Eritrea, 194
ethnicization and religious coloration, 279
Eurocentric and internal, 33
Eurocentric capitalist modernity, xxi, 24
Eurocentric intellectual conspiracy, 99
Eurocentric paradigms, 92, 93
Eurocentric scholars, 162
Eurocentric worldview, 99, 109
European colonial mission, 162
European colonies, 163, 179
European countries, 49–53, 225, 229, 230, 242
European courts, 229
European economic imperialism, 125
European history, 32, 99, 179
European intrusion, 91, 259
European knowledge and science, 98
Europeans, 44–47, 49–53, 92, 95, 97, 100, 126, 128, 159, 161–63, 196, 201, 228–30, 240, 241, 258, 260

Federal Government, 2, 12
federalism, 284
First World, 243
foreign debts, 149
frame development, 247
France, 25, 51–53, 97, 126, 176, 177, 180, 226, 228–30, 237, 271
French, 44–46, 49, 52, 53, 66, 68, 84, 86, 115, 116, 120, 123, 126–28, 176–78, 183, 229, 236, 282
French Algeria, 84, 126, 128
French colonies, 52
French Revolution, 176, 177
Fulani herdsmen, 279, 283, 284

Germans, 52, 178
Germany, 46, 51–53, 180, 226, 237
Ghana, 46, 92–94, 99, 133, 164, 186, 202

Ghanaian, 23
Ghanaian philosopher, 23
globalization, 40, 215, 221, 244
globalization theory, 244
government, 10, 12, 144, 189, 286
Great Zimbabwe monuments, 95, 99, 101, 108
Guardian, 49
Gulf countries, 187

Hausa, 227, 276, 279
hijab, 69, 79, 85, 229
Holland, 51, 177
Holy Roman Empire, 177, 178
Hong Kong, 38, 140
Hope City, 5
Houston, 75
How Europe Underdeveloped Africa, xxi, 43, 240
Human Development Index (HDI), 185
human society, 25, 171, 194, 218
hybridity, 23, 33, 35, 39

Igbo, 47, 50, 183, 197, 227, 274–76
Ikot Ekpene, 207
imperialism, 28, 44, 50, 179, 223
Import Substitution Industrialization, 129
India, 71, 101, 119, 140, 153, 160, 180, 181, 188, 220, 254
indigenous knowledge, 94, 95, 246–48
Indigenous Knowledge Systems (IKS), ix, 92–96, 98, 100–103, 105, 108, 109
Indigenous People of Biafra (IPOB), 272
Indigenous People of Biafra (IPOB)/ Eastern Security Network (ESN), 272
indirect rule, 127
Indonesia, 78, 186, 254
Internally Generated Revenue (IGR), 13
International Bank for Reconstruction and Development, 180
International Monetary Fund (IMF), 180, 225

International Organization for Migration (IOM), 227
International Political Economy (IPE), 145
Irish Republican Army, 53
ISIL, 224
ISIS, 32, 224
Islamic State, 279
Islamism, 68, 69, 72, 83
Islamist dogma, 69
Italy, 52, 53, 226, 230, 237

Japan, 32, 34, 52, 153
Joint Task Force (JTF), 278
Jordan, 216

Kaduna, 275, 276, 281, 282
Kantian cosmopolitanism, 31
Katsina State, 279
Keana Local Government Area (LGA), 279
Kenya, x, 49, 52, 102, 128, 166, 170, 183, 186, 193, 194, 202, 207, 210, 224
Kick Against Indiscipline (KAI), 12
Konza Techno City, 5

la femme fatale, 69
Lagos, viii, 1–3, 5–17, 106, 144–46, 198, 201, 211, 258, 275, 286
Lagosians, 2, 6–9, 15, 16
Lagos Market Women's Association (LMWA), 201
Lagos Megacity Development Authority (LMDA), 2
Lagos Plan, 106, 144, 145
Lagos police force, 3
Lagos State Development and Property Corporation (LSDPC), 9
Lagos State Economic Empowerment and Development Strategy (LASEEDS), 10
Lagos State Ministry of Economic Planning and Budget, 2
Lagos State Waste Management Authority (LAWMA), 12

Lagos State Waterfront and Tourism Development Corporation, 13
Lagos waterfronts, 1, 13, 15
Latin American, 24, 32
law and order, viii, ix, 11, 43, 44, 48, 118, 259
Lewisian, 106
Liberia, 47, 53, 224
Libya, 224
London, 5, 49, 211

Makoko-Iwaya Waterfront, 11
Malawi, 94, 97
Malaysia, 140, 254
marketing boards, 49, 128
Marxian historiography, 25
Marxian internationalism, 31
Marxist humanism, 25
Mauritania, 224
Mbaise, 207
Mbano, 207
Middle East, 186
migration, 216, 217, 227, 269, 271, 273, 275, 277, 279, 281, 283, 285
Migration Policy Institute, 227
Ministry of Physical Planning and Urban Development, 15
Ministry of Waterfront Infrastructure Development, 13–15
misogyny and backwardness, 84
missionaries, 98
Mission to Kala, 160
modernity, 109, 242
modernization, xxiii, 241, 242, 256
modernization theory, 241, 242, 256
moral economy, ix, xiv, 113, 114, 120–24, 131, 133, 134
Moroccan Green City, 5
Movement for the Actualisation of a Sovereign State of Biafra (MASSOB), 272
Movement for the Emancipation of the Niger Delta (MEND), 272
Mozambique, 52, 194
Muslim North, 281

Nailia Dance, 75
Nailiyat, ix, 65, 67–75, 77–79, 81–83, 85
Nairobi, 5, 168
Namibia, 52, 194
Nassarawa State and Safana LGA, 279
National Council of Nigeria and the Cameroons (NCNC), 275
nationalism, 23, 25, 27, 29, 31–33, 35, 37, 39–40, 173, 175–79, 181, 183, 185, 187, 189–90
Native Revenue Ordinance, 206
Nativism, 23
Ndebele, 99
neocolonialism, 50
Neolithic revolution, 65
Netherlands, 25, 229, 230
New Partnership for Africa's Development (NEPAD), 106, 140, 147, 149, 152
New rubber plants, 50
New/Satellite Town Development Scheme, 2
New World Order (NWO), 216
New Zealand, 95
Ngwaland, 207
Niger, 224, 258, 272, 277, 278, 281–83
Niger Coast Protectorate, 258
Niger Delta, 272, 277, 278, 282
Niger Delta Avengers (NDAs), 277
Niger Delta crisis, 277
Niger Delta youths, 278
Nigeria, x, xi, 10, 12, 13, 17, 47, 48, 93, 103, 107, 128, 275–86
Nigerian geographical space, 280
Nigerian institutions, 279
Nigerian military security, 279
Nigerian women, 47, 201, 210, 211
Ni Una Menos, 38
non-governmental organizations (NGOs), 147
North African, 53, 226, 236
North America, 46, 50, 51, 76, 93, 97, 181, 242
North Central and North West Zones, 279

North East, 272
Northern Nigeria, 183, 258, 277, 282
Northern People's Congress (NPC), 275
Northern Province, 258
North Korea, 34
Nosotras Paramos, 38

Odi Bayelsa State, 282
oil-producing African countries, 186
Oil Rivers Protectorate, 258
Old Bende Division, 206
Old Calabar Province, 207
Oniru Private Housing Estate, 9
ontological contentment, 74
Organisation of African Unity (OAU), 144
Orientalism, xxii, 68, 72–75
Orientalist gaze, 66, 75
Orientalist layers, 75
Orientalizing gaze, 82, 84
orthodox Muslim theologians, 69
Ouled Nail, 65, 67, 71–73, 75, 81, 82, 84–86
Oxford University, 45, 49

paradigms, viii, 149, 187, 241
peasant colonial economy, 128
perpetual peace, 26
Petals of Blood, x, 159–61, 163, 165, 170
Philippines, 38, 186
plantation economy, 128
political administration, 17, 104, 197
poor governance, 149, 277
poor Lagosians, 1–3
Portugal, 52, 53, 97
postcolonial Africa, vii, x, xii, xxiv, 16, 17, 43, 92, 94, 96, 100, 102, 106, 113, 114, 117, 130–34, 139–42, 210, 211
postcolonial African development, 113, 114, 130, 148, 149, 153, 154
postcolonial African society, 165, 211
postcolonial identity, viii, xix
postcolonial nationalism, 24, 40, 83

postcolonial urbanization, viii
postcolonial world, 23, 24, 29, 33
production communities, 123

radical feminists, 195
reformation thinkers, 177
Republic of Africa, 44, 58–60
Rhonda Kingdoms, 197
River Niger, 258
Rivers State, 278
Roman Catholic Church, 178, 179
Rostowan, 106
rural agricultural economy, 121
Rwandan model, 106

Second World War, 106, 259
settler, 52, 128, 220
settler agricultural economy, 128
settler colony, 128
shallowly sensual, 72
Shona people, 99
Singapore, 5, 140, 151
Small and Medium Enterprises (SMEs), 131
Social and Economic Rights Action Center, 11, 14
social entrepreneurship, ix, 113, 114, 118, 123, 124, 130–34
South Africa, 45, 47, 48, 50, 51, 53, 97, 99, 107, 115, 128, 197, 202, 236
South East Asia, 121, 256
South Eastern Nigeria, 206, 274
Southern Nigeria, 206, 258
Southern Rhodesia, 46, 52
South Korea, 34, 140, 151
South Yemen, 216
Spain, 177, 226
Special Anti-Robbery Squad (SARS), 282
State fragility and forced migration, 269, 270
Sudan, 151, 205, 216, 224, 240, 285
sustainable development, ix, 43, 114, 130, 185, 236, 247–49

sustainable development goals (SDG), 44
Sweden, 177, 230

Taiwan, 34, 38, 140
Tanganyika, 52, 202
Tanzania, 52, 94, 106, 189, 202
Texas, 75
THAAD missile system, 34
theorization, 28, 35, 40
Things Fall Apart, 160
Third World, xv, xxvi, 28, 29, 173, 174, 180, 181, 184–87, 196, 223, 241–43, 245
the Third World, 117, 221
Third World countries, 185, 187, 223, 245
Third World states, 173
Town Councils, 54
Treasure Islands, 254
Trojan horse, 5
Tswana, 197

UAE, 187
uncivilized, 117, 258
unequal exchange, 125
uniform, 128, 184
Union of Soviet Socialist Republic (USSR), 228
United Gold Coast Convention (UGCC), 202
United Kingdom, 53, 226–28, 237, 270
United Nations, xxiii, 11, 144, 146, 147, 179, 185
United Nations Development Programme (UNDP), 185
United Nations Economic Commission for Africa (UNECA), 144
United Republic of African States, 43
United States, 46, 47, 50, 51, 53, 188, 189, 223, 226, 230, 237
urban fantasies, 1, 3, 6

Vietnam War, 53
Viva Nos Queremos, 38

waḥdat al-wujud, 69
Warrant Chiefs, 206, 207, 211
West Africa, 3, 8, 48, 51, 52, 94, 115, 116, 126, 128, 184, 202, 223, 224, 275, 279, 282
West African Pilot, 8
West Africa Province (ISWAP), 279
Western capitalists, 164
Western development concepts and models, 247
Western Europe, xvii, 24, 25, 92, 96, 100–104, 109, 181, 228, 240, 242
Western imperialism, 28, 31
Western media, 226, 228
Western nation-states, 24
Western Province, 258, 262
Western science, 246
Western values, 99, 166
Western Zimbabwe, 99
We Strike, 38
White, xii, xviii, 32, 45, 46, 52, 100, 102, 105, 116, 117, 169, 170, 208, 220, 223
Wizard of the Crow, 161
World Bank, 2, 12–14, 106, 146, 148, 180, 184, 185, 187, 225, 239
World Trade Organization (WTO), 151, 180
World Wars, 49, 126

Yaba Local Government Authority, 11, 12
Yoruba, 108, 183, 197, 198, 211, 227, 275

Zenata Eco City, 5
zerna, 76, 80, 81, 86
Zimbabwe, 46, 52, 92–95, 97–102, 107, 128, 151, 240
Zimbabwe Curriculum Framework, 99

About the Contributors

Dr. Fidelis Allen is a professor of Development Studies in the Department of Political and Administrative Studies, University of Port Harcourt. He is former acting director of the Centre for Ethnic and Conflict Studies (CENTECS), and Centre for Conflict and Gender Studies (CCGS) of the same University. He was visiting scholar at the Centre for Civil Society, Howard College, University of KwaZulu-Natal South Africa. Allen examines doctoral and master's thesis for several universities, including Northwest University Mafikeng, University of Johannesburg, University of Pretoria, Babcock University, and University of Nigeria. He is also editor-in-chief of *Journal of Political and Administrative Studies* as well as a member of many journals' editorial boards, including that of Australia based *Cosmopolitan Civil Societies*. His articles have appeared in several local and international peer-reviewed journals and edited books, including the *International Encyclopedia of Political Science*. He has served as guest lecturer and speaker in many academic and civil society settings, including University of Bonn and Tata Institute of Social Sciences, Mumbai. Allen is an active member of Midwest Political Science Association (MPSA); Nigerian Political Science Association (NPSA); and International Political Science Association (IPSA). He is fellow of the Gender Studies Association of Nigeria and author of *Implementation of Oil-Related Environmental Policies in Nigeria: Government Inertia and Conflict in the Niger Delta*, published in the UK by Cambridge Scholars Publishing. Allen was a recipient of Canada's International Development Research Centre's Doctoral Award managed by United Nations University for Peace Africa Programme in Addis Ababa, in 2007. He was also recipient of University of KwaZulu-Natal's Doctoral Scholarship. Allen is currently non-residential Fellow of the *African Polling Institute,* Abuja on the *Nigeria Social Cohesion Project 2020* funded by Ford Foundation. Allen's research covers the areas of development, environmental politics and security, conflict, gender, and intersectionality. He is currently serving as Head of the Department of Political and Administrative Studies, University of Port Harcourt.

Dr. Luke Amadi holds a PhD in Development Studies from the University of Port Harcourt, Nigeria. He is currently guest editor, Cambridge Scholars Publishing, UK. His areas of research interest include globalization, postcolonial studies, political economy, economic development, ecological justice, and alternative development theory. Amadi is widely published in reputable journals. He has also edited some volumes and contributed chapters in seminal books. His recently edited volume in 2019 (with Dr. Fidelis Allen) is *Global Food Politics and Approaches to Sustainable Consumption: Emerging Research and Opportunities,* published by IGI Global Publishers, in Pennsylvania, USA. His works have been primer for undergraduate and graduate students of leading Universities in Africa, Europe, America, Asia, and North America, including University of Birmingham, UK and the University of Western Ontario, Canada. His recent journal publication (2020) is *Globalization and the Changing Liberal International Order: A Review of the Literature* published in London by Elsevier's *Research in Globalization.* He is a member of several professional bodies, including Nigerian Political Science Association (NPSA).

Dr. James Olusegun Adeyeri holds a PhD in History from the University of Ibadan, Nigeria. He is the immediate past associate editor of LASU *Journal of Humanities*, Lagos State University (LASU), Ojo, Nigeria. His teaching and research focus is mainly on African History, Peace, and Conflict Studies, and Human Rights Studies on which he has published extensively in both local and foreign journals/books, such as *Conflict Studies Quarterly*, *Yonsei Journal of International Studies*, *Africa Development,* and book chapters in Palgrave *Handbook of African Politics, Governance and Development* (2018), *Leadership and Complex Military Operations* (2016), and *Capacity Building for Sustainable Development* (2018). He has also contributed entries in *Encyclopedia of Psychology and Contemporary Religion, The British Empire: A Historical Encyclopedia,* and *Religion and Contemporary Politics: A Global Encyclopedia.* Dr. Adeyeri is a grantee of several scholarly awards, most recently, Visiting Fellowship of the Center for the History of Global Development, Shanghai University, China (Virtual). He is currently the co-coordinator of the PhD and MPhil/PhD History and Diplomacy programs, and the Coordinator of Master in International Relations and Strategic Studies, LASU.

Dr. John Ebute Agaba is a professor and lecturer in the Department of History, Benue State University, Makurdi, Nigeria. He obtained his PhD in

History and International Studies from University of Jos, Nigeria. He has published many articles in both national and international journals and books. He has attended conferences in many different African and European countries. Agaba is a CORDESRIA-SEPHIS Laureate. He is a pioneer member of Historical Fiction Research Network, United Kingdom. His research interests are in Economic and Social History as well as Migration, Conflict, Gender, and Development Studies. Agaba served as the Head of History Department, Benue State University, Makurdi, Nigeria between 2014 and 2019. He is currently on a sabbatical in the Department of History and International Studies, Federal University Lafia, Nasarawa State, Nigeria.

Dr. Biko Agozino is a professor of Sociology and Africana Studies, Virginia Tech, Blacksburg, VA, USA. He is the author of the following books—*Critical, Creative and Centered Scholar-Activism: The Fourth Dimensionalism of Agwuncha Arthur Nwankwo* (2016); *ADAM: Africana Drug-Free Alternative Medicine*, 2006; *Counter-Colonial Criminology*, 2003; *Pan African Issues in Crime and Justice* (co-edited), 2004; *Nigeria: Democratising a Militarised Civil Society*, (co-authored) 2001; *Theoretical and Methodological Issues in Migration Research* (edited), 2000; and *Black Women and the Criminal Justice System*, 1997. He is also the director-producer-editor of "Reparative Justice," 30 minutes, color, African Independent Television, Lagos, Nigeria, 2002; director-producer of *CLR James: The Black Jacobins Sociology* Series, 2008; director-producer of *Shouters and the Control Freak Empire*, Winner of the Best International Short Documentary, Columbia Gorge Film Festival, USA, 2011. He is editor-in-chief of the *African Journal of Criminology and Justice Studies*, and series editor, Ashgate Publishers Interdisciplinary Research Series in Ethnic, Gender and Class Relations, continued by Routledge. Ph.D. (Edinburgh); MPhil. (Cambridge); B.Sc. First Class Hons (Calabar).

Dr. Olayinka Akanle is a research associate in the Department of Sociology, Faculty of Humanities, University of Johannesburg, South Africa and a Lecturer in the Department of Sociology, Faculty of Social Sciences, University of Ibadan, Nigeria. He was a postdoctoral fellow at the South African Research Chair Initiative (SARChI) in Social Policy, College of Graduate Studies, University of South Africa (UNISA), South Africa. He has won other scholarly awards like being a World Social Science Fellow (WSSF) of The International Social Science Council (ISSC), Paris, France, Laureate of the Council for the Development of Social Science Research in Africa (CODESRIA), and University of Ibadan Postgraduate School Prize for scholarly publication awardee. He is a scholar and an expert on International Migration, Policy, Practice, and Sustainable Development in Nigeria and

Africa. Dr. Akanle has attended many local and international scholarly conferences and has published widely in local and international journals, books, technical reports, and encyclopedia. He is the author of Kinship Networks and International Migration in Nigeria and has co-edited books, including T*he Development of Africa: Issues, Diagnosis and Prognosis.*

Adebisi Alade is a trillium scholar and currently a PhD candidate in the Department of History, McMaster University, Canada. His research interest is at the intersection of environment, health, and development histories, focusing on how subaltern politics and resistance has historically shaped development. Previously, he was a Water Without Borders student at the United Nations University, Institute for Water, Environment, and Health (UNU-INWEH) where he studied International Public Policy Development. He has published in reputable journals, contributed book chapters, and is currently co-editing a volume on *Histories of Health and Environment across Borders*. Adebisi is the coordinator of Confronting Atrocity (a transnational project on restorative justice) at McMaster University and a member of the McMaster University Participedia research team.

Dr. Solomon Awuzie currently teaches Literature and Creative Writing at the Department of English, Edo University Iyamho. He had his first degree at the department of English and literary studies, Imo State University Owerri, his Master's degree at the department of English, University of Ibadan, and his PhD at the Department of English Studies, University of Port Harcourt. He has publications in reputable journals.

Dr. Fred Ekpe F. Ayokhai is a senior lecturer in the Department of History and International Studies, Federal University of Lafia, Nasarawa State, Nigeria. He holds a PhD and Master of Arts degree in History from the Department of History, Nasarawa State University, Keffi, in addition to a Postgraduate Diploma in Education (PGDE) from the Usmanu Danfodio University, Sokoto and a Bachelor of Art (Hons) Degree from the Bendel State University, Ekpoma, Edo State, Nigeria. He is also the immediate past acting chairperson of the Academic Staff Union of Universities (ASUU), Federal University Lafia Branch and a member of the Historical Society of Nigeria (HSN). His area of research specialization is in African Economic and Development History. He has also worked on issues of peace, conflict, women, and security in the Niger Delta area of Nigeria. He is the major editor of a book titled *Concepts in Historiography: Essays in Honor of Olayemi Akinwumi* (2008). His recent areas of research interest span Pan-Africanism, Nationalism, Governance, and Leadership issues in Africa. He has published over fifty essays in both local and international academic journals and peer-reviewed books.

Chukwuka Blessing Chidiogo is a lecturer in the Department of Sociology, Faculty of The Social Sciences, University of Ibadan, Nigeria.

Dr. Jairos Gonye holds a PhD in English (University of Venda, South Africa). He is currently an associate professor in the Department of Curriculum Studies at Great Zimbabwe University, Zimbabwe, where he teaches English. He is also a research associate in the English Department of the University of the Free State, South Africa. His research interests include postcolonial literature, representations of dance, pedagogy, and popular culture. He has published in international journals such as *Pedagogy, Culture and Society, Dance Research Journal, Journal of Black Studies, Research in Dance Education, SARE*, and *Imbizo*. He has book chapter publications with the University of Zimbabwe and Palgrave publications, respectively. Gonye is also head of the technical team for Great Zimbabwe University's new journal called *Journal of New Vision in Educational Research* (JoNVER).

Dr. Nick T. C. Lu received his PhD in English in Fall 2018 from the University of North Texas (UNT). He has taught literature and writing courses for more than five years at UNT as a graduate teaching fellow and an adjunct faculty since 2015. Lu's research and teaching interests include postcolonial theory, globalization, nationalism, Marxist theory, critical geography, and world literature with a regional emphasis on transnational Asian and African cultures and literatures. His most recent publication underscores the pioneering role of Flora Nwapa's debut novel *Efuru* in Nigerian feminist culture. Building on his doctoral dissertation which traces in Taiwanese colonial literature the discursive construction of Taiwan as a nation, Lu is now preparing his book manuscript which seeks to unveil the various ways in which the cultural image and geopolitical materiality of the "island" influence the formation of national culture and consciousness in Taiwan since colonial times to the neocolonial present. Lu's other scholarly works on Taiwanese literature, ecocriticism, and Asian critical regionalism were presented at several national and regional conferences in the United States in the past few years.

Dr. Fouad Mami is a professor of English at the Department of English, University of Adrar (Algeria). He graduated from the University of Algiers with a thesis on the oeuvre of contemporary Ghanaian novelist, Ayi Kwei Armah. Working principally on contemporary African fiction, he singles out themes such as illegal immigration, development, and state formations in the Maghreb—deploying the self-moving dialectic of world capitalism— as a framework of analysis. His research has appeared in *Amerikastudien/*

American Studies, *The Journal of North African Studies*, *African Studies Review*, and other outlets.

Dr. Nathan Moyo works as a senior lecturer in Curriculum Studies at the Robert Mugabe School of Education, Great Zimbabwe University, in Zimbabwe. He holds a PhD from the University of Johannesburg, South Africa, and M.Ed. in Curriculum Studies as well as a B.Ed. in History Education from University of Zimbabwe. His initial qualification is a Certificate in Education (Secondary), after which he taught History in various secondary schools in the country. Moyo's research interests are in history and history education, indigenous knowledges, and curriculum theory and transformative pedagogies. Nathan Moyo has published articles and book chapters in international journals and books. Moyo is a founding editorial board member of *African Journal of Education in Rural Contexts* (AJERC) launched in 2018. In 2020, Moyo published a book chapter in *The Palgrave Handbook of History and Social Studies Education*.

Dr. Mike O. Odey is professor of Economic History and Development Studies. His research foci revolve around agricultural History and food security systems, poverty issues, gender-related matters, entrepreneurship, and political economy. He has published over 80 peer-reviewed essays in international/local journals and book chapters. He is editor of several journals. He has written two major books, namely, *The Development of Cash Crop Economy in Nigeria's Lower Benue Province, 1910–1960* and *Food Crop Production, Hunger, and Rural Poverty in Nigeria's Benue Area, 1920–1995*, published by Carolina Academic Press, Durham, USA. Odey is a regular attendee and paper presenter in numerous international conferences, including, Africa Conference Series at University of Texas, Austin, USA (2009–2013); AG Hopkins' Conference at the University of Texas, Austin (2011). He was also a paper presenter in the Africa-Berlin Conference in Germany (2012). In July 2014, Odey attended and presented two groundbreaking essays in TOFAC International Conference, in Durban, South Africa, and another conference, on Innovation and Entrepreneurship conference in Durban (March 2015). Odey teaches in the Department of History, Benue State University, Makurdi, Nigeria, where he headed the department for four years and has also served the same University in various capacities. He was external Assessor for the promotion of eight Professors and five Associate Professors in other Nigerian Universities. Odey has also been an external examiner for both undergraduate and postgraduate students in nine different Nigerian Universities. Odey was a visiting professor in the University of Nigeria Nsukka, and Taraba State University, Jalingo. He has been on Nigeria University Commission Accreditation Team since 2015, and currently is a member of Governing Council, EVANGEL University, Akaeze, Ebonyi State.

Dr. Matthew Dayi Ogali is a senior lecturer in the Department of Political and Administrative Studies, University of Port Harcourt, Nigeria. Ogali has several publications in national and international journals to his credit and currently serves as associate editor, *Nigerian Journal of Oil and Politics*.

Victor Ikechukwu Ogharanduku is researcher at the Micheal Imoudu National Institute for Labour Studies, where his research is centered on social protection and development. He is a member of the Development Studies Association, UK, a fellow of the French Institute for Research in Africa (IFRA), and a member of the International Network For Economic Research (INFER). He has published in peer-reviewed journals such as *Peace Review* and *Peace and Conflict Studies* and contributed chapters to edited books. His research interests include the transformative role of social protection in development in fragile, conflict, and violent settings; the influence of social protection on social cohesion, inequality, peace, conflict, social exclusion, resilience, and social justice.

Dr. Emmanuel Steelman Okla is a lecturer in the Department of History and International Studies, Edo University, Iyamho, Nigeria. He earned his PhD in History from Benue State University Makurdi. He has published several articles in journals and contributed chapters in many book projects. His research interests are in Social, Diplomatic, Military History, and Refugee/Migration Studies.

Dr. Olanrewaju Faith Osasumwen holds a doctorate degree in International Relations. She is a researcher and faculty in the Department of Political Science and International Relations, Covenant University, Nigeria. Over the years, she has conducted extensive quantitative and qualitative studies on Displacement, Migration, Conflict, and Human Rights. Through her research, she has upheld intense advocacy toward vulnerability awareness and need-based humanitarian intervention for vulnerable groups, especially displaced people, toward the promotion of the United Nations Universal Declaration of Human Rights and the actualization of Sustainable Development Goals (SDGs). She is a member of academic (professional) associations such as the International Sociological Association and International Political Science Association, as well as research groups such as the Covenant University Cluster on Africa Development Issues, the Covenant University Centre for Economic Policy and Development Research (CEPDeR), and the Covenant University Research Cluster on Women Development and Human Security

Initiatives. She is a reviewer for journal publishers such as the *Journal of Internal Displacement*, *Third World Quarterly*, *Cogent Social Science*, and *Sage Open* which are indexed in Scopus.

Dr. Moses J. Yakubu is a senior research fellow at the Institute of African and Diaspora Studies, Faculty of Arts, University of Lagos, Akoka, Lagos, Nigeria. He holds a PhD degree in History and Strategic Studies. He holds a Certificate of Completion of Course on the Implementation of the UN Security Council Resolutions on the Women, Peace and Security Agenda in Africa, jointly awarded by the Peace Operations Training Institute and UN women; and a Certificate of Completion of Course on Conflict Analysis from the U.S. Institute of Peace. His research interests include peace, and conflict studies, development studies, and gender/women studies. In 2020, he won the University of Edinburgh Grant to participate in a workshop entitled: "Micro Dynamics of Armed Conflict and Political Violence in West Africa, jointly organized by the Postgraduate School of the Niger Delta University (NDU) and the Department of Political Science, Lagos State University (LASU), under the platform of the University of Edinburgh's Catalyst Regional Workshop for West Africa. In 2010, he won the Sexuality in Africa Award, organized by the African Regional Sexuality Resource Centre, Lagos, Nigeria, funded by the Ford Foundation. He has attended and presented papers at both national and international conferences, and published in several edited books and journals within Nigeria and beyond.